RECOVERING INTIMACY IN LOVE RELATIONSHIPS

The Family Therapy and Counseling Series

Series Editor
Jon Carlson, Psy.D., Ed.D.

Kit S. Ng
Global Perspectives in Family Therapy: Development, Practice, Trends

Phyllis Erdman and Tom Caffery
Attachment and Family Systems: Conceptual, Empirical, and Therapeutic Relatedness

Wes Crenshaw
Treating Families and Children in the Child Protective System

Len Sperry
Assessment of Couples and Families: Contemporary and Cutting-Edge Strategies

Robert L. Smith and R. Esteban Montilla
Counseling and Family Therapy with Latino Populations: Strategies that Work

Catherine Ford Sori
Engaging Children in Family Therapy: Creative Approaches to Integrating Theory and Research in Clinical Practice

Paul R. Peluso
Infidelity: A Practitioner's Guide to Working with Couples in Crisis

Jill D. Onedera
The Role of Religion in Marriage and Family Counseling

Christine Kerr, Janice Hoshino, Judith Sutherland, Sharyl Parashak, and Linda McCarley
Family Art Therapy

Debra D. Castaldo
Divorced without Children: Solution Focused Therapy with Women at Midlife

Phyllis Erdman and Kok-Mun Ng
Attachment: Expanding the Cultural Connections

Jon Carlson and Len Sperry
Recovering Intimacy in Love Relationships: A Clinician's Guide

RECOVERING INTIMACY IN LOVE RELATIONSHIPS

A CLINICIAN'S GUIDE

Edited by

JON CARLSON AND LEN SPERRY

Routledge
Taylor & Francis Group
New York   London

This book is part of the Family Therapy and Counseling Series, edited by Jon Carlson.

Routledge
Taylor & Francis Group
270 Madison Avenue
New York, NY 10016

Routledge
Taylor & Francis Group
27 Church Road
Hove, East Sussex BN3 2FA

© 2010 by Taylor and Francis Group, LLC
Routledge is an imprint of Taylor & Francis Group, an Informa business

Printed in the United States of America on acid-free paper
10 9 8 7 6 5 4 3 2 1

International Standard Book Number: 978-0-415-99253-4 (Hardback)

Library of Congress Cataloging-in-Publication Data

Recovering intimacy in love relationships : a clinician's guide / edited by Jon
  Carlson and Len Sperry.
    p. cm.
    ISBN 978-0-415-99253-4 (hardback : alk. paper)
    1. Marital psychotherapy. 2. Intimacy (Psychology) 3. Man-woman
  relationships. I. Carlson, Jon. II. Sperry, Len.

BF575.I5R43 2010
616.89'1562--dc22   2009045291

Visit the Taylor & Francis Web site at
http://www.taylorandfrancis.com

and the Routledge Web site at
http://www.routledgementalhealth.com

Contents

Series Editor's Foreword

> ... to have and to hold from this day forward, *for better, for worse,* for richer, for poorer, in sickness and in health ...
>
> **—Book of Common Prayer**

Intimacy and connection are what makes life worth living. When they are absent, a void or even a pain exists. Both joy and pain are part of loving partnerships. The idea that relationships are for both "better and worse" has been accepted for many years but what should the couple do when their relationship sinks into despair and intimacy disappears? How can a therapist help them? Are there models of recovery that take into account the various sources of disruption as well as cultural views?

This book addresses these questions and helps couples who have "come apart" to find connection and restore intimacy. Most readers are familiar with how sexual infidelity can damage relationships but today's "affairs" often have different sources. Seemingly positive things like cell phones, money, children, work and friends are also capable of eroding intimacy. The authors in this volume describe ways to restore intimacy with various sources of crisis and also to understand how intimacy and recovery varies according to many factors including gender, culture, religion, and class.

The methods and skills that are provided will help couples with their pain, anxieties, depressed mood and damaged hopes about the possibility of an intimate relationship. Clinicians seem to know about how to help their clients remove the problems and pain but this book also shows how to facilitate a recovery that leaves the couple with intimacy completely restored. This is not an easy task. As Harry J. Aponte wrote in the Foreword to *The Intimate Couple:*

"As therapists, we are speaking to intimacy and, consequently, also to love. As scientists, we are daring to address nature, a reality that is not just a subject of our work, but also something we live. As people who, by our very nature, live within a moral framework, we are treating of love that is not just emotion but also moral choice. In writing about love and intimacy, we are considering as rich and complex a subject as there is."

I hope that the readers enjoy this book on both a personal and professional level and use the ideas to enhance all the relationships.

Jon Carlson, PsyD, EdD
Series Editor

Preface

Intimacy is one of the most gratifying, endearing, and affirming of all human endeavors. It is one of the most treasured of all gifts that one can share with another. Yet it is also one of the most delicate and brittle of gifts; it can too easily be lost, diluted, or destroyed if not prized and nurtured. Although infidelity—sexual or emotional—is commonly considered the main cause of loss of intimacy, there are many other reasons why intimacy cools or is lost. These include physical or emotional violence, work demands, poor health, financial problems, divergent interests, unhealthy narcissism, or unrealistic expectations of the other. These factors are now being recognized as significant—and in many cases difficult to treat—issues in the context of couples therapy. Accordingly, the focus of this book is the restoration and recovery of intimacy. Most books stop at problem resolution or problem acceptance and miss the next step of restoring intimacy and happiness.

Needless to say, recovering and restoring the gift of intimacy can be an exceedingly difficult ordeal and process. Not surprisingly, therapists are often enlisted in this recovery process. Yet, therapists who deal with this therapeutic challenge typically find few relevant and available professional resources to consult. Partly, this is due to deficits in graduate training programs, but it is also due to the limited view many researchers and clinicians have held regarding intimacy and its treatment. Fortunately, a fresh vision has emerged in the past decade. Central to this fresh vision is an expanded view of intimacy as multifaceted: sexual, emotional, sensual, social, intellectual, aesthetic, and spiritual. Also there is the recognition that, in many relationships, intimacy is underdeveloped due to arrested development or benign neglect, as when a couple becomes overly focused on "bills and babies" and then neglects to nurture their relationship with each other. Another emerging recognition is that many current couples' communication programs are not sufficiently focused on intimacy development and recovery. Finally, as Alfred Adler has stated, "It is always easier to fight for one's principles than live up to them."

Much has changed since our previous book, *The Intimate Couple*, was published nearly a decade ago. In that volume we highlighted clinically relevant theory, research, and practice strategies to assist couples in developing intimacy, which at the time was framed quite narrowly.

Our goal in this book is to present a multifaceted view of intimacy as well as the latest advances in research and clinical practice regarding intimacy. We wanted to provide clinical treatment guidelines, including evidence-based ones, for dealing with recovery of intimacy in the context of infidelity and noninfidelity. We also wanted to highlight key cultural, gender, and religious factors in working with couples' intimacy issues. Finally, we wanted to showcase the most recent and noteworthy contributions of intimacy researchers and clinicians. These include David Burns, Frank Pittman, Harville Hendrix, Paul Peluso, Brent Atkinson, and Fred Luskin.

This book should be of particular interest to clinicians who work with individuals in close, intimate relationships, whether in an individual or couples therapy context. It could also be used in marital and couples therapy and family therapy courses in various professional training programs such as counseling, counseling and clinical psychology, marital and family therapy, nursing, or psychiatry.

The book is arranged in two sections with an appendix as well as interviews with leading thinkers in the world of love relationships. Part I, "Intimacy Overview," begins with Len Sperry providing an overview of the definitions and contexts for understanding intimacy as well as some clinical and research models of intimacy. Steven Solomon and Lorie Teagno provide their comprehensive model for doing infidelity couples therapy. Their approach views facilitating intimacy as the key ingredient to prevent affairs or recover from them. Dennis Bagarozzi shows how assessment can be used to tailor treatment for couples. Specifically, he demonstrates how the Intimacy Needs Survey can be used in clinical practice. In the final contribution to this section, W. Jared DuPree and Mark White look at the supportive research evidence for the treatment of infidelity and describe their practice-based evidence approach.

Part II of the book, as its title suggests, is devoted to "Clinical Considerations in Recovery from Emotional Infidelity." Jill Savege Scharff describes how the object relations approach directly addresses the loss and recovery of healthy attachments. Stephen Fife and Gerald Weeks describe the interpersonal and intrapersonal barriers that work against the attainment and maintenance of intimacy. The types of intimacy and various fears are utilized in the clinical process. Healthy attachment is necessary for intimacy in relationships. Katherine Helms offers treatment guidelines for addressing the increasing issue of Internet infidelity and what exactly constitutes infidelity. Byron Waller highlights the (often unrecognized) impact of financial deception upon intimacy. He describes the various types of financial infidelity and deception and provides treatment guidelines. Maureen Duffy describes how changes in work and friendships can negatively impact couples' intimacy. She provides treatment guidelines that address these areas when restoring intimacy with couples. J. Maria Bermúdez and Michele Parker describe how context and culture impact the treatment of intimate partner infidelity. They present a treatment model that helps the couple create a meaningful intimate relationship. Shea Dunham and Cyrus Ellis describe the unique features in helping African American couples restore intimacy. Robert Smith and Esteban Montilla describe the unique cultural, religious, and gender considerations when working with Latino couples. Kok-Mun Ng, Paul Peluso, and Shannon Smith address the important factors in working with Asian populations. They address marital satisfaction, intimacy, culture, relationship stress, and *enqing*. Jill Duba concludes this section with her chapter exploring how religion and faith impact the recovery of intimacy. She offers clear treatment guidelines for addressing this important variable.

In the Appendix, we review popular self-help books that might be useful for clinicians and clients.

We thank our editors at Routledge, George Zimmar, Dana Bliss, Dawn Moot, and Anna Moore. You continue to support our ideas and help to make them meaningful and accessible to others.

A special thank you goes to the many contributors to this volume. Each has taken an important area and applied their clinical excellence.

Finally, we thank our life partners Laura and Patricia who have helped us to learn the importance of restoring intimacy whenever the inevitable setbacks impact. They remind us of what Phyllis Bottome (1937) stated, "Conduct springs from contact. There are no virtues on an empty island."

Jon Carlson, Psy.D., Ed.D.
Lake Geneva, Wisconsin

Len Sperry, M.D., Ph.D.
Boca Raton, Florida

Contributors

Dennis A. Bagarozzi, Sr., MSW, Ph.D., is a licensed psychologist and licensed marriage and family therapist in Georgia. He is a Fellow in Family Psychology in the American Psychological Association and a Fellow in the American Association for Marriage and Family Therapy. He is on the editorial boards of numerous professional journals and is the editor of the "Family Measurement Techniques" section of the *American Journal of Family Therapy*. He has authored 70 journal articles and book chapters and seven texts. He is in private practice in Atlanta and Athens, Georgia.

J. Maria Bermúdez is an assistant professor of marriage and family therapy at the University of Georgia in the Department of Child and Family Development. She is a licensed marriage and family therapist and a clinical member and approved supervisor of the American Association for Marriage and Family Therapy. Her work is based on social constructionist, feminist informed and culturally responsive approaches to therapy, research, and supervision. She is originally from Honduras and her research and clinical work address conflict resolution and communication processes among Latino couples and families and experiential approaches to narrative therapy. (http://www.fcs.uga.edu/cfd/faculty.php?id=264 mbermude@uga.edu)

Jill D. Duba is an associate professor in the Department of Counseling and Student Affairs at Western Kentucky University. Her areas of focus include marital satisfaction, the role of religion in counseling couples and families, the role of religion in counselor education, and treating older clients. Her most recent publications include a book titled *The Role of Religion in Marriage and Family Counseling* and various refereed journal articles including "Therapy with Religious Couples"; "Treating Infidelity: Considering Narratives of Attachment"; and "Teaching Gerontology in Counselor Education." In addition, she was granted a research grant to study satisfaction among long-term couples and received the 2007 Journal Award for Outstanding Publication in the *Adultspan Journal*. She also has a private counseling practice in Bowling Green, Kentucky.

Maureen Duffy, Ph.D., is a consultant and family therapist in private practice in Miami Shores, Florida. She is coeditor of the *Qualitative Report* and the *Weekly Qualitative Report* and serves on the editorial boards of the *Journal of Marital and Family Therapy*, the *Family Journal*, and the *Journal of Systemic Therapies*. She is president of the International Institute for Human Understanding and is an associate of the Taos Institute. She is a member of the virtual faculty for the graduate program in discursive therapies of Massey University in New Zealand.

Shea M. Dunham, MSW, MS.Ed., Ph.D., is an assistant professor at Governors State University in the Division of Psychology and Counseling. She has degrees in the fields of social work, marriage and family therapy, counselor education, and supervision.

W. Jared DuPree, Ph.D., IMBA, LCMFT, is an assistant professor of marriage family therapy at the University of Houston–Clear Lake. He also maintains a small private practice and consulting firm in League City, Texas. He engages in research related to couples intimacy, Latino families, organizational innovation, and international family therapy. (www.drjaredupree.com)

Cyrus Marcellus Ellis, Ph.D., is an associate professor of counselor education at Governors State University. He earned his doctorate from the counselor education program at the Curry School of Education at the University of Virginia. He is the recipient of the William Van Hoose Memorial award from the Curry School Foundation and the OHANA award from Counselors for Social Justice. He is a counselor educator focusing on recovery, race relations, counselor training, and diversity.

Stephen T. Fife, Ph.D., is an assistant professor of marriage and family therapy at the University of Nevada, Las Vegas. His research interests include the treatment of infidelity, facilitating forgiveness in therapy, and processes of change in psychotherapy. He has published his work in a variety of psychotherapy journals and has presented extensively at local, national, and international conferences. He also has a private practice in Las Vegas.

Katherine M. Helm, Ph.D., is the director of graduate programs in psychology and an associate professor of psychology at Lewis University. She is a licensed clinical psychologist and has worked in community mental health, psychiatric hospitals, and university counseling centers. She is currently the supervisor of clinical training at Governors State University in the counseling center where she supervises practicum and internship graduate students' clinical work. Her research and practice interests include the provision of couples and individual psychotherapy, best pedagogic practices in teaching graduate and undergraduate students, multicultural issues, and teaching and supervising counselors in training. (helmka@lewisu.edu)

R. Esteban Montilla, Ph.D., is the coordinator of counseling education for Latin America and assistant professor of counseling with St. Mary's University of San Antonio, Texas. He is a graduate of Texas A&M University–Corpus Christi and a professional member of the American Counseling Association. He is the general secretary of the Sociedad Interamericana de Counseling and a diplomate with the College of Pastoral Supervision and Psychotherapy. He is also a Latin American theologian recognized for his ability to integrate spirituality into the practice of counseling and psychotherapy. He is the author of several books including *Pastoral Counseling with Latinos and Latinas* (2005) and *Viviendo la Tercerad Edad* (2004). (rmontilla@stmarytx.edu http://www.stmarytx.edu)

Kok-Mun Ng is an associate professor in the Department of Counseling at the University of North Carolina at Charlotte, North Carolina. His research and clinical interests include marriage and family, attachment, psychological assessment, well-being, emotional intelligence, counselor education and supervision, and multicultural and cross-cultural counseling issues. He is a licensed professional counselor in North Carolina, Texas, and Malaysia.

Michele L. Parker, M.S., LMFT, earned her master's degree in marriage and family therapy from Oklahoma Baptist University. She is currently a doctoral candidate in the marriage and family therapy program at the University of Georgia. She is currently a licensed marriage and family therapist in the state of Georgia and has worked with both couples and families on a range of clinical concerns. Her primary research focus includes the role of adult attachment in couples and family therapy. (1lparker.myweb.uga.edu)

Paul R. Peluso, Ph.D., is currently doctoral program coordinator at Florida Atlantic University. He is the coauthor of *Couples Therapy: Integrating Theory, Research, & Practice* (Love Publishing) and *Principles of Counseling and Psychotherapy: Learning the Essential Domains and Nonlinear Thinking of Master Practitioners* (Routledge Publishing), as well as the editor of the book *Infidelity: A Practitioner's Guide to Working with Couples in Crisis*

(Routledge Publishing). He is the author of over 25 articles and chapters related to family therapy, couples counseling, and Adlerian theory.

Jill Savege Scharff, M.D., is chair of the International Institute for Psychoanalytic Training at the International Psychotherapy Institute; clinical professor of psychiatry, Georgetown University; and teaching analyst, Washington Center for Psychoanalysis. She is the coauthor with David Scharff of many books, including *Object Relations Family Therapy* (1987), *Object Relations Couple Therapy* (1991), *A Primer of Object Relations Therapy* (1992), *Object Relations Therapy of Physical and Sexual Trauma* (1994), *Object Relations Individual Therapy* (1998), and *Tuning the Therapeutic Instrument* (2000). She practices psychoanalysis and psychotherapy with children and families in Chevy Chase, Maryland.

Robert L. Smith, Ph.D., CFT, FPPR, is professor and chair of the Department of Counseling and Educational Psychology at Texas A&M University–Corpus Christi. He received his Ph.D. from the University of Michigan. He is one of the founders of the International Association of Marriage and Family Counselors and currently serves as its executive director. He is a board member and director of research for the Sociedad Interamericana de Counseling. He has been the recipient of several research awards and has published over 70 refereed articles and a dozen textbooks and manuscripts, including *Counseling and Family Therapy with Latino Populations: Strategies that Work.*

Shannon D. Smith is an associate professor in the Department of Counselor Education at the University of Nevada, Las Vegas. He has worked as a child and family therapist in community mental health, director of child counseling clinic (Mansfield, Ohio), and as a school counselor in the public school system. His research interests include multicultural counseling and development, issues of diversity and social advocacy, child and family therapy, school counseling, and play therapy.

Steven D. Solomon, Ph.D., is the cofounder and codirector of the Relationship Institute (www.therelationshipinstitute.org) in La Jolla, California, where he and his professional partner, Lorie J. Teagno, developed the Intimacy Therapy program and wrote their popular book *Intimacy after Infidelity: How to Rebuild and Affair-Proof Your Marriage.* He has been in private practice as a clinical psychologist for over 25 years and specializes in couples' therapy. He has been married to his wonderful wife, Esther, for 24 years, and they live in San Diego where they have the great fortune of raising their son, Lewis.

Jonathan J. Sperry, M.S.W., is a staff therapist at Broward House, a holistic drug treatment program for individuals who are HIV positive. He is also a doctoral student in mental health counseling at Florida Atlantic University in Boca Raton, Florida. His clinical work focuses on substance abuse, group therapy, and therapy utilizing music modalities, including drumming. His research involves addictions, personality assessment, self-transcendence, and social interest.

Len Sperry, M.D., Ph.D., is professor of mental health counseling at Florida Atlantic University and clinical professor of psychiatry at the Medical College of Wisconsin. He is board certified in clinical psychology, psychiatry, and preventive medicine and has 500 publications, including 55 professional books. He is on the editorial boards of the *Journal of Marital and Family Therapy,* the *Family Journal,* and the *American Journal of Family Therapy.*

Lorie J. Teagno, Ph.D., is a licensed clinical psychologist and cofounder of the Relationship Institute and Intimacy Therapy program. She has been in practice in southern California for more than 25 years. She has coauthored the book *Intimacy after Infidelity* and the online course "Making Up Is Hard to Do" (www.ContinuingEdCourses.net) with her colleague and partner, Steven D. Solomon, Ph.D. She and her partner also train therapists in Intimacy Therapy and their unique and effective approach to dealing with infidelity.

Byron Waller, Ph.D., LCPC, is an associate professor of psychology and counseling at Governors State University and a licensed clinical professional counselor at Refuge Christian Counseling in South Holland, Illinois, where he works with individuals, couples, and families. He has written and presented in several areas, including forgiveness in relationships, self-efficacy and career development, depression relapse and mindfulness, multicultural issues, and spirituality.

Gerald R. Weeks, Ph.D., ABPP, is professor and chair of the Department of Marriage and Family Therapy at the University of Nevada–Las Vegas. He has published 19 books in the field of individual, couple, sex, and family therapy.

Mark B. White, Ph.D., LMFT, is an associate professor of medical family therapy and marriage and family therapy at East Carolina University. He has also taught at Auburn University and Kansas State University. He has served as an associate editor for the *Journal of Marital and Family Therapy* and has been active as an educator, researcher, and family therapist since 1992. His current research interests include family therapy process and outcome and couples living with chronic illness. (http://www.coupleslivingwithms.com/)

PART I

Intimacy Overview

CHAPTER 1

Intimacy

Definition, Contexts, and Models for Understanding
Its Development and Diminishment

LEN SPERRY

A book or treatise about the recovering of intimacy presumes that the experience of intimacy has already been achieved, but that somehow it has cooled or even been lost. Today, unfortunately, this experience of diminishment and loss of intimacy has become all too painfully common. Needless to say, the results and consequences of this loss can be devastating for couples.

Subsequent chapters in this book describe and illustrate the process of recovering intimacy. However, before turning to these chapters, it may be useful and reasonable to first address the matter of intimacy itself: what is it, how it develops, and how it becomes diminished and lost. The purpose of this chapter is to address these questions. Accordingly, it provides an overview of definitions and contexts for understanding intimacy. It then describes some developmental and diagnostic models of intimacy that have considerable clinical value and utility for clinicians working with couples. Finally, it sketches some of the many causes of the loss and diminishment of intimacy that are further elaborated in subsequent chapters.

Defining Intimacy and Its Contexts

In everyday conversation intimacy has come to mean a close and even a sexual relationship. The *Random House College Dictionary of the English Language* (1983) defines intimacy as a "close, familiar, and usually affectionate or loving personal relationship with another person" entailing a "detailed knowledge or deep understanding" of that person.

Implied in this definition is that there is a developmental aspect of intimacy in which such detailed knowledge and deep understanding occur. It is fascinating to note that since the publication of our book *The Intimate Couple* (Carlson and Sperry, 1999), the situation has changed little in that most professional articles and books on intimacy discuss it without formally defining it. It seems that intimacy is a lot like pornography. Most of us know what it is when we see it, but precisely defining it and differentiating it from other related constructs continue to be quite challenging. Generally speaking, clinicians, writers, and researchers are reluctant to define intimacy, presumably because even operational definitions are difficult to formulate.

That being said, we hazard the following definition and description of intimacy. We consider intimacy to be the ability—and the choice—to be close, loving, and vulnerable. Intimacy is a dynamic process that evolves over time and for which mutual trust is essential for its continued development; and intimacy presumes the capacity for self-knowledge and for self-disclosure. Self-knowledge makes it possible to be oneself in an intimate relationship without taking over the other or losing oneself to the other—called symbiosis. Instead, intimacy involves the capacity to be separate and together in an intimate relationship—called self-differentiation. Self-disclosure is the capacity to share one's self, including one's deepest fears and dreams, with another. A lack of the capacities for mutual trust, self-knowledge, self-differentiation, and self-disclosure reflects a symbiotic rather than an intimate relationship. There are several dimensions to intimacy, including emotional, physical, sexual, spiritual, aesthetic, social, recreational, and intellectual aspects. Among these, emotional and sexual are the most commonly described by clients, clinicians, and researchers. Furthermore, it is important to note that each partner also needs to focus on creating a safe nonjudgmental accepting environment for his or her partner for this to occur.

Marriage can be a particularly close intimate relationship. It is a relationship in which the partners can strive to know and trust each other and share deep personal information without fear of ridicule or reprisal. Psychological safety is the precondition for intimacy, and unless partners make it safe for the other to be him- or herself, intimacy is impossible (Hendrix, 1988/2008).

Because intimacy demands trust, deep sharing, and vulnerability, relatively few couples experience intimacy as an ongoing, sustained state. In fact, most couples experience it episodically and imperfectly, if at all (Welwood, 2005). Also because of its demands, betrayal of intimacy can be a traumatic experience. Furthermore, because intimacy requires nurturing to sustain itself, several circumstances can cause it to cool or be lost. Needless to say, the restoration and recovery of the former level of intimacy can be exceedingly difficult, particularly since so many individuals and couples continue to believe in the fallacy of romantic love and infatuation as the basis for intimacy.

The construct of intimacy is similar to but can and should be differentiated from related constructs such as love, passion, power, boundaries, autonomy, closeness, and commitment. The rest of this section provides a context and conceptual boundaries for understanding intimacy and its related constructs. These contexts include mature and immature intimacy; love and intimacy; intimacy, passion, and commitment; and boundaries, power, and intimacy.

The first context is that of mature and immature intimacy. Husband–wife relationships are capable of mature intimacy, whereas mother–child relationships are not capable of mature intimacy. Obviously, the couple's relationship can be characterized by immature intimacy, despite their capacity to relate maturely, whereas immature intimacy is the only capacity for mother–child relationships. In this regard, the dictionary definition given earlier does not distinguish between mature and immature intimacy. On the other hand, Welwood (2005) distinguishes mature or perfect love from immature love. Beavers (1985) and Napier (1996) assume this distinction by specifying that individuals have equal overt power or are emotionally differentiated persons. L'Abate (1997) implies such equality. Whitaker and Ryan (1989) add that intimacy develops in tandem with self-autonomy and that autonomy increases as a function of intimacy.

A second context involves the distinction of love and intimacy. L'Abate and Talmadge (1987) describe love as a development process consisting of three elements: behavioral, cognitive, and emotional. The behavioral element consists of the capacity to be caring and to accept care. The cognitive element consists of the capacity to see good in another and the capacity for forgiveness. The emotional element is, of course, intimacy. Intimacy consists of the capacity to be dependent on the other, the capacity of receiving love and accepting the partner's love. It also consists of the capacity to express, withstand, understand, and resolve the conflict and hostility that occur in intimate relationships. Needless to say, this is exceedingly difficult in a culture that promotes independence and self-sufficiency.

A third involves the relationship of intimacy to passion and commitment. Sternberg (1986, 1987) describes what he calls the "triangle of love."

It consists of three components: commitment, passion, and intimacy. For Sternberg intimacy encompasses the affects and feeling states of closeness, connectedness, and bondedness. Passion is described as encompassing the drive that leads to physical attraction, romance, and sexual consummation of the relationship. Commitment differs from passion and intimacy in that it involves short-term and long-term decisions. The short-term decision is to love the other individual, while the long-term decision is to maintain that love. Developmentally, intimacy, passion, and commitment change in degree or level during the course of an ongoing relationship (Sternberg, 1986). Passion becomes increasingly intense early in the relationship in conjunction with a rapid rise in intimacy. Commitment, however, develops much more slowly and steadily. As the relationship continues to develop, commitment rises to match the level of intimacy, while the level of passion often decreases significantly. Accordingly, when a couple complains that their "love has cooled" or "the romance is gone," what they are really saying is that a change in the level of passion in their relationship has occurred. When passion decreases but the levels of intimacy and commitment remain adequate, the relationship is not in jeopardy, but rather one element of it has changed.

A fourth context involves the relationship of intimacy to power and boundaries. Bennan and Leif (1975) were the first to differentiate power and boundary dimensions from intimacy. The intimacy dimension involves self-disclosure, friendship, caring, and appreciation of individual uniqueness. It involves negotiating both the emotional and physical distances between partners, so as to balance the need for autonomy with the need for belonging. Boundary issues in couples' relationships center on membership and structure: membership in terms of who is involved in the couples' system and to what degree, and structure in terms of the extent to which partners are part of, but at the same time apart from, the couple subsystem. Boundary also refers to the degree of intrusiveness that will be accepted in the relationship. For married couples, commitment to their marriage is the core boundary issue, along with related commitments to jobs, friends, extended family, and outside interests. Power issues include responsibility, discipline, control, role negotiation, and decision making. Couples' relationships continually involve both overt and covert efforts to influence decisions and behaviors of the partners. Power issues are tied to money, privileges, and rewards. They are also more subtly manifest in struggles for control of the relationship, including one-upmanship efforts and escalation of conflict. The power dimension "predicts" who will pursue and who will distance in the relationship. In marital conflict it "determines" who tells whom what to do in specific situations. The power dimension greatly impacts both boundaries and the level and nature of intimacy. Optimal couple functioning and self-differentiation result when boundary and power issues are reasonably resolved so that the partners can relate in a healthy and intimate manner (Doherty & Colangelo, 1984).

In short, the construct of intimacy is similar to but can be differentiated from related constructs such as love, passion, power, boundaries, autonomy, closeness, and commitment. Now we turn to a discussion of various clinical and research models for understanding the process of how intimacy develops, fails to develop, and diminishes.

Models of Intimacy

You now have a cross-sectional perspective on intimacy. This perspective is useful in defining the term and differentiating from others, but it is an insufficient perspective. To more fully understand and appreciate intimacy one must also have a longitudinal perspective and a diagnostic perspective. This section describes both of these. First, two developmental models usefully describe the trajectory intimacy takes if it does develop and mature. As previously noted, the development of maturity appears to be rather uncommon for couples. Next, two diagnostic models are offered. The first is the underlying theory for the second. The second is the Global Assessment of Relationship Functioning (GARF) scale, which became a part of the *Diagnostic and Statistical Manual of Mental Disorders* fourth edition (*DSM–IV*) and the current *DSM–IV–TR*. Although it appears that far too few clinicians who work with couples utilize this rather sophisticated diagnostic device, GARF does possess considerable clinical value in quickly and accurately assessing a couple's level of intimacy, both emotionally and sexually.

Developmental Models

There are at least two developmental models of the stages of long-term relationships such as marriage. The first to be briefly described are the four stages of a close love relationship described by Sperry (1978) and his colleagues (Sperry & Carlson, 1991; Sperry, Carlson, & Peluso, 2006). These stages are described in terms of the developmental process of growth from the symbiotic-like quality of new relationships through other stages requiring considerable growth and differentiation of both partners in intimacy. Four stages distinguish various points on this developmental journey: dependence, counterdependence, independence, and interdependence. Most couples begin at the first and quickly move to the second where they may become stuck for a long time and may not proceed beyond this stage without significant personal and relational growth, often requiring effective therapy to continue on this journey.

Dependence

In the dependence stage, which spans first attraction to the end of the honeymoon, both individuals seek a sense of mutual completeness, or symbiotic striving, and total happiness, which they wrongly and blindly assume is achieved simply by being in the presence of the other. As one or both relinquish their allegiance to this myth, the relationship shifts to the next stage.

Counterdependence

Also called negative independence, the counterdependence stage is marked by disillusion, discontent, and discord. Blaming and relinquishment of personal responsibility become mutually alternative behaviors. Couples reflect their discontent directly by demanding, fighting, and competing with each other, or more indirectly with passive aggression or by leading lives of unhappiness and quiet desperation. Efforts at autonomy are in stark conflict with mutuality, and thus, infidelity, separation, and divorce are common at this stage.

Independence

Also called positive independence, the independence stage is marked by the recognition that demands for mutual completeness and total happiness are unrealistic and acceptance that growth in autonomy, self-knowledge, self-disclosure, and self-differentiation are necessary for growth and intimacy. This is a transitional stage in which the needs for autonomy and mutuality are recognized but only tentatively met.

Interdependence

The interdependence stage is marked by the integration of autonomy and mutuality. Both partners develop and express a heightened sensitivity to the rhythmic pattern of pain and joy and can more easily forgive and risk sharing their deepest fears and longings. Needless to say, relational satisfaction is high as both partners grow and develop the uncompleted parts of themselves and have no need for the symbiotic striving that characterized their initial attraction to each other.

Solomon and Teagno (2006) describe a developmental model of long-term close relationships that is remarkably similar to the model just described. They note that long-term love relationships grow and develop over time in definable, predicable stages and have observed four stages of love in such relationships. They describe these stages as: sweet symbiosis; soured symbiosis; differentiation; and synergy.

Sweet Symbiosis

Sweet symbiosis is the initial, honeymoon phase of falling in love. In this process of merging, the other's imperfections are not seen or at most minimized, leading to the "blindness" of love. It lays the foundation of the affectional bonding and investment in the relationship, which is tested in later stages, and lasts approximately 18 months.

Soured Symbiosis

In the soured symbiosis stage the emerging awareness of differences between the partners are experienced as hurts and disappointments. Nearly all couples who seek therapy do so because of arrested development at this stage. Also, most infidelities occur here.

Differentiation

In the differentiation stage couples begin to regain their separate sense of self. They experience differentiation in conflict, accept their differences, and feel their bond of love deepening. Maintaining this mature development over time leads to the next stage.

Synergy

In the synergy stage couples are very comfortable together; they view the other's strengths and weaknesses clearly, respect each other's separateness, possess the ability to confront challenges, and can easily share feelings of love (Solomon & Teagno, 2006).

Diagnostic Models

The GARF scale is a clinician-rated instrument for assessing couple and family functioning on a continuum from optimal to severely disturbed (American Psychiatric Press, 2000). GARF permits clinicians to rate the degree to which a couple meets the affective or instrumental needs of both individuals with regard to the dimensions of problem solving (i.e., negotiation, communication, conflict resolution), organization (i.e., boundaries, power sharing, responsibility), and emotional climate (i.e., empathy, commitment, sexual functioning) on a 1 to 100 scale, with five increments of 20 points. It is important to note that GARF was informed by theory and extensive research of the family competence model (Beavers, 1985; Beavers & Hampson, 1990).

In his book *Successful Marriage*, Beavers (1985) describes five levels of competence among couples, similar to the five ranges of functioning of GARF. These levels range from the severely disturbed, borderline, mid-range, and adequate to the optimal levels of competence. He notes that partners typically come from families with about the same degree of distance, trust, and toleration of intimacy. Furthermore, he noted that individuals tended to marry partners who had similar family rules regarding distance and intimacy. These levels of couple functioning are briefly described along with a notation of the emotional climate dimension of GARF at the corresponding range of functioning.

Severely Disturbed

Among the couples considered severely disturbed, coherence and hope were the primary deficiencies, although enmeshment, lack of gratification, nonexistent choice, and unresolved ambivalence characterized these couples. Couples with enmeshed styles tended to deny the need for warmth and closeness, whereas those with more detached styles tended to deny anger and a desire for separateness. Beavers noted that being loving meant that both partners believed they had to think and feel the same way. Psychosis was occasionally an issue in the severely disturbed marriages, and in addition to medication, couple's work focused on relationships, communication, boundaries, and choice. Triangulation, particularly involving the couple, a parent, or a child, were ordinarily tenacious and persistent in these couples (Beavers & Hampson, 1990). Little if any sense of attachment, commitment, or concern about the partner's welfare is noted on corresponding range of the emotional climate dimension of GARF (American Psychiatric Association, 2000).

Borderline

Couples considered borderline comprised about 40% of Beavers's practice. They are the most difficult of the groups to treat, many of them having had several previous treatment experiences. These couples were identified with an extreme concern with control, often of a bizarre nature. Although in borderline couples detached styles were unlikely to remain in treatment after a crisis was settled, those with enmeshed styles tended to be involved in more intensive treatment, and a central issue in therapy was the power struggle (Beavers & Hampson, 2003). Significant ongoing, unresolved conflict and sexual dysfunction are noted on the corresponding range of the emotional climate dimension of GARF (American Psychiatric Association, 2000).

Midrange

Beavers notes that the midrange group comprised about 40% of his practice, and they were the easiest and most gratifying to treat. As with other types of couples, the midrange couples with detached styles seldom needed long-term treatment, while those with more enmeshed styles were less demoralized. He also noted these couples had more successful experiences with intimacy than severely disturbed or borderline couples. With these couples, Beavers tied the control issue to the intimacy issue and helped the individuals to see that intimidation was a method that ultimately reduced and eliminated any possibility of intimacy (Beavers & Hampson, 2003). Pain, anger, or emotional deadness interferes with couple enjoyment, and troublesome sexual difficulties are noted in the corresponding range of the emotional climate dimension of GARF (American Psychiatric Association, 2000).

Adequate

Unlike couples at the preceding three levels of functioning, couples in the adequate group are able to communicate reasonably and deal with their problems, although some conflicts remain unresolved without disrupting couple and family functioning. If they seek out couples therapy, it is typically situation specific, such as a death in the family, job loss, and so forth (Beavers & Hampson, 2003). Caring, warmth, and sharing are mixed with frustration or tension, with some reduced or problematic sexual activity noted in the corresponding range of the emotional climate dimension of GARF (American Psychiatric Association, 2000).

Optimal

Couples at the optimal level of competency rarely seek couples therapy because of their level of differentiation and competence. These couples have the capacity to experience intimacy on an ongoing basis (Beavers & Hampson, 2003). Optimism, caring, warmth, and sharing are present, and satisfactory sexual relations are noted on the corresponding range of the emotional climate dimension of GARF (American Psychiatric Association, 2000).

Clinical Implications of These Models for Intimacy

Beavers's model and GARF suggest that relatively sustained and satisfying emotional and physical intimacy are possible only at two ranges of couple functioning: the adequate and optimal levels. A basic premise is that a couple must experience a rather consistent degree of coherence or structural stability as well as control with regard to equity and power sharing in order to experience sustained levels of intimacy. In short, sustained levels of coherence and control in a relationship are prerequisites for intimacy (Beavers, 1985). While some degree of intimacy occurs at the midrange level of couple functioning, little, if any, is likely at the borderline and severely disturbed levels (Beavers, 1985). This is not to say that couples at the midrange, borderline, and severely disturbed levels do not have intimacy problems and concerns; they do. Rather, it is that basic structural and coherence problems are operative; and for the severely disturbed couples and lower functioning borderline couples, the primary focus of treatment has to be directed toward establishing or reestablishing boundaries and hierarchical structures. Similarly, in higher functioning borderline couples and midrange couples, the primary focus of treatment has to be directed toward control issues and power sharing. Only after couples

Table 1.1 Comparison of Developmental and Diagnostic Models of Intimacy

Sperry (Solomon & Teagno, 2006)	Beavers (1985)	GARF Scale
Interdependence (Synergy)	Optimal	80–100
Independence (Differentiation)	Adequate	61–80
Counterdependence (Soured Symbiosis)	Midrange	41–60
	Borderline	21–40
	Severely Disturbed	1–20

have achieved sufficient coherence or structural stability and control with regard to power sharing is it realistic to focus therapy primarily on intimacy issues.

The stage model of long-term relationships described by Sperry (1978) and his colleagues (1991, 2006) seems to align reasonably well with some of the other stage models, particularly those of Solomon and Teagno (2006) and Beavers (1985). By extension, it should also align with GARF. Table 1.1 compares these four models specifying differing levels of intimacy.

Reasons for the Diminishment and Loss of Intimacy

As noted earlier, it is commonly believed that sexual and emotional infidelity is the primary cause of the loss of intimacy. There are, however, several other reasons why intimacy diminishes or is lost. These include physical and emotional violence, use of Internet pornography and cybersex, work demands, poor health, financial problems, divergent interests, unhealthy narcissism, or unrealistic expectations of the other. These factors are increasingly being recognized as significant, and in many cases difficult to treat, issues in the context of couples therapy.

Needless to say, recovering and restoring the gift of intimacy can be an exceedingly difficult ordeal and process. Not surprisingly, therapists are often enlisted in this recovery process. Yet, therapists who deal with this therapeutic challenge typically find few relevant and available professional resources to consult. This is partly due to deficits in graduate training programs and partly due to the limited view many researchers and clinicians have held regarding intimacy and its treatment. Fortunately, a fresh and new vision has been emerging in the past decade. Central to this new vision is an expanded view of intimacy as multifaceted: sexual, emotional, sensual, social, intellectual, aesthetic, and spiritual. As noted earlier, there is also increasing recognition that, in many relationships, intimacy is underdeveloped due to developmental arrest or benign neglect, as when a couple becomes overly focused on "bills and babies" and then neglects to nurture the relationship with each other.

Concluding Note

This overview of intimacy and related constructs includes several models and allows us to posit a number of observations about intimacy. First, current theory and research is not particularly consistent with the general public's view of intimacy and perhaps even that of some or many clinicians. In clinical language, the term intimacy is a much more circumscribed construct than that of popular parlance. Second, intimacy is not an ability that most individuals and couples exhibit or possess. Third, sustained periods of intimacy are not present in most couples' relationships, meaning many do not consistently experience it. This is not to suggest that intimacy is an all-or-nothing phenomenon wherein certain individuals can rather consistently experience it, while other individuals never experience it. There is also a group of individuals who are capable of occasionally experiencing it, such as in times of crisis such as funerals or following a serious accident. Rather, it appears that there are discrete levels of relational functioning that have been noted in individuals and couples. Fourth, there is clinical utility and value in assessing intimacy in terms of levels of competence. Specifically, the GARF scale provides a clinically useful scale for rating relational behavior, including intimacy. Hopefully, clinicians will utilize it concurrently with the Global Assessment of Functioning (GAF) on Axis V. Fifth, intimacy problems will often present alongside more basic relational issues, such as structural, hierarchical, and boundary problems, and control and power-sharing problems and concerns. These more basic and underlying problems must be adequately addressed before intimacy issues can become the primary focus of therapy.

With this discussion as a backdrop, we can now turn to a more detailed description of the process of recovering intimacy. Subsequent chapters will describe several factors that lead to the diminishment or loss of intimacy as well as interventions to foster the recovery of intimacy.

References

American Psychiatric Press (2000). *Diagnostics and statistical manual of mental disorders* (4th ed., Text rev.). Washington, DC: Author.

Beavers, R. (1985). *Successful marriage: A family systems approach to couples therapy*. New York: Norton.

Beavers. W.R., & Hampson, R. (1990). *Successful families: Assessment and interventions*. New York: Norton.

Bennan, E., & Leif, H. (1975). Marital therapy from psychiatric perspective: An overview. *American Journal of Psychiatry, 132*, 583–591.

Carlson, J., & Sperry, L. (Eds.). (1999). *The intimate couple*. New York: Brunner/Mazel.

Cusinato, M., & L'Abate, L. (1994). A spiral model of intimacy. In S. Johnson & L. Greenberg (Eds.), *The heart of the matter: Perspectives on emotion in marital therapy* (pp. 108–123). New York: Brunner/Mazel.

Doherty, W., & Colangelo, N. (1984). The family FIRO model: A modest proposal for organizing family treatment. *Journal of Marital and Family Therapy, 10*, 19–29.

Gottman, J. (1994b). *Why marriages succeed or fail.* New York: Simon and Schuster.

Hendrix, H. (1988/2008). *Getting the love you want: A guide for couples.* New York: Holt.

L'Abate, L. (1997). *The self in the family: A classification of personality, criminality and psychopathology.* New York: Wiley.

L'Abate, L., & Talmadge, W. (1987). Love, intimacy, and sex. In G. Weeks & L. Hof (Eds.), *Integrating sex and marital therapy: A clinical guide* (pp. 23–34). New York: Brunner/Mazel.

Napier, A. (1996). Of men and intimacy: A contextual approach. In L. Vandecreek, S. Knapp, & T. Jackson (Eds.), *Innovations in clinical practice: A source book* (pp. 467–480). Sarasota, FL: Professional Resources Press.

Soloman, S. D., & Teagno, L. J. (2006). *Intimacy after infidelity: How to rebuild and affair-proof your marriage.* Oakland, CA: New Harbinger Publications.

Sperry, L. (1978). *The together experience: Getting, growing, and staying together in marriage.* San Diego: Beta Books.

Sperry, L., & Carlson, J. (1991). *Marital therapy: Integrating theory and technique.* Denver: Love Publishing.

Sperry, L., Carlson, J., & Peluso, P. (2006). *Couples therapy: Integrating theory and technique*, 2nd ed. Denver: Love Publishing.

Sternberg, R. (1986). A triangular theory of love. *Psychological Reviews, 93*(2), 119–135.

Sternberg, R. (1987). *The triangle of love: Intimacy, passion, commitment.* New York: Basic Books.

Welwood, J. (2005). *Perfect love, imperfect relationships: Healing the wound of the heart.* Boston: Trumpeter.

Whitaker, C., & Ryan, M. (1989). *Midnight musings of a family therapist.* New York: Norton.

CHAPTER 2

Recovering From Sexual and Other Types of Infidelity, Part I

A Typology of Infidelities

STEVEN D. SOLOMON and LORIE J. TEAGNO

Although love and commitment are absolutely necessary conditions of long-term love relationship (LTLR) formation and continuation, they are not sufficient to produce lasting LTLR success. True intimacy is the key factor that makes love relationship fulfillment over the long term possible. Intimacy is the catalyst that enables love and commitment to last a lifetime, and it is the fuel that sustains a love relationship in its journey through the years.

Not surprisingly then, just as the many couples we have worked with have taught us about the significance of intimacy to their LTLR health, we have also learned from numerous couples that there is a striking correlation between intimacy and infidelity: a striking and strong inverse correlation. That is, infidelity occurs when a couple has either never achieved a significant level of real intimacy in their LTLR or when they have built a sturdy intimacy structure in their relationship but for whatever reason that structure has been dramatically weakened or damaged.

It follows then that the key to not only enabling a couple to heal from the traumatic wound of infidelity but also to empower them to rebuild their relationship so that it is so healthy that they are unlikely to ever have to worry about infidelity again is for the couple's therapist to focus on assisting the couple achieve real intimacy. Although it is essential to address

Doing the former can be very helpful to the couple in their immediate dilemma, but it does not do much to assist them in the long term. Where couples need help is in learning how to do the process of conflict well. Once they have acquired these tools, they will be positioned well psychologically to come together around a resolution. The value of helping couples acquire this skill as opposed to providing them with specific conflict solutions is addressed in the Confucian axiom that relates the greater ultimate value of teaching a person to fish instead of giving a person a fish.

The third of the three intimacies is what we call affection intimacy (AI). This is actually what many laypeople picture when they think of intimacy. AI is defined as a couple's expressions of love for each other. We identify four types of AI: verbal, actions, sexual, and nonsexual physical. Healthy AI is of course essential to ongoing LTLR health.

Both the couple and each partner can be assessed as to the relative strengths in the four subtypes of AI, although in TRI couples therapy, and especially infidelity couples therapy, AI is rarely a main focus of therapy until the middle and later stages of a couples therapy. The tendency to focus prematurely in therapy on AI is another common couples therapy error. The time to fully address AI is after significant progress has been made in helping the couple enhance their SI and CI, especially the latter. Focusing on AI first is like treating the symptom rather than the disease.

In our work with infidelity couples, a conceptual understanding of the three intimacies is essential in two ways. First, knowledge of what the three intimacies are and how they govern LTLR health provide insight into what causes a partner to be unfaithful; particular weaknesses in the three intimacies create the vulnerability to infidelity. More specifically, the failure by a couple to develop strong Conflict Intimacy inevitably creates the buildup of negative feelings between the two partners. When this is combined with their loss of Affection Intimacy, which results both from such low Conflict Intimacy as well as from the weak Self Intimacy that underlies it, the couple becomes susceptible to infidelity.

An understanding of the three intimacies also provides the therapist a key to guide the infidelity couple in restructuring their LTLR in order to create a healthier relationship after the excruciating trauma of infidelity. By helping them to build real strength in each of the three intimacies, we are empowering them, inoculating their LTLR against the dangers that led them to be vulnerable to infidelity. Assisting them in achieving healthy SI and strong CI fuels a resurgence in their AI. It enables them to grow truly intimate in both the light and the dark sides of their passion. This is what enables a couple to feel truly fulfilled, a couple that is grateful to be together. And that is what provides immunity to infidelity. But getting there is of course a process, which leads us to the next part of our theoretical model.

The Developmental Model of Long-Term Love Relationships

Building on the incisive work of Bader and Pearson (1988), a central tenet of the TRI model of LTLR is that these relationships are marked by a developmental growth process. We define this process as proceeding through four stages of growth. LTLR growth is defined by the couple's progression from more symbiotic functioning to more differentiated functioning.

Movement along the developmental LTLR path is bidirectional; although there is a natural push for growth, regressions in LTLR functioning to earlier, less mature levels also occur. One mark of the heuristic nature of the TRI model is evident in noting that it is the three intimacies, or lack thereof, that govern any couple's progress in this developmental process of navigating from symbiotic to differentiated functioning. CI plays a particularly pivotal role here.

The four stages of the TRI developmental model of LTLR are:

1. Sweet Symbiosis
2. Soured Symbiosis
3. Differentiation
4. Synergy

Sweet symbiosis is the initial, honeymoon phase when two people fall in love. It is one of the most wonderful, magical times in anyone's life. Here there is a great deal of symbiotic merging taking place in which the other's imperfections are not seen or at most minimized, leading to the "blindness" of love. This is symbiosis at its beautiful, powerful best, aided by eons of evolution and the resultant bonding catalyzed by "love chemical" neuronal flooding (Fisher, 1992). In our profession, symbiosis is too often viewed as purely pathological. Here we can see that symbiosis is not always unhealthy. In this first stage of a LTLR, symbiosis is not only wonderful to experience, it is also an absolute necessity in providing the strength of bonding in the relationship that will be greatly needed in later stages in which the LTLR is severely tested.

Sweet symbiosis turns into soured symbiosis when the previously unseen or ignored failings and differences between the partners begin inevitably to emerge through the experience of hurts and disappointments. In our experience, 95% of the couples who seek couples therapy do so because their LTLR development has gotten arrested in soured symbiosis, and most all infidelities occur in couples stuck in this stage.

The ability to move through and beyond soured symbiosis is completely dependent on the couple's ability to develop CI. CI skills are what enable the couple to become differentiated in conflict in spite of the pull for symbiosis that the emerging differences and negative affect create.

Couples who are able to develop CI then move into the third stage, differentiation. This is the stage in which couples begin to be able to have the best of both worlds; they are able to experience differentiation in conflict, work their differences through, and in so doing feel their bond of love deepening.

Maintaining this mature development over time leads a couple into the synergy stage, where the growth they have made is solidified and regression back to soured symbiosis, even under great stress, rarely happens. These are couples who are very comfortable together. They see each other's strengths and weaknesses clearly, respect each other's separateness, are confident in their relationship's ability to confront challenges, and are good at sharing and feeling their love. They are strong in all of the three intimacies.

The Three Deal Breakers

Before we begin to focus specifically on infidelity, there is an additional concept that is important to cover here. One of the most significant judgments that the couples therapist makes with any couple is whether or not there is hope for the LTLR. One of the most remarkable findings that we have made from our years of working with couples is that there are very few things that a LTLR cannot overcome. The resilience of LTLRs and the incredible strength of love established in sweet symbiosis are not to be underestimated.

In fact, we have found only three things truly doom a LTLR. In order of increasing frequency they are:

1. One or both partners never truly loved the other when the commitment to the relationship was made.
2. Too much anger, pain, or damage has been inflicted by one partner on the other or by both on each other that for one or both partners the love they once had for the other no longer exists.
3. One or both partners are unwilling to own his or her part of the problems in the LTLR or are unwilling to commit to trying his or her best to overcome these issues.

We seldom find the first deal breaker to be the reason for the ending of a relationship. The second deal breaker occurs quite often. But by far the most common reason we find that LTLRs fail is due to the third deal breaker. Our experience tells us that a large percentage of the marriages that end in divorce in our society do so not as a result of "irreconcilable differences" but due to this third deal breaker, the unwillingness to own and overcome one's contribution to the relationship problems. That is, if not for the third deal breaker, many of these couples would have found that their differences were indeed reconcilable.

All too often partners run rather than face their own weaknesses and their own demons. All too often they convince themselves that the grass is greener on the other side of the fence, that they will not have these problems when they find the "right" spouse. They may indeed find a better match in their next partner, but unfortunately, if they fall victim to the third deal breaker, their own issues will resurface and hinder or damage their next LTLR just as they did their previous one.

Theory: The TRI Infidelity Typology

The Three Types of Infidelity

Just as working from a heuristic model of LTLR is essential to effective couples therapy work, it is equally vital, when working with an infidelity couple, for the therapist to have a strong, clear conceptual framework regarding infidelity. This is what enables the therapist to evaluate and understand the dynamics of the couple's infidelity, including its causes and its likely remedy.

Consequently, a number of our colleagues have developed interesting and insightful infidelity typologies (Brown, 2001; Lusterman, 1998). Most of the useful models are quite complex since their typologies are defined by the multiplicity of factors, both intrapsychic and interpersonal, involved in infidelity causation. We have found that a simpler model of infidelity typing is more helpful for us; it allows us to see clearly why the infidelity occurred within the larger context of the couple's LTLR, and it points the way for us in seeing what work the couple needs to do to heal and create a new, healthier LTLR.

Most important to the understanding of this typology is our assertion that all infidelities have the same cause: significant unresolved negative affect. An individual in a LTLR ends up engaging in infidelity only when he or she has allowed negative emotions to build up inside him or her. By not working through these negative emotions, this partner unwittingly sets him- or herself up for having his or her actions hijacked by the festering negative affect. The acting out behavior of infidelity is the result.

Given this understanding of infidelity causation, and thanks to what we have learned over the years from working with infidelity couples, we have concluded that there are three types of infidelity. Each type is defined by the specific negative emotion that is the primary unresolved affect that led the betraying partner to be unfaithful. The three types of infidelity are:

1. Infidelities of Fear
2. Infidelities of Loneliness
3. Infidelities of Anger

LTLR partners who experience increasing amounts of fear, loneliness, or anger and who do not consciously acknowledge and then deal successfully with these particular three negative emotions are at high risk for infidelity.

Unresolved, the negative emotion will become so strong within these individuals that they become vulnerable to having their integrity overridden; the power of their fear, or their loneliness, or their anger silences their conscience and so they choose to either seek out or simply acquiesce to an opportunity to be unfaithful. We assert that this intrapsychic dynamic underlies every infidelity.

This typology has proven to be especially powerful in our work with infidelity couples due to its congruence with our overarching LTLR conceptual model. Both the TRI model of LTLRs and TRI's three types of infidelity typology are based on the primacy of intimacy, especially emotional intimacy. Just as our model of LTLRs defines healthy LTLR functioning as being based on strength in the three intimacies, so too our infidelity typology is defined by how weakness in the three intimacies (specifically SI and CI) underlies LTLR breakdowns and ultimately results in infidelity. This theoretical cohesiveness brings clarity to our work with infidelity couples, even with all of their complexities. As a result, we find the heuristic nature of this theoretical model to be a powerful catalyst for success in treatment of these challenging couples.

Before getting into the specifics of the three types of infidelity, we need to define infidelity. As we use the term here, infidelity refers to any action taken unilaterally by a partner in a committed love relationship that violates the explicit or assumed agreement of sexual or emotional exclusivity between the two partners. This definition includes two subtypes of infidelities: affairs and sexual liaisons. Having an affair denotes involvement in an affectional relationship that may or may not include sexual relations, while having a sexual liaison is an interpersonal relationship or interaction entered into expressly for the purpose of sexual satisfaction. One-night stands can be either an affair or a sexual liaison, but most often are the latter. An infidelity relationship that continues over time can be either subtype as well, although more frequently are affairs.

The Infidelity of Fear: Running From Old Pain

Fear is a powerful, primal emotion. Acting on fear can save one's life, but living in the thrall of fear diminishes one's life. In fact, one way of looking at the work we do as therapists is to see it as assisting our clients to increase their awareness of their fears while simultaneously working with them to decrease the extent to which they are controlled by their fears.

The failure of a partner in a LTLR to accomplish the latter goal leads to the scenario that plays out in an infidelity of fear. They have a deep-seated fear associated with being in a love relationship. As their involvement in the LTLR grows, so does their fear. At some point, if their fear is not resolved, it will become so strong that it takes control of their behavior, just as fear takes control of any of us if we find ourselves in a situation that is terrifying. Their fear causes them to act out in a desperate attempt to escape from the situation that is frightening them: the love relationship itself. All too often, the escape is the LTLR "weapon of mass destruction" (Ceo, 2005), infidelity.

In order to be able to identify a betrayal as an infidelity of fear, it is important for the therapist to remember that the partner who has had an infidelity of fear has the following characteristics:

1. Low SI, particularly when it comes to being aware of and dealing with the emotion of fear.
2. Long-standing, deep-seated fear of one of the following:
   a. the fear of intimacy, sometimes experiences such as the fear of losing him- or herself and his or her independence in a love relationship,
   b. a fear of commitment, fueled by a primal fear of choosing wrongly or of making a mistake,
   c. the fear of being unworthy of love.

So an infidelity of fear results when a LTLR partner has one of these three strong, old fears about him- or herself and love and he or she is unable or unwilling to confront those fears (low SI) within him- or herself.

Understanding and recognizing these three specific fears that, when activated by increasing involvement in a LTLR, drive a partner to engage in infidelity is vital for the therapist to be able to assist the infidelity of fear couple. The roots of each of these deep-seated fears always extend back to the betraying partner's family of origin and his or her attachment history.

But simply having one of these fears will not necessarily lead to infidelity. The partner gripped by one of these fears will only betray his or her partner if he or she also has significantly low SI, particularly when it comes to being aware of and dealing in the LTLR with the fear. These partners will be unfaithful if they repress or deny their fear. Even if they do have some awareness of their fear, if they do nothing to work it through they are also likely to betray. Here we can see how the two components of SI, emotional self-awareness and the sharing and working through of emotion, are so vital to LTLR health. Low SI is the catalyst of an infidelity of fear. And as will be discussed more fully in the section on treatment in the next chapter, the key to an infidelity of fear couple's becoming invulnerable to a recurrence of an infidelity is to increase the SI of the betraying partner so that he or she can work through and resolve the deep-seated fear that caused the partner to betray.

That fear long predates the current relationship, originating in early attachment wounds. In fact, of the three types of infidelity, the infidelity of fear can be seen to have the least to do with the dynamics of the LTLR that is betrayed and the most to do with the betraying partner's own psyche and history. One result of this, that the betraying partner comes into the LTLR with this infidelity inducing fear, is that infidelities of fear usually occur, or start occurring early on in the LTLR, sometimes months, weeks, or even just days into the relationship. Also, infidelities of fear often occur serially, not usually consisting of a single infidelity, and they are just as often short-lived sexual liaisons as they are emotional affairs.

The Infidelity of Loneliness: Running Toward Awakening

Mutually falling in love, the state of being in sweet symbiosis, can be described as a time in a person's life when one feels the perfect opposite of loneliness. But after the inevitable end of sweet symbiosis, feelings of loneliness often develop in one or both LTLR partners.

This is a sign that something is wrong in the relationship. It is not a sign that the LTLR is fatally flawed but rather an indication that the relationship needs to grow and change. Unfortunately, it is common that a partner in whom a sense of loneliness is growing will do nothing about his or her loneliness. Some of these individuals have not developed enough SI to be consciously aware of this uncomfortable feeling or deny or repress it because they think they "should not" be feeling it and so are afraid to acknowledge it. Others, though aware of it, do nothing because they do not know what to do to attempt to address it or do nothing because their attachment history causes them to expect to feel lonely and thus have no hope that anything can be done to resolve and make the feeling go away. Others do try to address their loneliness in various ways with their partner but find that their attempts do nothing to beat back their increasing sense of isolation and estrangement.

As a result, due to their inaction or their failed action, this partner's sense of loneliness grows. And a lonely person, a really lonely person, is really vulnerable to the one thing that will most powerfully take his or her loneliness away: falling in love again. This is the very process that leads to so many affairs. These are infidelities of loneliness.

How does the therapist determine when an infidelity was one of loneliness? The conditions that underlie and define an infidelity of loneliness are:

1. The development of the LTLR has been arrested, usually for years or even for decades, at stage two, soured symbiosis, by the failure to ever develop healthy CI.
2. Due to this low CI the partners have grown apart, causing deterioration in AI.
3. This lack of closeness over time has resulted in the betraying partner feeling increasingly unloved and deeply lonely.
4. The betraying partner has low SI, which contributed to the buildup of the unchecked loneliness within him- or herself.

Whereas low SI is the key underlying an infidelity of fear, in the infidelity of loneliness low LTLR CI is the catalyst of betrayal. The couple's inability to deal effectively with their inevitable differences, their failure to resolve their conflicts, not only results in increasing, unresolved negative feelings within and between both of them, but it also creates distance between them that with time grows into a yawning gulf. These are the couples that come into therapy speaking of having "grown apart." Low CI, not bad sex, not financial problems, not alcohol or drug addiction, not the kids, not lack of date nights, not anything else is the cause. Over time, low CI, whether the couple has been mired in either the conflict avoidant or the hostile dependent maladaptive conflict styles, will result in a relationship awash in loneliness with partners starving for love. This is the fertile ground from which an infidelity of loneliness springs.

Unlike infidelities of fear, infidelities of loneliness usually do not occur at the beginning of a LTLR. Because it takes time for loneliness to build to the point that it is strong enough to overshadow the love that the LTLR was built upon, infidelities of loneliness usually do not occur for at least a few years after the beginning of the LTLR. Affairs are most often an infidelity of loneliness, while sexual liaisons usually are either infidelities of fear or of anger. After all, it is the emotional attachment and succor of an affair that assuages loneliness much better than the alluring yet ephemeral pleasures of sex.

Another characteristic of an infidelity of loneliness is that most often the betraying partner does not actively seek it out. To the contrary, these partners frequently are taken by surprise by both their attraction to the other person and the subsequent actions they take driven by that attraction. Infidelity of loneliness betraying partners have described this experience as going from feeling numbed or deadened by their loneliness and then feeling suddenly, shockingly awakened by their intense desire.

The key to assisting a couple who has experienced such a LTLR shattering "surprise" to never have to worry about it happening again is to help them build such strong CI that their sense of intimate closeness with their partner makes loneliness impossible. With such intimacy, the vulnerability to seeking out love from another evaporates. But sometimes it is impossible to get to this work with infidelity of loneliness couples because the very real love the betraying partner felt for his or her affair partner cannot just be turned off. Until that emotion has significantly faded, the betraying partner's earnestness and motivation to heal the LTLR is necessarily in doubt.

The Infidelity of Anger: Running for Revenge

When individuals who have never learned how to work constructively through their anger come into a LTLR they are like a time bomb and the relationship has just triggered the countdown on the timer. The explosion is going to happen; the only questions are how long before it takes place and what form is it going to take. Sometimes it takes the form of infidelity, the infidelity of anger. This is infidelity as the ruinous tool of revenge.

The characteristics of an infidelity of anger are:

1. The betraying partner has low SI, particularly when it comes to dealing with situations in which he or she feels hurt or disappointed.
2. Due to this low SI, the betraying partner has a great deal of hurt and disappointment built up inside (much of it predating the LTLR and originating in a pathological early attachment history), creating a reservoir of anger.
3. The betraying partner has unrealistic and immature expectations of a LTLR, often defined by the expectation that all his or her needs should be met and as a result has a very low tolerance for disappointment.
4. There is low CI in the LTLR, defined by either a strong conflict avoidant or a strong hostile dependent conflict process style.

Infidelities of anger are the most primitive of the three types. Their roots lie in the betraying partner's childhood. The arrested, immature nature of the betraying partner's dynamics is evident in the therapy room. With this type of infidelity, it is the combination of low SI in the betraying partner and then low CI in the couple that potentiates the betrayal.

While infidelities of loneliness manifest later in a LTLR, infidelities of anger often occur quite early in the relationship since the lion's share of the anger that fuels the betrayal is frequently already festering within the betraying partner before the LTLR begins. This is not always the case, however. In some cases the infidelity of anger only takes place after repeated unresolved hurts and disappointments in the LTLR itself have built up, fueling the rage that seeks release in revenge.

In either case it is vital to note that it is the betraying partner's failure to develop healthy SI in dealing with his or her hurts and disappointments that gives the partner over to out of control anger. This dangerously low SI also inhibits infidelity of anger betraying partners from being able to attain any measure of CI. Some of them are typically explosive hostile dependent individuals, but just as many are less obviously angry conflict avoidant repressors and deniers.

A tip off that the therapist is looking at an infidelity of anger case is the occasion when the betraying partner relates how over time he or she felt more justified in being unfaithful, due to the supposed misdeeds of the partner. One result of this is that infidelities of anger are often multiple in number and most commonly sexual liaisons. Another identifying feature of an infidelity of anger is the betraying partner's need to have the infidelity revealed. Revenge, whether it is the conscious or unconscious intent of the betraying partner, is not secured unless the betrayal is revealed and its pain inflicted. Frequently infidelity of anger betraying partners will leave numerous and obvious clues to their betrayal.

Helping the betraying partner develop real SI so is it possible to heal his or her attachment wounds is the first major task necessary to overcome an infidelity of anger. The other therapeutic undertaking centers around assisting the couple to build strong CI to enable them to avoid the buildup of hurt, disappointment, and the resultant anger and resentment that could refuel another infidelity of anger in the future. Now we will get to the specifics of how we assist couples in just these ways.

TRI Treatment Guidelines for Recovering Intimacy After Infidelity

The Basics

Working with couples who have initiated therapy in response to the discovery or revelation of infidelity requires a delicate touch since it is therapy performed within an extremely highly charged emotional environment. We have found, therefore, that it is especially important for the therapist to be well grounded in four basic precepts of couples therapy.

First, as always in couples therapy, it is absolutely essential that the therapist work to avoid any experience of favoritism for either partner. Few things will cause a couple to drop out of therapy quicker than the therapist's failure to avoid being triangulated.

But infidelity couples present with a heightened, built-in danger of bias for the therapist; one partner, after all, is the betrayed and the other is the betrayer. It is easy to see one partner as the victim and the other as the perpetrator, one partner as the good guy and the other as the bad guy. If the therapist gives any hint that this is the way he or she sees them, the therapy is over before it begins.

On the other hand, it is absolutely essential that the therapist clearly establishes at the outset of the therapy that the partner who engaged in infidelity is alone responsible for it and for its painful and damaging effects.

So it is a very fine line that the therapist must walk in these cases. We find that treating both partners with respect, separating what they have each done from who they each are, and looking for opportunities to give each of them honest positive as well as negative feedback enables us to effectively align with both partners.

Also important for the therapist to remember is that just as with any other couple, it is essential with infidelity couples to focus more on helping them with conflict process than with conflict resolution. Infidelity couples, like all couples, most need our help in learning how to do conflict well, how to fight well. They are more than intelligent enough to come up with good enough solutions to their differences.

Though it is seductive for the couples therapist to provide couples with "ingenuous" answers to their problems by being a font of "wisdom," doing so does not serve couples well in the long term. Doing so does not equip couples to be able to handle their future difficulties and crises. But if we help them learn to wield the tools of healthy conflict process, they will be able to resolve issues on their own going forward.

At the outset of infidelity couples therapy, the couple, especially the betrayed partner, may need the therapist's more direct involvement and guidance in order to help stabilize themselves and the situation. But it is not long before the couple is best served by the therapist bringing the focus onto the conflict process.

A related pitfall to be avoided is the therapist prematurely focusing on rekindling the feeling and expression of love and affection between partners. This is a common couples therapy mistake but one that is especially counterproductive in infidelity couples therapy.

As discussed in the sections on the three intimacies, for true long-term growth and change in LTLRs it is necessary to make significant headway in working through the underlying causes of relationship distress first before directly and fully addressing how they feel and express their loving feelings. Date nights and roses are not the first order of business. Focusing at the outset on "loving well" with couples in trouble is like slapping a bandage on a gaping, infected wound. It might feel like help in the short term but in reality it is just covering over deeper problems that will only get worse.

This is especially true in traumatized couples like infidelity couples. First, these couples need to be focused by their therapist on the work of building up their SI and their CI or they will have no chance of their AI returning to life.

The final basic couples therapy issue to address is that of the therapist's own level of LTLR maturity. As with any type of guide, it is difficult for anyone to lead others where he or she has never been. The most effective couples therapists are those who through their own personal work and LTLR experiences have at times achieved at least stage three in a LTLR. The intimacy maturity gained from this enables these therapists to truly show their clients the way to achieve this same personal and LTLR growth. It enables these therapists to be able to create a calm and safe environment for couples to bring their toxic conflicts into. Without this, the therapist's discomfort with a couple's anger or rage will fatally hinder the work the couple needs to do.

The therapist's intimacy maturity and the extent to which he or she has worked through his or her own past LTLR wounds is especially called into play when working with infidelity couples. Since the primal emotions triggered by this most basic of betrayals are so strong and deep, and since most of us at one time or another during the course of our own romantic relationship history have experienced being unfaithful or a partner being unfaithful to us, strong transferential reactions can easily be produced. These, of course, are major impediments to the therapist's ability to give the infidelity couple the help they so desperately need.

Therefore, it is vital that therapists working with infidelity couples not only have journeyed to at least stage three at some time in their LTLRs past or present, but that they have also worked through whatever infidelity experiences they have had. Otherwise, the therapist is setting up him- or herself to fall victim to the first basic couples therapy misstep we mentioned above: aligning him- or herself with one partner and against the other.

Early Infidelity Couples Therapy Treatment Issues
Absolutely critical to success in the therapeutic process of assisting a couple recover intimacy after infidelity is the therapist's ability to adroitly manage the early phase of the therapy. The fragility and volatility of infidelity couples during initial consultation and early therapy makes this especially challenging for the therapist.

Therefore, as a framework with which to aid the therapist in strategizing and intervening, we have identified three major infidelity couples therapy tasks facing the therapist as he or she begins working with a new infidelity couple. They are:

1. Dealing with the betrayed partner's devastation,
2. Determining the betraying partner's earnestness,
3. Assessment of the LTLR and of the infidelity.

Dealing With the Devastation   Aside from the standard tasks inherent to the beginning of any psychotherapy, the first order of business in working with a couple coming in for therapy shortly after the discovery or revelation of infidelity is crisis management work. Before either individual or dyadic healing can begin to take place, the therapist has to move to stop the bleeding, especially that of the betrayed partner.

From the first minutes of the first session, the therapist intervenes in a number of ways to stop further deterioration in the LTLR and to establish a foundation of safety and healing for the therapy. There are a few distinct components of this initial work.

Most immediate of these is the need to assist the couple, especially the betrayed partner, deal with the devastating and often overwhelming emotions that he or she is feeling in response to the infidelity. Principal among these, of course, is profound hurt, sorrow, fear, and rage of the betrayed partner. The betraying partner's emotions, such as guilt and fear, though real, are not the focus of this initial crisis management work since it is the betrayed partner whose reality and whose heart have been shattered. From the initial session and for some time afterward, he or she is in dire need of assistance from the therapist in dealing with and managing the maelstrom of painful and hostile feelings and impulses swirling within and threatening to sweep him or her away.

Simply having the therapist hear the pain, disorientation, and devastation helps this partner. Validating all of the emotions that he or she is feeling is important, as is normalizing the partner's reaction. Assuring the betrayed partner that the breadth and strength of the emotions and thoughts that he or she is experiencing are absolutely normal for someone going through what he or she is going through helps the partner bind his or her anxiety. It also enables the person to begin to feel an inkling of normalcy after finding him- or herself flailing wildly about, adrift in what he or she used to "know" as his or her world, now turned upside down.

Simultaneously, the therapist needs to assess the ego strength of the betrayed partner, particularly evaluating his or her ability to self-soothe. Helping this partner to heighten his or her ability to self-soothe during this agonizing time can be vital not only for his or her subjective experience but also in enabling the person to have the strength to manage the pain and anger so that he or she can productively work in the couples therapy.

Doing early didactic work with the couple about infidelity and about LTLR in general helps them begin to feel like they have a grasp on a situation that previously felt totally out of control, unexplainable, and overwhelming. Teaching them about the three types of infidelity helps them to understand what happened and see that they are not alone.

This can also help them start to see a ray of hope, which is always one of the therapist's most vital tasks to accomplish at the outset of any therapy. Beginning to believe that perhaps he or she will actually be able to heal and overcome this trauma provides particularly the betrayed partner a tentative but huge sense of relief. Didactic review can also spark the first stirrings of each partner's hope for his or her relationship's healing and survival.

So early in their therapy, usually beginning in the first session, one of the primary means by which the therapist begins to provide hope is by sharing with the couple his or her understanding of their situation within the context of the three types of infidelity and the TRI model of LTLR. One of the strengths of these TRI conceptual formulations is that they are not complex or technical. They are easy for the therapist to explain to clients, and their relative simplicity makes them easy for couples to grasp and relate to their own LTLR and infidelity experience. We find that sharing the LTLR model and the infidelity typology with couples stirs hope within them in that it brings understanding to replace their confusion and begins to show them the path out of the hell they have descended into.

In addition, for infidelity couples in great pain, often at war with each other, and usually filled with confusion, their therapist's expertise and insight as demonstrated by command of LTLR and infidelity theory, which makes sense to them, begins to build hope in the couple that this therapist can help them and just maybe they can get past this trauma. And of course, that hope is vital to both partners staying in and doing the difficult work of their infidelity couples therapy.

That therapy takes time, so it is also important for the therapist to let the couple know that typically infidelity couples therapy takes between 6 and 18 months to complete. The structure that this timeframe provides helps the couple accept that there are no quick fixes and that the commitment they are making is both a significant one but also one with a definite endpoint.

Another task for the therapist during this initial crisis management stage is to inhibit the destructive anger expression that often erupts out of the betrayed partner's devastation. Validating the betrayed partner's rage is vital, but so is defining a clear line in the sand over which neither partner is allowed to go in expressing anger. Teaching the couple the difference between standing up for oneself in expressing anger versus expressing anger in such a way so as to inflict pain on the other is one of the important early lessons of infidelity couples therapy.

It is also important that early on the therapist assess for suicidal or homicidal ideation; a large percentage of crimes of passion are the result of infidelity. Infidelity is such a profound betrayal and causes such deep hurt that the desire for retribution can become overpowering. The therapist must help the betrayed partner know that it is normal to feel this impulse for revenge; in helping him or her to verbally express and examine this desire the therapist assists the client not to act on it. This is of particular consequence when children are involved. Impulsively using one's children to get back at the betraying partner makes these innocents victims of betrayal as well.

In fact in general one of the other key aspects of the initial crisis management work of infidelity couples therapy is helping the partners resist the lure of making any such impulsive decisions. The often desperate desire to escape from the pain and anguish they are experiencing predisposes infidelity couple partners to want to take quick action. Their judgment is impaired by the powerful negative emotions that are clouding their minds.

This is especially true of betrayed partners. Helping them to see that they have time to make important decisions calms them. It is also important to help them acknowledge that their judgment is not as sound as it normally is, and understandably so. We encourage these clients not to make hasty decisions or quick, radical changes to their lives. Such changes may eventually need to be made, but they usually do not need to be made right away.

These are some of the most common issues that arise initially in treating the infidelity couple, particularly the betrayed partner, and in dealing with the shattering emotional effects of infidelity. Unless the therapist focuses right away on stabilizing the emotional turmoil that betrayed partners are enduring, it is likely their hope for personal and relationship recovery will dim and that those negative emotions will come to control them, resulting in destructive acting out behavior. On the other hand, by working to stop their emotional bleeding the therapist will enable betrayed partners to stabilize and the couple to gain the hope and strength necessary to do the work of healing their relationship.

Determining Earnestness   Another major issue that needs to be attended to early in infidelity couples therapy is the threshold issue of earnestness. This is an issue that pertains particularly to the betraying partner. After being unfaithful, is he or she sincerely committed to the LTLR? Determining the answer to this question is one of the primary tasks of the couples therapist in the first few therapy sessions. It is a question that is understandably uppermost in the betrayed partner's mind; he or she needs to have it answered as soon as possible, even though he or she may not like the answer.

Obviously, if the answer to this question is "no," the therapist needs to change the focus of the therapy away from working to heal and rebuild the LTLR. Sometimes this situation arises when the betraying partner agrees to come in for couples therapy out of guilty feelings for the terrible pain he or she caused the partner. Other times the betraying partner agrees to couples therapy not out of a desire to repair the LTLR, but as a delaying tactic to keep the options open and the partner's wrath mollified while he or she figures out how best to get out of the relationship.

But we find that a majority of betraying partners who present with their spouses for infidelity couples therapy are in fact earnest in their desire to heal their LTLR. This, however, does not eliminate the need for therapists to address this issue explicitly at the outset of their therapy. Betrayed partners need this reassurance that they are not again "being a fool," and the therapist needs to clearly establish the motivations of the partners to assist in determining how best to work with them.

Earnest betraying partners feel extremely guilty, knowing the pain they have caused their partners. They are angry and disappointed with themselves for causing such pain. These partners want to understand why they ended up betraying both their partners and themselves. They are willing to do just about anything in an attempt to try to make amends for what they have done to their partners. They are motivated to do their part, which after an infidelity is much more than 50%, in healing and rebuilding the relationship.

How is this earnestness determined? In two main ways. First, the therapist needs to start assessing up front, beginning in the first session, if the betraying partner is able to explicitly, unequivocally, and sincerely state both his or her total commitment to the partner and the LTLR, as well as state his or her pledge to do whatever can be done to heal and rebuild that relationship.

It goes without saying that this includes the assurance that their infidelity relationship or relationships are over. If the betraying partner has not ended those relationships, no real work to heal and rebuild the LTLR can take place, and the therapist runs the risk of the therapy becoming complicit in a continuing betrayal. If the betraying partner does not provide his or her spouse with convincing evidence that the infidelity is over, then it is likely best to suspend the couples therapy until such time as he or she does so.

But if the betraying partner does make clear his or her sincere commitment to the LTLR through verbal statements, the therapist needs to assess the earnestness of that commitment in the betraying partner's actions. This is the second means of earnestness assessment. As mentioned above, the first test of this is whether or not the infidelity relationship has ended. Beyond that, however, the therapist needs to use the extent to which the betraying partner engages in the work of the therapy, the work of healing the LTLR, to determine if his or her earnestness is real or not. This work can be divided into three main areas of betraying partner behavior:

1. Expressions or regret and remorse,
2. Trust-building behaviors,
3. Involvement in therapy.

One sign of real commitment to the LTLR in the betraying partner is their willingness and desire to express regret and remorse repeatedly for the betrayal and how it has devastated the partner. If the desire and willingness to express these sincere emotions is not present or is minimally present, this is a clear sign that the betraying partner's commitment to the relationship is tenuous at best. In order for real healing from the wound of infidelity to occur, such expressions of regret and remorse need to occur repeatedly and frequently, especially when that wound is still fresh. If true, deep regret and remorse are in fact felt by the betraying partner, such expression is not a problem and this becomes clear early on in the therapy.

Of course, many, if not most, betraying partners at some point in the healing process find themselves feeling frustrated and impatient with their partner's inability to "get over it already." But if their motivation to rebuild the LTLR is true, they are able to overcome that frustration. Early signs of an unwillingness to repeatedly be the object of their partner's expressions of hurt and rage and also to respond to such episodes with repetitions of their expressions of regret and remorse are a clear indication of a weak or insincere commitment to the LTLR. This is especially true when it occurs even after the therapist has attempted to assist the betraying partner to recognize the necessity of these behaviors and he or she still fails to engage in them or only does so intermittently and resentfully.

Likewise, early signs of an unwillingness to "bend over backward" to do things to earn back trust is also an indicator of an insincere commitment to the LTLR on the part of the betraying partner. The betrayed partners' acts have shattered the trust of their partner; the only way to rebuild that trust is also through the reassurance of their totally trustworthy actions going forward. So the betraying partner must be willing to be completely transparent and disclosive of their day-to-day actions.

Also, the betraying partner needs to be willing to be proactive in behaving in ways that are reassuring and trust inducing for the partner. Such trust-building behaviors are outlined in Janis Spring's book *After the Affair* (1996) and include both low-cost and high-cost behaviors. We often use Spring's list with clients and have added to it. We have clients look over the list and use it to determine which types of behaviors the betrayed wants his or her partner to agree to. This list changes over time for the couple. From the outset of therapy, employing it can help the betrayed partner begin to feel there are demonstrable boundaries that help him or her begin to build trust and confidence in both self and partner. The unwillingness of the betraying partner to engage in any such trust-building behaviors calls into serious question his or her commitment to the LTLR.

Finally, the failure of betraying partners to engage fully in the work of their infidelity couples therapy is another indicator of a lack of earnest commitment to the LTLR.

Infidelity couples therapy is demanding for both partners. The therapist challenges each person to grow, to be honest and open, to own his or her own weaknesses and mistakes, and to work on the relationship both in and outside the office. Often, the therapist's first sign that the betraying partner's expressed commitment to their LTLR is not sincere or as strong as he or she espouses is when the person repeatedly fails to really work in the therapy. This can manifest as a failure to open up emotionally, a failure to self-disclose sincerely, lying, refusing to answer the partner's questions about the infidelity, or a failure to do either assigned work between sessions or take other actions he or she committed to take. The therapist must be watchful for such behavior and determine if it does indeed indicate a lack of earnest LTLR commitment or is a manifestation of resistance deriving from some other cause.

If, as a result of any of these three types of behavior taking place, the therapist comes to question the earnestness of the betraying partner's commitment to the LTLR, he or she needs to bring this issue up in the therapy to be discussed and if necessary, acted upon. Such action includes either or both partners deciding to end the LTLR when it becomes clear that the betraying partner's earnest commitment does not exist. Or the indicated action may be the betraying partner bringing his or her actions into alignment or congruence with the actual, heartfelt commitment to the relationship. Either way, this issue of the betraying partner's earnestness needs to be dealt with early and explicitly.

Using the TRI LTLR model, we see the question of the betraying partner's earnestness as the evaluation of whether any of the three deal breakers apply to him or her. For if any of the three deal breakers does apply to the betraying partner, he or she will not be able to make or maintain an earnest commitment to the LTLR.

Most often, the deal breakers involved here within the betraying partner are either the second ("Love has died") or the third ("Won't take responsibility"). The therapist must be careful in concluding that the second deal breaker applies. Quite often infidelity couples partners, especially betraying partners, come into therapy no longer able to feel or access love for his or her partner and thereby conclude that the love in the relationship is dead. But we have learned from these couples that in fact often in these cases their love is not dead. It is just covered over, buried under a mountain of pain and resentment. If the couple is able to dig out from under that mountain by developing healthy CI so they can work through the built up negative feelings toward each other, they often find their love coming back to life.

Even more common in cases of the betraying partner being unable to make an earnest commitment is the third deal breaker being the cause of this failure. An unwillingness to take responsibility for one's self and one's part in the LTLR problems, by far the most common reason for LTLR failure, here manifests as the unwillingness to commit to the work of healing. In these cases, the betraying partner would rather end the LTLR than take responsibility for examining self and engaging in the work of rebuilding the relationship. Usually in these circumstances (i.e., when the third deal breaker applies to the betraying partner), his or her involvement in the infidelity itself served unconsciously as a means toward escaping from the pain and difficulties of the LTLR by sabotaging it. These are Brown's (2001) "Exit Affairs." As with any couple in which the third deal breaker applies, the therapist better serves the couple in assisting them in working on a good divorce and not a good marriage.

LTLR and Infidelity Assessment   The last major task for the TRI therapist in the early phase of infidelity couples therapy is the assessment of both the LTLR and the infidelity. As in any type of psychotherapy, incisive initial evaluation is vital to effective treatment.

In addressing the betraying partner's earnestness and the betrayed partner's devastation we have already dealt with certain initial evaluative issues. But one of the strengths of the TRI approach is that it provides a strong heuristic framework that the therapist can use to get a clear picture of the couple's relationship and of the infidelity. This enables the therapist to see where the couple is stuck in the LTLR developmental process, what the couple's intimacy strengths and weaknesses are as defined by the three intimacies, and what kind of infidelity has occurred. All this information gives the therapist the data he or she needs in order to develop a clear understanding of why the infidelity occurred and what work the couple needs to do in order to both heal their LTLR in the short term and rebuild it so it will flourish for the long term.

In assessing the couple's LTLR the TRI therapist uses the two main TRI LTLR constructs: the developmental model of LTLR and the three intimacies. Determining where an infidelity couple is developmentally is usually quite simple since the vast majority of infidelity couples are stuck at the same point in the developmental process: soured symbiosis. Though couples take varying routes to get there, almost all couples presenting for infidelity couples therapy have become arrested in soured symbiosis, unable to progress into the differentiation stage. Some have regressed from differentiation to soured symbiosis due to a failure to deal well with major stressors, but most infidelity couples have never been able to mature past soured symbiosis. They have never been able to navigate through the Scylla and Charybdis of conflict avoidance and hostile dependence to reach CI. For the TRI therapist the key question then becomes determining which of these two maladaptive conflict styles the couple uses when dealing with their differences. Further, whichever conflict style, the therapist needs to look at each partner's conflict process tendencies, strengths, and weaknesses.

This leads to the other major area of initial infidelity couple LTLR diagnostic assessment, the three intimacies. Determining where the couple and each partner is in each of the three intimacies provides the TRI therapist with a clear picture of the structure of the LTLR and its weaknesses and strengths. This powerful information gives the TRI therapist the lion's share of what he or she needs to know in order to fashion a treatment plan for the couple.

First in this process is the assessment of each partner's level of SI. A useful way to approach this assessment process is to use the three questions of the Emotional Self Awareness (ESA) exercise (Solomon & Teagno, 2006) to identify three relevant SI variables. That is, how strong is each partner's ability to be consciously aware of and identify his or her emotions (Question 1), how much insight does he or she have into the causes of their emotions (Question 2), and how strong is he or she in taking constructive action to stand up for his or her feelings, rights or needs (Question 3)? Since we know that SI forms the most basic foundational layer upon which LTLR intimacy rests, identifying each partner's SI strengths and weaknesses is essential in enabling the therapist to determine what therapy work needs to be done later by each partner.

Ascertaining which conflict process style the couple engages in, conflict avoidance, hostile dependence, or a cycling between the two, hybrid style, has a major impact on TRI infidelity couples therapy work. As referenced earlier, a great deal of the actual therapy work session after session with these couples is work in the Initiator and the Inquirer (I-to-I) CI developing exercise developed by Bader and Pearson (1988). In order to be effective in helping the couple with this work, it is essential that the therapist have a clear understanding of the couple's conflict process style and each partner's conflict process strengths and weaknesses. These strengths and weaknesses become quite clear to the TRI therapist once each partner has been placed in both the initiator and the inquirer roles of the I-to-I exercise within the first few sessions of their infidelity couples therapy.

Bader and Pearson's I-to-I exercise is a powerful tool because it focuses on conflict process, not conflict resolution. The I-to-I exercise is the tool we use to teach clients how to express their feelings constructively, how to listen well to their partner's feelings, and how to manage the tension within themselves that conflict creates (Solomon & Teagno, 2006). As partners develop their capacity for CI, it enables them to escape from their intimacy killing toxic conflict pattern, whether it is conflict avoidant or hostile dependent.

The I-to-I exercise places each partner in one of two roles, the initiator or the inquirer. The initiator shares to be self-revelatory and intimate, to stand up for the self, and to hopefully learn more about him- or herself. The inquirer's responsibility is to listen well to the partner, to tell the other what he or she has heard, and to ask questions designed to deepen his or her understanding of the partner's reality, questions that ultimately assist the initiator in understanding more about him- or herself. This exercise pushes the initiator to be more self intimate and differentiated while it pushes the inquirer to maintain differentiation instead of devolving into defensiveness.

Assessing the couple's AI is important in completing the picture of their LTLR's structure. Though AI work is not focused on early in infidelity couples therapy, determining the strengths and weaknesses of an infidelity couple's AI often speaks volumes about how they got into the painful straits in which they find themselves.

The key for the therapist is to assess each partner's abilities and tendencies within the LTLR to both give and receive the four types of AI: verbal, actions, nonsexual physical, and sexual affection intimacy. Getting a clear view from the couple of how their AI progressed over time in their LTLR is useful since the TRI therapist is not only looking at postinfidelity revelation AI functioning but also at earlier AI functioning. Past LTLR AI functioning information gives the therapist an idea of the partners' AI capabilities. This can be used eventually in their therapy to help the couple build upon after they have done a good deal of infidelity healing work and CI work.

Concurrent to the assessment of the couple's LTRL, it is essential that the therapist also determine the type of infidelity or infidelities that have occurred. By utilizing the descriptions outlined above of the defining characteristics of each type of infidelity, the infidelity couples therapist can analyze and identify the infidelity type. Knowing which type of infidelity took place gives invaluable information to the therapist; as discussed earlier, determining whether the betraying partner's infidelity was one of fear, of loneliness, or of anger is essential to the identification of the main weaknesses in the LTLR. This then informs the therapist's insight into what therapy work the couple needs to focus on in order to restructure and rebuild their LTLR so that the fertile ground upon which infidelity grows is never again present within the couple's relationship.

References

Bader, E., & Pearson, P. (1988). *In quest for the mythical mate: A developmental approach to diagnosis and treatment in couples therapy.* New York: Routledge.

Bowlby, J. (1969). *Attachment.* New York: Basic Books.

Brown, E. (2001). *Patterns of infidelity and their treatment.* Philadelphia: Brunner-Routledge.

Ceo, M. (2005). *Couples and affairs: Managing the clinical challenges.* Memphis, TN: Cross Country Education, Inc.

Fisher, H. (1992). *Anatomy of love: A natural history of mating, marriage and why we stray.* New York: W.W. Norton.

Lusterman, D. (1998). *Infidelity: A survival guide.* Oakland, CA: New Harbinger Publications.

Solomon, S., & Teagno, L. (2006). *Intimacy after infidelity.* Oakland, CA: New Harbinger Publications.

Spring, J. (1996). *After the affair.* New York: HarperCollins.

CHAPTER 3

Recovering From Sexual and Other Types of Infidelity, Part II

Treatment Guidelines and Strategies

STEVEN D. SOLOMON and LORIE J. TEAGNO

Once the early infidelity couples therapy work of attending to the betrayed partner's devastation has begun, once the betraying partner's earnest commitment to the long-term love relationship (LTLR) has been affirmed, and once the initial assessment of the LTLR and of the type of infidelity have been accomplished, the work of rebuilding the LTLR's intimacy structure needs to commence. This work is defined by two major related goals: significantly increasing three intimacies (as outlined in the previous chapter) functioning and reestablishing trust as a given in the LTLR. The accomplishment of these two therapy goals results in the creation of a LTLR that is so strong in its intimacy that it is infidelity proof.

The paths to achieving these two longer-term infidelity therapy goals are intertwined. Reestablishing a high level of trust in the LTLR is enabled by a combination of growth in the three intimacies in the relationship over time as well as by the consistent integrity and trustworthy behavior of the betraying partner displayed over time.

Periodically, mistrust and suspicion will erupt in the betrayed partner. At times frustration in the betraying partner's continued lack of trust arises. Incidents may need to be reviewed and worked through in therapy. Trust-building guidelines need to be revisited and adjusted, and the importance of the betraying partner's transparency often needs to be reiterated. The fragile, slow process of rebuilding trust needs to be closely attended to

A sure sign that this is happening is when affectional feelings begin to reemerge. As discussed earlier, when the dark side of a couple's passion (CI) begins to be openly wrestled with and worked through, the light side of their passion (affection intimacy [AI]) will begin to thrive. So when the infidelity couple has made substantial progress in growing their SI and CI, the therapist considers starting to work with them on their AI.

Helping them to assess the AI structure of their relationship is useful here. The therapist can have each partner rate both him- or herself and his or her partner in the four types of AI. Having them share their ratings with each other and talk about them can be very powerful. Often partners are completely unaware of which of the four types of AI is most meaningful to their partner, that most makes them each feel loved and important. So helping them to draw this type of AI map of their LTLR can have a great impact on helping them to learn where they need to make extra AI efforts. Assigning AI homework can be useful in this process.

Summary of General Treatment Guidelines

- Work assiduously to avoid any appearance of favoritism for either partner.
- Establish early and clearly that the partner who engaged in infidelity is alone responsible for it.
- Focus the work of therapy on the couples' conflict process, not on conflict resolution.
- Avoid prematurely focusing on rekindling AI.
- The most effective infidelity couples therapists have achieved LTLR stage three experience in their own lives and have worked through their own infidelity experiences and issues.
- The two major tasks of infidelity couples therapy are assisting the couple heal from the shattering effects of the infidelity and helping them build a healthy and stable intimacy structure in their LTLR.
- There are three major infidelity couples therapy jobs confronting the therapist at the outset of therapy:
  1. Dealing with the betrayed partner's devastation,
  2. Determining the betraying partner's earnestness,
  3. Assessment of the LTLR and of the infidelity.
- The longer-term work of helping the couple rebuild their LTLR's intimacy structure so as to achieve LTLR health and minimize the chances of a reoccurrence of infidelity is defined by two related goals:
  1. Significantly increasing three intimacies functioning,
  2. Reestablishing trust as a given in the LTLR.

Specific Treatment Guidelines for Each Infidelity Type

This section will provide an overview of the general treatment guidelines we use in working with all infidelity couples on rebuilding the intimacy structure of their LTLR after an infidelity. But how we work with these couples is greatly impacted by which one of the three infidelities the betraying partner engaged in.

Infidelity of Fear

Of the three types of infidelity, we have found that successful treatment of infidelities of fear couples depends on change from the betrayed partner the least. Although the betrayed partner has a role in helping to create the changes necessary so that the partner never again commits an infidelity of fear, that change is much more about the betraying partner than it is about the relationship with his or her partner.

The work of the betraying partner is primarily to acknowledge the deep fear that is driving him or her, whichever of the three fears (commitment, intimacy, worthiness) it is. Then that partner has to work it through, deal with it, unmask the false beliefs about him- or herself and about love relationships that it is based on, and replace these with healthier beliefs. The betraying partner's fear will never completely disappear, but by confronting this fear and wrestling with it, he or she will become stronger and the fear will become weaker. If the betraying partner has enough courage to do this work, the fear will lose its strength to control him or her; it will no longer have the power to drive the person to betray.

As the betraying partner works on him- or herself, he or she needs to include the partner in the process by being self intimate with both him- or herself and his or her partner. The betraying partner needs to talk with his or her partner about this fear. This practice pushes at both SI and CI as it raises the tension and challenges both partners to differentiate.

The therapist's role in this process is to provide a "holding frame" for the couples work. As you guide the betraying partner to confront his or her fears and discuss them, you also support him or her. You will simultaneously support the betrayed partner to hear his or her partner's reality without getting defensive. This partner will need to be able to self-comfort just as the other partner will need to do the same as his or her level of fear is activated. The betraying partner will be expecting to be criticized, attacked, or humiliated.

Infidelity of Fear Case Example   This first case presentation exemplifies the type of work the TRI therapist conducts during the first session of infidelity couples therapy as well as some of the dynamics evidenced by an infidelity of fear couple. Transcribed dialogue alternates with bracketed comments, which illustrate the assessment methods being utilized, explicate the therapist's thoughts, and gives reactions to material presented. Some sections of dialogue are summarized for the sake of brevity.

Joan and Suzy have been together 10 years and have been registered domestic partners for 9 of those years. The therapist had seen Joan individually for several sessions after the couple had worked with a different couples therapist for three sessions. Joan came to therapy after Suzy cut off their relationship and saw this therapist's colleague briefly for individual therapy as she tried to decide how to deal with the betrayal. Neither felt the previous couples therapy was helpful in clarifying their decisions or dilemmas.

Therapist: Suzy, as you know I have met with Joan for three months so I would like to start with you and ask you what is the most pressing thing for you to learn today in this meeting?

Suzy: You know about Joan's betrayal with our mutual friend. I am devastated and have decided that the relationship is over. I believe that she has always lied to me and continues to lie. But I wanted to come in because Joan keeps asking me to give us another chance and promises that she wants to change. I have read your book and if I decide to work on the relationship or not, I want to learn to take better care of myself and figure out how we got to this place. I thought we had a loving, strong and committed relationship! I don't understand how this happened!

T: You're feeling the devastation of the betrayal and while a part of you feels that Joan and the relationship won't change, another part of you wants to understand how you could have felt so strong and good in the relationship while Joan was feeling differently and you did not sense this. What you would like to learn is how you two got to this place and how you did not see it as it happened. Is that right?

S: Yes. I am confused, hurt, untrusting, and devastated.

T: And, for good reasons; not only have you been betrayed by the person you have loved and created a life with for 10 years, but it seems your instincts did not help you out?

[Therapist normalizes client's deep hurt and confusion.]

S: I guess so or maybe I did not pay enough attention until too late.

T: So another part of you also wonders if your instincts might have worked, but you did not listen? You'd like to learn how to better hone your instincts?

[Suzy's ambivalence is normal for the betrayed partner. She wants to protect herself by leaving the relationship but her investment and love

for Joan still exists, so that part of her wants to explore the possibil-
ity of the relationship continuing. Conflict avoidance is likely as well
as low SI and CI. Note that she is focused on what she did not see
or intuit, but has not yet noted her partner's role in withholding the
expression of her feelings. Possible dynamic is that Suzy avoids Joan's
feelings, becoming a "lie invitee" (Bader, Pearson, & Schwartz, 2000).
Low CI]

S: Maybe. I thought that our loss of sexuality was normal; that all couples
lose this after 10 years and we're both going through menopause. I thought Joan and I saw this the same way. *[turning to*
Joan] When I asked you if it was a problem, you said it wasn't.
You would still tell me you loved me. Why?

J: I do still love you. I'm sorry. But things were not always good between us.
We both knew that.

[Therapist notes that Joan has not offered Suzy comfort or taken
ownership for her part in the hurt. While this is not unusual when
the betrayal is being spoken of it may indicate Joan's limited ability to
take responsibility, and a limited ability to be empathetic.]

T: *[Redirects Joan to self-disclose and "tests" her SI and capacity for CI with*
her partner.] Joan describe to Suzy when your loving feelings
started to change and what you were feeling that contributed to
these changes.

J: I felt like my opinions were dismissed over big things. When I disagreed
with your reasoning I felt you did not pay attention. I did not
like what became priorities in our life and that kept happening.
I felt alone and empty.

[Joan is fairly vague about her emotions, indicative of low SI as she
places more weight on Suzy's actions that her own.]

T: Suzy, would you tell Joan what you heard her say; just summarize?

[Suzy does and then Therapist asks her what she is curious about that
keeps the focus on Joan's experience. Therapist is doing early indirect
teaching of the I-to-I to assess clients' abilities to assume each role
and to assess for each partner's struggle with the roles, giving an indi-
cation of their level of symbiotic vs. differentiated functioning.]

S: Joan, how long did you feel dismissed and what did you do when you
felt that way?

J: I have felt that way for the past 6 years. I tried to speak up and get you
to listen, but when you did what you wanted anyway, I just went
along with things because I hate to argue.

T: So would it be fair to say that when you felt dismissed you had other feelings that grew and became stronger over time but you did not voice them to Suzy?

J: Yes.

S: Why didn't you tell me? I want to know how you feel! I'd rather fight over those things than this: an affair! Look what has happened! I don't know if I can ever trust you again and why should I?

[Long pause. Therapist lets the tension sit in the room. Suzy is clearly angry, hurt, and desperate and indirectly asking for succor and some explanation. Joan is clearly uncomfortable, and does not respond to her partner's request. Therapist waits.]

J: Maybe we can't fix this. *[Conflict avoidant response, attempting to get Suzy to back off.]*

S: Maybe we can't.

[Long pause]

T: Suzy, you stated that what you want from this meeting is to stand up for yourself and know how you and Joan got to this place of possibly ending your relationship over an infidelity. What have you learned about yourself so far? *[Therapist wants to return to test Suzy's commitment to self-evaluation and sticking to her stated goals. Is she more symbiotic with Joan that she recognizes?]*

S: I have learned that I am really hurt and angry. I don't really want to listen to her reasons for the affair. Is that wrong? *[Client has heard and acknowledged her feelings, indicating some SI and ownership for how her reaction affects her partner.]*

T: Joan, what are your thoughts about your partner's question? *[Therapist is testing to see if Joan can or wants to soothe her partner, to test her empathic capacity, get a sense of whether she can take responsibility for the pain inflicted and see if Joan can assume a more self-defined vs. reactive position with Suzy.]*

J: I can understand that you don't want to hear my complaints about our relationship. I did not tell you what was going on for me. I should have, but when you get mad at me I stop talking. I am sorry that I have hurt you, but there are things about the relationship that I did not like.

[Joan's capacity for ownership appears to be limited: possible presence of the third deal breaker. Her level of SI and CI are also compromised by her fear. She has difficulty making space for her partner's feelings by suspending her own.]

T: I hear the pain and discomfort you have both been experiencing and especially Suzy's pain at learning about the infidelity. Joan it sounds like you're caught between wanting to hear the pain you've caused Suzy and wanting to talk with her about the uncomfortable feelings you have had in the relationship over the past 6 years. And, for you Suzy, you want to talk with Joan about your pain, yet you are not prepared to hear about her feelings yet. I imagine that this dilemma reflects some of what you two have struggled with over the years, each wanting to be heard, but not knowing how to have the conversation without an argument or resentment. Is that accurate?

[Both nod yes.]

T: What I can offer each of you is a safe place to discuss Suzy's intense pain over your infidelity, Joan, and a way to hear each other's feelings about the relationship now and in the past. I will teach you both how to deal with your differences, tension, and pain successfully so that you can each learn more about yourself and your partner. If you are both willing to commit to working in therapy for 3 months to do the hard work that it takes to deal with the deep hurt, the real anger, and the fears that are dominating your relationship right now and that actually have been percolating for a number of years, by the end of 12 weeks you will both have a clearer sense of what you are personally capable of regarding forgiving the other, taking responsibility for your own part in the difficulties, and then determining if you want to continue to invest time, love, and growth to reconstructing this relationship. Does that interest you?

[Therapist introduces to clients the time frame and contract for the therapy work. Therapist is not shrinking from labeling the work difficult and giving a realistic time period that will require stamina and personal work on the part of each partner. Differentiation is underscored by the therapist's talk of learning more about self rather than reinforcing focusing on the partner's commitment and effort. Also included is "informed consent" about the fact that after 12 weeks each can be clearer in her thinking and no promise is made that all will be corrected, but that the decision making will continue. This is an example of holding the tension while creating hope and a safe place where new ways of communicating can occur.]

[Both say yes.]

T: I look forward to seeing you both next time. I admire your desire to understand your relationship and the hurts and stuck spots you have both struggled with. It says a great deal about both of you that you are here, trying to save your relationship, rather than doing the easy thing, which would be to just give up and run away from the pain and the hard work of healing these deep wounds. I appreciate the opportunity to help you both develop the skills that will make you each feel stronger and become more of the partner you each aspire to be. In preparation for that meeting I have some handouts for each of you. They talk about assumptions I make about how relationships change and grow [TRI, Assumptions for Relationship Growth, 2007], what each of you will need to do to prepare for each session [The Couples Institute, How to Get the Most from Couples Therapy, 2007], some immediate homework that helps you each learn how to be more aware of your feelings [TRI, Emotional Self Awareness Exercise handout, 2007] and a questionnaire for each of you about the history of your relationship [TRI, Couples Intake Questionnaire, 2007]. I often include readings and homework as part of therapy; are you both motivated to follow through on assigned homework?

[Therapist establishes that there will be teaching as well as therapy and that the commitment to work on self exists both inside and outside the office. All along, the therapist is measuring each partner's ability to keep her word to self and her partner. Therapist is also putting responsibility for the sessions and relationship work squarely in the laps of the clients.]

Developmental Assessment of the Relationship   This couple came out of sweet symbiosis as their differences and tensions over how to spend money and leisure time emerged. Neither woman knew how to discuss and work through these differences successfully. Soured symbiosis appeared early as the couple avoided their differences (conflict avoidant CI style), not knowing how to resolve them in a successful way.

Three Intimacies Assessment   Both partners struggle with low SI and very limited CI. AI is significantly compromised. They generally have a conflict avoidant style. As Suzy became more frustrated, she viewed Joan as selfish and unreliable. Joan, in turn, viewed Suzy as rigid and demanding. And, in response to Suzy's expressions of frustration and anger, Joan withdrew with resentment that remained unexpressed. As a result of their impaired CI, their AI dramatically decreased.

Infidelity Diagnosis   This turned out to be an infidelity of fear. Joan has a history of previous infidelities and may have flirted or been inappropriate with others. What later became clear to be her fear of unworthiness is signaled by her talk of feeling empty. Despite her ambivalence about recommitting to Suzy and her expressed desire to end her relationship with the other woman, she could not face the idea of being alone. Her "cut off" relationship with her dad when she was younger reinforces a struggle with worthiness. Her especially significant avoidance of conflict and preference for giving up (though resentfully) reinforce her need to be with someone, presumably to have a sense of self, at "any" cost.

Possible Deal Breaker   The third deal breaker appears to be most likely applicable of the three. Both partners' strong conflict avoidance and lack of accountability for their contribution to the relationship weaknesses are poignant.

Outcome   The third deal breaker did become the death knell for the relationship. In the end, no matter the work on CI and SI, Joan would not do the work to face her fears. She was unable to find the courage to develop a clearer, more honest sense of self and hold that self in relation to Suzy. She would not admit to Suzy that she was still communicating with the other woman. Eventually Suzy made the decision to end the relationship because there was no indication that Joan was earnest in her effort to grow and rebuild the relationship. Joan then chose to return to the other woman and the sweet symbiosis and conflict avoidance of that relationship rather than challenge herself to tolerate and accept the normal tension and differences of a LTLR. She chose ephemeral symbiotic intimacy over the immediate uncomfortable tension and discomfort that could eventually bring stable, resilient intimacy.

Specific Treatment Guidelines for Infidelity of Fear Couples
- Successful treatment of these couples depends the most on change in the betraying partner.
- The primary work of the betraying partner is to acknowledge and work through whichever of the three deep-seated fears (commitment, intimacy, or worthiness) motivated the betrayal(s), replacing the false beliefs the fear is based on with healthier, more emotionally mature beliefs about self and LTLRs.
- Work on increasing the betraying partner's SI is vital to this work, enabling the betraying partner to become fluent in emotional self-awareness, both with self and with the LTLR partner.
- The therapist works to provide a holding frame for these couples, both pushing and supporting the two partners in their work on SI and CI.

Infidelity of Loneliness

With infidelity of loneliness couples, work on developing great CI is the key to eliminating the loneliness that overtook the LTLR and powered the betrayal. However, SI work is also important here. The betraying partner's personal work is to become reliably self intimate since it was his or her weak SI that allowed the loneliness to grow unchecked to the point that it came to overwhelm and control him or her, leading to the infidelity. So this partner must fully commit to work on building up his or her SI, not only so that he or she becomes highly aware of what emotions he or she is feeling, but also so that he or she becomes able to and does talk with the partner about those emotions, whether good or bad. If the betraying partner does not do this he or she is setting him- or herself up for another infidelity of loneliness in the future.

Concurrently, the betrayed partner must work on his or her self to become a partner who serves to create a sense of safety in the LTLR so that the partner can reliably share his or her feelings. The betrayed partner must expand his or her expectations of a love relationship to include separateness and disappointment and must come to be able to accept and respect the range of emotions his or her partner's newfound SI enables him or her to share with the partner, and vice versa.

This then leads to the therapist having to address the low CI that led to the growth of distance between the couple. This is what gave birth to the loneliness that enabled the infidelity. The therapist assists the couple in closing the gap between the two of them by guiding them through the process of facing and overcoming their differences.

This is accomplished by focusing the infidelity of loneliness couple on developing strength in CI so they can work through the great deal of hurt, disappointment, and resentment that have piled up between them not only as a result of the infidelity, but just as if it had not happened. After all, it was the couple's inability to deal constructively with and resolve those negative feelings that sowed the seeds of the loneliness that led to betrayal. These negative feelings from the past have to be dealt with. Much like with an infected wound, in order to heal, the couple has to clean out the pain, the fears, and the anger that have been festering in their LTLR.

Then the healing will begin and the loneliness will start to fade as both partners begin to feel the stirrings of their love reawakening as they begin to experience real, mature intimacy with their long-lost partner. As the infidelity of loneliness couple learns through this process of building a solid three intimacies structure in their LTLR, the real antidote to loneliness for the betraying partner specifically and both partners in general is the rediscovery that the person that each fell in love with is still there and still loves them. Through the achievement of strong SI and CI, infidelity of loneliness couples can reawaken their AI, recapture their connection, and deepen it. That is what happens when a couple becomes truly intimate.

Infidelity of Loneliness Case Example   This case presentation illustrates midphase CI work with an infidelity of loneliness couple. Stu and Chelsea have been married 8 years and have two children ages 3 and 6. They have been using the I-to-I format since the second therapy session to develop greater CI. This is the eighth session and each partner is asked to choose an I-to-I developmental goal before they begin their discussion in the I-to-I format. Chelsea has offered to be the initiator on the topic of being more honest with Stu about the affair. Stu agreed to be the inquirer.

Chelsea: My goal is number 5: to think about what is bothering me and why before I speak. I know that I start to talk and then the dam opens and I am all over the place and end up accomplishing nothing for myself or in our communication. I need to talk about my affair.

Stu: My goal as the inquirer is number 8: To remain calm, not take it personally and continue to think productively and ask more questions. This may be a challenge as we discuss the affair, but I'm going to push myself.

C: Since we started working on the relationship in therapy I found great relief in being able to be honest with you. I feel less fearful and lighter. I have been scared to be brutally honest. Scared of your anger and I have not wanted to hurt you more. But I am feeling safer and some hope for more honesty. I think before I could not be honest because I knew you did not trust me and rightly so, but I would get frustrated and hopeless when I would tell you the truth and you would not believe me.

S: You're feeling safer so that's allowing you to be more honest. In the past you were afraid of my reaction and of hurting me. You also stopped yourself from being honest because I would not believe you were telling me the truth. Is that right?

C: Yes. I also think that early in our relationship I tried to talk with you about my negative feelings about your mother and we'd always get in a fight and I'd feel shut down, frustrated, and eventually hopeless. So I think I have just continued that pattern in our relationship. I stopped trying to change things; I stopped trusting that we could improve.

S: Because we could not make any progress about my mom, you thought we couldn't make any progress in other areas of our relationship and especially about the affair?

C: Yes

S: You have kept your feelings to yourself, so how has that made you feel inside?

[Instead of reacting emotionally, Stu is pushing himself to ask Chelsea about her feelings and how her actions affect her sense of self and her feelings.]

C: I have felt confused, angry, disappointed, hopeless, and I guess I decided that especially because of the affair, I had no right to talk about all these feelings since I had devastated you.

S: You have had many negative feelings, but decided that you had no right to share them because you had been unfaithful.

C: Right now I feel ready to talk with you about these feelings. I also feel proud of myself for coming clean and I feel excited and hopeful that I can change, and maybe we can.

S: You are feeling optimistic, proud, and excited.

C: I have missed being able to talk with you. I really appreciate your help listening to me.

[Therapist notes that Chelsea also wanted to discuss the affair but has avoided that subject. Using the soft moment to help them stretch themselves into more difficult terrain the therapist pushes the following:]

Therapist: Stu can you summarize for your wife what she started with and what she has said so far?

S: You wanted to organize your thoughts and feelings before you spoke; you are wanting to be more honest about the affair than you have been in the past, and you want to speak honestly and not worry about whether or not I am able to believe you.

C: Yeah, I guess I need to get focused and talk about the affair. First, before I do that I want to say that I do not want to hurt you more than I already have. You have been asking why I did what I did and I want to answer your questions to help you decide if you can forgive me.

T: Are you wanting to know if Stu is ready to hear this?

C: Yes. Is that okay with you Stu?

S: I have no choice because if I don't hear it I will only wonder, but I believe that hearing it will help me, as you said decide, see if I can get over this. I do believe that you have not continued to have contact with Pete, but I am not sure I believe what you tell me about the past. So, I am ready to listen.

C: Okay, here goes. For many years I have felt single, lonely, frustrated, and angry over our differences regarding your mother. I felt unprotected and not understood by you. Over time and no resolution

I began to focus more on the kids and then I got in touch with how depressed I was. When I got into individual therapy I learned that I had been struggling with depression since I was a kid. I started to focus on myself, work, and the kids and did not feel I had the energy to also deal with the marriage.

S: Can I tell you what I heard because you have said a lot of things?

C: Yes.

S: Since the problems with my mother and our arguments about this you have felt frustrated, angry, and essentially single. Oh, and unprotected by me. You then put your energy into the kids and work, but then you realized that you felt very depressed. You got into therapy and then the focus was on trying to understand and fix the depression. You did not have the energy for the marriage.

C: Yes, that sounds accurate, but I hear how I shut you out. I think I had given up on us and any changes. By the time I met Pete I was already emotionally out of the marriage. I did not look for an affair. I found myself feeling alive on the one hand, but also not depressed, but guilty and ashamed of myself. I didn't even admit the affair to my therapist.

S: You shut me out but had also given up on our marriage. I really want to react to this, but I won't. [He recalls his goal and due to the work they'd already done on CI in their previous sessions, he is able to not take it personally (so far) and ask more questions.] You did not look for an affair, but it made you feel good even though you also felt guilty and ashamed.

C: Yes.

T: Stu, is there anything Chelsea said that you're curious about, that you'd like to ask her about that keeps the focus on her and her feelings?

S: Let me think; there's so much. If you knew it was wrong why did you do it anyway?

T: Stu, can you ask that in a more open way that helps Chelsea learn about herself?

S: How did you make it okay with yourself to meet him, kiss him, then have a sexual relationship? [He has opened up the question, actually asked a more difficult question that requires she consider her motivation and conflicting feelings.]

C: I no longer had romantic feelings for you. I decided our marriage was over and I did not think that you would find out. I hate saying that out loud. I don't want to hurt you and I don't like what this says about me.

S: You kept telling yourself that our marriage was over and you believed I would never know.

C: Yes.

S: When did you decide that you did not love me anymore and did you try to tell me?

C: I tried to tell you one Christmas when we were arguing over your mother again. But the truth is I assumed you knew by the way I was act- ing. I was avoiding you, avoiding being sexual with you, and we fought a lot.

[Therapist notes Chelsea's past ambivalence about pushing herself to ask for more from herself or her husband.]

S: This is hard! You think because it was clear to you that it was clear to me. I will never understand if you knew it was wrong how you did it anyway! You lived in a fantasy that only you knew about. That's unfair to me and us and our kids!

[Stu loses differentiation in the face of his understandably strong emotions concerning her infidelity and reacts defensively, turn- ing the conversation to his reality instead of staying with his wife's reality. This is an example of losing the ability to be "curious, not furious" in conflict.]

C: This is why I don't talk to you. You punish me for telling you the truth. I don't want to hurt you. You wanted answers. I am trying to tell you how I did what I did. I don't expect you to agree with me or say it is okay. I know I did the wrong thing. I will always regret this and not like myself for this. I am sorry. I am very, very sorry for hurting you.

[Therapist notes that Chelsea became reactive and lost her focus but was able to recover to talk about her feelings and refocus on her objective while tolerating his negative feelings.]

S: I don't think this conversation helps. Maybe I am not ready to hear this. Maybe I don't want to know who you were back then and who you became. I can't get past the hurt and betrayal.

[Stu has some self-awareness in knowing he is breaking from the role, is able to express his feelings and own his limitations and challenges while also challenging his partner to withdraw from the conversation. He uses some intimation while really needing to ask for soothing and help. His fear of asking for more from his wife is normal at this point in therapy.]

[Therapist waits to see if Chelsea can continue to calm her reactiv- ity to his hurt and angry feelings and if she can continue to offer him succor but not at her own expense. Therapist also waits to see if Stu

can self-soothe, return to the inquirer role, and tolerate hearing the answers to his questions.]

[Long pause. Chelsea starts to pout, appears to feel defeated while Stu appears to feel sorry for himself and defeated.]

T: This is hard and painful work for both of you. The truth is difficult but as you both have previously stated, it is essential to know in order to heal and make the difficult decisions that stand before you both. Chelsea, is there something you want to ask Stu about his pain?

C: What can I do to help you? I want to help you with this.

S: I don't know that there is anything you can do now. I don't know if I can hear this.

[Therapist notes that Stu is at a crossroads: to stay stuck in certain pain or to stretch himself to experience his pain, fear, and hurt while remaining open to his wife and even let her (who hurt him) offer him reassurance.]

[Long pause]

T: Stu, right now you stand at a crossroads; can you define it?

[Therapist pushes him toward his I-to-I goal to continue to think.]

S: I'm stuck between just hurting and protecting myself against Chelsea hurting me anymore or hearing what she's done and why and risking more hurt. I think that's it.

T: Does it look that way to you, Chelsea?

[Therapist is pushing clients to use each other as a resource; indirectly teaching them to push past their old survival skill of withdrawing and relying only on self.]

C: You want to understand what I did, but can't imagine being able to do that without feeling more hurt ... and anger?

S: Yeah, I am fighting, getting more and more angry with you.

C: I think that you're going to feel angry and I am going to have to learn how to handle your anger without withdrawing.

S: Hmmm ... *[He's thinking about what she's offered.]*

T: I think this is a good place to stop. Chelsea, how did you do sticking with your goal as an initiator?

C: I think I got off track a couple of times, but I feel really good about being able to hear Stu's anger and not withdraw. I tried to organize my thoughts and feelings better rather than just reacting.

T: Stu, how did you do with your goal?

S: I had a hard time. Early on I was able to get back on track, but at the end I just couldn't.

T: You both struggled as anyone would with such difficult topics. You both stretched yourselves. You are trying to build trust after so many years of living separately while together, living without sharing, without being able to wrestle with your differences and arrive together at solutions that work. You both worked hard. This is and will continue to be a difficult topic. You both tried to recover. You both worked earnestly. You both did better than you would have done just a few weeks ago.

T: Take the developmental I-to-I handout home. I call it the "Roadmap to Emotional Maturity." My suggestion is that you set goal number 5 for both the initiator and inquirer as your default setting for productive discussions. That means, as either of you recognize that you are not able to stay in a conversation in a productive way, that you tell your partner and ask to table the discussion for an hour, until the evening or to "sleep on it." This is not done as a threat but a means to protect the relationship and "do no harm." And I'd like you to formally do the I-to-I exercise twice before I see you next week, for at least 20 minutes each time.

T: Lastly, I recommend that you let this discussion percolate for 24 hours before returning to the discussion. Use that time to think about what you said and what you heard. Think about what you can do better and where you want this conversation to go.

Developmental Assessment of the Relationship   They dated 1 year and lived together almost 2 years before marrying. They have been married for 7 years. Both report the first 2 years as being "issue free" as they enjoyed each other's company, had a good connection, and a good, frequent sex life. They enjoyed a wonderful period of sweet symbiosis but brought little experience with effective CI. Consequently, the couple has become entrenched in a conflict avoidant cycle that has them arrested within soured symbiosis. The first disillusionment or sustained tension and growth pull toward CI involved in-law difficulties for Chelsea. Both partners cite this as the beginning problem that has never been resolved and eventually pulled them apart. So while the couple did have a healthy period of sweet symbiosis, little or no development toward successful differentiation has been accomplished since their entrance into stage two, soured symbiosis.

Three Intimacies Diagnosis   Chelsea has been low in SI while Stu is somewhat more developed in this area, but mostly limited to the expression of his negative emotions. Chelsea is stuck in an anger cycle, feeling victimized and blaming her partner. She is mostly unaware of her more vulnerable feelings and needs, and does not know how to express them to Stu.

Therefore, they are locked into a low CI, conflict avoidant pattern not knowing how to effectively navigate the sharing of their emotions. So by default they do not bring up their negative feelings, hoping that by ignoring them they can minimize the hurt feelings and the tension between them. Unfortunately, the long-term result is the ever-growing distance between them, the resulting backdrop of resentments and loneliness, as well as a gnawing feeling of resignation. AI has become significantly lower over the years as the resentments growing out of their CI have been poisoning and weakening their caring for each other.

Infidelity Diagnosis   Chelsea has had an infidelity of loneliness fueled by the growing distance in the relationship and her sense of separateness. Chelsea's inability to be more emotionally self-aware or self intimate made her vulnerable to an affair. She felt increasingly separate and alone in her marriage and did not have enough SI to push her to take effective action that would have been congruent with her values and marital commitment to combat her loneliness.

While she did not seek an affair, the reawakening of feelings with Pete became too alluring for her to resist. To make it "okay" for her to be unfaithful, she convinced herself that by the time she was attracted to Pete her marriage was already over. This is a common self-justification in infidelities of loneliness. We find that in many infidelity of loneliness cases the love is not in fact dead, but has been starved by the lack of SI and CI and the resulting loss of AI. As a consequence of this weakening of love and how it is "covered over" by the buildup of negative emotion toward the partner and so not readily felt, it is easy for the betraying partner to convince him- or herself that the love is gone, and therefore the infidelity is "justified." In other infidelity of loneliness cases, the love actually has been starved "to death." But this usually takes at least 7 to 10 years of being stuck in stage two for love to truly be gone.

Possible Deal Breaker   The second deal breaker ended up applying to Stu and Chelsea; the loss of their love was caused by negligence on the part of both partners. Interestingly, we find that when the second deal breaker applies to a couple, dooming their LTLR, it is more common that their love died as a result of the "starvation" of love caused by conflict avoidance than by the "murder" of their love caused by the abuses of hostile dependent conflict process.

Outcome   Currently this couple has decided to separate. Stu has moved toward divorce proceedings. He is unable to accept, tolerate, and rebuild trust in Chelsea. She reinforces his fear by struggling to hold on to herself when he gets angry and instead withdraws from him. She often takes his anger personally and expresses ambivalence about the relationship. The couple has remained in individual therapy and stayed in touch with the marital therapist.

Specific Treatment Guidelines for Infidelity of Loneliness Couples
- Therapeutic work on developing strong CI is the key to eliminating the loneliness that overtook the LTLR and powered the betrayal.
- The betraying partner must work to become reliably self intimate, as her lack of true acknowledgment of her loneliness led to the infidelity.
- The betrayed partner must work on SI and CI to help create a sense of safety in the LTLR.
- The betrayed partner must expand his expectations of his LTLR to include separateness and disappointment.
- Transforming their low CI to high CI enables the couple to work through the hurt, disappointment, and resentment that has grown between them over the years and that led to the betrayal.
- With the growth in CI there follows a growth in AI that the therapist needs to foster and guide.

Infidelity of Anger
Much like with an infidelity of loneliness couple, tailoring the therapy to the needs of the infidelity of anger couple centers on both of the partners developing greater CI as well as on the betraying partner overcoming his or her low SI. But in these couples, the betraying partner must commit to work on growing SI particularly in regard to how he or she handles anger and the emotions of hurt and disappointment, which are what fuels the rage. He or she has to develop in-the-moment awareness of these emotions (ESA exercise) and then practice talking with the partner constructively, in a nonblaming way about them (I-to-I exercise).

The infidelity of anger betraying partner must do the hard SI work necessary to identify and work through the pain and anger he or she has built up from the past. Doing this personal work will enable him or her to change the fundamental motivational stance in the LTLR from one of individual survival to one of relationship survival. It will also transform his or her experience of love, from being mostly about his or her own safety to being about intimacy and willing vulnerability. Only after the betraying partner does these things will he or she be safe from being hijacked by anger in the future. Only then will the danger of the anger controlling him or her, causing the person to act out for revenge, be eliminated.

The therapist also must work with the couple to develop CI around past and present issues in the relationship. It is essential that the therapist challenge the couple to change their toxic communication style, whether it is hostile dependent or the conflict avoidant style. This task is especially challenging for the betraying partner, who will reflexively see, interpret, or experience the betrayed partner's words as attacking. The betrayed partner has to learn to overrule his or her individual survival reflexes. The infidelity of anger betraying partner will need the therapist's help to pull him or her back from withdrawing or attacking.

The therapist is teaching these couples a new behavior that feels very foreign and dangerous to them: one of observing, suspending one's views, being empathetic while having separate though unrepresented or unvoiced thoughts and feelings in the moment. This is a challenging emotional and psychological task for both partners. The therapist needs to be strong and clear in his or her thinking to be able to effectively understand what each partner needs in order to differentiate, self-define, and be present, especially with the latent if not overt hostility that these couples bring into therapy.

The therapist guides the infidelity of anger couple through this process toward becoming adept at dealing with their negative feelings as a team. Instead of reacting to them in an attacking, defensive way or in an avoidant, minimizing, or "brush it under the rug" way, they will come to do so openly and constructively, with each taking responsibility for his or her part in the problems and each expressing caring and regret for the pain caused to the partner. When the couple has achieved this ability, anger will no longer have the power to hijack their LTLR by causing an infidelity of anger. Anger will no longer be the enemy. Anger will no longer be in control of the betraying partner. Their ability to be intimate will prove to be more than a match for any anger, hurts, or disappointments that arise.

Infidelity of Anger Case Study   Terry and Debbie have been married for 22 years and have one young adult child. This couple had been in to see this therapist 5 years previous to this because of marital problems related to their parenting style differences. During previous therapy with this therapist the couple was willing to do some work to rebuild a marital connection. Debbie had reported in the therapy that Terry had "hit" on women since they were first married. He denied this. Debbie let the subject drop, and once the acute relationship pain was decreased, the couple left therapy. At the last session, the therapist suggested that though they were feeling relieved since the crisis had passed, the therapist did not believe that they had enough skills to achieve the conflict process resilience that they would need down the road.

The couple returned after 5 years because Debbie discovered that Terry had been using the services of prostitutes. She had previously suspected that he had been sexually inappropriate with other women, an allegation he denies. She learned about the prostitutes when she discovered a receipt.

When she confronted him he denied it, but as she continued to press him, he eventually admitted to these betrayals. She did a lot of research and discovered his use of Craig's List to meet women. He admits to the prostitutes, but denies the other accusations. The couple had briefly seen three other therapists over the past 10 years, and Debbie reports that they have told her they believe Terry has had multiple affairs.

This I-to-I dialogue takes place in a session during the later midphase of therapy after the couple had been practicing the I-to-I both inside and outside the sessions, using the developmental I-to-I goals, and having agreed to a list of trust-building behaviors.

Debbie: I have something I would like to work on; it's my continued lack of trust in you and that I find it difficult to have tough discussions with you. Is that okay if we work on this?

Terry: I think things have been going better, but if you want to talk about this, it's okay.

[Despite his anxiety about the topic he is willing to push himself.]

D: While we were on our vacation there were a couple of times when I felt hurt by what I saw as your insensitivity to me. For example, when you took photos of topless women in France and I told you I did not like it, you got angry at me and we had an argument. I want to be able to bring up these topics and talk them out.

[She is doing a good job with emotional self-awareness, demonstrating improved self-differentiation and a willingness to be conflict intimate.]

T: You were hurt by the photos I took and felt I was defensive and did not listen to your feelings. You want us to be able to discuss these things without an argument.

D: Yes, and I want to know that my sensitivity to feeling embarrassed or being reminded of your unfaithfulness is also important to you. I don't necessarily think that you'll do something inappropriate with women, but I need you to keep in mind my hurt, fear, and fragile trust.

[She is questioning his earnestness in rebuilding trust and she is willing to ask him to help her with this.]

T: So, it's not so much the photo taking, but that I did not think about how my actions might affect you. You want to know that I think about how I have hurt your trust of me. Is that right?

[Expressed, ongoing awareness of the hurt he has caused, and willingness validate his partner's pain are both powerful ways to rebuild his integrity as well as her trust in him.]

D: Yes. I guess if you would keep in mind how things might affect me and if I bring up a hurt that it will matter to you enough to listen, care about the affect, and want to help me feel more secure. I want to trust you again, but I worry that you think that because we are still together that this issue is over. It will take time for me and I need you to be patient with me as well as help me with this by staying aware of my insecurity and sensitivity.

[Debbie is doing a good job asking for help, being vulnerable to her partner while holding on to herself.]

T: I am sorry that I took the photos; I forgot to consider your feelings. I will do better. I have a hard time revisiting my mistakes, and I wonder if you will ever forgive me or if this will constantly come up and you'll never be able to let it go.

[Terry is demonstrating differentiation with empathy and not losing a sense of self and is able to be both self intimate and conflict intimate by bringing up his concerns about his partner's possible limitations.]

D: It sounds like you are having trouble trusting me and my ability to forgive you. You also have trouble being reminded of your hurtful actions. Did I get that right?

[This couple is able to move between the roles of initiator and inquirer with ease, an advanced skill. She is also able to be empathetic to his emotional sensitivities as well as her own.]

T: Yes.

D: I admit that I have obsessed over the prostitutes. I think I have because over the years I have suspected you of cheating because I have seen you behave too sexually with other women when I have been present. When I have asked you about this, you always sloughed it off and said I was crazy. But now I know more of the truth so my obsessing is probably my way of trying to deal with the truth and protect myself by not ignoring again my instincts. Does that make sense to you?

[Debbie is remaining aware of more vulnerable feelings and continues to bring up difficult issues while not blaming her spouse. She is questioning the value of obsessing and its limitations.]

T: It does, but at the same time I have known you to get angry and not be able to forgive.

[He is able to empathize and recap while simultaneously raising his concerns and increasing the tension.]

D: That's fair. I guess I will have to figure out when I am obsessing to check out my instincts and when I am obsessing out of fear or to punish you out of my insecurity. Will you trust me and help me do that?

[*She continues to share the fruits of her self intimacy and asks for assistance without asking her partner to give up a part of himself; differentiation and individuation are maintained. A differentiated connection is requested.*]

T: I'd like to say unequivocally yes, but I can't promise that I won't get defensive and impatient sometimes. But I will try to remind myself that I have caused you pain and that you aren't meaning to lash out at me.

D: That would help me a lot to rebuild my faith in you, see you as earnest in wanting to change to be true to me, to improve the relationship, and help me to trust my instincts.

T: I am sorry that something I did that was so selfish continues to cause you pain. It is hard for me to see how much, how often, and how deeply my stupid choices continue to hurt you. I appreciate you struggling with this, staying with me and our marriage, and again I promise that I am committed to you and to us. I will keep working on myself.

D: I appreciate your words. They help me.

Developmental Assessment of the Relationship   Terry and Debbie dated for 2 years when they met in their mid-20s. Both described the early years as fun. Sweet symbiosis seems to have been positive but marred early on by her suspicions that he was not completely honest with her. They also struggled with his career and limited money early in the marriage. They were not able to stay mutually supportive in the face of these stressors, and soured symbiosis occurred early in the relationship while both minimized its presence. As a result they have never been able to move beyond stage two.

Three Intimacies Assessment   Both have had low SI and ineffective CI. In spite of this, their AI has remained fairly strong; it appears to have been the bond between them. Both partners have been locked in a competitive, untrusting relationship with each other. As Debbie became angrier at Terry's inappropriate actions with women and his lack of support toward her regarding the raising of their daughter, she became stuck in a hostile dependent cycle with him. Terry viewed his wife as rigid, neurotic, and angry, and he admitted to staying away from home to avoid her and the relentless arguments. She would make openly disparaging remarks about him while he would behave with other women in ways that were disrespectful of his marital relationship.

Infidelity Diagnosis   Terry's history of inappropriate interactions with women, the current involvement with prostitutes, and his indirect expressions of anger toward Debbie suggest an infidelity of anger. In the course of therapy he spoke of his expectations that his wife should agree with him, that life at home should be easy. He acknowledged his expectation that arguments and tension should be mostly nonexistent in marriage, and that eventually he began to see his wife as purposely hurting him and defying his requests. His early family history includes a hostile, competitive father and a fearful, compliant mother. For her part, Debbie comes from a family that did not discuss problems, but that could be very biting and indirect with their anger.

Outcome   This couple came to therapy locked in an angry, attack and defend hostile dependent conflict process pattern. Debbie was devastated, relieved, and angry with Terry when his infidelities were revealed. Terry was embarrassed, relieved, and defiant. While she wanted to save the marriage, he was more ambivalent. He stated that he did not want to save the marriage if it did not improve. He stated in later therapy sessions that a turning point for him was seeing and feeling the depth of Debbie's pain and hurt. As she stopped leading with her anger and spoke more about her sense of loss and hurt, he was able to hear that she did love him. With that he recalled his love and connection with her and started to examine his selfishness and how he had let his passive anger determine his choices. This couple continues to work in therapy and reports that their marriage is more loving, connected, and genuine than it has ever been.

Specific Treatment Guidelines for Infidelity of Anger Couples
- Working with these couples to help them build strong CI is central.
- The therapist much challenge both partners to work to leave behind their entrenched toxic conflict process pattern, whether it be hostile dependent or conflict avoidant.
- The betraying partner must also be focused on overcoming his low SI, particularly in regard to how he or she handles anger and the emotions of hurt and disappointment, which are what fuel the rage.
- This SI work must also delve deeply into the past, where the source of most of the anger and the maladaptive defenses used to deal with it lies.
- The therapist must assist in this SI work, since this will enable the couple to change the fundamental motivational stance in the LTLR from one of individual survival to one of relationship survival.

Conclusion

In the end, TRI infidelity couples learn that the secret to success in a LTLR is true intimacy. For the therapist who is called upon to assist the couple whose LTLR has been imperiled by infidelity, it is vital to make the struggle to build a sound intimacy structure into the couple's relationship central to the therapeutic work of recovering from infidelity.

At TRI we erect that structure upon the pillars of the three intimacies using the blueprints provided by the TRI model of LTLRs and our infidelity typology. We find that the true intimacy afforded by strength in the three intimacies allows the love of the infidelity couple partners to once again flow and be returned in its fullness. It enables them to thrive as a couple in spite of the past infidelity and buttresses them against future relationship breakdowns in the face of the inevitable challenges that await them as they travel through life together. As such, we have found that this approach to infidelity couples therapy empowers the therapist to effectively meet the challenges of this daunting work by providing both a model that brings clarity to chaos as well as powerful clinical tools with which to help the couple recover intimacy after infidelity.

References

Bader, E., Pearson, P., & Schwartz, J. (2000). *Tell me no lies*. New York: St. Martin's Press.

The Couples Institute. (2007). How to get the most from couples therapy handout. www.thecouplesinstitute.com

The Relationship Institute. (2007). TRI therapy handouts and questionnaires. www.therelationshipinstitute.org

Solomon, S., & Teagno, L. (2006). *Intimacy after infidelity*. Oakland, CA: New Harbinger Publications.

CHAPTER 4
Interview With Frank Pittman

Frank Pittman, M.D., is a noted Atlanta psychiatrist and family therapist specializing in family crises, men's issues, marriage, and infidelity. His books include *Private Lies: Infidelity and the Betrayal of Intimacy*; *Man Enough: Fathers, Sons and the Search for Masculinity*; and *Grow Up! How Taking Responsibility Can Make You a Happy Adult*. For 25 years he has written the film column for the *Psychotherapy Networker*.

Eds: Since infidelity—sexual or emotional—is common in problematic relationships, how do you deal with situations in which one partner discloses the infidelity to you privately? The ethics books say that therapists cannot agree to keep such a "secret" from the other partner. In theory that sounds fine, but it can be a challenge with certain couples. How do you handle this matter and keep the couple in therapy?

FP: I try not to get trapped in a conspiracy to keep affairs secret from one of the spouses. That is disorienting and crazy making and, what's more, it is anti-therapeutic. I see couples together for the first session and I bring up questions about infidelity at that time, treating it as something that can be and must be discussed, somewhat like domestic violence or abuse. When infidelity has occurred you can smell it in the waiting room. I can say: "When other people are seriously talking divorce for vague reasons, like not being in love, they are usually sitting on a secret infidelity. Are you?" I might then ask the spouse, "What would you do if this were revealed?" If none of this works, you can use a Madanes pretend technique to warm up the room for a little truth. Just remember: a secret affair is far more dangerous to a marriage than an angry battle. It is rare for couples to divorce after a first affair that has been stopped, is fully disclosed and discussed with a sincere apology.

Eds: In the 1970s it was not uncommon for therapists to give permission for couples to separate and divorce. The pendulum seems to have swung to other end of the continuum lately. What is the place of the moral dimension in couples work, as exemplified by Bill Doherty and others?

FP: Therapy involves helping couples see what would happen to them and to their children if they pursued the divorce. Divorce is not a benign procedure and families will suffer for generations. The research consistently confirms this. We therapists have been here before and can see over the next hill; patients in crisis may be caught up in their feelings of the moment without concern for the long-term effects of their course of action. So we must make sure they know what we know. Non-directive therapy may be irresponsible if it does not inform and educate the people making decisions in a state of crisis. Anger is disorienting.

CHAPTER 5

Recovering Intimacy

Using Assessments to Pinpoint Treatment

DENNIS A. BAGAROZZI

Couples enter therapy with a variety of presenting problems. One of the most common is poor communication. Upon closer examination and assessment, however, one discovers that when couples complain about not being able to communicate effectively, they are actually saying they are unable to communicate intimately and meaningfully. The reasons for couples not identifying intimacy difficulties as their major concern is that they often think of intimacy as applying only to sexual relations. In order to help couples broaden their definition of intimacy to include more than sexual interactions and to pinpoint more accurately the sources of their dissatisfaction, therapists might consider using the Intimacy Needs Survey (Bagarozzi, 1990) as part of their pretreatment assessments. A brief discussion of this instrument and its development is presented below, followed by case illustrations selected to demonstrate its clinical uses.

Historical Background and Discussion

The intimacy needs' system evolves out of the more primary and fundamental evolutionary and biologically determined attachment behavioral system that is essential for the survival of the species. However, as Main (1999) has stressed, the term "attachment" is a unique form of affectional bond that should not be used or confused with affectional bonds in general. Bowlby (1969/1982) also made the distinction between the attachment behavioral system and the affiliative behavioral systems that emerge later in the life cycle. Conceptually and theoretically, therefore, intimacy between adults is best thought of as falling within the realm of affiliative relationships.

The *Random House Dictionary of the English Language* defines intimacy as a "close, familiar and usually affectionate or loving personal relationship with another person." This close relationship entails a "detailed knowledge" of the other person as well as a "deep understanding" of that individual. Inherent in this definition of intimacy is the notion of interaction and reciprocity as evidenced by the proactive sharing of one's thoughts, feelings, beliefs, and so forth in response to those of the other.

Early research into the realm of interpersonal intimacy treated intimacy as if it were a unidimensional construct (Alford, 1982; Braiker & Kelley, 1979; Guerney, 1977; Miller & Lefcourt, 1992; Orlofsky & Levitz-Jones, 1985; Walker & Thompson, 1983). Other investigators, who recognized the multidimensional nature of the construct, elected to study only certain components (Berscheid, Snyder, & Omoto, 1989; Derogatis, 1980; Hudson, 1982; Lo Piccolo & Steger, 1974; Tesch, 1985; Ting-Toomey, 1983a, 1983b). Olson (1975, 1977) was the first clinical researcher to conceptualize intimacy as having a number of different components (i.e., emotional, social, intellectual, sexual, recreational, spiritual, and aesthetic).

Schaefer and Olson (1981) conducted a factor analytic study using a 75-item questionnaire administered to 192 married couples. The items in this instrument addressed the seven a priori categories previously identified as being component parts of the intimacy construct. Five empirically derived factors were produced (emotional, social, sexual, intellectual, and recreational). They used the highest loading items contained in each of the five factors for inclusion in the 50-item Personal Assessment of Intimacy in Relationships (PAIR) inventory. The current version is a 36-item scale that contains six items from each subscale and a six-item conventionality subscale.

The PAIR inventory has a number of shortcomings. First, it assumes that, for a given individual, the strength of each intimacy need component is the same across all five factors. Second, it does not address the fact that intimacy needs strengths differ from individual to individual. Third, it focuses solely on the respondent's satisfaction with how receptive his or her partner is to the expression of a felt need. Finally, it does not adequately address the issue of reciprocity (i.e., how satisfied the respondent is with his or her partner's degree and quality of involvement and self-disclosure in each component area).

To remedy these shortcomings, the Intimacy Needs Survey was developed (Bagarozzi, 1990). Bagarozzi returned to the seven a priori components of intimacy identified by Olson (1975, 1977) and added two additional dimensions: physical intimacy and psychological intimacy. Physical intimacy was added in order to help individuals differentiate physical closeness from physically intimate behavior that is specifically designed to be sexually stimulating and arousing. Time as a factor was introduced to help respondents consider the amount of time they would like to spend on a daily basis with their spouses or significant others in order to feel that their intimacy needs were being satisfactorily fulfilled.

In order to deal with the shortcomings of the PAIR inventory outlined above, the Intimacy Needs Survey addresses the issues that are discussed in the sections that follow.

Total Intimacy Needs Strength

For each component need identified in the Intimacy Needs Survey, a definition of the particular component need is given. The respondent is then asked to answer five Likert-type questions about the particular component need under consideration. For example, the definition of intellectual intimacy would be: Intellectual intimacy is the need to communicate and share important ideas, thoughts, beliefs, and so forth with your partner.

The first two Likert-type questions for this component are:

(a) In general, how strong is your need to communicate and share important ideas, thoughts, beliefs, and so forth with your partner? (Circle only one number)

1	2	3	4	5	6	7	8	9	10

Not a Strong Need   An Extremely
At All   Strong Need

(b) How important is it for you that your partner listens to you whenever you share ideas, thoughts, beliefs, and so forth that are meaningful to you? (Circle only one number)

1	2	3	4	5	6	7	8	9	10

Not a Strong Need   An Extremely
At All   Strong Need

The product of answers (a) × (b) represents the need strength score for each component need. The total Intimacy Needs Strength score for an individual is determined by summing all eight component needs' strength scores. Total Intimacy Needs Strength scores range from 8 to 800. For individuals seen in marital or couple's therapy, average scores range from 400 to 650.

Receptivity Satisfaction

Receptivity satisfaction is the subjective satisfaction one experiences with the degree and quality of acceptance, empathy, and understanding that his or her partner shows in response to one's intimate self-disclosures and expressions of felt need. For the component of intellectual intimacy, the question designed to assess receptivity satisfaction is:

(c) To what extent is your partner able to meet and satisfy your need for intellectual intimacy? (Circle only one number)

1	2	3	4	5	6	7	8	9	10

Not At All Able to   Totally Satisfies
Satisfy This Need   This Need

Reciprocity Satisfaction

Reciprocity satisfaction is the subjective satisfaction one experiences with the depth, extent, and quality of one's partner's self-disclosures and expression of felt need in the same component need area. The last two questions are used to assess this aspect of intellectual intimacy:

(d) How important is it for you and your satisfaction with your partner that he/she communicates and share with you his/her ideas, thoughts, beliefs, etc? (Circle only one number)

1	2	3	4	5	6	7	8	9	10

Not At All   Extremely
Important   Important

(e) To what extent is your partner able to meet and satisfy your expectations for sharing and communicating his or her ideas, thoughts, beliefs, and so forth? (Circle only one number)

1	2	3	4	5	6	7	8	9	10

Not At All Able to   Totally Satisfies
Satisfy This Need   This Need

Receptivity and Reciprocity Satisfaction Scoring

For each of the eight component needs of intimacy, receptivity and reciprocity scores are computed for each partner. These are reported as percentages. For example, a receptivity percentage score of 85% means that one's partner is perceived as being receptive to one's self-disclosures and felt need in the area of intellectual intimacy at a fairly high level of satisfaction. Little or no change in one's partner's behavior in the area of intellectual intimacy may be desired or requested. On the other hand, however, the same person may perceive his or her partner as meeting the need for reciprocal exchange at only a 50% level of satisfaction in the area of intellectual intimacy, and a great deal of change may be desired and requested.

Each of the remaining seven components of intimacy is treated in the same way in the Intimacy Needs Survey. Definitions of these seven component needs are presented below accompanied by a brief case example. The reader will note that some of the examples include elements of more than one component need. It is not uncommon for more than one component need to be expressed during an intimate exchange between spouses.

Emotional Intimacy

Emotional intimacy is the need for communicating and sharing with your partner all your feelings, both positive (e.g., happiness, joy, elation, gladness, excitement) and negative (e.g., sadness, unhappiness, fear, anger, guilt, shame, loneliness, boredom, fatigue).

Example of Emotional Intimacy   Sarah has just been promoted to chief financial officer. That evening she tells her husband, George, that she is both excited and somewhat frightened about her new responsibilities. George congratulates her, then says, "Sarah, I am confident that you will do a superb job."

Psychological Intimacy

Psychological intimacy is the need to communicate, share, and disclose personal material, information, and feelings about the self to one's partner. Psychological intimacy also includes the need for disclosing and sharing one's hopes, dreams, fantasies, aspirations, and plans for the future as well as sharing one's fears, concerns, and insecurities with one's partner.

Example of Psychological Intimacy   Michael is in deep thought. Jane asks him what he is thinking about and Michael says: "I was just thinking about my sister. When we were children, she was always there for me. No matter what difficulties I faced, she was always helpful. I think I learned a lot about caring and empathy from her." Jane inquires as to whether Michael has ever shared these insights with his sister. Michael responds: "Not really." Jane suggests: "Perhaps she would like to know how important she is to you and what kind of impact she has had upon you and your life." Michael looks at Jane and says: "Thank you, I think I will talk with her about this when we visit my family for the holidays."

Sexual Intimacy

Sexual intimacy is the need for communicating, sharing, and expressing thoughts, feelings, desires, and fantasies that are of a sexual nature. Sexual intimacy includes sharing erotic experiences together (e.g., watching erotic films, listening to erotic music, reading erotic materials). Sexual intimacy also includes the need for physical closeness, body contact, involvement, and interactions that are especially designed to be sexually arousing, stimulating, exciting, and satisfying (e.g., erotic kissing, petting, hugging, dancing, fondling, bathing). Sexually intimate behavior may or may not lead to sexual intercourse or orgasm for one or both partners involved.

Example of Sexual Intimacy Debbie and Charles are contemplating marriage, but Debbie has some reservations. She feels unfulfilled sexually. After some time of thoughtful consideration, she voices her concern: "Charles, there are some things about our love making that I'd like to talk with you about." Charles responds: "What's wrong?" Debbie answers: "Well, most of the time when we have sex our love making is over right after you come, and I rarely have an orgasm. This is very frustrating for me." Charles is silent. Debbie continues: "Would you be open to trying some new sexual positions that would make it easier for me to have an orgasm?" "Yes," says Charles, "What do you have in mind?" Debbie is straightforward in her response: "Charles, I find it easier to come when I'm on top. I can move more freely and position myself better." Charles smiles, takes Debbie by the hand, and leads her to the bedroom. "Okay," he says, "let's give it a try."

Physical (Nonsexual) Intimacy

Physical intimacy is the need for physical closeness and body contact with one's partner. Physical closeness includes such experiences as holding hands, cuddling, slow dancing with one's partner, nonsexual touching (e.g., patting, caressing, hugging), kissing that is not a prelude to sexual relations, sleeping in the same bed with one's partner, walking together arm-in-arm, and so forth.

Example of Physical (Nonsexual) Intimacy John is having difficulty sleeping. Pain from old football injuries is keeping him awake. His wife, Julie, moves closer to him in their bed. She begins to massage his lower back. John whispers: "Thank you, honey. That feels so good. It is just what I need right now."

Social and Recreational Intimacy

Social and recreational intimacy is the need to engage in playful and enjoyable activities and experiences with one's partner. Social and recreational intimacy includes activities and experiences such as exchanging jokes and humorous stories, sharing one's daily experiences, and discussing daily events with one's partner, sharing meals, snacks, and refreshments with one's partner, exercising together, playing sports and games together, sharing hobbies, dancing together for pleasure and enjoyment, vacationing together, and so forth.

Example of Social and Recreational Intimacy   Joe and Joan have been married for 20 years. For the past 6 weeks, they have been taking ballroom dancing lessons. As they practice twirling, Joan laughs and looks deeply into Joe's eyes. She says: "Oh, Jose, how you can Tango! You sweep me off my feet." Joe responds "Ole."

Aesthetic Intimacy

Aesthetic intimacy is the need and desire to share with one's partner feelings and experiences that are considered to be beautiful, breathtaking, or awe-inspiring, such as the wonder of nature and the cosmos, music, art, poetry, literature, and so forth.

Example of Aesthetic Intimacy   Cindy comes home with a new CD, *La Boheme*, she has purchased for Mark's birthday. After dinner, Cindy puts on the disc while she and Mark relax in their living room. As Luciano Pavarotti begins "Che gelida manina," Mark whispers: "This is just beautiful." Cindy puts her head on Mark's shoulder, closes her eyes, and says in a soft voice: "Yes, it is beautiful."

Spiritual Intimacy

Spiritual intimacy is the need to share one's thoughts, feelings, beliefs, and experiences with one's partner that have to do with religion, the supernatural, moral values, the meaning of existence, life after death, one's relationship to God, and so forth. Spiritual intimacy also includes the joint practice and participation together with one's partner in religious activities, rituals, celebrations, experiences, and so forth. Spiritual intimacy between two people does not necessarily require that they share the same religion.

Example of Spiritual Intimacy   Susie and Tom have been dating for several months, and she thinks that Tom would be a wonderful husband and father. Saturday evening, over dinner, Susie invites Tom to accompany her and her parents to Sunday church services. Tom declines and Susie is puzzled. She asks: "Tom, why don't you want to come to church with us? Do you have other plans?" Tom responds: "No, Susie, I don't have other plans, but I don't believe in organized religion." This surprises Susie so she presses Tom for more details. She asks: "What is it about organized religion that you don't like?" Tom answers: "I don't think that a person has to go to church to be a good human being. I am honest, ethical, moral, and kind. I do what I believe to be the right thing. I don't believe I need a priest, minister, or rabbi to tell me how to live my life or to be an intermediary between God and me. I'm sorry if my views offend you, Susie, but this is what I believe. Susie is silent for a while and then says: "Tom, you are a very good and decent man, but I don't think I can be comfortable in an intimate relationship with someone who does not share my religious beliefs. My faith is very important to me. It is at the core of who I am." Tom says: "Susie, I respect you and your views, and I would never expect you to change them." Susie responds: "Tom, I respect you too and I would not expect you to change your philosophy, and it is very hard for me to say this, but I think it is best that we don't continue to see each other any more." Tom responds: "Yes, Susie, I agree. I hope we can still remain friends."

Intellectual Intimacy

Intellectual intimacy is the need to communicate and share important ideas, thoughts, beliefs, and so forth with your partner.

Example of Intellectual Intimacy   Kathy is reading the community newspaper. She turns to her husband and asks: "Andy, what do you think about the referendum being proposed approving a liquor-by-the-drink ordinance? Andy replies: "I think it is a good idea. It will bring in more business, more revenue, and our taxes won't go up." Kathy says: "Well, I disagree. I think it is a very bad idea. We live in a quaint little community. I think that having establishments that serve liquor by the drink will change the very nature of our town. I think our community will lose its rural charm." Andy is thoughtful for a moment then responds: "Maybe you're right. I need to think about this some more." Kathy smiles and says: "Thanks for hearing me out."

Time and Intimacy

How much time a person would like to spend interacting with a significant other in order to feel intimately connected to that person differs from individual to individual. This aspect of intimacy can be assessed through a series of questions. For example:

> Is the amount of time that you now spend with your partner sufficient for you to feel that your intimacy needs are being met satisfactorily: Yes _____ No _____ Undecided _____
>
> If your answer to the above question is either no or undecided, please check below those need components where more time together would be desirable and then indicate the amount of time *per day* you would like to spend with your partner for each component area.

Need Component	Desired Time Each Day	
1. Intellectual	Hours _____	Minutes _____
2. Emotional	Hours _____	Minutes _____

Need Component	Desired Time Each Day
3. Psychological	Hours _____ Minutes _____
4. Sexual	Hours _____ Minutes _____
5. Physical	Hours _____ Minutes _____
6. Spiritual	Hours _____ Minutes _____
7. Aesthetic	Hours _____ Minutes _____
8. Social/Recreational	Hours _____ Minutes _____
Total	Hours _____ Minutes _____

Intimacy Needs Survey: Current Empirical Status

At this time, a clinical sample of approximately 125 couples has completed the Intimacy Needs Survey. The author is in the process of identifying a sample of nonclinical couples willing to participate in a study designed to investigate whether clinical and nonclinical samples respond differently to the instrument. Once these data have been collected, tests for validity and reliability will be performed. For the moment, the Intimacy Needs Survey remains a clinical tool, the validity and reliability of which have yet to be established.

Assessment Procedures and Diagnostic Considerations

Couples seeking relationship or marital therapy are required to participate in a six-session assessment and diagnostic process. The first session is a joint session during which both partners are interviewed together. During this initial session, the couple's ability to identify the presenting problem and the couple's communication style are assessed. Next, the couple's ability to negotiate conflicts, problem solve, and plan joint activities is evaluated. Each partner then is interviewed for two individual sessions. During these two sessions, personal histories and histories of significant relationships are gathered. Diagnostic formulations are also made at this time. The couple is given a battery of assessment instruments to complete based on the nature of the presenting problem or problems. Usually, the assessment instruments couples are asked to complete focus on the couple's relationship. However, in certain situations, personality tests and measures may also be included. For the purposes of this chapter, only two assessment instruments are discussed in detail—the Intimacy Needs Survey and the Spousal Inventory of Desired Changes and Relationship Barriers (SIDCARB). The latter is used only when spouses have been legally married. The reasons for this are self-evident.

Spousal Inventory of Desired Changes and Relationship Barriers   SIDCARB (Bagarozzi, 1983; Bagarozzi & Atilano, 1982; Bagarozzi & Pollane, 1983) was developed to help therapists gain a multidimensional view of marriage. SIDCARB is based on social exchange theory. The major theoretical constructs operationalized by this instrument are: (a) each spouse's subjective satisfaction with his or her partner in 10 areas of marital exchange, (b) the amount of behavior change desired of one's partner in these 10 areas of the relationship, and (c) each spouse's subjective perception of two classes of barriers to separation and divorce, that is, internal psychological barriers (commitment to marriage vows, religious beliefs, obligations to children, and concerns for parents and in-laws), and external circumstantial barriers (job, legal, and financial considerations and concerns for friends and neighbors).

Based on a spouse's responses to SIDCARB questions, three types of marriage perceptions are possible: mutually rewarding and satisfying marriages, unsatisfying marriages with low barriers to separation and divorce, and unsatisfying marriages with high barriers to relationship termination. This latter perception is referred to as a *nonvoluntary marriage*. More will be said about the implications for treatment when marriages are perceived as nonvoluntary later in this chapter.

Unrecognized Intimacy Needs Differences During the Courtship Process

It would be erroneous to assume that significant needs strength's differences between dating partners are readily apparent during the courtship process. Unfortunately, this is not always the case. Important differences may go unrecognized until after the couple marries or the partners begin to live together.

Long-distance relationships and whirlwind romances are two of the most common reasons for couples not recognizing major differences in their intimacy needs. In situations where couples have children shortly after they marry, differences in intimacy needs strengths may not become apparent until after the last child leaves home.

In some cases, intimacy needs' differences may be ignored or denied by one or both partners during courtship for psychological reasons (e.g., personal insecurities, unresolved unconscious conflicts). The deliberate falsification of one's intimacy needs and needs strengths in order to win over an unsuspecting partner is an unfortunate occurrence, but it does happen from time to time. Such deceit is frequently symptomatic of a personality disorder.

Factors Affecting Intimacy Needs Strengths and Their Fulfillment

Changes in the strengths of intimacy needs can come about with the passage of time and the development of the relationship. Such changes are often seen in the area of sexual intimacy. For example, since women and men reach their sexual peaks at very different times during their lives, a woman's true need for sexual intimacy and intercourse may not emerge until she is in her late 30s or early 40s. By the time a man is 40, in many cases, his need for sexual intimacy will have decreased to some extent. Women who discover that they have strong sexual needs, in their 30s and 40s, may find their husbands' need for sexual intimacy diminished, resulting in a serious and frustrating desire discrepancy. The desire for sexual involvement and intercourse also may decline, for some women, after childbirth or after menopause. This may be an unexpected and upsetting occurrence for both spouses that has negative repercussions for other areas of intimacy.

The discovery of previously unrecognized intimacy needs in areas other than the sexual dimension of a relationship can lead to a marital crisis. The awareness of unfulfilled needs (e.g., intellectual, psychological, spiritual) may cause the dissatisfied spouse to seek out other individuals who are perceived as being able to meet these needs more fully. New relationships cultivated to meet these needs may be perceived as threats to the marriage by one's partner.

Although intimacy needs strengths may not change quantitatively over time, the desire to have these needs fulfilled by one's partner may change. The loss of desire for intimate involvement with one's spouse may come about for a number of reasons (e.g., long-standing unresolvable conflicts and disputes, chronic patterns of negative interaction cycles, infidelity, physical or emotional abuse).

Interpreting Assessment Findings in Light of Diagnostic Formulations

The first thing to consider when reviewing the total intimacy needs strength score of a spouse or partner is whether the score falls within the average range of possible scores. Extremely high scores or extremely low scores should be suspect since they may be symptomatic of a *Diagnostic and Statistical Manual of Mental Disorders* fourth edition (*DSM–IV*) Axis I condition or and Axis II disorder. Very low scores may also signify that a spouse has completely withdrawn from the relationship and does not wish to rekindle intimacy. In some instances, very high scores or very low scores may simply represent a respondent's tendency to use the extreme ends of a Likert scale. When extreme scores are encountered, the therapist should take the time to explore the possible reasons for such extremes.

Widely different total needs strength scores between spouses or partners are not a common occurrence. Typically, significant differences between partners' scores are found in component needs strengths. It is important to keep in mind that component needs strength's differences are not necessarily problematic for couples. Spouses with similar component needs strengths may still feel that their intimacy needs are not being met satisfactorily (i.e., receptivity and reciprocity satisfaction) since need fulfillment is subjectively evaluated.

Treatment Format

After formal assessment procedures have been completed, couples are given detailed feedback about the status of their relationship. All instruments that couples have been asked to complete are reviewed and interpreted. Couples' strengths and weaknesses are outlined and problematic areas of the relationship are underscored. Treatment goals are then discussed. Once treatment goals have been established, couples are taught functional communication skills and conflict negotiation strategies, followed by empathy training. When intimacy is identified as the presenting or major problem, the Intimacy Needs Survey is used to help pinpoint treatment.

Treatment Guidelines: Overview

Decisions about the conduct and course of treatment are made based on an integrative model of marital and family therapy developed by Bagarozzi and his colleagues (Anderson & Bagarozzi, 1983, 1988a, 1988b; Bagarozzi, 1980, 1981, 1982; Bagarozzi & Anderson, 1982, 1988, 1989; Bagarozzi & Giddings, 1983a, 1983b). The decision procedure is as follows:

- Begin treatment with a straightforward educational, behavioral, social skills training approach designed to teach functional communication, problem solving, and conflict negotiation skills. Homework assignments are an integral part of this process.
- Couples who learn these skills and who are able to utilize them to resolve differences and conflicts related to intimacy difficulties in their relationship can usually benefit from this approach. Such couples are presented as case examples in this chapter.
- Couples who are unable or unwilling to learn new skills and couples who are unable or unwilling to complete homework assignments may require strategic interventions to dismantle their resistances. The therapist might consider using some of the following techniques to overcome resistances:
  1. Positively reframing the couples' resistance to learning new skills or completing homework assignments as the couple's unique and creative way of becoming more "intimate" by their joining together against the therapist.
  2. Predicting noncompliance and relabeling noncompliance as understandable caution before trying something new.
  3. Prescribing resistance by asking the couple to use all the means possible to avoid completing assignments so that they can identify how they work together as a team to avoid doing tasks that they both consider to be unpleasant or that may threaten the fragile intimacy that they do share.

4. Asking couples who only partially complete in-session tasks or homework assignments to "go slow" and to "take their time" so as not to become "too intimate too fast." A common restraining strategy for dealing with a desire discrepancy between spouses who present with sexual intimacy as their chief complaint is to prescribe sensate focus homework assignments with the stipulation that the couple refrain from having sexual intercourse during the sensate focus process.

5. If strategic interventions prove not to be successful in overcoming resistances, the therapist should consider the possibility that external systems or factors are interfering with therapeutic progress. For example, negative influences from parents, in-laws, siblings, friends, or others who see therapy as a sign of weakness, a waste of time and money, or who wish to sabotage the couple's success for reasons of their own may make it very difficult for young couples, especially, to follow through with treatment. Incomplete separation and enmeshment with families of origin may make intimate commitment to one's spouse impossible in some instances. Under such circumstances, an intergenerational approach designed to resolve loyalty and allegiance conflicts may be required before the therapist can deal successfully with the couple's intimacy problems.

6. If strategic measures fail and external factors are found not to be interfering with treatment progress, insight-focused interpretations might be in order. Insight-focused interpretations may target specific unconscious couple defenses such as unconscious collusions against the therapist, mutual projective identifications and reciprocal transference phenomena, acting out for one's spouse, acting out with one's spouse, and so forth.

7. If resistance continues even after discrete dyadic defenses are uncovered and interpreted, unearthing the couple's unconscious contracts (Sager, 1976) may be the next step. Identifying, outlining, interpreting, and editing dysfunctional themes in the couple's mythological system (Anderson & Bagarozzi, 1983, 1988a, 1988b; Bagarozzi & Anderson, 1982, 1988, 1989) can also be used to overcome couples' resistances by therapists who are comfortable conducting intensive forms of treatment.

When little or no resistance to a straightforward, learning, behavioral social skills training approach to recovering intimacy is offered, the procedures outlined in the following case examples are appropriate. A summary of the interventions used in each case example appears in the clinical notes coda.

Case Examples

Whirlwind or Long Distance Romance

John and Kathy met on a singles cruise. They were passionately attracted to each other and spent the entire trip together. After the cruise, they corresponded electronically and nightly telephone conversations were the norm. Since they lived in adjacent states, they saw each other every other weekend. This dating pattern continued for several months until Kathy relocated to live with John. Difficulties began shortly after the couple became engaged. John was on a partnership track with a prestigious law firm. His workday usually began at 7 a.m. and ended around 8 p.m. Saturdays were often spent at the office or playing golf with colleagues and clients. This was the state of affairs when the couple contacted me.

Kathy's total intimacy needs score was 625; John's was 531. While both scores are within the average range, John's score is considerably lower than Kathy's. Reciprocity and receptivity satisfaction percentage scores for the couple are shown in Table 5.1.

Receptivity and reciprocity satisfaction scores that fall below 75% are considered to be problematic. For John, both receptivity and reciprocity in the sexual area are perceived as unsatisfying and social/recreational receptivity is seen as problematic. For Kathy, five receptivity and four reciprocity scores fail to meet the criterion level of 75%. Time needed to feel intimately connected also differed considerably for the couple. For John, 30 minutes a day was sufficient. Kathy desired at least 90 minutes each day.

Table 5.1 Reciprocity and Receptivity Satisfaction Percentage Scores for John and Kathy

	John		Kathy	
	Receptivity	Reciprocity	Receptivity	Reciprocity
Emotional	85	90	60	60
Psychological	80	90	65	65
Intellectual	85	90	70	80
Sexual	70	70	90	85
Spiritual	100	100	100	100
Aesthetic	90	90	40	40
Social/Recreational	80	50	40	40
Physical	80	80	80	90

Treatment Both John and Kathy were distressed by these findings. They were told that the 94-point difference in their total needs strength's scores was due to very low component needs strength's scores for John in the same areas where Kathy's needs strength's scores were high (i.e., emotional, psychological, intellectual, and aesthetic). Component needs strength's scores in the area of sexual intimacy were found not to be very different. However, Kathy's lack of sexual interest was interpreted as a loss of desire due to the depressing state of the couple's relationship. The couple was told that component needs strengths tend to remain fairly stable over time, but that this fact should not be disheartening since some changes are possible and that the couple may be able to achieve satisfaction if both partners are willing to make adjustments and compromises. John and Kathy agreed that they would like to try to see if their intimate relationship could be improved.

Training in functional communication skills and empathic listening began. The couple was asked to practice these skills for 45 minutes twice a week. The focus of each homework discussion was a specific component need that was identified as a cause for concern for each partner; for example, emotional, psychological, intellectual for Kathy, and sexual and social/recreational for John. The couple was instructed to begin discussing the component need perceived to be the least problematic. More difficult areas became the focus of discussion as the couple progresses successfully.

Prescribing such homework assignments immediately increases the amount of intimate time the couple spends together. For this couple, the question was whether the time spent together each week was sufficient to satisfy, to some degree, Kathy's need to spend more time with John. It is not uncommon to find that such a simple and straightforward behavioral exercise also increases receptivity and reciprocity satisfaction for the more dissatisfied partner and increases the overall level of satisfaction for couples, like John and Kathy, who do not have major problems in other areas of their relationship, who are voluntarily committed to change, and who are not struggling with issues of power and control.

As time went by, Kathy and John made important gains in their relationship. Kathy was able to accept less time with John than she had initially requested. Her depression lifted and their sex life improved. Kathy's aesthetic and social or recreational needs were met by friends, and she no longer looked to John to fulfill them. Treatment ended after 8 months with the couple planning to marry.

Clinical Notes Total needs strength's differences were dealt with through normalization in order to help the couple become more receptive to treatment, that is, Kathy and John were told that it is not unusual for couples to differ in the strengths of their component needs.

Kathy's lack of sexual interest was interpreted as being symptomatic of her depression. What is implied here is that once the couple's relationship improves, Kathy's sexual desire will return with the lifting of her depression. This is an example of indirection.

Engendering hope is another strategy used in the above example. Although the therapist says that component needs strengths tend to be stable, he does say that changes are possible if both partners are willing to make adjustments and compromises. It has been my experience to find that individuals are more likely to make changes when they interpret these to be changes in how they behave as opposed to changes in who they are, the latter being more threatening.

Earlier, I said that the approach used in this chapter is that of straightforward educational, behavioral, and social skills training that requires practice and the completion of homework assignments. In this example, the therapist uses a basic learning strategy of having couples work on their problems incrementally (i.e., from the least problematic in difficulty to problems that are more complex and challenging). The more successful (reinforced) couples are at the outset of treatment, the more likely they will be to continue in therapy and to proceed to more difficult levels of problem solving and conflict resolution.

It is also important to understand that out-of-session practices and homework assignments always increase the amount of time couples spend together. In many instances, such restructuring of the time couples spend together doing homework assignments need not be mentioned by the therapist. This is especially true if time spent together has been an issue of conflict for the couple in the past. If the additional time spent together is felt to be rewarding for both spouses, it will continue.

The Emergence of Unrecognized Intimacy Needs and the Differentiation of the Self

Ashley and Willie were high school sweethearts who began to date during their sophomore year. Ashley got pregnant when they were seniors, and she dropped out of school to have their son. When their child was in middle school, Ashley completed her education and then went on to college. By the time Ashley received her bachelor's degree, Willie had built a very successful construction business and had become a wealthy, high-profile figure in their community. Shortly after their son left for college, Ashley became depressed. She entered individual psychotherapy in order to alleviate this condition. After several months of individual treatment, her therapist recommended marital therapy since many of her problems were seen as conjugal in nature. Ashley called for an appointment 3 months later. Her husband reluctantly agreed to complete the assessment process but would not commit to following through with therapy.

SIDCARB scores revealed that Ashley perceived her marriage to be an unhappy nonvoluntary relationship. Willie, on the other hand, perceived his marriage as voluntary and satisfying. He could not understand why Ashley was so unhappy.

Ashley's total intimacy needs strength score was 590; Willie's was 459. Clinically significant component needs strength's differences were found between Ashley and Willie in the following areas of intimacy: emotional, psychological, intellectual, aesthetic, and social/recreational. In these five areas, Ashley's needs strengths scores were considered to be moderately high, while Willie's were very low. Receptivity and reciprocity satisfaction percentage scores in all five areas were extremely low for Ashley (ranging from 44–67%). The only component needs areas where Willie experienced dissatisfaction were in sexual intimacy and social/recreational intimacy. Receptivity and reciprocity satisfaction scores for these two areas did not reach 50%.

Treatment   Reviewing assessment findings only served to bring into consciousness what Ashley had felt for some time (i.e., she had married a man who was unable to meet her basic intimacy needs). For Willie, however, the solution to their marital difficulties was simple. He would be satisfied if Ashley "just gave me more sex."

It is countertherapeutic to interpret a spouse's high-barrier SIDCARB scores as signifying the spouse's perception of the marriage as being nonvoluntary. Doing so does not encourage hope for success, nor does it increase spouses' motivation to continue in therapy. A more fruitful approach is to reframe high-barrier strength scores as commitments to the marriage. This was how Ashley's scores were treated. This reframe had a positive impact on Willie. He agreed to consider committing to 12 weeks of marital therapy. He was adamant, however, that he was not interested in any therapy that would change his personality. He said he was happy with himself the way he was.

The fear that therapists possess secret skills, techniques, or powers that they can use to change people against their will is sometimes encountered at the outset of therapy and can be a major cause of resistance and defensiveness. To overcome these fears, Willie was told that changes in one's personality or one's personality traits take a considerable amount of time and could only be brought about with the person's full cooperation. It was further explained that such changes usually require long-term intensive individual psychotherapy and that personality change is not the goal of marital therapy—the focus of marital therapy being to learn more effective communication and conflict negotiation skills and to improve marital intimacy. This clarification put Willie at ease, and he agreed tentatively to the 12-week course of therapy with the proviso that he could terminate therapy at any time if he felt no progress was being made. Ashley agreed to this contract.

Ashley was pleasantly surprised by Willie's ability to learn the communication skills and empathic listening procedures taught during the first 2 weeks of therapy. She was even more surprised by his willingness to complete homework assignments. Willie's attentiveness paid off for him in a very important way; Ashley became more receptive to him sexually.

The next improvement for the couple came in the area of social/recreational intimacy. Ashley agreed to go on fishing excursions with Willie in exchange for his accompanying her to cultural events (e.g., museum visits, art exhibits, and the symphony). Ashley experienced little change in the areas of emotional, psychological, and intellectual intimacy. These three component needs remained unfulfilled.

When it becomes clear that one's spouse is unable to satisfy core intimacy needs, the problem of differing needs strengths must be dealt with forthrightly. The therapist should approach personal needs differences in a matter-of-fact manner by explaining that it is highly unlikely that one single individual will be able to meet and satisfactorily fulfill all the intimacy needs of his or her partner. To expect one's partner to do so only sets one up for disappointment and frustration. It is also important for the therapist to help couples understand that differences in needs strengths are simply that—differences. Some individuals may have a tendency to pathologize these differences. Spouses with relatively high needs may be labeled "needy, dependent, clinging, or controlling" by their partners. Spouses with relatively low intimacy needs may be characterized as "aloof, withdrawn, disinterested, or withholding."

Willie told Ashley, on a number of occasions, that her needs for emotional, psychological, and intellectual intimacy were symptomatic of her "extreme neediness." However, the truth of the matter was that her requests for more intimacy made him feel inadequate. One way to depathologize intimacy needs strengths differences is to talk about these differences as possibly being constitutionally determined. Comparing intimacy needs strengths differences to differences in sex drives often resonates with couples. If couples can accept this rationale, they can begin to deal with their differences more creatively.

Willie said that he understood this sexual analogy very well since his need for sexual intimacy was considerably stronger than Ashley's need as evidenced by their Intimacy Needs Survey scores. He would not characterize himself as being "sexually needy" but considered himself to be "virile." Having made this cognitive shift, Willie was able to discuss ways in which Ashley might be able to have these other needs fulfilled. In subsequent sessions, Ashley began to talk about her need as unactualized aspects of her self.

Sometimes when couples date exclusively during high school and then marry, separation from their families of origin may be incomplete and personal identity formation may be affected. In some instances, individual and couple identities become so entangled and enmeshed that ego boundaries become blurred. For Ashley, the dawning awareness that her husband could not meet core intimacy needs was her first realization of their differences and separateness. This recognition, coupled with her perception of her marriage as nonvoluntary, was seen as contributing significantly to her depression.

When this phenomenon is encountered in marital therapy, the therapeutic challenge is whether the spouses can strengthen their individual identities and function as autonomous persons within the mutually agreed upon boundaries of a committed relationship. Some couples can achieve these developmental goals and tasks, while others cannot develop a sense of self within what they perceive as a confining relationship.

Dealing with their differences in the areas of emotional, psychological, and intellectual intimacy required a series of emotionally charged sessions during which contingency contracts were negotiated. These contracts introduced significant structural and process changes into the couple's relationship. The terms of the contracts were as follows.

Willie agreed that Ashley could pursue a master's of fine arts degree with the expectation that her needs for intellectual intimacy and psychological self-fulfillment would be met through her studies. Willie's major concern, however, was that Ashley might also seek fulfillment of her emotional needs through relationships with other men that she would befriend at the university. This was the major stumbling block for Willie. Ashley explained that she believed that Willie could satisfy her emotionally if he would simply spend more time with her (using the communication and empathic listening skills they had learned) talking about what she was learning and her academic experiences.

In exchange for these requests, Willie asked for the following:

1. A continuation of the same level of sexual involvement that the couple had established over the course of therapy.
2. That Ashley accompany him on one of his extended fishing trips to Alaska.
3. That they would purchase season tickets and attend all home games of the university's football team.

It is important to keep in mind that behavioral contracting with couples will tend to be successful if the exchanges agreed upon by the partners incorporate structural and process changes in the couple's system (Bagarozzi, 1983) and that the exchanges themselves have symbolic significance for the partners (Bagarozzi, 1981). With the formalization of these agreements, the treatment was concluded.

Clinical Notes   The first thing to note in the above case example is how reviewing assessment findings can often bring about insightful discoveries for spouses. In Ashley's case, her preconscious knowledge that she and Willie were mismatched became readily apparent. In addition, perceiving her marriage to be nonvoluntary did not help the matter. Her depression was clearly understandable given her marital situation. The spouse who perceives the marriage to be nonvoluntary is usually the spouse who is more motivated to enter treatment. When this occurs, the therapist must devise an intervention strategy that will induce the less-interested spouse to participate in the therapeutic process. Reframing Ashley's high-barrier scores as evidence of her commitment to the marriage worked to some degree with Willie, but he was still skeptical about the therapist's intentions. In order to allay his fears and reduce his defensiveness, a very simple straightforward educational discussion about the nature and goals of marital therapy was offered. By giving Willie the option of terminating therapy at any time during the 12-week trial process, he felt in control of the process. This made him more receptive to the therapist and the therapy itself.

Positive reinforcement by the therapist for the couple's completing homework assignments is standard procedure and should continue throughout the course of therapy. It is mentioned here simply as a reminder for the reader.

It is not uncommon for success in one area of the relationship to have positive ramifications in other areas of intimacy that have not been directly targeted. For example, Willie's completing homework assignments and thereby spending more time with Ashley resulted in her becoming more sexually responsive to him. When couples report such occurrences, the therapist should treat them as further examples of therapeutic progress and the couple's newly found ability to work more cooperatively as a team.

Contingency contracts are at the heart of this approach to couple's therapy. Such contracts can be formal or informal. The couple should decide how formalized contracts between the spouses should be. For some couples a simple verbal agreement will suffice. For others, contracts may need to be written so that the spouses can refer to them if uncertainties arise. For Ashley and Willie, both formal and informal contracts were negotiated.

Depathologizing intimacy needs differences is often required when large discrepancies exist. How the therapist deals with this problem is a matter of creativity and style. In Willie and Ashley's case, differences in constitutional makeup were used to explain assessment findings. In situations where extreme scores are found, it is not uncommon for the spouse who has a lower (or in many instances an average) need for intimacy to feel inadequate. When such circumstances arise, the therapist still may be able to normalize extreme scores by relabeling them as manifestations of a more encompassing personality style (i.e., introversion or extraversion). Essentially, depathologizing and normalizing techniques are employed to help spouses become more accepting of differences.

The Deterioration of Intimacy Over Time

This final case example is one that demonstrates how intimacy can erode over time and how a couple can choose to deal with the loss of intimacy in their relationship. This is not an example of a therapeutic success story in the sense that marital satisfaction was regained and intimacy was rekindled. It is, however, a story of pragmatic compromise.

Mr. and Mrs. Newson were married for 41 years. Mrs. Newson was 59 and her husband was 61. They had three married children and four grandchildren. Mr. Newson called for an appointment. His attorney suggested that he and his wife try marital therapy before filing for divorce. The couple had separated 6 months earlier.

In the couple's initial interview, Mr. Newson stated that he had lost all feelings for his wife. He said he cared about her and her welfare, but that was the extent of his feelings for her. Mrs. Newson, on the other hand, said that she was angry with her husband because of his ambivalence about staying married to her, but she still hoped that his feelings for her would return. She had not given up on the relationship or her husband.

Mr. Newson's SIDCARB profile revealed that he perceived his marriage to be voluntary. Although he did identify some areas of exchange dissatisfaction, he desired no change from his wife. Mrs. Newson also perceived her marriage to be voluntary but, unlike her husband, she was very dissatisfied and desired a considerable amount of change in his behavior toward her.

The total intimacy needs strengths scores for Mr. and Mrs. Newson were 336 and 641, respectively. For Mrs. Newson receptivity and reciprocity dissatisfactions were seen in the following areas: emotional, psychological, sexual, spiritual, social/recreational, and physical intimacy. For Mr. Newson, receptivity and reciprocity dissatisfactions were found in the areas of psychological, sexual, aesthetic, social/recreational, and physical intimacy. Again, however, Mr. Newson said that he did not desire that his wife make any changes toward him in the areas of intimacy dissatisfaction.

Mr. Newson's lack of interest in having his wife meet any of his unfulfilled intimacy needs was considered to be symptomatic of marital disaffection (i.e., the gradual loss of emotional investment in one's spouse). It includes a decline in caring, emotional estrangement, increased apathy, and indifference. When disaffection is suspected, therapists may consider administering the Marital Disaffection Scale (Kayser, 1993) to estimate each spouse's investment in the marriage and willingness to work toward a more satisfying intimate relationship. The Marital Disaffection Scale's scores range from 21 to 84. The higher the score, the higher the disaffection. Mr. Newson's score on this measure was 72, Mrs. Newson's score was 23.

Mr. Newson spoke openly and honestly about his loss of desire to be sexually intimate with his wife. He characterized his wife's criticism of him and his devotion to his businesses, for the past 10 years, as having a corrosive effect upon him and his desire for her. Mr. Newson revealed that he and his wife had come to this same exact crisis point in their marriage 10 years earlier, but he could not end the marriage for a number of reasons (i.e., he perceived it to be nonvoluntary). Now, circumstances had changed and he was seriously considering divorce. Mrs. Newson was distraught. She said she did not want the marriage to end, but she knew that the decision was not hers to make. It was up to Mr. Newson.

Interpreting Assessment Findings and Devising Treatment Strategies Although both Mr. and Mrs. Newson's SIDCARB profiles showed them to perceive their marriage as voluntary, this was not totally accurate. In one difficult session several weeks into the treatment, Mr. Newson told his wife that he feared that if he divorced her she would have a "nervous breakdown." In response to this, Mrs. Newson said that she would be able to handle that situation if it came to pass. When asked for his professional opinion concerning Mrs. Newson's mental health, the therapist said that Mrs. Newson would be understandably depressed if Mr. Newson chose divorce, but she seemed very capable of handling such a situation appropriately and without undue stress.

In a later session, Mr. Newson expressed his concern that his children would be devastated if their parents divorced. In order to deal with this issue, several family sessions were held with Mr. and Mrs. Newson and their children. During these sessions, Mr. Newson was assured by all three children that their lives would go on and that they would rather see their parents divorce than watch them struggle with this issue for "another 10 years."

Although one might expect there to be some movement in one direction or another by Mr. Newson after these family sessions, he still was ambivalent. Several factors were seen as contributing to Mr. Newson's ambivalence: (a) the obsessive compulsive nature of Mrs. Newson's personality, (b) his fear of making the wrong decision, and (c) loss of control.

In subsequent sessions, it was revealed that Mr. Newson was planning to retire within the year, and that he would be relinquishing control of his businesses to his partners and his children. Essentially, he would have much more free time, and he feared that his wife would expect him to spend that time with her. When one considers the major differences in the Newson's needs for intimacy, it is easy to understand why Mr. Newson would want to gain some physical and interpersonal distance from his wife. Without business obligations to keep him away from home several days each week, Mr. Newson would feel trapped.

When this issue was presented to Mr. and Mrs. Newson for discussion, Mr. Newson said that he would not mind spending time with someone who would not be so critical, but he could not envision himself spending all that time with Mrs. Newson. He said that he would prefer to have whatever little need for intimacy he possessed met by someone else. Mrs. Newson began to cry. She said that she did not want to live with someone who no longer wanted to be around her. Mr. Newson said that he did not mean to hurt her but that he was simply being "honest." At this point, the therapist intervened by saying that it seemed that Mr. Newson had three possible options. He could:

1. Recommit to his wife and work toward improving their marriage and developing a more intimate relationship.
2. Divorce Mrs. Newson and try to find happiness and greater intimacy with someone else.
3. Continue living with Mrs. Newson in a platonic relationship, if she agreed to do so.

The therapist added that if Mr. and Mrs. Newson agreed to the third option that Mr. Newson should discontinue sharing his ruminations and ambivalences about this decision with his wife and that he should refrain from telling his wife that he no longer had any desire to be sexually intimate with her. These suggestions were made in order to curtail, as much as possible, Mr. Newson's passive-aggressive and thinly disguised expressions of anger toward his wife.

Mr. Newson said that he needed some time to think about his options, and therapy was temporarily put on hold. Two months later, Mr. and Mrs. Newson returned for their final session. They had agreed to remain together and to live as roommates. Mr. Newson had moved into a separate wing of their home and as far as their children knew, the matter was closed.

Clinical Notes The Newson's case, on the surface, appears to be one where the therapist's role is that of a facilitator who helps the spouses make some difficult decisions about the future of their relationship. On one level, this is so, but much more is going on in these sessions than meets the eye. First of all, Mr. Newson's SIDCARB scores are suspect. According to Mr. Newson, his marriage is perceived to be voluntary. However, as therapy progresses, he begins to rationalize his inability to leave Mrs. Newson by claiming concern for her sanity if he were to leave her. Assurances from the therapist that Mrs. Newson would be able to handle their divorce appropriately made it difficult for Mr. Newson to use this defense again. With this defense having proven ineffective, Mr. Newson then projected his own fears on to his children, saying that they would be "devastated" if he were to leave their mother. The therapist dealt with this defense by convening family sessions.

The defenses of rationalization and projection were used by Mr. Newson to deal with his basic need for intimacy and his fear of becoming intimate. For some individuals, too much closeness to another human being raises the spectre of being engulfed and controlled by the other, too much distance, on the other hand, raises the fear of abandonment and isolation.

The final contract arrived at by Mr. and Mrs. Newson should be seen not only as a quid pro quo agreement between two spouses concerning how they will live out the rest of their lives together, but as a restructuring of interpersonal space and a conscious agreement about the intimacy they will share as a couple.

Concluding Thoughts

The focus of this chapter was to demonstrate how the Intimacy Needs Survey can be used to help couples improve their relationship when intimacy problems are the chief complaint. The importance of systematic assessment of the couple's relationship was stressed since intimate behavior takes place within a larger relationship context. The degree to which both spouses perceive their marriage to be voluntary or nonvoluntary will greatly affect their desire to work toward restoring, increasing, or improving intimacy in their marriage. Even though a dissatisfying marriage may be perceived as voluntary, a spouse who believes that more fulfilling relationships are possible still might decide to work to improve the marriage. Dissatisfied spouses who perceived their marriage to be nonvoluntary may also decide to work toward improving intimacy and relationship satisfaction, since doing nothing only promises a life of frustration and unhappiness. One should not assume that a particular marital structure predetermines a spouse's willingness to work toward a more satisfying and more intimate relationship.

Personality factors play a significant role in an individual's willingness and capacity to engage in intimate relationships, and they should not be underestimated. Mr. Newson's ability to be intimate was limited, to some degree, by the presence of certain obsessive-compulsive personality traits. While it would be inaccurate to say that Mr. Newson suffered from an obsessive-compulsive personality disorder, his ruminations, perfectionism, ambivalence, and need to control certainly affected his decision making concerning divorce. Similarly, a spouse's interpersonal style and the way he or she deals with conflict also must be taken into account. Again,

Mr. Newson's approach to conflict resolution was avoidance. He separated from his wife in order to avoid unpleasant discussions. In addition, he had not learned how to express negative feelings directly and constructively. As a result, he developed a passive-aggressive interpersonal style. Training in functional communication, conflict negotiation, and assertion helped Mr. Newson deal more directly with his wife. It did not, however, affect his lack of desire to engage in more intimate and sexual relations with Mrs. Newson. Sometimes, when "the thrill is gone" it is "gone for good." Just ask B. B. King.

References

Alford, R. D. (1982). Intimacy and disputing styles within kin and nonkin relationships. *Journal of Family Issues, 3,* 361–374.

Anderson, S. A., & Bagarozzi, D. A. (1983). The use of family myths as an aid to strategic therapy. *Journal of Family Therapy, 5,* 145–154.

Anderson, S. A., & Bagarozzi, D. A. (1988a). Family myths: An introduction. *Journal of Psychotherapy and the Family, 3–4,* 3–16.

Anderson, S. A., & Bagarozzi, D. A. (1988b). Family myths: Psychotherapy implications. *Journal of Psychotherapy and the Family, 3–4,* .

Bagarozzi, D. A. (1980). Holistic family therapy and clinical supervision: Systems, behavioral and psychoanalytic perspectives. *Family Therapy, 2,* 153–165.

Bagarozzi, D. A. (1981). The symbolic meaning of behavioral exchanges in marital therapy. In A. S. Gurman (Ed.), *Questions and answers in the practice of family therapy* (pp. 173–177). New York: Brunner/Mazel.

Bagarozzi, D. A. (1982). Contingency contracting for structural and process changes in family systems. In L. A. Wolberg & M. L. Aronson (Eds.), *Group and family therapy 1982: An overview* (pp. 245–261). New York: Brunner/Mazel.

Bagarozzi, D. A. (1983). Methodological developments in measuring social exchange perceptions in marital dyads (SIDCARB): A new tool for clinical intervention. In D. A. Bagarozzi, A. P. Jurich, & R. W. Jackson (Eds.), *New perspectives in marital and family therapy: Theory, research and practice* (pp. 48–78). New York: Human Sciences Press.

Bagarozzi, D. A. (1990). Intimacy needs questionnaire. Unpublished instrument, Human Resources Consultants, Atlanta.

Bagarozzi, D. A., & Anderson, S. A. (1982). The evolution of family mythological systems: Considerations for meaning, clinical assessment and treatment. *Journal of Psychoanalytic Anthropology, 5,* 71–90.

Bagarozzi, D. A., & Anderson, S. A. (1988). Personal, conjugal and family myths: Theoretical, empirical and clinical developments. *Journal of Psychotherapy and the Family, 3–4,* 167–194.

Bagarozzi, D. A., & Anderson, S. A. (1989). *Personal, marital and family myths: Theoretical formulations and clinical strategies.* New York: W. W. Norton.

Bagarozzi, D. A., & Atilano, R. B. (1982). SIDCARB: A clinical tool for rapid assessment of social exchange inequities and relationship barriers. *Journal of Sex and Marital Therapy, 8,* 325–334.

Bagarozzi, D. A., & Giddings, W. C. (1983a). The role of cognitive constructs and attributional process in family therapy: Integrating intraperson, interpersonal and systems dynamics. In L. A. Wolberg & M. L. Aronson (Eds.), *Group and family therapy 1983: An overview* (pp. 207–219). New York: Brunner/Mazel.

Bagarozzi, D. A., & Giddings, C. W. (1983b). Behavioral marital therapy: Empirical status, current practices, trends and future directions. *Clinical Social Work Journal, 11*, 263–280.

Bagarozzi, D. A., & Pollane, L. (1983). A replication and validation of the Spousal Inventory of Desired Changes and Relationship Barriers (SIDCARB): Elaboration on diagnostic and clinical utilization. *Journal of Sex and Marital Therapy, 9*, 303–315.

Berscheid, E., Snyder, M., & Omoto, A. M. (1989). Issues in studying close relationships. In C. Hendrick (Ed.), *Close relationships* (pp. 63–91). Newberry Park, CA: Sage.

Bowlby, J. (1969/1982). *Attachment and loss,* Vol. I: *Attachment.* New York: Basic Books.

Braiker, H. B., & Kelley, H. H. (1979). Conflict in the development of close relationships. In R. L. Burgess & T. L. Huston (Eds.), *Social exchange and developing relationships* (pp. 135–168). New York: Academic Press.

Derogatis, L. R. (1980). Psychological assessment of psychosexual functioning. *Psychiatric Clinic of North America, 3*, 113–131.

Guerney, B. G., Jr. (1977). *Relationship enhancement: Skill training program for therapy, problem prevention and enrichment.* San Francisco: Jossey-Bass.

Hudson, W. W. (1982). A measurement package for clinical social workers. *Journal of Applied Behavioral Science, 17*, 229–239.

Kayser, K. (1993). *When love dies: The process of marital disaffection.* New York: Guilford.

Lo Piccolo, J., & Steger, J. C. (1974). The sexual interaction inventory. A new instrument for the assessment of sexual dysfunction. *Archives of Sexual Behavior, 3*, 585–595.

Main, M. (1999). Epilogue. Attachment theory: Eighteen points with suggestions for future studies. In J. Cassidy & P. R. Shaver (Eds.), *Handbook of attachment: Theory, research and clinical applications* (pp. 845–887). New York: Guilford.

Miller, R. S., & Lefcourt, H. M. (1992). The assessment of social intimacy. *Journal of Personality Assessment, 46*, 514–518.

Olson, D. H. (1975). *Intimacy and the aging family: Realities of aging.* Minneapolis: University of Minnesota Press.

Olson, D. H. (1977). Quest for intimacy. Unpublished manuscript. University of Minnesota, Minneapolis.

Orlofsky, J. L., & Levitz-Jones, E. M. (1985). Separation—individuation and intimacy capacity in college women. *Journal of Personality and Social Psychology, 49*, 156–169.

Sager, C. J. (1976). *Marriage contracts and couples therapy: Hidden forces in intimate relationships.* New York: Brunner/Mazel.

Schaefer, M. T., & Olson, D. H. (1981). Assessing intimacy: The PAIR inventory. *Journal of Marital and Family Therapy, 7*, 47–60.

Tesch, S. A. (1985). The psychosocial intimacy questionnaire: Validation studies and an investigation of sex roles. *Journal of Personal Relations, 2*, 471–488.

Ting-Toomey, S. (1983a). The analysis of verbal communication patterns in high and low marital adjustment groups. *Human Communication Research, 9,* 306–319.

Ting-Toomey, S. (1983b). Coding conversation between intimates: A validation study of the Intimate Negotiation Coding System (INCS). *Communication Quarterly, 31,* 68–77.

Walker, A. J., & Thompson, L. (1983). Intimacy and intergenerational aid and contact among mothers and daughters. *Journal of Marriage and the Family, 46,* 841–849.

CHAPTER **6**

Interview With Frederic Luskin

Frederic Luskin, Ph.D., is the director of the Stanford Forgiveness Projects and the author of the best-selling *Forgive for Good* and *Forgive for Love*.

Eds: What are some of the common misconceptions that couples have about forgiveness?

FL: 1. That it is the same as condoning ... that you either condone or forgive. Forgiving starts with thinking something is wrong.

2. That you only forgive big things. It is better to get in the habit of forgiving small offenses so your partner feels accepted.

3. That you have to tell your partner you have forgiven. Often it is better to just let it go.

4. That forgiveness is the same as being a doormat. When you forgive you can still be assertive in trying to change improper behavior.

Eds: Is it the same as forgetting?

FL: Sometimes with small things it is the same as forgetting. For larger offenses what happens is you remember differently. You remember without the need for an enemy and without the negative charge.

Eds: What is forgiveness? What is forgiveness not?

FL: Forgiveness is remaining at peace even though your partner did something you did not want them to. It is not condoning or reconciliation or for their well-being. It is a way to stay at peace and connected even though you think your partner did something wrong.

Eds: Can you describe the seven steps in your model?

FL: *The 7 Steps to Forgiveness in a Committed Relationship* (Frederic Luskin, Ph.D., *Forgive for Love* [Harper One, 2008]):

- *YOU CHOSE THEM:* The first and most important step is to honor the fact that the person sleeping next to you did not get there by accident. You may not have chosen wisely or your partner may have changed over time, but please do not blame them for being the person with whom you tried to make a committed relationship work.

- *RECOGNIZE THAT EVERYONE IS FLAWED, INCLUDING YOU:* No matter how hard you try to hide from this discovery you are going to be in a relationship with a human being. You will find all human beings to be flawed and bring all sorts of weird habits and annoying traits with them. Making it more difficult for you and your partner is you too are flawed and therefore even your perspective will be off. So, please be gentle and patient with both of you.

- *LET YOUR PARTNER KNOW HOW BLESSED YOU ARE TO BE WITH THEM:* Your lover has many good traits. The health of your relationship requires you to spend your time noticing and acknowledging their good qualities rather than to dwell on their flaws. Give your partner praise and thanks on a regular basis.

- *TO KNOW THEM IS TO LOVE THEM:* The most important contribution you make to a successful relationship is to be your partner's friend. This means to know them well enough so what they do makes sense even if you do not like it. In that way you see things from their point of view, which allows you to negotiate from the place of a deep and sustaining friendship.

- *ACCEPT WHAT YOU CAN'T CHANGE AND GRIEVE YOUR WOUNDS:* Sometimes our partner has deeply hurt us or they have truly terrible habits. Remember, forgiveness comes at the end of the grief process and not before. This means you may feel real pain from some losses and mistreatments. You then have to decide whether or not you choose to stay. If your answer is yes understand you are accepting the thorns that your human rose bush comes with.

- *DECIDE TO RECOMMIT:* After you have grieved your losses then you have to act in accordance with your decision to recommit to the relationship and your partner. That means you need to be present and kind.

- *PLEASE GIVE YOURSELF A BREAK:* Through the whole process be gentle with yourself and get support where needed. That means to remember your good points, accept your limitations, and agree to be kind to yourself as you try to make a relationship work. Regularly forgive yourself. No one said relationships are easy but good evidence shows them to be well worth it.

Eds: Is it possible to recover intimacy after a betrayal?

FL: Yes … it takes time to grieve the loss or wound first. Then it is helpful to express how you feel betrayed and hurt. Then give the offender a chance to offer an apology and/or change. Finally decide to recommit to the relationship if that is in your best interest.

CHAPTER 7

Recovering Intimacy After Infidelity
A Practice-Based Evidence Approach

W. JARED DUPREE and MARK B. WHITE

Infidelity is a common presenting problem that therapists encounter. The general public is cognizant of the issue as well; a recent USA Today/Gallup poll found that 54% of Americans know someone who has an unfaithful spouse (Jayson, 2008). Because studies that attempt to describe the prevalence of infidelity have used different samples and varying definitions of infidelity, it is difficult to determine how many couples in the United States are affected by infidelity. Estimates range from less than one fourth of committed relationships (around 16% of respondents in a recent ABC News national survey, Langer, Arnedt, & Sussman, 2004); 25% of married men and 15% of married women (Laumann, Gaugnon, Michael, & Michaels, 1994), 25–50% of women and 50–65% of men (Lawson, 1989), to 70% of all Americans at some point during their marital life (*Marriage and Divorce Today*, 1987, cited in Fisher, 1992). The rates are estimated to be higher for cohabiting couples (Laumann et al., 1994; Treas & Giesen, 2000), while there simply are not enough data to estimate the rates for committed gay and lesbian couples.

Historically, infidelity has been defined as participating in a sexual encounter outside of an exclusive relationship. More recently, Piercy, Hertlein, and Wetchler (2008) asserted that definitions of infidelity have expanded to include a wide range of behaviors, including sexual intercourse, cybersex, viewing pornography, kissing and holding hands, and even emotional intimacy with another person to the detriment of the primary relationship. At the most basic process level, infidelity could refer to any behavior that breaks the contract two people have with each other (Lusterman, 1998). Although different articles use different terms and definitions of infidelity (e.g., extramarital affairs, emotional infidelity, sexual infidelity), we will generally use the term infidelity to refer to any breach of the primary couple relationship (sexual or emotional) that couples are seeking treatment to deal with. In addition, we have adopted the language used by Gordon, Baucom, and Synder (2004) and refer to the person having the affair as the *participating party*, while the nonparticipating partner is referred to as the *injured party*.

Blow and Hartnett (2005b), in a review of literature on factors that contribute to infidelity, reported that lower levels of marital commitment, marital satisfaction, and sexual satisfaction may influence the likelihood of infidelity. Other factors related to infidelity include length of the primary relationship, lower levels of religiosity, higher income, parental divorce, past divorce, remarriage, attachment style, and age; however, it is important to note that many of these factors are based on studies with small sample sizes and mixed conclusions. Overall, our understanding of factors that lead to infidelity based on empirical studies is limited. Piercy et al. (2008) outlined factors that may contribute to infidelity based on current treatment patterns and environmental influences, including attachment, trust, cultural myths about marriage and relationships, systemic dynamics, and levels of differentiation. They also recognize that with the onset of the Internet, the opportunity to engage in extradyadic relationships has increased. Cyberspace changes the landscape of how, when, and where infidelity could occur.

The current emphasis in mental health delivery systems includes a focus on treatment guidelines. There is a growing body of literature that emphasizes empirically supported treatments, evidence-based practice, and best practice guidelines (e.g., Carlson & Ellis, 2004; Larner, 2004; Patterson, Miller, Carnes, & Wilson, 2004). The essence of this literature is that therapists use the results of clinical research, or at a minimum the consensus of experienced therapists, to inform their clinical practice. Practice-based evidence has emerged as a method of gathering data from practicing clinicians to inform treatment guidelines. This chapter will distill and disseminate such aggregated wisdom related to treating infidelity into a practice-based evidence model.

Practice-Based Evidence

Efforts have been made over the past decade to identify treatments for specific presenting problems that have been shown to be efficacious through empirical support (Bruce & Sanderson, 2005). Traditionally, an established hierarchical ranking of "grades of evidence" has been used to establish evidence with randomized controlled trials and empirically supported treatments at the high end and observational studies at the low end (Krakau, 2000). Sprenkle (2002) suggested that empirically supported treatments are a valuable resource to the practitioner who has a client with a presenting problem and is searching for a treatment that is shown to be effective in treating it. However, he points out that empirically supported treatments can be misleading and often do not give a full account of what could be helpful in treating a certain presenting problem. Stiles and colleagues (2003) also noted that researchers and reviewers have voiced concerns about whether phenomena observed in efficacy studies are representative of actual practice patterns. Thus, effectiveness studies have been conducted to evaluate already efficacious treatment in real-world applications (Bruce & Sanderson, 2005).

Agras and Berkowitz (1980) presented a model of research that outlined the process for developing and evaluating promising treatments. They indicated that the first step in developing evidence-based treatment guidelines is to examine the current status of the interventions used in the field. In order to do so, they acknowledged the importance of clinical observation and basic research as a means of examining current practice patterns.

Most studies typically focus on basic research or theoretical models to understand treatment guidelines as one develops evidence-based treatment. Little emphasis is placed on the observations from practicing clinicians. However, more emphasis has recently been placed on methods that implicitly link research to practice as a means to narrow the practitioner–researcher gap (e.g., Fox, 2000; Hays, 2005). These methods allow researchers to obtain a more realistic picture of current practice patterns since the information comes directly from clinicians. Once these practice patterns are defined, basic research and existing theoretical models can be used to formulate treatment guidelines that can be tested. Recently, the fields of psychiatry and psychotherapy have begun to use the term "practice-based evidence" to refer to methodologies that inform the researcher by "gathering good-quality data from routine practice" (Margison et al., 2000, p. 123; Lucock et al., 2003). Practitioners identify important clinical phenomenon and then use that knowledge to inform and validate clinical models and manuals (Johnson, 2003).

Benefits of a practice-based evidence approach include: (a) the researcher–clinician gap is narrowed as researchers and clinicians collaborate on research (Barkham & Mellor-Clark, 2003; Fox, 2000), (b) researchers can tap into years of expertise and knowledge from clinicians that work in real-world settings rather than blindly forming treatment guidelines, (c) clinicians can offer insights to nuances that researchers may not be aware of due to a lack of clinical experience in different areas, and (d) clinicians are more likely to use practice-based evidence research to inform practice patterns (Luckock et al., 2003).

Because the current status of treatment for infidelity lacks sufficient quantitative evidence to create an empirically supported treatment or MAST, we have approached the literature in this area using a practice-based evidence lens in order to offer clinical guidelines and awareness for infidelity treatment. Hopefully, these guidelines can later be tested and compared in order to begin the process of reaching an evidence-based form of treatment for infidelity. A practice-based evidence model offers initial themes and patterns of practice through key principles, interventions, and areas of assessment that can be tested and compared in order to inform future direction. Using years of clinical experience in the form of books and articles, a practice-based evidence approach provides valuable insights as the field moves toward an evidence-based practice set of guidelines for the treatment of infidelity issues.

Review of the Literature

We reviewed three classes of literature in the process of developing the best practice guidelines. First, we examined journal articles relating to the treatment of infidelity. Second, we reviewed foundational books written by professionals (e.g., Glass, 2003; Moultrup, 1990; Pittman, 1989). These books were considered foundational based on the number of times they were cited in the literature and recent publications as well as the fact that they were some of the first books written on treating infidelity. Third, more recent books written by professionals were also included and analyzed. It is important to note that we did not review all professional books written on infidelity. Books that were written by laypersons, self-help books solely for individuals coping with infidelity, and scholarly examinations without a clinical focus were not included in our review.

In our search for infidelity treatment studies, we identified one outcome study (Atkins, Eldridge, Baucom, & Christensen, 2005), which extracted a sample of 19 couples dealing with infidelity from a larger study comparing Traditional Behavioral Couple Therapy and Integrative Behavioral Couple Therapy. In addition, we also reviewed a study testing a theoretical model of infidelity treatment that used a small sample of six couples (Gordon et al., 2004). A number of qualitative and theoretical articles have been written that provide some guidelines in treating infidelity (Afifi, Falato, & Weiner, 2001; Atwood & Seifer, 1997; Blow & Hartnett, 2005a, 2005b; Elbaum, 1981; Gordon & Baucom, 1998, 1999; Gordon et al., 2004; Johnson, Makinen, & Millikin, 2001; Olson, Russell, Higgins-Kessler, & Miller, 2002; Penn, Hernandez, & Bermudez, 1997; Previti & Amato, 2004; Schneider & Corley, 2007; Shackelford & Buss, 1997; Silverstein, 1998).

Once we identified a core set of clinical recommendations that was similar across sources, we stopped reviewing additional books as we determined that we had reached saturation. Similar to qualitative interviewing, the notion of saturation suggests that increasing the sample size of the books analyzed would not produce additional significant findings. In other words, the themes and common threads of the analysis had reached a clear demarcation. Thus, after examining the foundational books and articles, we began to examine more recent books written by professionals. After analyzing several recent books, the same themes and patterns were discovered. We stopped the analysis process when we judged additional books would not add significant insight. Thus, a total of 10 books or book chapters were used in the analysis of this study (Abrahms Spring, 1996; Brown, 2001; Glass, 2003; Glass, & Wright, 1997; Johnson, 2008; Lusterman, 1995, 1998; Moultrup, 1990; Pittman, 1989; Weeks, Gambescia, & Jenkins, 2003) in addition to the quantitative and qualitative journal articles (Afifi, Falato, & Weiner, 2001; Atkins et al., 2005; Atwood & Seifer, 1997; Blow & Hartnett, 2005a, 2005b; Elbaum, 1981; Gordon & Baucom, 2003; Gordon et al., 2004; Hertlein & Weeks, 2007; Penn et al. 1997; Previti & Amato, 2004; Schneider & Corley, 2002; Shackelford & Buss, 1997; Silverstein, 1998).

Articles, chapters, and books were analyzed by two faculty members and two doctoral students. Based on our understanding of the different facets of clinical work, we began the review process by creating matrices and then distilling the information obtained into the following categories: treatment engagement, assessment, process and intervention, treatment adherence, and relapse prevention. In addition, two additional themes emerged during the review of literature: therapist attributes and areas of debate. It is important to note that although all the books and chapters mentioned how clinicians could use the information to guide infidelity treatment, some of the books were clearly directed more toward the layperson experiencing infidelity. Thus, some of the books provided little or no information in regard to certain aspects of treatment. In addition, other books offered indirect information about areas of treatment through the use of case examples or anecdotes. Only information related to infidelity treatment was analyzed.

Following the creation of the matrices, areas of treatment were compared and contrasted to find common threads among all perspectives. These common threads were then summarized as best practice guidelines. In addition, areas of debate were noted, suggesting the need for further research to more clearly understand best practice guidelines in particular areas.

Infidelity Treatment Guidelines

According to Olson et al. (2002), couples experiencing infidelity need a map from which they can work in order to understand the process of recovery. Blow and Hartnett (2005b) suggested that treating infidelity is very different from other couples' issues and needs special attention in regard to treatment guidelines. The best practice approach described below was designed to provide a map from which the therapist can guide the treatment process.

The best practice guidelines are divided into several areas: goals of treatment, treatment engagement, treatment format, assessment, process and intervention, treatment adherence, and relapse prevention. In addition, cultural and ethical considerations are listed. Finally, a section addressing online infidelity treatment considerations is provided. These guidelines are summarized in Table 7.1.

Goals of Treatment

The different clinical approaches to treating infidelity share the following common goals for treatment:

1. Create a safe, trusting environment for the clients to examine and explore their relationship.
2. Provide a structured environment for the clients to feel equally validated and guided in the process of therapy.
3. Examine the emotional, behavioral, and cognitive reactions to the trauma of infidelity.
4. Explore past and present patterns of the relationship.
5. Explore past and present expectations and meanings of the relationship.
6. Provide a structured process of self-disclosure to allow for understanding and a means of rebuilding attachment and trust.
7. Examine new patterns, meanings, and expectations of the relationship on a structural, behavioral, emotional, and cognitive level in order to maintain trust.
8. Explore the process of forgiveness and mutual healing.

Treatment Engagement

Treatment engagement refers to the therapist's role with the clients and the treatment structure. In addition, a third theme of therapist attributes was evident following the analysis relating to the therapist's role.

In regard to the therapist's role, nearly all the models describe a therapist as one who is direct, active, collaborative, flexible, and gives advice. Furthermore, many of the models recommended that therapists should have certain traits or attributes. Clinical experts recommend that therapists be nonjudgmental, willing to focus on the affair, patient, validating, understanding, observant, and able to provide hope and reassurance in order to provide effective treatment.

Table 7.1 Themes in Clinical Guidelines for Treating Infidelity

I. Treatment Engagement

1. *Role of the Therapist*	a. Direct, active, collaborative, guide, flexible, advice-giving.
2. *Treatment Structure*	a. Provide plan, b. Set boundaries.
3. *Modality*	a. Couple, couple/individual, and sometimes individual.*

II. Assessment

1. *Cognitions/Emotions*	a. Thoughts/emotions before and after the affair, b. Level of crisis, c. Possible mental health disorders (e.g., major depression, bipolar disorder, addictions, personality disorders).
2. *Couple/Family Relationship*	a. Current and past relational patterns of the couple, b. Family of origin.
3. *Trauma Event(s)**	a. Type and length of affair(s) (disclosed in individual and/or couple sessions),* b. Reactions to the affair.
4. *Life Cycle*	a. Stage of life, b. Outside events and stressors.

III. Interventions

1. *Deescalation*	a. Reduce emotional crisis level, b. Engage both partners through validation.
2. *Cognitive Reframing*	a. Understand meaning of affair in light of past expectations and patterns.
3. *Systemic Restructuring*	a. Create safety for restructuring of thoughts, behaviors, and attachments, b. Create new patterns of interaction and communication while setting boundaries to reduce risk of repeat trauma(s).
4. *Attachment Rebuilding*	a. Strengthen new patterns of relationship, b. Use new patterns to express hurts, forgive, and rebuild new meaning in relationship.

IV. Treatment Adherence

1. *Needs of Clients*	a. Consistently reexamine needs of clients, b. Collaborate with treatment process, c. Clearly communicate treatment plan.
2. *Therapist Attributes*	a. Nonjudgmental, b. Understanding, c. Ability to focus on the affair, d. Validating, e. Observant, f. Flexible, g. Provide hope

V. Relapse Prevention

1. *Restructuring*	a. Restructuring of relationship patterns, irrational thoughts, and family structures.
2. *Rebuilding*	a. Rebuilding emotional bonds, level of hope, and positive behaviors.

Continued

Table 7.1 Themes in Clinical Guidelines for Treating Infidelity (*Continued*)

	VI. Cultural Considerations
1. *Religion/Culture*	a. Examine beliefs, expectations, and contexts that may influence meanings of infidelity and intimacy.
	VII. Ethical Dilemmas
1. *Secrets**	a. Overall, keeping secrets seems to be harmful. Disclosure to the partner seems to be beneficial when seeking relationship improvement.
	b. Keeping secrets may be needed when there is a risk of physical violence. Some believe that ancient affairs do need to be disclosed.*
	c. When the court system is involved due to custody or divorce issues, keeping secrets needs to be assessed in regard to benefit of all members.
2. *Confidentiality*	a. Providing confidentiality guidelines upfront helps avoid ethical or legal problems.

* Areas of debate (modality–couple vs. couple/individual vs. individual; amount disclosed about affair).

The importance of the therapist establishing structure within the treatment process also was emphasized. The literature reviewed suggested that it is important for the therapist to establish clear boundaries from the beginning in regard to both the couple's relationship (e.g., stopping the affair, knowing where each person is during the day, managing relationships) and the process of treatment (e.g., providing an outline for treatment, role of clients and therapist, maintaining neutrality between partners, avoiding triangles). Finally, two interventions seem to help solidify the treatment structure throughout the process: emotional validation and joining. Thus, as the therapist validates both partners while maintaining a neutral stance between partners through joining and boundary setting, clients feel more engaged and are willing to take more risks as they delve into the painful process of rebuilding trust.

Treatment Format

Further research is needed to understand the differences in effectiveness between individual, individual and couple, couple, and group treatments. The majority of sources recommend couples treatment in combination with individual treatment as needed. If individual therapy is used, it appears that clear boundary setting would be important to avoid triangulation or disintegration of treatment progress. Brown (2005) suggested that individual therapy is recommended when the participating party is engaged in a split self affair. In other words, the participating party is in a long-term serious relationship stemming from an internal split between doing things "right" and the emotional self. Long-term individual therapy is recommended, augmented by couples treatment as needed.

Assessment

In the beginning of treatment, a number of assessment areas provide background information in order to understand some common patterns and traits of the couple's relationship. Other areas of assessment appear to be important throughout the treatment process.

First, it is important to assess the degree to which the couple desires to improve the relationship and move toward a healing process. Some couples may be struggling with whether or not they want to salvage the relationship. It is not uncommon for one party to want to work on the relationship and the other to want out. If a couple has not made the decision to improve the relationship, some time may be needed to explore options for treatment, including possible individual treatment or divorce adjustment if that is the direction the couple decides. However, the beginning processes of treatment discussed below provide a backdrop to explore commitment issues. It may be beneficial to explain to the couple that a decision to stay in the relationship may not be needed in the beginning of treatment but that these issues will be explored. For example, in the model of forgiveness by Gordon et al. (2004) the decision to stay or leave is decided in the final stages of treatment. Lusterman (1995) also used a model that helps the couple move toward either a better marriage or a better divorce. Other models seem to assume that the couple wants to maintain or improve the relationship. Careful examination of this issue is important in order to tailor treatment as an exploratory process, a reconciliation process, or a combination of both.

Important areas to assess in regard to background information include family of origin patterns (e.g., couple or family boundaries, triangles, levels of intimacy, a family history of infidelity) attachment and relationship patterns, and developmental life cycle characteristics. Understanding relationship patterns provides a systemic context that can guide treatment and help the couple focus on process issues rather than content.

Throughout treatment it is important to be aware of the level of crisis (e.g., suicidality, homocidality, depression), emotional trauma, and couple or family boundaries as well as comorbidity issues (e.g., substance abuse). Lusterman (2005) recognized that the discovery of infidelity by the injured party often produces a posttraumatic reaction; however, he noted that such a reaction is normal and not seen as pathological. Lusterman also identified the phenomenon of a delayed traumatic reaction in which the discoverer does not experience the full "trauma" of the infidelity until a significant amount of time has passed. He encouraged therapists to be aware of the differences between pathological trauma and anxiety symptoms that are common among discoverers of infidelity.

Finally, the characteristics of the affair itself need to be assessed. This appears to be important in order to understand levels of emotional distance, patterns of the relationship, and what needs to occur for reconciliation to take place. A number of models acknowledge the different types of affairs (sexual, emotional, virtual) individuals may have been involved in. Other models suggest it may be important to have individual sessions to understand the motives and depths of the affair before dealing with the affair within conjoint therapy. There are differences of opinion as to how much needs to be shared about the affair itself. Some clinicians have reported that the one who has had the affair should share every detail of the affair (e.g., length of the affair, details of the sexual interaction, places of the affair), while other clinicians to do not emphasize such a detailed approach. Schneider, Irons, and Corley (1999) did find that revealing information about the affair over time rather than in the beginning produced adverse effects for several partners in their study. Schneider and Corley (2002) recommended that the participating partner should disclose at least the broad outline of all significant sexual activities in the beginning of treatment and that further discussion with a therapist could help determine how much more needs to be shared. In addition, Atkins et al. (2005) found that couples who kept infidelity a secret did not improve in treatment (had poorer outcomes than those who revealed the affair prior to or in the initial stages of therapy).

It appears to be important for the involved partner to disclose information about the affair. Disclosure may be helpful because of the impact it has on changing the negative interaction cycle. Keeping the infidelity a secret may reinforce old patterns, while disclosing could help form new patterns of interaction that lead to a more trusting relationship. More research is needed as to how much should be disclosed and the timing of the disclosure. Furthermore, a number of studies and clinicians suggest that different types of affairs (emotional vs. sexual) may need to be disclosed and dealt with differently (Glass & Wright, 1985; Thompson, 1984). However, a lack of research in these areas makes it difficult to provide any conclusive guidelines.

Processes and Interventions

Processes refer to those patterns of treatment that seem to be common across models. *Interventions* refer to specific strategies of treatment implemented during the process of treatment. There were a number of common threads evident in the literature that seem to exemplify the process of therapy when treating couples who are dealing with infidelity. It is important to note that although the following information is presented in a stage format, the stages are designed to guide the clinician through key processes rather than suggest a step-by-step method common to manualized treatment models.

The initial stage of treatment seems to focus on three main areas: deescalation, assessment, and treatment planning. Through deescalation, the therapist attempts to reduce the level of emotional crisis, engage both partners through validation, and build trust with both partners while maintaining a neutral stance (which may require helping one partner become more engaged or bringing one partner's level of emotional intensity down). Typically, it appears that the participating partner is withdrawn, while the injured partner exhibits high levels of emotional intensity.

During assessment, the therapist assesses for current reactions to the affair, goals and desires for therapy, and emotional and cognitive meanings of the affair. In addition, gathering data about each client's family of origin (FOO), current and past relationship patterns, and the details about the affair itself seems to be important for more effective treatment. This can help reduce blaming or distancing patterns as well as place the infidelity within the context of relational processes.

Treatment planning also appears to be important for couples dealing with infidelity in order to provide structure and "a map" for the couple. Areas to address during the treatment planning stage may include current boundary issues at home and in therapy, establishing goals at the individual and relational levels, and providing an outline for treatment in addition to explaining the therapy process.

The second stage of treatment appears to emphasize cognitive reframing and restructuring emotional attachments. The process of cognitive reframing appears to follow a pattern of (a) gathering meanings associated with the affair from both partners, (b) examining past expectations and influences regarding the relationship, (c) exploring patterns of behavior in FOO and current or past relationships, and, (d) normalizing and reframing behaviors into new meanings of the current and future relationship. Thus, understanding the affair within the context of past expectations and old patterns of relationship behaviors helps the couple reframe the meaning of the affair and redefine new meanings of the relationship. For example, a couple dealing with an ongoing affair in which the husband is the participating partner may discover that the affair is part of an interaction pattern that has been reinforced for years. They may discover that the husband withdraws during times of conflict because he has a high self-expectation for perfection, while the wife attempts to address tension areas in the relationship. Their interaction pattern would reinforce a typical pursuer–distancer relationship within the context of the husband having unrealistic expectations of perfection. Thus, the couple may reframe their relationship and discuss how they were trapped in a pattern of interaction in which pursuing and distancing did not allow for emotional connection and unrealistic expectations for perfection sabotaged any chance for closeness.

In addition to cognitive reframing, emotional attachment restructuring helps the couple heal the wounds of the affair by treating the infidelity as an emotional trauma or attachment injury. Important aspects of building and structuring healthy attachment patterns are: (a) identifying negative interaction cycles, (b) identifying the level of attachment injury, (c) examining roles of each partner in the interaction cycles, (d) exploring FOO issues related to the patterns, and (e) establishing new ways of expressing affect, thinking differently about the relationship, and making behavioral changes in order to form a positive interaction cycle.

The final stage of treatment is focused on solidifying the forgiveness process as well as examining how the couple will move forward in their new relationship. The forgiveness process appears to take place by helping the couple form new patterns of expressing feelings and thoughts in order to understand and validate the cognitive and affective meanings behind the affair. Using the previous example, the husband may communicate how his high expectations for perfection discourage attempts to deal with conflict in the marriage because of his fear of being wrong or rejected. He may share how he feels distant and lonely when he withdraws, yet he feels "leery" of getting close out of a fear of being rejected. He may express his guilt of having the affair and communicate how his fear of bringing up yet another failure reinforced continuing the affair. The wife may express her anger and hurt in finding out he had an affair when she has tried to "fix" the relationship so many times in the past. The wife possibly would share her feelings of betrayal and feeling alone. Both partners would express how they feel and try to understand how the other feels in regard to the affair within the context of specific relationship patterns. The couple may realize that they were experiencing similar feelings in the relationship before the affair and even similar feelings of loneliness after the affair, even though they each reacted to these feelings in different ways. Thus, helping partners mutually validate each other's experience helps begin the forgiveness process. Case (2005) suggested that expressions of forgiveness are much more powerful after the couple has gone through a process in which they recognize their role within the context of the affair and have expressed underlying feelings.

There seems to be a natural progression in the process of therapy in which the experiences and feelings have been shared and the couple begins to examine the future of the relationship in terms of either pursuing the relationship and changing old patterns and expectations or starting a separation process. Exploring how the current relationship will change appears to help solidify the onset of the forgiveness process. In addition, helping the couple explore future goals of the relationship, reexamining what has worked and not worked in the relationship, and discussing future treatment options help provide closure and future direction for further treatment or termination.

When a couple decides to pursue the relationship, treatment direction shifts to a relationship-enhancement process while reinforcing the forgiveness process. If the couple decides to separate, dealing with the forgiveness process may need to happen within the context of individual therapy.

Treatment Adherence

The majority of the models examined for this study did not address treatment adherence (therapists' ability to follow therapeutic guidelines). However, some general principles indirectly surfaced following analysis. First, it appears that paying attention to the role of the therapist and providing clients with "a map" for treatment at the beginning of therapy help the therapist plant the seeds for an effective therapeutic alliance. Second, collaboratively working with the couple and reexamining goals throughout the process seem to help the treatment progress in an effective manner. Finally, it appears important that therapists display the common attributes discussed above in order to facilitate successful client engagement in therapy.

Relapse Prevention

Although the majority of the models did not address relapse prevention, all the models appear to focus on a second order change mentality as a means to prevent relapse. Thus, rather than focusing on simple behavioral change in which structural measures are made to prevent relapse (e.g., curfews, avoiding certain places or friends, avoiding business travel), processes are changed through cognitive reframes, emotional attachment healing, and systemic restructuring. Relapse prevention seems to depend on whether the couple is able to examine the patterns of the relationship, heal broken bonds, and form new processes of expressing feelings and thoughts as well as new ways of behaving within a systemic framework.

Therapists' ability to prevent relapse may be enhanced as we understand more about predictive and protective factors of infidelity. Although little research has been done in these areas (Blow & Harnett, 2005b), there are some initial findings that can help guide treatment. Previti and Amato (2004) reported that infidelity is both a cause and consequence of relationship deterioration. Thus, infidelity seems tied to the quality of the relationship itself. Shackelford and Buss (1997) also found that certain factors seem to cue infidelity, including emotional disengagement, reluctance to spend time with partner, sexual disinterest, and argumentativeness. The majority of the factors identified suggest that relationship patterns and behaviors seem to cue infidelity. Addressing the relationship's patterns of emotional engagement and behaviors itself seems integral in preventing relapse. The empirical findings of Atkins et al. (2005) suggested that focusing on the relationship rather than the infidelity itself appears critical to the treatment process.

As stated, Blow and Hartnett (2005b) suggested that possible predictors of infidelity include parental divorce, past divorce, remarriage, and attachment style. In addition, Weeks and colleagues (2003) commented that clients suffering from bipolar disorder, depression, personality disorders, and addictions may be more susceptible to engage in infidelity. Thus, possible protective factors may be to deal with attachment patterns, past relationship patterns, FOO issues, and individual mental disorders. In addition, Weeks et al. (2003) asserted that helping clients develop empathy, humility, commitment, understanding, healthy communication, and hope may help in the long-term forgiveness process and prevent relapse.

It is important to note that the majority of the models suggest that infidelity treatment focus on dealing with the trauma of infidelity. However, once the crisis of the affair has been addressed, it is generally recommended that treatment progress to dealing with other relationship issues. Thus, although the trauma of infidelity has been processed and interventions have been made, additional treatment, possibly dealing with intimacy, relationship enhancement, communication, impulse control, or mood disorders, is appropriate.

Cultural Considerations

Penn et al. (1997) provided clinical guidelines when treating infidelity within the context of certain ethnicities, religions, and philosophies. It is important to note that these guidelines were not based on empirical studies; rather, guidelines were derived from personal communications with other clinicians and existing literature addressing general mental health guidelines within the context of culture. In addition, much of their recommendations have the risk of encouraging stereotypes. The following guidelines are issues to be aware of and may not apply to one's clients. Schwartzman (1983) provided helpful insight suggesting that therapists use an "inside-out" approach when considering cultural context. Oftentimes, therapists take an outsider's view in which the therapist learns cultural principles and traits from an outside source (e.g., books, articles) and applies those principles to his or her client without considering unique differences. The "inside-out" approach invites clients to help the therapist understand their culture by providing an insider's view through the therapist's questions about the culture rather than making assumptions. The purpose of this section is to offer possible themes to be aware of when examining the context of culture, while still maintaining an inside-out approach.

Religion

Penn et al. (1997) suggested that when working with clients with a strong religious background, it may be important to address infidelity within the context of their established religion. They suggest it may be more effective to work in collaboration with their clients' religious leaders and take a "one-down" position in which the clients become experts on their religion. In addition, addressing how particular religious beliefs view infidelity may be necessary to understand the context of infidelity (e.g., examining the feelings of shame and guilt within Islam or other Eastern philosophies, openly discussing religious sanctions).

Ethnicity

Unfortunately, the guidelines provided by Penn et al. (1997) for ethnicity are speculative due to the lack of research in this area. However, some theoretical guidelines were presented. For African Americans, they suggested that the joining process and focusing on respect are critical steps due to the lack of trust for therapists among African Americans as well as the trust and respect issues raised by the infidelity. In addition, the authors suggested using family and religion to support the process of rebuilding committed relationships. For Hispanic Americans, the authors noted that dealing with "dirty laundry" may be uncomfortable for the couple. Thus, avoiding harsh judgments and helping the couple feel understood and respected in the process appear to be important. In addition, addressing gender roles, acculturation levels, and expectations of the marriage is essential for this cohort. For Asian Americans, addressing issues of shame, guilt, and blame seems to follow the traditional views of Eastern philosophy and would apply when addressing infidelity. It was also recommended that therapists be aware of gender roles and that acculturation levels are also important when treating Asian Americans.

Ethical Considerations

Secrets

A number of ethical dilemmas may arise when treating infidelity. First, it is not uncommon for individuals in therapy to disclose a past infidelity that has not been previously discussed with his or her partner. A couple of studies provide some guidelines for these situations. As mentioned above, Atkins et al. (2005) found that those couples who disclosed an infidelity within treatment progressed faster than couples who kept the infidelity a secret. In fact, many of the couples that kept infidelity a secret got worse. Schneider and Corley (2002) found that among sex addicts, disclosure of extramarital sex produced positive results overall based on both the participating partner's and the injured partner's point of view. In addition, they found that staggered disclosure (disclosure over time) seemed to produce negative results in the relationship. Afifi et al. (2001) found that among dating couples there were four possible types of self-disclosure: (a) *unsolicited partner discovery*, which includes situations in which the participating partner disclosed the infidelity without solicitation, (b) *solicited partner discovery*, those instances in which the injured partner discovers infidelity after questioning the participating partner, (c) "*red-handed*" *discovery*, cases in which the injured partner catches his or her partner during an act of infidelity, and (d) *unsolicited third-party discovery*, which occurs when a third party discloses the infidelity to the injured partner. Afifi et al. (2001) found that unsolicited partner discovery produced the least amount of negative results in the relationship. Solicited partner discovery produced more negative results in the relationship; however, red-handed discovery and unsolicited third-party discovery produced the most negative results. Thus, current research would suggest that the relationship may benefit from relatively early and full partner disclosure. Disclosing within the process of therapy may provide a more structured, safe environment for this to occur.

Confidentiality

A second issue that arises when an individual discloses infidelity within the context of therapy is the ethical dilemma of confidentiality. Weeks et al. (2003) asserted that being upfront with clients about confidentiality is the most effective way to avoid legal issues or ethical dilemmas. They provided three possible confidentiality guidelines that are presented to couples at the beginning of treatment: (a) all information from any source is confidential, (b) all information from any source must be shared, and (c) therapists choose to keep the secret information confidential for a specific time period with the understanding that conjoint treatment will end if the client refuses to be accountable. Weeks et al. (2003) provided a detailed approach to this third option through a series of steps: (a) the therapist does not divulge the secret and in return expects accountability for the behavior(s); (b) accountability means taking responsibility for any conduct that violates the couples agreement about intimacy and exclusivity; (c) the individual is told that an active affair or other forms of infidelity will make couples therapy impossible; (d) the participating partner must choose between the infidelity and the partner; (e) the therapist gives the partner a deadline to stop the affair or conjoint therapy will cease; (f) the therapist requires individual sessions to understand motives behind infidelity; (g) if the participating partner refuses to share the infidelity, conjoint therapy is ended by explaining to both partners that an issue in individual therapy has been discussed, making it impossible to conduct couples therapy; and (h) if the partner ceases infidelity, individual sessions are needed concurrently with the other marital partner in order to gain enough insight that the affair will not occur again.

When Not to Disclose

Brown (2001) offered guidelines about when not to disclose an affair. First, in situations in which the disclosure of an affair may increase the likelihood of violence, it would be imperative to address issues of domestic violence before addressing infidelity issues. Second, if the couple is seeking divorce, revelation of an affair may not be necessary due to the fact the disclosure may be used for revenge purposes. In addition, Brown noted that adultery may influence the court system's ruling on custody issues and financial decisions. Thus, addressing the revelation of infidelity when dealing with the court needs to be thoroughly assessed before going through the disclosure process. Finally, Brown suggested that some therapists feel that ancient affairs do not need to be revealed. Weeks et al. (2003) contended that the only time a therapist should insist on the revelation of an affair is if the affair is ongoing or if the past affair is getting in the way of treatment. However, they recognized there is considerable debate about this issue and more research is needed.

Countertransference

Personal biases and identifications that occur through countertransference may impede effective treatment (Bettinger, 2005; Silverstein, 1998; Weeks et al., 2003). Silverstein (1998) argued that clinicians be aware of biases that may stem from dealing with a betrayal in their own past, moralism and religious beliefs, gender bias, and conflict-avoidant patterns of doing therapy. Talking about infidelity and sex may be uncomfortable for some clinicians, while other clinicians may have difficulty controlling angry, righteous, or guilty emotions. Consciously being aware of biases, seeking consultation and supervision, and continually working out personal issues have been identified by several authors as the ethical responsibility of clinicians working with infidelity.

Internet Infidelity Considerations

Atwood (2005) recognized that Internet infidelity is different from traditional infidelities in that it appears to be anonymous and relatively safe, as it can be pursued in the privacy of one's own home or office. She defines *cybersex* as the behavior of seeking sexual satisfaction through the Internet rather than from his or her partner, while a *cyber-affair* is defined as one partner sharing an emotional connection with a participating cyber-friend on the Internet. A cyber-affair may or may not engage in cybersex, although it often occurs; however, the cyber-affair suggests that the relationship is taking away from the relationship with his or her own partner.

In regard to treatment, it is important to be aware of factors that set the stage for Internet infidelity, including: (a) cyber-infidelity is anonymous;

(b) the cyber-surfer projects an ideal mate; (c) cyber-infidelity often attracts those with intimacy issues; (d) cyber-infidelity can be used to regulate anxiety; (e) cyber-infidelity becomes a source of communication; and (e) cyber-infidelity can lead to Internet addiction (Atwood, 2005). Nelson, Piercy, and Sprenkle (2005) conducted a multiphase Delphi study with expert practitioners and researchers who examined the treatment of Internet infidelity. They found that many of the experts treated couples who were dealing with Internet infidelity in a similar manner to how they treated couples who were experiencing traditional infidelities. Thus, it is not surprising to find that many of the treatment recommendations for Internet infidelity are similar to traditional infidelity models. Atwood (2005) suggested that Internet infidelity includes crisis intervention, addressing self-esteem, facing the trauma of the act, dealing with the loss of the cyber-lover, addressing underlying patterns, improving communication, rebuilding couple trust, and constructing new stories. It appears that a possible difference between Internet infidelity treatment and traditional infidelity treatment might be addressing minimization or denial issues related to the cyber-affair. In other words, some partners may not view the cyber-affair as an affair at all since there is no physical contact. It may be important for clinicians to explore the meaning behind the behaviors within the context of the relationship to help both partners understand the impact the cyber-affair has had on the primary relationship.

Case Illustration

The following case illustration is based on a compilation of cases seen by the first author (names used in the case study are pseudonyms). Steve and Lisa had been married for 8 years and have three children ages 4, 10, and 12. The two older children came from Lisa's previous marriage in which she had been married for 3 years. Lisa called to set up an appointment stating that her husband had been having an affair for the past 8 months with an acquaintance of hers. When Steve and Lisa came for their first session, Lisa seemed anxious and victimized, while Steve seemed distant and slightly embarrassed. Lisa sat at the edge of her seat explaining the horror of discovering the affair was with someone she briefly knew through the Parent Teacher Association. As Lisa expressed her anger and frustration, Steve sat back with a note of exhaustion. I validated Lisa's feelings, explaining that I cannot know how she feels, but invited her to help me understand the depth and range of emotions she felt after learning about the affair.

After the initial validation occurred, Lisa sat back in her chair as if to say that some of what she needed at that moment had been met through the validation. Time was spent at that point getting to know the couple and trying to take some of the heat off the trauma of the affair. I found out that Steve was a mechanic for a local shop that specialized in working on semitrucks. Lisa was an administrative assistant for a law office in town. They had met through a singles event at their church and married 6 months later. They described the relationship as very passionate in the beginning with occasional bouts of jealousy and anger. Lisa also explained that her previous marriage had ended due to her ex-husband's drinking habits. Both Lisa's and Steve's parents lived nearby, with Lisa's parents living within a mile of the home. Steve seemed appreciative that time was spent away from the affair getting to know the couple. He seemed a little more engaged; yet, he still seemed to be preparing for another "round" of something.

After the initial joining, the couple was told that some information needed to be gathered to help better understand their situation. The level of crisis was assessed by asking questions associated with anxiety, depression, suicidality or homocidality, and trauma. It appeared that Lisa was experiencing some significant anxiety symptoms as she described difficulty sleeping, loss of appetite, and irritability. It was explained that experiencing anxiety after the discovery of an affair is normal and should subside over time.

FOO and relationship patterns were also explored. Lisa seemed enmeshed with her mother and often talked on the phone with her about the couple's marital problems. She also seemed very close with her two older children, while having problems with the youngest boy. Steve seemed more distant from his extended family, although he enjoyed going to his parent's house once a month for a Sunday family meal. He also reported feeling distant from most relationships he has had in his life. In regard to their interaction cycle, it became clear that Lisa would often pursue during arguments, while Steve would want to distance or withdraw. He would often physically leave the house to work on a project following intense arguments.

Finally, cognitions and emotions were assessed surrounding not only the affair but the relationship in general. Lisa felt unappreciated and rejected, stating she took care of the household chores even though she worked a full-time job as well. She also thought the affair represented a similar feeling she had with her ex-husband, stating that he also left her through an affair with alcohol. Steve, after some probing, was able to state that he felt judged and attacked. He felt that he had tried to please her in many aspects of their life but always fell short. He also stated that he thought Lisa was more worried about what other people thought rather than the actual hurt of the affair. Once again, emotions were validated on both sides in order to avoid any triangulation between therapist and clients.

Following the assessment phase, questions were asked regarding what they would like to get out of therapy. Following some collaboration that led to no firm conclusions, a plan was proposed that suggested the couple use this time to explore the relationship's viability as they attempt to heal through the experience of therapy. In addition, some initial boundaries were proposed to help reduce Lisa's anxiety as well as to reduce the likelihood that the affair would continue. Some of these boundaries included a complete cutoff in communication with Steve's lover and more open communication regarding where Steve and Lisa were during the day and when they would be home. Steve also agreed to let Lisa randomly check his cell phone usage. The couple agreed with the proposed plan followed by a brief "advice-giving" discussion in which hope was instilled by stating that many couples can heal following an affair and that many couples become even stronger.

The first session often seems like wrestling a two-headed bull as one tries to find some control among the volatile emotions and establish some structure while avoiding triangulation. There were a few times that a self-righteous Lisa sought to punish Steve for the affair. Steve tended to respond to these verbal lashings with either guilt and shame or defensive anger. Fortunately, Lisa's anger seemed spent by the end of the session, and both parties agreed to focus for the next few sessions on the dynamics of the relationship and refrain from agonizing about the affair. With the structure established, the first phase of treatment could occur. During the next three to four sessions, Steve and Lisa's relationship patterns were explored along with the validation of emotions surrounding those patterns. It became clear that Steve and Lisa had not differentiated from their families of origin, with Lisa still being caught in a triangle with her own mother and father, while Steve seemed to distance from his mother because of her controlling, passive-aggressive nature. It also became clear that Lisa and Steve's relationship mirrored their parents' relationships. The insight gained through examining FOO issues led them to an expression of resentment and hurt about the relationships they had with their own families. During this exploration time, boundaries surrounding the affair were still encouraged, and there were times that feelings came up about their relationship and the affair. Rather than ignoring these emotions and experiences, time was spent to explore and validate emotions and thoughts surrounding the affair. However, these thoughts and emotions were always tied into the relationship patterns of the couple in order to help the couple begin to see how the affair was a symptom of a negative interaction cycle fueled by FOO patterns.

The second phase of treatment led to the setting of boundaries among the generations along with the invitation to open up dialogue about relationships they would like to improve. Lisa began to set boundaries with her mother by not speaking with her about either their own marriage or the parent's marriage. In addition, Lisa began to seek out her husband during times of stress and anxiety rather than her children. Steve also began to be more assertive with his own mother in expressing his feelings as well as letting go of some of the baggage he had carried regarding his mother. Steve also began to reach out to the older children and spend more time at home engaging in family activities. It was interesting to watch the couple experience each other taking emotional risks within each other's family of origin. This seemed to send a message to the other that their relationship was important. Finally, Steve and Lisa agreed to begin going on a date night, while allowing for both Lisa and Steve to have alone times as well to spent on hobbies or exercise. The restructuring stage led to the development of a safer environment to explore more of the hurt and constructs surrounding the affair.

During the beginning of the third phase of treatment, which occurred around the eighth session, Steve and Lisa questioned whether they needed to come to therapy anymore. They both reported higher levels of satisfaction and less arguing. We explored termination at this time and questions were posed regarding the hurt surrounding the affair. It was interesting that both seemed to want to avoid the hurt, although they both knew the hurt was still there. It was suggested that the couple could terminate if they wanted to, but that if they continued the third phase of treatment could benefit their relationship in the long term through a more complete healing process. It was explained that some of their old symptoms could return temporarily as they seek to reduce their anxiety and levels of hurt through old patterns as they heal, but that if they were willing to experience the entire process, their relationship could become more fulfilling.

The couple decided to begin the attachment-building process and for the next six sessions the pain and emotions surrounding the affair and the relationship in general were examined more deeply. Different from the beginning phase, the couple was able to interact within a safer structure along with new patterns of communication and validation, allowing for a more thorough process exploration. Intensity was very high at times and feelings were expressed openly, but each partner allowed the other to feel, express, and receive validation. In addition, more details surrounding the affair were communicated, which led to more feelings of anxiety and rejection at times. However, each sent the message to the other that they wanted to understand where the other was at and allow the other to be and feel where the other was at. There were times that Steve wanted distance and Lisa wanted to blame, but with minor suggestions and holding true to the structures established, the couple was able to engage in new patterns of interaction and form new attachment cycles.

Toward the end of therapy, the couple began to examine the forgiveness process. They explored their decision to remain together. They explored the journey they experienced of differentiating, understanding, and seeking to connect rather than distancing or becoming enmeshed. The last sessions were devoted to looking forward and describing what their marriage and relationship meant in light of their new lens of understanding and stronger emotional bond.

This example was based on a number of couples the first author has worked with over the past 7 years. Overall, many of the couples experienced a stronger attachment following the therapy experience; however, it is important to note that some couples decided not to experience the third phase of treatment, while others terminated treatment early on. It is not known what happened to these couples, but one might expect they experienced an emotional distancing effect over time as unresolved hurts remained hidden. Others moved toward divorce therapy or individual therapy as they chose to separate. In all cases, focusing on previous patterns and examining new patterns were crucial to prevent the repetition of negative interaction cycles. In addition, other couples did not have as many FOO issues as the case illustration presents, but the structuring of new patterns within the system seemed to be important across cases.

In summary, the process of treatment relating to infidelity is based on both a collaborative and direct approach with more structure being present in the beginning phases of treatment. Similar to other crises, providing structure in the beginning allows for a safer environment to explore a couple's hurts and constructs surrounding the affair. Validating emotions while avoiding triangulation is a delicate and important balance to maintain. Once restructuring has occurred in which boundaries have been set to avoid further attachment injuries and space is given to allow for both differentiation and attachment building, the couple can begin to explore the pains of infidelity in a more process-focused manner. It is common during this time for couples to experience high levels of emotional intensity paired with a return of symptoms temporarily; however, if the couple can experience the process of forming a more positive interaction cycle through the expression and validation of each other's emotions and constructs, it is likely that the relationship will be able to move beyond the affair.

Future Research

Future research is needed to empirically test the common themes and patterns presented. It is likely that many of the effective treatment interventions and modalities found in common couples therapy will transfer to infidelity treatment; however, lack of research makes it difficult to make such conclusions. There does seem to be a difference related to the trauma-like effect associated with the discovery of the infidelity and other problems that couples may present. In addition, the Internet creates a unique context for infidelity that needs closer examination.

Some also may argue that the attachment injury associated with infidelity may be difficult to heal due to the level of injury associated with the affair.

Recent research on softening techniques as related to marital therapy may provide greater insight on how to heal couples who experience difficulty moving past the attachment injury (cf. Bird, Butler, & Fife, 2007). Softening is a technique used to help couples break a negative interaction cycle and "soften" toward each other through an increased willingness to understand, comfort, and validate (Johnson, 2004). Anderson, Butler, and Seedall (2006) found that volatile couples generally viewed carefully structured enactments of softening as more helpful. Because couples addressing infidelity may experience more emotional volatility, structured softening techniques may be one intervention that could help couples begin to heal the attachment injury. However, more research is needed to examine softening interventions as associated with couples experiencing the pains of infidelity.

Finally, more research is needed to examine cultural, religious, and ethnic differences when treating infidelity. For example, Bettinger (2005) maked some suggestions on how to work with gay male couples in relation to infidelity; however, very little is known about same sex couples and infidelity treatment. Equally, racial and ethnic differences in regard to infidelity treatment are lacking.

Note

Portions of this chapter were previously published in DuPree, W. J., White, M., Olson, C., & Lafleur, C. (2007). Infidelity treatment patterns: A practice-based evidence approach. *American Journal of Family Therapy, 35, 4,* 327–341. Taylor & Francis Ltd., http://www.informaworld.com. Reprinted by permission of the publisher.

References

Abrahms Spring, J., with Spring, M. (1996). *After the affair: Healing the pain and rebuilding trust when a partner has been unfaithful.* New York: HarperCollins.

Afifi, W. A., Falato, W., & Weiner, J. (2001). Identity concerns following a severe relational transgression: The role of discovery method for the relational outcomes of infidelity. *Journal of Social and Personal Relationships, 18,* 291–308.

Agras, W. S., & Berkowitz, R. (1980). A progressive model of clinical research. *Behavior Therapy, 11,* 472–487.

Anderson, L. G., Butler, M. H., & Seedall, R. B. (2006). Couples' experience of enactments and softening in marital therapy. *American Journal of Family Therapy, 34*(4), 301–315.

Atkins, D. C., Eldridge, K. E., Baucom, D. H., & Christensen, A. (2005). Behavioral marital therapy and infidelity: Optimism in the face of betrayal. *Journal of Consulting and Clinical Psychology, 73,* 144–150.

Atwood, J. D. (2005). Cyber-affairs: "What's the big deal?" *Journal of Couple and Relationship Therapy, 4*(2-3), 117–134.

Atwood, J. D., & Seifer, M. (1997). Extramarital affairs and constructed meanings: A social constructionist therapeutic approach. *American Journal of Family Therapy, 25*, 55–75.

Barkham, M., & Mellor-Clark, J. (2003). Bridging evidence-based practice and practice-based evidence: Developing rigorous and relevant knowledge for the psychological therapies. *Clinical Psychology and Psychotherapy, 10*, 319–327.

Bettinger, M. (2005). A family systems approach to working with sexually open gay male couples. *Journal of Couple and Relationship Therapy, 4*(2–3), 149–160.

Bird, M. H., Butler, M. H., & Fife, S. T. (2007). The process of couple healing following infidelity: A qualitative study. *Journal of Couple and Relationship Therapy, 6*(4), 1–25.

Blow, A. J., & Hartnett, K. (2005a). Infidelity in committed relationships I: A methodological review. *Journal of Marital and Family Therapy, 31*, 183–216.

Blow, A. J., & Hartnett, K. (2005b). Infidelity in committed relationships II: A substantive review. *Journal of Marital and Family Therapy, 31*, 217–234.

Brown, E. (2001). *Patterns of infidelity and their treatment* (2nd ed.). Philadelphia: Brunner-Routledge.

Brown, E. (2005). Split self affairs and their treatment. *Journal of Couple and Relationship Therapy, 4*(2–3), 55–69.

Bruce, T. J., & Sanderson, W. C. (2005). Evidence-based psychosocial practices: Past, present, and future. In C. E. Stout & R. A. Hayes (Eds.), *The evidence-based practice: Methods, models and tools for mental health professionals* (pp. 220–243). Hoboken, NJ: Wiley.

Carlson, J., & Ellis, C. M. (2004). Treatment agreement and relapse prevention strategies in couple and family therapy. *Family Journal: Counseling and Therapy for Couples and Families, 12*, 352–357.

Case, B. (2005). Healing the wounds of infidelity through the healing power of apology and forgiveness. *Journal of Couple and Relationship Therapy, 4*(2–3), 41–54.

Elbaum, P. L. (1981). The dynamics, implications, and treatment of extramarital sexual relationships for the family therapist. *Journal of Marital and Family Therapy, 7*, 489–495.

Fisher, H. (1992). *Anatomy of love: The mysteries of mating, marriage, and why we stray.* New York: Fawcett Columbine.

Fox, N. J. (2000). Practice-based evidence: Towards collaborative and transgressive research. *Sociology, 37*(1), 81–102.

Glass, S. (2003). *Not just friends: Protect your relationship from infidelity and heal the trauma of betrayal.* New York: Simon and Schuster.

Glass, S. P., & Wright, T. L. (1985). Sex differences in type of extramarital involvement and marital dissatisfaction. *Sex Roles, 12*, 1101–1119.

Glass, S., & Wright, T. (1997). Reconstructing marriages after the trauma of infidelity. In W. K. Halford & H. J. Markman (Eds.), *Clinical handbook of marriage and couples interventions* (pp. 471–507). Chichester, England: Wiley.

Gordon, K. C., & Baucom, D. H. (1998). Understanding betrayals in marriage: A synthesized model of forgiveness. *Family Process, 37*, 425–450.

Gordon, K. C., & Baucom, D. H. (1999). A forgiveness-based intervention for addressing extramarital affairs. *Clinical Psychology: Science and Practice, 6*, 382–399.

Gordon, K. C., & Baucom, D. H. (2003). Forgiveness and marriage: Preliminary support for a synthesized model of recovery from a marital betrayal. *American Journal of Family Therapy, 31*, 179–199.

Gordon, K. C., Baucom, D. H., & Snyder, D. K. (2004). An integrative intervention for promoting recovery from extramarital affairs. *Journal of Marital and Family Therapy, 30*, 213–232.

Hays, R. A. (2005). Introduction to evidence-based practices. In C. E. Stout & R. A. Hayes (Eds.), *The evidence-based practice: Methods, models and tools for mental health professionals* (pp. 1–9). Hoboken, NJ: Wiley.

Hertlein, K. M., & Weeks, G. R. (2007). Two roads diverged in a wood: The current state of infidelity research and treatment. *Journal of Couple and Relationship Therapy, 6*(1–2), 95–107.

Jayson, S. (2008, March 19). Poll: Infidelity is common knowledge in the USA. Retrieved November 20, 2009, from http://abcnews.go.com/Health/Sex/Story?id=4480097&page=1

Johnson, S. (2003). The revolution in couple therapy: A practitioner-scientist perspective. *Journal of Marital and Family Therapy, 29*, 365–384.

Johnson, S. M. (2004). *The practice of emotionally focused couple therapy* (2nd ed.). New York: Brunner-Routledge.

Johnson, S. M. (2008). Broken bonds: An emotionally focused approach to infidelity. In F. Piercy, K. Hertlein, & J. Wetchler (Eds.), *Handbook of the clinical treatment of infidelity* (pp. 17–30). New York: Haworth.

Johnson, S. M., Makinen, J., & Millikin, J. (2001). Attachment injuries in couple relationships: A new perspective on impasses in emotionally focused marital therapy. *Journal of Marital and Family Therapy, 27*, 145–155.

Krakau, I. (2000). The importance of practice-based evidence. *Scandinavian Journal of Primary Health Care, 18*, 130–131.

Langer, G., with Arnedt, C., & Sussman, D. (2004, October 21). Primetime Live poll: American sex survey. Retrieved November 20, 2009, from http://abcnews.go.com/Primetime/PollVault/story?id=156921&page=1

Larner, G. (2004). Family therapy and the politics of evidence. *Journal of Family Therapy, 26*, 17–39.

Laumann, E. O., Gagnon, J. H., Michael, R. T., & Michaels, S. (1994). *The social organization of sexuality: Sexual practices in the United States*. Chicago: University of Chicago Press.

Lawson, A. (1989). *Adultery: An analysis of love and betrayal*. New York: Basic Books.

Lucock, M., Leach, C., Iveson, S., Lynch, K., Horsefield, C., & Hall, P. (2003). A systematic approach to practice-based evidence in a psychological therapies service. *Clinical Psychology and Psychotherapy, 12*, 241–253.

Lusterman, D. D. (1995). Treating marital infidelity. In R. Mikesell, D. D. Lusterman, & S. McDaniel (Eds.), *Integrating family therapy: Handbook of family psychology and systems theory* (pp. 259–269). Washington, D.C.: American Psychological Association.

Lusterman, D. D. (1998). *Infidelity: A survival guide*. Oakland, CA: New Harbinger.

Lusterman, D. D. (2005). Marital infidelity: The effects of delayed traumatic reaction. *Journal of Couple and Relationship Therapy, 4*(2–3), 71–81.

Margison, F. R., Barkham, M., Evans, C., McGrath, G., Mellor-Clark, J., Audin, K. et al. (2000). Measurement and psychotherapy: Evidence-based practice and practice-based evidence. *British Journal of Psychiatry, 177*, 123–130.

Moultrup, D. J. (1990). *Husbands, wives, and lovers.* New York: Guilford.

Nelson, T., Piercy, F. P., & Sprenkle, D. H. (2005). Internet infidelity: A multi-phase Delphi study. *Journal of Couple and Relationship Therapy, 4*(2–3), 173–194.

Olson, M. M., Russell, C. S., Higgins-Kessler, M., & Miller, R. B. (2002). Emotional processes following disclosure of an extramarital infidelity. *Journal of Marital and Family Therapy, 28*, 423–434.

Patterson, J. E., Miller, R. B., Carnes, S., & Wilson, S. (2004). Evidence-based practice for marriage and family therapists. *Journal of Marital and Family Therapy, 30*, 183–195.

Penn, C. D., Hernandez, S. L., & Bermudez, J. M. (1997). Using a cross-cultural perspective to understand infidelity in couples therapy. *American Journal of Family Therapy, 25*, 169–185.

Piercy, F. P., Hertlein, K. M., & Wetchler, J. L. (Eds.). (2008). *Handbook of the clinical treatment of infidelity.* New York: Haworth Press.

Pittman, F. (1989). *Private lies: Infidelity and betrayal of intimacy.* New York: Norton.

Previti, D., & Amato, P. R. (2004). Is infidelity a cause or a consequence of poor marital quality? *Journal of Social and Personal Relationships, 21*, 217–230.

Schneider, J. P., & Corley, M. D. (2002). *Disclosure of extramarital sexual activities by persons with addictive or compulsive sexual disorders: Results of a study and implications for therapists.* In P. Carnes & K. Adams (Eds.), *The clinical management of sex addiction* (pp. 137–162). New York: Brunner-Routledge.

Schneider, J. P., Irons, R. R., & Corley, M. D. (1999). Disclosure of extramarital sexual activities by sexually exploitative professionals and other persons with addictive or compulsive sexual disorders. *Journal of Sex Education and Therapy, 24*, 277–287.

Shackelford, T. K., & Buss, D. M. (1997). Cues to infidelity. *Personality and Social Psychology Bulletin, 23*, 1034–1045.

Silverstein, J. L. (1998). Countertransference in marital therapy for infidelity. *Journal of Sex and Marital Therapy, 24*, 293–301.

Sprenkle, D. H. (Ed.). (2002). *Effectiveness research in marriage and family therapy.* Alexandria, VA: American Association for Marriage and Family Therapy.

Stiles, W. B., Leach, C., Barkham, M., Lucock, M., Iveson, S., Shapiro, D. A. et al. (2003). Early sudden gains in psychotherapy under routine clinical conditions: Practice-based evidence. *Journal of Consulting and Clinical Psychology, 71*(1), 14–21.

Schwartzman, J. (1983). Family ethnography: A tool for clinicians. In J. C. Hansen & C. J. Falicov (Eds.), *Cultural perspectives in family therapy: The family therapy collections* (pp. 122–135). Rockville, MD: Aspen.

Thompson, A. P. (1984). Emotional and sexual components of extra-marital relations. *Journal of Marriage and the Family, 46*, 35–42.

Treas, J., & Giesen, D. (2000). Sexual infidelity among married and cohabiting Americans. *Journal of Marriage and the Family, 62*, 48–60.

Weeks, G. R., Gambescia, N., & Jenkins, R. E. (2003). *Treating infidelity: Therapeutic dilemmas and effective strategies.* New York: Norton.

PART II

Clinical Considerations in Recovery From Emotional Infidelity

CHAPTER 8

An Object Relations Approach to Intimacy

Loss and Recovery

JILL SAVEGE SCHARFF

Intimacy and How It Is Achieved

Intimacy is a sense of closeness and connection with another. The first image of intimacy that comes to mind is the intimacy of a couple. The woman and her husband or partner come together because they feel deeply connected and committed to each other, and they cement their bond as they care for their child. The first experience of intimacy happens between infant and mother, a pair who have had 9 months to relate to each other before birth and months of close physical dependency afterward, all of which creates a strong foundation for feeling connected. As the infant communicates with the mother and meets her response, the infant feels protected and understood. The mother feels in tune with her infant and becomes a mother. The mother's husband or partner supports their intimacy and reaches into their circle to form a bond with the infant too and becomes a father or second mother. They all have intimacy. Husbands and wives, partners, mothers and babies all want to have that special feeling. Patient and therapist, teacher and student may have a kind of emotional and intellectual intimacy, but it can never have the depth of connection that grows with love that includes physical and sexual interaction. On the other hand, being part of a couple does not mean that you automatically have intimacy. Some people cannot achieve intimacy with their partners, no matter how hard they try, and some avoid it out of fear or disgust.

Having intimacy is not some great miracle, although it does feel like a great gift when it happens. A couple achieves intimacy by spending time together, building trust, offering the security of commitment, and negotiating the daily trivia of their lives in a respectful way. An intimate couple may have separate interests, different types of work, and minds that function in opposite ways, but they set their priorities for being together and they have shared goals. The partners may come from different cultures, but they share the goal of establishing a shared multicultural identity. They listen, they learn about each other, they negotiate, and they celebrate their differences.

Conscious Compatibility, Similarities, Complementarities

Intimate partners come together on the basis of conscious perceptions and experiences of dating. They look for similarities or attractive differences. They marry within their own culture or outside it. Either way, they find a measure of complementarity that lets each of them become a better person, richer than before. They develop a physical relationship of concern for the pleasure they may give and receive from looking and touching each other and eventually experience sexuality together. These conscious factors are important, but the long-term fit of their partnership, the feeling of intimacy they can enjoy, will depend on factors they may be unaware of at the time of their commitment. These factors stem from the repressed areas of their personalities (Dicks, 1967). The couple relationship offers hope that these areas can be refound in the partner or in the self in relation to the support of the partner and then reintegrated into the self. Intimacy fosters that development, but failure to find the lost parts of the self can spoil the bond and break the hope of intimacy (Scharff & Scharff, 1991a).

Sexuality

Good enough sex is important in maintaining the couple's relationship, but physical competence is not enough to create a sense of intimacy. The couple bond forms on a good relationship in which the partners feel not only that their physical cues are responded to with pleasure and release, but that their emotional needs are met by their partner's concern and interest, and even that their feelings are inquired about proactively. This makes the sexual compatibility more complete. There is a physical and emotional interpenetration that is deeply gratifying and supportive of adult development. The term *psychosomatic partnership* is borrowed from Winnicott (1971) who described the physical and psychological components of the mother's holding and handling of her infant. The couple's psychosomatic partnership recalls the bliss of infancy, but it also stirs up any problems left over from that period of development. These old problems can interfere with intimacy, but intimacy can provide a new experience, similar but not the same, that helps to heal these old wounds. Intimacy allows for a reworking of early development (Scharff, 1982).

Unconscious Factors

Unconscious resonance is the basis of intimacy. The partners develop a shared personality greater than the sum of its parts, and they feel more complete together. They fit. People sometimes refer to this by saying "we just click" or "we have chemistry." What they mean is that their internal worlds have parts that fit together like locking pieces, or like a molecule bonding with another molecule for which it has a valency to combine. This interlocking and shifting of the boundaries of the self within the umbrella of the couple relationship is a wonderful opportunity for growth. If the lock is too tight, it restricts growth and blocks a feeling of safety, openness, and intimacy; these are the couples who seek help.

Why Intimacy Falls Off

Intimacy requires a person to be alert, considerate, attentive, focused, respectful, and devoted. Intimacy needs to be nourished and guarded. Intimacy is highly prized, and when it is lost, the couple feels tremendous loss. Its erosion can happen suddenly or gradually. As life goes on there are many pressures that take each member of the couple off in various, different directions. Couples need to be on the lookout for pitfalls that could interfere with their intimate relationship.

Holding a Secret

When one partner is troubled by a memory or a thought too shameful or too precious to share with the other, the relationship is in trouble: One cannot tell and the other does not want to know; one is preoccupied and the other is inquisitive; one feels ashamed and the other judges harshly. Secrecy sets up a vicious cycle of withholding and ignoring or intruding and then more secrecy. Intimacy requires openness, honesty, and acceptance.

Preoccupation With Work

It usually takes two incomes to maintain the desired standard of living in our society, and this means that work and domestic chores fill the time and create pressure to keep up with daily living. Stress leads to argument, blame, tuning out, and self-medication. When it is time for bed, sleep seems more important than talking and touching, and intimacy is forgotten.

Preoccupation With Another Person

One partner may become preoccupied with another person, as if that relationship will be easier or more immediately rewarding than the couple relationship. Most obviously, a person may look for an affair so as to find a spurious kind of intimacy there when it is lacking at home or to hurt or jolt a spouse who is not attentive. But the other person may not be a sexual object. For instance, some women knock themselves out for their children and forget to take care of themselves and their partner. A man may get so focused on a child's sports team that he misses an important anniversary. Divorced parents may feel so guilty about leaving the home, and so sad about missing their children, that they overdo the visits to the exclusion of their new partner or may even be caught up in memories of a lost love or a departed spouse.

Sexual Involvement in an Extramarital Affair

Some couples believe that sexual involvement with others adds to their enjoyment of intimacy, but these are not the couples we tend to see clinically. We see couples whose relationship has suffered from the inclusion of a third party into the sanctity of the committed relationship. Sexual involvement may be with another person, same sex or opposite sex, same age, older, or younger. It may be with a living person in personal contact by choice or for a fee, with a voice on the telephone, or an image on the Internet. The actual person carries more risk to the marriage, but all are a betrayal of the commitment to love and honor the partner, and all of them corrupt any level of intimacy the couple thought they had achieved.

In therapy after an affair, we ask for full disclosure. We work with the couple to understand what the affair offered that was missing in the marriage, and we cannot get that understanding unless there is total honesty in the revelation. Without that, apology is useless and forgiving impossible. Not that we think of the one who had the affair as the culprit: The couple has to understand how each partner contributed to the problem that led to the affair. Rebuilding trust takes time. The outcome of treatment depends on whether the motivation behind the affair is relatively benign (an attempt to bring excitement in to maintain the marriage) or totally malignant (an attack on it to torment the other or destroy the marriage) and whether or not the marriage was reasonably good before the affair (Scharff & Scharff, 1991b).

Unresolved Mourning

A loss can bring a couple together as the partners support each other and grieve together. However, some losses have a disruptive effect on intimacy. The loss or illness of a parent can draw energy from the couple. When a husband and wife are enjoying sexual intimacy and then lose a fetus or a newborn, their intimate relationship comes under strain if they do not realize that this is a loss to be mourned. The intimate couple who has infertility problems struggles to maintain intimacy in the face of prescribed sex, intrusive medical interventions, and the fear of never having a child.

Preoccupation With Oneself

People who are preoccupied with themselves cannot reach out to their partners. They may be suffering from chronic physical illness in which case pain and fatigue interrupt intimacy. They may be suffering from emotional stress or mental illness—narcissistic, depressive, manic, borderline, hysterical, obsessive, or addictive in type. When a partner turns to substances for relief, the addictive process may set in and take on a life of its own. The substance is more reliable and immediate than the partner. The substance is more important than the marriage. Depression may result from or cause problems in intimacy. Depressed people may spoil the gains of their current couple relationship because they are silently sad and angry about earlier losses or lack of connection in the current relationship. People with borderline personality disorder may be too reactive and too irrational to stop and think through the problems. Narcissistic people may be too selfish to care about the person they are with. At the least, they are most concerned with their own perspective and cannot engage in negotiation of any meaningful sort. Narcissism is at the root of all couple relationship problems (Scharff & Bagnini, 2003).

Retreat From the Partner's Unwelcome Qualities

Untreated symptoms of mental illness, personality disorders, abusive behavior, and disturbing habits of mind may drive a partner away or may be unfairly blamed as the partner's excuse for withdrawing. Sometimes retreat is really a form of punishment of the other, even if it begins as a defense of the self.

Strategies for the Recovery of Intimacy

The main strategy for helping couples to recover intimacy is to offer them understanding as the vehicle for relating. From this, they learn to listen to and understand each other. Therapists help them to see how their patterns of protecting themselves interfere with relating. By tuning in to their feelings, we show them how to tune in to each other and how to bear their feelings. We hold their anxiety in our minds and help them find ways to think about it and master it. We help them to own their part in causing problems, and so see each other more clearly as individuals. We get in touch with unconscious factors that need to be brought to awareness for each of the partners to be more fully alive and more able to participate in the creative melding of personalities that the couple relationship brings. We teach them to think about their relationship as an entity to consider and cherish.

Using Object Relations Theory

The object relations approach relies on a psychoanalytic theory called Object Relations Theory, a terrible name for a very human set of ideas (Scharff & Scharff, 2005, 2008). It is believed that at birth each person faces the loss of the illusion that all needs will be met automatically, and then becomes totally dependent on the devoted care of another person. The infant experiences hunger and must be fed, experiences distress and must be soothed, experiences danger and must be protected. However well intentioned she or he is, the mothering person inevitably falls short of the ideal of total immediate need eradication. Infants must learn to accept delay and soothe themselves, but some are more able than others in their ability to manage, and they all become overwhelmed at times. They experience their good mothers as bad objects.

The infant takes in an image of the frustrated mother and pushes that image out of awareness because it is painful. This is called *the rejecting object*; part of the infant's mind called the antilibidinal ego pushes it away, binds itself to it by intolerable feelings of disappointment, rage, and abandonment, and drops it into the unconscious layer of the personality. This constellation of ego-object-affect is called an *internal rejecting object relationship*. The more the infant longs for his or her needs to be met, the more the mother seems out of reach. We call this image *the exciting object* for which the infant craves most painfully. Another part of the mind, called *the libidinal ego*, splits off to repress this image as well, bound to it by feelings of dissatisfaction and craving. This constellation is *the exciting object relationship*. The main part of the ego experiences the mother as good, kind, loving, and gratifying of needs and is full of satisfaction. This *central ego* stays conscious of that positive, confidence-building view of the mother as a good object with a happy baby by pressing out of consciousness the views of her as mean and too exciting. But the rejecting and exciting object relationships always seek to reemerge and be integrated into the personality. According to object relations theory, the self is a system of internal object relationships in a dynamic balance. The healthy person has access to the rejecting and exciting object constellations because they are not too intolerable. The unhealthy person lives in a closed system, opposed to the expression of any feelings of rage, hurt, need, or longing. This makes it difficult to feel whole or to share in a couple relationship.

Mutual Projective Identification

The man who cannot allow the expression of any feelings may choose a partner like himself, two preoccupied people living on a restricted emotional plane and not rocking the boat. They rub along well enough, but they do not enjoy great intimacy. On the other hand, he may choose someone who is fully expressive of feelings because he envies her freedom to feel. In the best scenario he may learn from her that it is safe to express his feelings, but if he chooses someone who is, or later becomes, overly expressive, or terrifyingly expressive, he finds reason to stay shut down. This drives her to greater demonstration of her frustration and despair, and a vicious cycle begins. Why would the man choose such a wife? Most often it is because he is looking for someone with qualities the same and different from the figures in his early life, in relation to whom he learned to repress his feelings. Why would she choose him? Most often because she wants a man who is steady and controlled, who she hopes can meet her needs calmly, and so contain her reactivity and emotionality. In this way they both re-find in each other a lost part of themselves (their repressed internal objects and parts of ego), and this gives hope of reintegration.

Transference and Countertransference

The man has a transference to his partner: She reminds him of figures from his past. The woman has a transference to her partner: He reminds her of figures from her past. In relation to their partners, the embodiment of these imagos, they repeat scenes from earlier in their lives. Each sees the partner in the light of earlier imagos projected onto him or her. The process being reciprocal, they create a mutual projective identification process that is characteristic for their marriage. Each couple creates a unique projective identification process, and as the partners of each couple find parts of themselves in each other, they establish a unique joint object relations set.

The therapist helps them to untangle the superimposed views of each other, and in so doing draws to herself similar transferences. These transferences resonate with the imagos the therapist carries herself from earlier experiences with caring figures in her life. The couple's unconscious object relations set resonates especially with the therapist's *internal couple*, an internal object that forms from reactions to couples at every stage of development while the therapist was growing up and in her clinical practice. What the therapist feels in response is her countertransference. Since she has had years of clinical experience, years of being in her own therapy or analysis, and she does not have the vulnerable situation of being in love with either of them, she can see more clearly what she is being drawn into, comments on it, and so provides an example for how to deal with being in the grip of projections, and helps the couple take back their projections and to own their repressed objects, revisit them, and modify them in the light of new experience.

Holding, Containment, and Interpretation

The therapist works according to a theory of technique based on object relations theory. She provides a good holding environment just as a mother provides a secure base for her child (Winnicott, 1965). She provides good centered holding, just as a mother tunes in to her baby, engages, follows the baby's lead, and provides a focus for the baby. She conveys the baby's value and meaning. She provides the stuff out of which the infant builds a self. She provides good containment of her child's anxiety by holding it in her mind and ponders what can be wrong. She considers the possibilities and arrives at a way of proceeding to soothe and settle the child. She subjects the infant's experience, and her own empathy for it, to process and review, and so makes the intolerable anxiety of her dependent infant something that can be thought about and managed. Like a good mother, the therapist offers a reliable environment and a personal willingness to engage in the necessary interactions for revealing the source of the couple's problems. In her countertransference, she receives the problem and mulls it over, and returns it to the couple in a verbal form for further inquiry and discussion. Once she understands the couple from deep inside her own experience, she is in a position to offer an interpretation of the difficulties. Interpretation shows the partners how their projective identification system is a way of defending themselves, of expressing needs, of trying to grow, but tending to stay the same to avoid individual and shared anxieties. Interpretation is geared at giving insight that the object relations therapist believes is essential for securing the level of change that will allow a return to full intimacy.

Sexuality

A couple can get along well, but, without a satisfying sexual bond, the partners feel something is missing. The center will not hold. Shared pleasure should be a right, a reliable actuality, a memory, and a hope. It keeps the partners connected, returning to each other for joy. The interpenetration of body parts for hetero- and homosexual couples not only provides stimulation of erogenous zones, it is the physical correlate of their emotional and spiritual joining. As the partners age, it is harder to maintain frequency because of increased demands from the emotional and financial needs of children, increased responsibility at work, and later, the less reliable sexual responsiveness of the aging body. Then they have to plan for time alone, and in between times they draw on their memory store. Their sexual relationship is important not just to the couple, but to the children in their family. Children need their parents to have a vital sexual bond so that the children can experience their own sexuality and romantic desires within the family without denial of their fantasies and without danger of their being enacted with a parent.

Clinical Practice Guidelines for Implementing Strategies for Recovery

Essentials of Technique

Working with the couple in the clinical setting is a matter of listening, responding, and trying to understand the situation intellectually and emotionally, historically and in the present. In object relations couple therapy, we do not suggest any particular exercises, we do not give homework, and we do not advise how to behave, think, or feel. We do not use paradoxical instruction to get the partners to do the opposite of what they think we want. We do not have a supervisor instructing us from behind a glass. We do not use genograms to nail down their history. We want to receive a living history as it emerges in its present form in the functioning of their relationship, with the emotional hot points leading to deeper layers of experience. As an observer, inquirer, and nonjudgmental helper, the couple therapist engages the partners in a psychological space where they can learn about each other and rebuild their relationship. Couple and therapist co-construct a reflective, transformative experience.

Setting the Frame

Offering the freedom to have an experience that is reflective and transformative calls for clear boundaries. The therapist sets up consultation sessions so that the partners have an opportunity to assess their goals and the therapist's ability to understand and be helpful. They agree on a mutually convenient time, duration, and frequency of therapy sessions to follow, and a fee that reflects the financial reality of couple and therapist. She explains her policies regarding payment schedule, dealing with the insurance company, and cancellation. If the couple has a history of violence, she explains that they may say whatever they want but they may not hit each other or her, and she agrees not to hurt them either. She cannot allow violence to anyone in her office. All these arrangements constitute the frame of the treatment and must be agreed to before the work can safely begin. The frame is firm for a reason. Strong emotions may be released on the way to the recovery of intimacy. The couple may express their difficulties in attempting to bend the frame, and if the frame is not secure, these manipulations will not be sufficiently evident, and the therapist will not be able to point them out and address the longing or fear that they represent.

Involved Impartiality

In the beginning of psychoanalysis, Freud recommended a therapeutic attitude of neutrality. He was referring to the unbiased attitude of the psychological researcher. As therapists, we are neutral in the sense that we do not judge what we hear: we simply record it and reflect on it. But unlike the researcher, we are an active part of the process, and that is what we are observing. (Even pure researchers now recognize that their participation affects their results.) We are neutral in that we do not take sides in the couple's dispute, and we do not identify with what we hear of their parents or children. We remain equidistant from each generation represented in their relationship.

Nevertheless we are thoroughly engaged with the couple at the deepest levels of experience, and so we may be pulled in reaction to one or the other member of the couple from time to time. This impact on us provides information about the partners' way of dealing with each other under the influence of internal imagos that seek expression in the couple relationship and in relationship to the therapist. This impact is what we are researching, and analyzing it is the basis of therapeutic action.

Psychological Space

The frame having been set, we now create an inviting but not seductive psychological space. We are neither cheerful nor grim. We are socially appropriate in a reserved way. Our attitude is one of involved impartiality, conveyed by our willingness to listen and inquire for clarification. But we do not crowd the space with questions to which we want answers to fulfill the requirements of history taking and record keeping. We simply want to hear what each partner wants to tell us. We follow their lead. We notice what they leave out. We give them choice and freedom to be themselves with us. We listen to their words, slips of the tongue, pauses, hesitations, and the quality of their silences. We notice their body language. We observe, inquire, and respond.

Negative Capability

Negative capability is a puzzling phrase that refers to the ability to respond without memory or desire and without any irritable reaching after fact and reason. This simply means that we can be in the moment and listen without wanting too much from the couple or controlling what we may hear or see. We do not reach for answers and reasons prematurely. We do not focus on any one thing: We take it all in and let it mature inside us, like wine in a cask until it is the right moment to bring it out into the open. We do not try to make sense of it and connect it to their histories: We wait for understanding to emerge from deep inside our own experience with the couple. We are connecting at the conscious level, but we are responding at the unconscious level, allowing resonance with our own internal object relations set.

Responding to the Unconscious: Body Language, Affect, and Dreams

The unconscious is expressed in feelings, in physical symptoms, in mistakes, and in relationship difficulties as the couple proceeds in daily life, and we learn about them by report in the therapy session. Unconscious wishes and fears also emerge directly in the session where we can have direct access to them. We become able to respond at the unconscious level by virtue of years of training, clinical experience, supervision, and most important of all, our own personal analysis or therapy. We know ourselves so we can come to know others. We reach the unconscious through various routes. It is conveyed in the atmosphere of the session, the quality of the silence, the sudden glance, a physical experience such as violent coughing or vomiting, and tears that connect to a deep emotion or a memory of an earlier relationship. We allow these things to happen, we feel them, we react, and we talk about what has happened and what occurs to each member of the couple about it. We look for the message in each event.

The unconscious is conveyed most vividly in dreams. Dreams are invaluable for reaching below surface communications. When a member of a couple talks about a dream, we respect the authorship of the dreamer and listen for his or her associations to the dream. Then we look for the spouse's associations. In the flow of their associations we decode the message from the unconscious. We regard the dream as a communication from and about the couple. The dreamer dreams the dream on behalf of the couple. For instance, a man who consciously longs for sex with his wife and feels deprived of sexual intimacy in his marriage because of her avoidance due to memories of sexual abuse dreams of himself as an adolescent joyfully seduced by a girl at the beach. Suddenly he realizes in horror that an alligator is approaching, abandons the girl, and runs home to his parents' house. His wife, whose abuse took the form of waking up as an adolescent to a relative performing oral sex on her, is empathic for his horror yet feels relieved to see her intuition validated that their avoidance of sex was not due to her alone. He too has underlying fears of being bitten. With a shared fear of sex acknowledged, the wife felt relieved of blame, and the couple could begin work on rebuilding their sexual relationship.

Transference and Countertransference

The couple relates to a therapist as they do to each other or to one or another of the important figures in the formative years. The transference is not any one way of relating. Transferences are multiple and may be quite subtle reactions to qualities perceived (or misperceived) in the spouse or partner and in the therapist, but they tend to cluster in forms that repeat often enough until you cannot miss them. As a female therapist you might find a wife connecting with you to the exclusion of her husband, a repetition of her bond with her mother who felt safer with her child than with her husband. You feel drawn to her friendship, which feels cozy, but unlike the wife's mother you do not want to be in a coalition of contempt for the man. So instead you connect the female bonding to its origins so that it becomes understandable. Or, if you are a male therapist you may feel rejected by the wife, unworthy of her attention, unable to connect to her. On the other hand, she may find in you a maternal quality this is lacking in her husband and connect with you as she would to a female therapist. Your counter-transference depends not only on your gender but on your identifications with male and female aspects of your parents and on the functioning of your internal couple and your internal rejecting and exciting object rela-tionships. Male or female therapist, you point out the destructive effect of exclusion and contempt on the intimacy that the couple wants to find, and through your personal engagement in the dynamic and your extrication from it, detoxify its effect on the wife and the husband.

Interpretation of Defense and Anxiety

Couples repeat the same arguments, and even when the thing they argue about shifts, the manner of their interaction does not. They have ways of doing things that irritate, or drive each other mad, and they keep repeating them. You may be stunned by them right away or may become gradually aware of them as they cycle by you or involve you in the interaction yet again. You step back and note what happened. You inquire as to why this interaction has to be this way. What does it defend them from? What more awful thing would happen if they stopped this way of relating? For instance, partners who tease and banter with the therapist in a lively way that is as entertaining as it is hurtful may need to do this to avoid a feeling of dead-ness at the center of their relationship. They will not give up hurting each other until the therapist can point this out, go with them to that inner place of sadness and futility, and help them mourn together, repair their hurts, and develop the concern that is the foundation for intimate relating.

Object Relations Approach to Dysfunction in Sexual Intimacy

The psychoanalytic approach combines with a behavioral format to create the object relations approach to sex therapy (Scharff, 1982). When a couple presents with a sexual dysfunction, the therapist may find that under-standing in therapy sessions has to be augmented by physical experience in a series of graded exercises performed in the privacy of the couple's home and reported on in the session, so as to highlight the underlying conflict expressed in the sexual arena and to open it to reworking. The rewarding effect of sexual pleasure drives the work along and reminds the couple of the healing value of sexual intimacy.

Working Through and Termination

The object relations approach is definitely not a quick fix. All this work takes time. The same patterns will repeat, and we will comment on our experience of, or involvement in, these interactions. The therapist's engage-ment breaks the patterns and throws them into chaos, freeing the couple from the old chains, but this may feel worse before it gets better. Then in relation to the therapeutic relationship, the couple is drawn to find new patterns (Scharff & Scharff, 1998). The goal is not symptom removal but an improved capacity to work and play together as a couple, enjoying daily life and sexual intimacy.

Research Support for Ideas on Intimacy

Freud's clinical research into the workings of the unconscious mind set the stage for the development of psychoanalytic theory of the individual. But rooted in the thinking of the 19th century, it remained a rather linear view of the individual mind dominated by instinctual sexual and aggressive drives being repressed to meet the demands of a sexually oppressive society. Freud gave to psychoanalysis the invaluable technical tool of free association, which is just as useful to the couple therapist—allowing the partners to say whatever occurs to them and following their lead, tuning our unconscious like a receiving apparatus to pick up the signals from the couple (Freud, 1933).

In the second half of the 20th century, psychoanalysts such as Fairbairn (1952) and Winnicott (1965) began to study not only the analysand before them, but also the nature of the relationship the analysand developed with the analyst, or to put it in technical terms, how the analyst was used as an object of desire, attachment, rejection, abuse, and so on. Again, this is a technique that we use in couple therapy, noting how the couple relates to the therapist and what they expect of us or fear from us. Studying the analytic relationship, these analysts saw the analysand's internal world writ large in interaction. From his study of many analytic relationships over his career as an analyst, Fairbairn (1952) developed object relations theory, a view of the self that is built from early relationships that are represented inside the self as a series of interlocking parts (parts of ego, objects, and affects) all in dynamic relationship inside the self, and all of them seeking expression in intimate relationships in which there is hope for their modification and reintegration. Derived from the study of relatedness, this concept of the origin and ongoing development of the self is what makes object relations theory so suitable for working with couples (and families, groups, and nations) (Scharff & Scharff, 1987). Henry Dicks (1967) was the one to realize that the Kleinian concept of projective identification could explain how two selves communicate in intimate relationship, leading to the formation of a joint marital personality in which each member of a couple finds lost parts of the self in the partner. The one then cherishes or denigrates the partner according to whether he or she repressed that part of the self, repressing it aggressively and thoroughly, or harboring it as a hidden ideal.

Projective identification is the concept for the mental mechanisms that foster the link between two personalities found in intimate partners. Klein

(1946) developed her ideas about projective identification from treating young children who were still in touch with how they perceived their parents. She thought that infants were born with quantities of life instinct and death instinct. She said that the infant full of death instinct at birth is full of anxiety about annihilation and gets rid of the feeling that is so threatening to the self by projecting it into the mother, but the downside of that maneuver is that she then seems to be the one causing the anxiety. Now the infant, faced with a mother who seems more persecutory that loving, deals with the new threat by taking in an image of her as a bad mother in order to control it inside the self. Fortunately, the infant under the influence of the life instinct also projects good feelings into the mother to keep them safe from the threat, and finds a good mother there to take in as well. It was Bion (1967) who realized that the mother had an important function in receiving these projections as communications of anxiety, using projective identification to understand what her child is going through, tolerating the projections in her more mature mind, and giving them back in the form of thinkable experience. So the infant learns how to manage anxiety and gradually realizes that the bad mother is the same person as the good mother.

Complex Attachment in Couples

Bowlby (1977) found a direct connection between broken attachment in infancy and later delinquent behavior among a group of what he called affectionless thieves. He went on to describe secure and insecure forms of attachment and their influence on the development of the self. Mary Ainsworth and colleagues (Ainsworth et al. 1978) picked up this theme and developed the Strange Situation Test in which she examined the behavior of toddlers on reunion with their mothers after a separation. From this she described their attachment as secure or insecure. If insecure, the toddler reacted either by avoiding the mother (dismissive insecure), by clinging to her in distress (preoccupied insecure), or got totally out of control (disorganized insecure). These studies do not tell us anything about the inner life. They simply give quantifiable measures of one dimension of early childhood experience that definitely bears upon the developing self. A secure attachment is the basis for the development of healthy object relations. Mary Main (Main and Goldwyn 1985) applied attachment research to adults and noted that the adult's attachment style predicted the infant's attachment style. For instance, parents who had been traumatized tended to have children whose reunion behavior fell in the disorganized group.

Attachment research has relevance for couple therapy. It validates the need to offer a secure base to which the couple returns in the therapy session. It shows therapists how to monitor the couple's reaction to our absence and behavior on reunion so that we can assess the partners' attachment styles. The next generation of researchers looked at the complex attachments of couples. Fisher and Crandell (1997) found that the attachment styles of intimate partners were predictive of the success of their pairing. For instance, two secure partners have a good chance of staying together; two insecure partners are likely to split up; and an insecure woman with a secure man will do better than an insecure man with a secure woman. The limitation of attachment theory is that it does not account for the role of fantasy and unconscious functioning in development, but the advantage is that it gives us a way of thinking about the contextual requirements in which to build a couple relationship and a therapy relationship.

Mirroring

Fairbairn (1952) based his ideas of the formation of personality on the need to manage affect, and now we have neuroscience findings that attest to the importance of affect in the regulation of the self (Fonagy, Gergely, Jurist, & Target, 2003; Schore, 1994). Emotions are experienced through internal body action. A mother mirrors her baby's facial gestures. In this way she conveys that she has received the smile or the grimace exactly as it was intended. As the baby gets older she mirrors it in a way that is similar to the original but not exactly the same. The older baby prefers this degree of freedom and responds as the mother up-regulates or down-regulates the force of the baby's experience. Gradually babies move from total dependency on the mother to regulate their affects and are drawn forward to self-regulation. The mother's attunement to the baby's affects and the timing of her response appropriate to the baby's needs and stage of development are crucial in securing healthy development of the infant self. In couples, both partners need to be in good attunement with each other, and each needs to be capable of self-regulation.

Right-Brain to Right-Brain Communication

The left brain is responsible for speech and verbal thinking, while the right brain (which is more developed at birth) deals with images and emotions. Recent neuroscience research shows that we are actually prewired at the neurological level to communicate and respond to emotion. Attunement occurs at the neurological level through the action of mirror neurons firing off in the right side of the brain of one person who is watching another person have an emotion (Galese, 2003; Rizzolatti, Fogassi, & Gallese, 2006). There is a neurological basis for projective identification, itself the basis for accurate empathy at the healthy end of the continuum and for delusional misperceptions at the unhealthy end. The right brain is the seat of the unconscious. Right-brain to right-brain communication (which happens 10 times faster than left-brain to left-brain communication) is the basis for the unconscious process of communication between intimate partners.

Clinical Example: Loss of Closeness and Its Recovery

Establishing the Reason for Treatment

Lily and Roger (names are pseudonyms) had been a couple for 2 years and had been talking of marriage for a year. Roger is a middle-aged widower. Lily, in her late 30s, has never been married but has had serial monogamous relationships. They find each other kind, attractive, and intelligent. Lily appreciates that Roger is well established in a prominent position and owns a beautiful 5,000-square-foot house. He is grateful that she brings culture into his life, especially opera. She appreciates that he helps her keep her medicines straight and generally stay focused. They are glad that they are both Catholics with good values (even though she resents that he will not go to her church where there is an excellent social program). He is delighted that she thinks about his grandchildren and knows how to amuse them and how to find gifts they would like. Although she complains about how much time he spends with his children, all of whom have problems, she enjoys the idea of being in a family, and she shares eagerly in his excellent relationship with his late wife's siblings, who accept her. They enjoy their sexual life, and it is unfortunate that conflicts interfere with their long-term commitment to an intimate relationship. They want to know if anything can be done to get them past that.

Opening the Psychological Space

I ask more about the sources of their conflict. Because of her attention deficit disorder, Lily asks for lists of directions for how to use appliances, which irritates Roger. It seems to him unnecessary because the manner of operation is simple or self-explanatory, and he does not want to explain things over and over. He does not know what she does all day at home, but having her there makes more work for him, more shopping, more cooking, and more cleaning up the mess that he would prefer to leave the way it is.

I think at first that their issues arise from the clash of their individual pathologies. Roger has obsessive-compulsive symptoms about having everything just his way, which works well for him at work but bothers Lily at home. Lily has rituals that prevent her from going to sleep, worries about contamination and cleanliness, and difficulty in carrying out complex instructions because of attention deficit disorder. Lily's obsessive-compulsive behaviors mainly do not bother Roger, but her sleep disorder makes him tired and late for work, and her attention deficit disorder annoys him because it makes her dependent on him, and he does not want to be her organizer. Lily finds Roger's compulsive behaviors sick, and she is hurt and frustrated by his refusal to help her out when she gets overwhelmed. Their presenting problem is that Roger is unable to commit to marrying Lily until her sleep disorder stops, which turns his life upside down, while Lily who wants to marry Roger is at the same time not sure if the relationship is good for her because he does not accept her vulnerabilities and support her.

Linking the Complaint With Defensive Patterns in the Session

Gradually the couple tells me more about the conflict. Lily complains that Roger keeps old papers and clothes all over the house, allowing dust and dirt to accumulate. She says that Roger stores old food in the refrigerator and allows any houseguest access to it. He asks what the problem with that is, and she explains that people should not put their fingers in the refrigerator and contaminate the food. She says she is the cook and she will protect the food. Lily feels that Roger does not eat enough good food and prefers to eat out, which deprives her of the joy of preparing safe food for him. From this discussion I think they both have concerns over being fed and taken care of and sharing the pleasure of eating.

Roger hates the fact that Lily goes to bed extremely late. He says that she delays him getting to sleep, which causes him to sleep late and arrive at work later than he wants to. Not only that, she takes an hour to shower because she gets lost in her thoughts, and so he feels he has to stay around to get her out of the shower. She counters with fury that he sees a therapist recommended by his brother, a behavioral psychologist, who advises him to bargain for behavioral improvements in her sleep habits, instead of changing himself. Worst of all, he does not make a commitment to marry her, in her opinion using the sleep disorder as an excuse. I see that each lacks empathy for the other and that they do not make room for my suggestions.

Lily begins to nag Roger about mess and dirt. He replies that he thinks she is obsessed with cleanliness. He does not understand why he cannot leave his papers around because there are plenty of rooms to put them in. Lily is irritated that he cannot understand that old papers collect dust, and moving them from one room to another does not accomplish the goal of reorganization and cleaning up.

Developing a Working Hypothesis

Lily and Roger have a strong foundation of compatibility in terms of values, culture, religion, and family. They share an obsessional defense system to guard them against unseen dangers. The problem arises when as a couple they repeat the same interaction compulsively, accusing and counterattacking the other's obsessions. It is not long before they are accusing me of an obsession over the frame of the treatment. Holding firm to the frame is what lets me see the first layer beneath their obsessional interactive patterns.

Reactions to the Therapeutic Environment

Roger and Lily need to call to confirm sessions that we have already arranged, often repeating the date and time two or three time after I have told them. They say that they want to respect my preference that we do our arrangements in the session instead of involving me in checking between times, but they are upset by it, and they find loopholes to justify their feelings of uncertainty. They have trouble leaving at the end of sessions and find just one more thing to say. Lily especially speaks for feeling interrupted and has trouble separating from the office space. She looks around the office, checking for lost items and asking questions to which she wants an answer but without leaving any space for an answer. She wants more time. She mourns the loss of her wonderful former therapists, one of whom would extend her session to two and a half hours for the usual hourly fee. My time boundaries and my fee continue to be difficult matters to accept and learn from. By holding the frame firm and working on their need for more time and connection across the spaces between sessions, I am able to understand and point out their fear of losing me, as Lily lost her former therapist and Roger lost his wife.

Defensive Patterns Emerge

Roger had been married for 30 years before being widowed 2 years ago. I ask about his late wife, and he tells me she was a wonderful woman, an excellent mother, adored by her children and loved by his family. She reminds him of his own mother who took good care of his father and all their children, and she took care of him totally. I ask about Lily's family and learn that she idolized her father, a prominent churchman who liked to spoil his only daughter, and she hated her mother whom she said was crazy. I see how each of them is looking for a lost object in the other, Lily to find a prominent man and get rid of the woman he is with, and Roger to find a new mother and wife. Roger says clearly that he wants to have a wife again, but for now he is not ready. I note that he is keeping Lily around but he is not committing to a date for marriage. I get the impression that he is auditioning Lily to fill the role, and although she gets the call back, she does not get the role. Lily likes being with Roger and living with him, but she seems less sure of whether she wants to be his wife. She is highly ambivalent about whether to stay with him or go back to her own church and meet new men. She says that this thought is in reaction to his ambivalence, but she seems to me to be in conflict over wanting to be compliant and wanting to control others, and she cannot reconcile this to being a wife. The couple has a shared obsessional defense system that works well when they agree—for instance, on the need to shop only for organic food or taking pills in the correct order and with proper spacing. It gets between them when they disagree over what to worry about, particularly in the areas of food, contamination, and cleanliness.

Lily returns to her concern about keeping food safe. She worries about catching a urinary tract infection from fingers that touch food in the refrigerator. Roger counters that you could more likely catch a urinary infection from a toilet seat. What he worries about is dirty hands touching his clean laundry. He boasts that he is expert in the properties of laundry detergents and temperatures for various fabrics, and he is extremely particular about the laundry. He says that he gets irritated having to explain to Lily how to operate the cycles of the washing machine, and yet he will not leave the laundry to the cleaning woman, because he certainly would not want her to sort the clean laundry with hands that had been cleaning the house. Lily says that she puts her laundered clothes in her drawers, but he leaves his piles of laundry gathering dust instead of in his drawers. They appeal to me to take sides, which I do not do. They compare me unfavorably to therapists who were much more sympathetic. The threat to find a new therapist embodies their ambivalence about being with me and being with each other.

Working With Countertransference

Working with my countertransference, I feel that I am not sufficiently sympathetic to their complaints, and that I am letting each of them down by not taking sides and championing the best obsessional defense. I feel as if I am an incompetent housekeeper who is not sufficiently alert to danger to myself and my family and who will spoil their things unknowingly. Each of them has an image of an unsatisfactory object that they project into each other, and now into me, so that I feel their disappointment. My interpretations do not move toward understanding. They are always followed by a return to concrete preoccupations and longing for an indulgent therapist. I wonder when they will dump me, get rid of me, kill me off totally, and find a better therapist.

The Underlying Anxiety

The argument about the cleaning of the clothes and my countertransference provides a segue to understanding the unconscious problem. Lily continues the argument, complaining that Roger's drawers are full of his late wife's possessions that he has not gotten rid of. Lily does not want the clean clothes in with them anyway because the wife died of cancer. Similarly, the late wife's perfume bottles are still in the bathroom for anyone to use, and Lily worries that a person who was tempted to use the perfumes could get cancer from them. Roger thinks that cancer from contagion is a ridiculous idea. She cannot fully express, and he completely ignores, her underlying sense of outrage at being forced to share space with a woman who is dead to her but not to him.

I ask what the clothes and the smell of her perfume mean to Roger. Lily replies for him, referring again to the actual clothes. Now she does express her anger that he has his late wife's jewels in the top drawer of the bureau that Lily uses for her clothes and that a dead woman's perfume bottles are kept in the powder room that visitors use. However, she thinks that it is not her place to tell Roger to get rid of his wife's things or what do with them. But she wishes they were not all around her, and asks him to box them up and put them somewhere else. She says again that she is terrified that they will give her cancer.

Interpretation

I say that the problem interfering with their relationship is that Roger is hanging on to closeness to his late wife and that Lily cannot stand being excluded by that. Referring to their obsessional fears and preferences, I notice that in each of the partners, there are worrisome characteristics that they value highly in themselves but denigrate in the other. Not only that, they project their ambivalence massively into the dead woman, Roger putting all that is good and worth hanging on to into the image and smell she has left behind, and Lily putting all her hate and frustrated longing to possess Roger into that image and smell.

Roger has not decided to let go of his attachment to his wife, and Lily has not decided if she can be with a man who has attachments to people other than her. The couple will have to own the meaning of their repetitive patterns of obsessional interaction and take back these projective identifications. Ultimately they will have to face their guilt that Roger was unable to keep his late wife alive and that Lily wants to get rid of her and replace her, and to connect this to their individual oedipal conflicts.

Goals of Treatment

As couple therapists, it is not our goal to keep a couple together but to help both partners differentiate their needs and choose to make the relationship better or let it go. If there is commitment to the couple relationship, dedication to the therapy, and the working through is sufficient, the couple is able to make a commitment to intimacy over the long term.

Concluding Note

The object relations therapist listens, responds, creates a safe space for psychological interpretation, demonstrates repeated defensive interactions, holds and contains anxiety, and works from the countertransference to arrive at a useful interpretation based on shared experience in the here and now. Asking about the couple's dream life and sexual experience amplifies our understanding. Therapists resonate at conscious and unconscious levels to figure out the partners' transferences to each other and to us and help them take back their projective identifications. The work done, the couple can re-find lost parts of themself and, with the pleasurable inter-penetration of physical and emotional parts now possible, enjoy full emotional and sexual intimacy.

References

Ainsworth, M. D. S., Blehar, M. C., Waters, E., and Wall, S. (1978). *Patterns of attachment: A psychological study of the strange situation*. Hillsdale, NJ: Erlbaum.

Bowlby, J. (1977). The making and breaking of affectional bonds. *British Journal of Psychiatry 130*, 201–210.

Dicks, H. V. (1967). *Marital tensions*. London: Routledge and Kegan Paul.

Fairbairn, W. R. D. (1952). *Psychoanalytic studies of the personality*. London: Routledge and Kegan Paul.

Fisher, J. and Crandell, L. (1997). Complex attachment patterns of relating in the couple. *Sexual and Marital Therapy 12*(3), 211–223.

Fonagy, P., Gergely, B., Jurist, F., & Target, M. (2003). *Affect regulation, mentalization, and the development of the self*. New York: Other Press.

Freud, S. (1933). New introductory lectures in psychoanalysis. *Standard Edition, 22*, 3–182.

Galese, V. (2003). The roots of empathy: The shared manifold hypothesis and the neural basis of intersubjectivity. *Psychopathology, 36*, 171–180.

Klein, M. (1946/1975). Notes on some schizoid mechanisms. In *Envy and Gratitude and Other Works: 1946–1963* (pp. 1–24). London: Hogarth.

Rizzolatti, G., Fogassi, L., & Gallese, V. (2006, November). Mirrors in the mind. *Scientific American*, 54–61.

Main, M. and Goldwyn, R. (1985). Interview based adult attachment classification related to infant mother and infant-father attachment. Unpublished manuscript, University of Berkeley, California.

Scharff, D. E. (1982). *The sexual relationship*. London: Routledge and Kegan Paul. (Reprinted Northvale, NJ: Jason Aronson, 1998)

Scharff, D. E., & Scharff, J. S. (1987). *Object relations family therapy*. Northvale, NJ: Jason Aronson.

Scharff, D. E., & Scharff, J. S. (Eds.). (1991a). *Object relations couple therapy*. Northvale, NJ: Jason Aronson.

Scharff, D. E., & Scharff, J. S. (1991b). The treatment of extra-marital affairs. In D. E. Scharff & J. S. Scharff, *Object relations couple therapy* (pp. 217–240). Northvale, NJ: Jason Aronson.

Scharff, J., & Bagnini, C. (2003). Narcissistic disorders in marriage. In D. K. Snyder and M. A. Whisman (Eds.), *Treating difficult couples* (pp. 285–307). New York: Guilford, 2003. (Reprinted in J. S. Scharff & D. E. Scharff (Eds.), *New paradigms for treating relationships* (pp. 323–344). Lanham, MD: Jason Aronson, 2006).

Scharff, J. S., & Scharff, D. E. (1998). Chaos theory and fractals in development, self and object relations, and transference. In *Object relations individual therapy* (pp. 153–182). Northvale NJ: Jason Aronson.

Scharff, J. S. and Scharff, D. E. (2005). The *primer of object relations: Second edition.* Jason Aronson: Lanham, MD.

Scharff, J. S., & Scharff, D. E. (2006). *New paradigms in treating relationships.* Lanham, MD: Jason Aronson.

Scharff, J. S., & Scharff, D. E. (2008). Object relations couple therapy. In A. Gurman (Ed.), *Clinical handbook of couple therapy* (pp. 167–195). New York: Guilford.

Scharff, J. S., & Varela, Y. (2000). Object relations therapy. In F. Dattilio & L. Bevilacqua (Eds.), *Comparative treatments for relationship dysfunction* (pp. 81–101).

Schore, A. (2003). *Affect regulation and the repair of the self.* New York: Norton.

Winnicott, D. W. (1965). *The maturational processes and the facilitating environment.* London: Hogarth.

Winnicott, D. W. (1971). *Playing and reality.* London: Tavistock.

CHAPTER 9

Interview With Paul Peluso

Paul R. Peluso, Ph.D., is an associate professor and doctoral program coordinator at Florida Atlantic University. He is the coauthor of *Couples Therapy: Integrating Theory, Research, and Practice* (Love Publishing) and *Principles of Counseling and Psychotherapy: Learning the Essential Domains and Nonlinear Thinking of Master Practitioners* (Routledge), as well as the editor of the book *Infidelity: A Practitioner's Guide to Working with Couples in Crisis* (Routledge). Dr. Peluso is the author of over 25 articles and chapters related to family therapy, couples counseling, and Adlerian theory.

Eds: We have titled this book *Recovering Intimacy in Love Relationships* because our premise is that most devitalized relationships can be reinvigorated, more committed, and more satisfying. In other words, we believe that intimacy that has been lost or dimmed can be recovered, and even enhanced. In your experience, how realistic is this premise?

PP: Personally, I think that you cannot be a competent clinician—especially in the practice of couples counseling—unless you believe that this is possible, and achievable. Having said that, I also think that clinicians have to acknowledge our limitations in helping couples recover intimacy. Namely, if one (or both) members of the couple are not willing to work, then we are seriously limited. For those couples who do want help, couples therapy has a lot to offer couples who no longer feel intimately connected to their partners.

The real dilemma is that most couples don't have a good grasp on what intimacy is, or how it progresses and develops. Each person may come in with some ideas, but frequently they have not communicated them to each other. It is something that is unspoken or "understood" in isolation from the other person. It is only when the other person fails to live up to some portion of their partner's idealized (and isolated) version of intimacy that doubt starts to creep in. Intimacy is lost when each person begins to doubt the commitment of the other, or when one person feels that they are sacrificing more than the other and not getting what they need in return. Often, this is a slow process that gets progressively worse, until one day one (or both) of the partners no longer recognizes their relationship as something vibrant and emotionally nourishing. At which point, they may come for treatment.

The other dilemma is that many counselors are not very well trained in addressing complex dynamics, like the ones presented by couples presenting with intimacy issues. [This is the subject of a new book that I have coauthored called *Principles of Counseling and Psychotherapy: Learning the Essential Domains and Nonlinear Thinking of Master Practitioners* (Routledge).] Specifically, when couples come to therapists for help, we have a critically short window to effect some change. If we are not successful in winning the clients over to the idea that they can recover, or begin the process of building intimacy again, then we run the risk of losing the couple for treatment, and possibly forever. In short, clinicians have to be able to quickly assess what the patterns and dynamics are, and dynamically intervene in a way that allows the couple to see some "light at the end of the tunnel" and leave hopeful about the relationship.

Eds: What about in couples that have or are experiencing infidelity—sexual, emotional, etc.—or substance abuse?

PP: Actually, in the case of infidelity, it can be easier to rekindle intimacy than with other couples concerns. Of course, this depends heavily on what kind of affair took place, and what the underlying dynamics were within the couple that contributed to the affair. This is work that Emily Brown developed that can be very useful for clinicians in helping to navigate through the challenges of helping couples dealing with an infidelity. For example, if the affair was an intimacy-avoidance affair, or a conflict-avoidance affair—where either intimacy or conflict is avoided by the couple, and the purpose of the affair may have been to bring it out into the open—then oftentimes the couple can heal and recover intimacy. However, if the type of affair is an exit affair (where the purpose of the affair is to end the relationship) then it may be far more difficult to recover intimacy [for more information on these and other issues related to infidelity, see Peluso, 2007].

I believe that there are two reasons why it can be easier to rekindle intimacy when a couple experiences infidelity. First is emotion. Couples who come to counseling following an affair are usually full of emotion. Often, in the beginning, it is negative emotion. Unfortunately, many couples counselors are uncomfortable with negative emotions, and, as a result, they try too hard to soothe the clients and smooth things other. That is the wrong thing to do. The couple will either stifle the (negative) emotion, or end therapy in frustration. Instead, the clinician needs to find creative and constructive ways of helping the couple channel and understand their emotional reactions, how it got them into their predicament, and how it can get them out it and into deeper intimacy. To do this, however, requires that couples counselors think in a different way about therapy and about emotions (again, part of some my writing has been devoted to this, but is beyond the scope of this chapter to expand on).

The second reason why it can be easier to rekindle intimacy in couples who are dealing with infidelity is the process of forgiveness. No treatment for infidelity can be successful without some forgiveness work. This means both partners acknowledging the roles that they played in relationship, and understanding (on a deep and profound emotional level) what impact that had on the other person. Only after that occurs can forgiveness really happen. However, if it does, then intimacy has a real chance to flourish.

So just as each of these two elements (emotion and forgiveness) are important pillars in working with infidelity in couples, they are also vital when trying to recover intimacy.

Eds: What is your therapeutic strategy or protocol for working with such couples to recover intimacy?

PP: I will speak more specifically about infidelity, though I think that the principles are similar for any couple that has experienced a loss of intimacy. I think that there are three important strategies that need to be addressed: 1. The decline in satisfaction, 2. Rebalancing power differentials, and 3. The role of fantasy.

Perhaps, with the exception of an infidelity that results from a sexual compulsion or addiction, all infidelities are associated with a decline in satisfaction with the relationship. Couples who are dissatisfied in their relationship are much more likely to engage in an infidelity. As a result, addressing the issue of satisfaction, the decline in satisfaction, and how this has played out in the relationship is the first step in working with couples in reclaiming or reviving intimacy.

One of the reasons for dissatisfaction is the lack of a balance of power in the relationship. Usually, one person feels that they don't have influence over the other person's actions (particularly with regard to decisions that affect the couple), or they feel that they sacrifice their needs and give into the other person's wants. Another way that the power balance is upset in a couple is when one partner triangulates another person in the relationship (i.e., children, parents, friends), which makes the other person feel "left out" or "ganged up on" when it comes to major decisions. As a result, an infidelity is often a way of rebalancing the perception of a power imbalance. It is a way to demonstrate to the other person that they have the power also, though it is expressed in a negative and destructive way. Exploring the power differential within the couple, how it relates to dissatisfaction in the relationship, and finding ways to rebalance the power in a relationship is another important strategy for recovering intimacy.

Lastly, the role of *fantasy* in infidelity (and intimacy) cannot be overemphasized. It is the thing that makes an affair so tempting, because it holds the promise of fulfilling something that seems to be missing in the relationship, or in the person. By contrast, the *reality* of the individual's present relationship is usually fraught with struggle, negotiation, disappointment, and conflict. In short, making *real* relationships work is hard *work*, while an affair (on the surface) seems to be easy, effortless, and enjoyable. Paradoxically, it almost never turns out that way, and after the act when the affair comes to light, the demands of the "other" person becomes "work" while the partner becomes the fantasy (i.e., "I never had it so good ..." "It was so comfortable back when ..."). I think that the key to recovering intimacy following an affair is to have the excitement of the fantasy that led to the infidelity align with the fantasy about the relationship that gets created in the aftermath for the person who had the affair. At the same time, it is crucial to tap into the partner's fantasies about the relationship. Unfortunately, these will be initially tied to some feelings of loss, sadness, grief, disgust, and anger. However, if the therapist can guide the partner through those emotions (again, part of forgiveness), then there may be room for growth and deepening intimacy. Gottman has an intervention he calls "dreams within conflicts" that can be very useful in making this connection for clients (he details this in his 1999 book *The Marriage Clinic*). The goal is to help the clients see that the conflict isn't something to avoid because it is destructive, but rather that the conflict has meaning and purpose in strengthening the relationship.

If these three objectives are met therapeutically, and if the couple has been able to tolerate the emotions contained as well as undergone some elements of forgiveness, then satisfaction in the relationship will increase, and the couple will have ways to discuss power differentials. At that point, both partners' fantasies about the relationship begin to merge together, and each gets the best of both worlds, thus recovering and deepening intimacy.

Eds: Do you utilize or see a place for adjunctive treatments like referral to a couples enrichment workshop, support group if substances are involved, bibliotherapy, etc.?

PP: Absolutely. I think that multimodal, multi-input approach is very helpful. First, couples counseling is limited to only 1 to 2 hours per week (or 1–2% of a person's waking hours each week). Second, adjunctive therapeutic activities can present (or reinforce) information that is being addressed in session, and it can do so in a creative way (especially in the case of movies, where the medium is visual and the audience participates vicariously through the characters). Therefore, these activities provide more *dosage* of the treatment (to borrow from medicine), and operate on several different levels (cognitive, emotional, experiential, visual, auditory), which can facilitate learning. From my perspective, why wouldn't you use them?

The only *caveat* to these adjunctive therapeutic activities is that they should be designed to work on the goal of bringing the couple together. It is incumbent on the therapist, however, to be aware of what the couple is engaging in, and how it impacts their treatment. Couples counselors should have lists of books (and movies) to recommend, and have either connections to or a working knowledge of the latest enhancement workshops/ groups out there. Too often, I think that couples counselors do not take the time to really look into those resources, and miss the opportunity to process the couple's experience when they engage in these adjunctive activities.

Eds: Since diversity is a given in couples work today, how do you proceed to tailor your therapeutic strategy?

PP: Culture cannot be ignored when doing any couples work, or any therapeutic endeavor. In the chapter that I coauthored in this volume, we discuss the *powerful* influence of the cultural construct of *enqing* (or strong mutual affection and admiration) in Asian couples, how it impacts marital satisfaction, and how clinicians should account for this. Other work has shown how culture can impact the universal patterns of attachment relationships, which, in turn, affects the couple relationship. So cultural values, how they are manifested in the couple's relationship, and what role they play in the couple's presenting concern is vital. However, the more important question isn't *if* cultural values are important, but *which* culture is most important (or impactful) for a particular couple. Is it the culture of one's ethnic identity, or origin, or the culture of the relationship that is a focus of concern? For example, perhaps the culture of the relationship is a pattern of "pursuer–distancer" and the couple has always interacted with each other in this fashion. That may be just as important as whether the couple comes from a more collectivistic versus individualistic ethnic culture. So the answer to the question of *which* culture is an important area of focus depends on the couple itself.

Another area that cultures can play an important role, and may be helpful to the clinician, is in the healing of the couple and the restoration of intimacy. Cultural values often contain the myths and ideals that capture the imaginations of people and can provide guidance or the model for change. Cultural values—from ethic to community to family of origin—are the seedbed from which ideas and ideals about how to be a man or woman, how to be a lover, or how to be successful in relationships comes from. In short, they can contribute a large part to a person's fantasies (whose importance is outlined above). These ideas and the failure to live up to them can often be at the heart of the couple's conflict. At the same time, bringing the couple back to those ideas and allow them the chance to decide how they might be able to better fulfill these images can be very powerful in transforming the couple's relationship. The culture may contain heroic stories of successfully transformation, or cautionary stories that warn individuals of the negative consequences of "wrong" behavior. Couples counselors who tap into these stories can find a powerful resource in bridging the emotional gulfs between partners, as well as restoring and deepening intimacy.

Reference

Peluso, P. R. (2007). *Infidelity: A practitioner's guide to working with couples in crisis.* New York: Routledge.

CHAPTER 10

Barriers to Recovering Intimacy

STEPHEN T. FIFE and GERALD R. WEEKS

Intimacy is an important part of human experience, with intimate relationship being "the principal arena within which adults live out their emotional lives" (Mirgain & Cordova, 2007, p. 983). Many researchers have argued that we have an inherent, universal need for closeness and connection with others (Aplerin, 2001; Popovic, 2005; Sullivan, 1953), particularly within couple and family relationships (Downey, 2001). The prevalence of dating, coupling, courtship, and marriage across cultures attests to the seemingly universal desire to be closely connected to another. Intimacy brings satisfaction and "is often considered as the essential factor in adults' health, ability to adapt, happiness, and sense of meaning in life" (Popovic, 2005, p. 35).

In spite of the widespread desire for intimacy, some people find it difficult to create intimate relationships with others. Additionally, some couples in committed relationships may have difficulty holding on to intimacy as it can be fragile and subject to change. It may be lost due to destructive relationship behaviors, such as infidelity or abuse. It may cool or wane because of distractions, neglect, or monotony.

Although the reasons that couples seek therapy may differ, they often come for counseling seeking to regain the love and closeness they once had for each other. They may talk about the loss of love or connection in their relationship, and they may express frustration or hopelessness that intimacy cannot be recovered (Weeks, 1995). Treatment for lost or diminished intimacy focuses on both problem solving as well as promoting growth

(Weeks & Treat, 2001). It involves identifying and removing individual and relationship barriers to the recovery of intimacy as well as facilitating the development of deeper and expanded closeness and connection.

Barriers to Recovering Intimacy

Intimacy in committed relationships can bring tremendous personal and relationship satisfaction. However, couple and family relationships can also be very emotionally challenging (Mirgain & Cordova, 2007). In spite of its seemingly universal nature, several factors may interfere with the recovery of intimacy once it has been lost (Downey, 2001). Intimacy has both an interpersonal dimension as well as an intrapersonal dimension to it (Alperin, 2006). Problems in one or both areas can become significant barriers to the recovery of intimacy for couples.

Interpersonal and Relational Barriers

Many couples struggle with relationship issues that disrupt feelings of closeness and prevent the rebuilding of intimacy. One couple sought therapy because they had drifted apart emotionally and felt disconnected from each other. Another couple on the brink of divorce expressed doubt that they could ever repair their relationship and regain the love they once had. When couples complain that they have "fallen out of love" or they do not feel as close as they used to, therapists should assess for interpersonal processes or relationship dynamics that are inhibiting them.

Neglect   Neglect is one of the most common reasons couples struggle to maintain intimacy. It can be a cause for the loss of intimacy as well as a hurdle that prevents couples from regaining intimacy. Partners may divert essential time and energy away from the relationship and become excessively engaged in their work, hobbies, children, or even other relationships. Couples who fail to give the relationship time and nourishment on a consistent basis unwittingly create patterns of independence and disconnect.

A variety of factors may play a role in relationship neglect. Research shows that the number of individuals who manage heavy family and work responsibilities is increasing (Emmers-Sommer, 2004). Partners may become overly focused on the business of running a family (i.e., managing the household, taking care of kids, paying bills, etc.) and as a result, give up time and energy for the marital relationship. They may also devote inordinate amounts of time to personal interests, hobbies, or recreation. For example, clients will often complain of their partner's obsession with the Internet, online chat rooms, or computer games. There also may be detrimental effects on intimacy from busy or conflicting work schedules (Emmers-Sommer, 2004). Other outside interests, such as friends, charity work, sports, education, and so forth, can also take away from a couple's time together. These are not inherently threats to a couple's intimate connection. However, when time and emotional commitment to outside interests become excessive, relationship closeness will suffer.

Recurring Violations of Trust   Because of the interdependent relationship between intimacy and trust, a violation of trust will produce negative consequences in a couple's intimacy. An obvious example is infidelity. A violation of a couple's commitment to emotional and sexual exclusivity has a negative effect on intimacy (Fife, Weeks, & Gambescia, 2008). However, other types of betrayals can also damage a couple's sense of closeness. For example, not following through on commitments or going against previously agreed upon standards may lead to emotional distance and decreased intimacy. One husband consistently undermined his wife's trust in him by spending large amounts of money without talking to her first, despite his promises to confer with her before making purchases. Each time he was caught, she felt betrayed and withdrew emotionally. The repeated violations of trust hindered the development of greater closeness in their relationship.

Violations of trust may occur in other areas of life, such as with parenting, excessive commitments to one's occupation or hobbies, or when boundaries with extended family or friends are inordinately open and diffuse. In one specific therapy case, a husband felt betrayed each time his wife talked to her mother and sisters about the conflicts or problems within their marriage. He would get angry and withdraw emotionally. She would, in turn, complain to her family about his emotional neglect, and the pattern would continue. As long as they persisted in these destructive behaviors, they perpetuated increasing emotional distance in their marriage and struggled to build the intimacy they desired.

Maladaptive Communication Patterns   Although there are a variety of definitions and understandings of intimacy, most share one particular characteristic: "a feeling of closeness and connectedness that develops through *communication* between partners" (Laurenceau, Barrett, & Rovine, 2005, p. 314, emphasis added). Therefore, it is no surprise that poor or ineffective communication may pose a significant barrier to intimacy (Gottman, 1994; Laurenceau, Barrett, & Rovine, 2005). Destructive communication may include patterns such as incessant speaking coupled with poor listening, ineffective ways of managing conflict or problem solving, persistent criticism, defensiveness, or cycles of demand and withdrawal. Each of these may inhibit the rebuilding of intimacy for couples.

One couple seeking treatment struggled immensely with listening. Both partners constantly spoke over each other, while disregarding their partner's thoughts and feelings. The pattern of mutual invalidation brought a loss of understanding and closeness in their relationship. Cases such as this illustrate that intimacy may be blocked when one or both partner's voice is marginalized by the other. Research has shown that when partners ignore or invalidate each other's feelings, it has a negative effect on their relationship satisfaction and negates the effect of positive interactions (Laurenceau et al., 2005). When both partners insistently voice their own positions, while ignoring or invalidating each other's feelings, each of them feels less and less that his or her needs are being heard or taken seriously. Patterns of interaction that take this form promote emotional distance and create considerable obstacles to rebuilding intimacy.

In addition to invalidation, other destructive communication patterns can inhibit closeness and connection. For example, patterns of demand and withdrawal have damaging effects on relationship quality (Gottman, 1994). Intimacy can also be blocked by persistent defensiveness or attempts to fix the situation, rather than listening to understand (Snyder, 2000). Partners may have interacted with each other in hurtful ways, leaving emotional scars, including a hesitancy to be vulnerable with each other due to a fear of being rejected or hurt. Ineffective ways of handling disagreements are also damaging. However, conflict itself does not preclude the recovery of intimacy (Clinebell & Clinebell, 1970; Gottman, 1994). Whether conflict results in closeness or distance depends more upon *how* the conflict is handled (Gottman, 1994). Gottman and Levinson (1999, 2002) identified five processes of conflict that lead to decreased closeness in relationships: contempt, criticism, defensiveness, stonewalling, and belligerence. On the other hand, conflict in which partners are supportive, warm, interested, and open to being influenced by the other deescalates problems and is associated with happy, stable relationships.

Narrow or Differing Definitions of Intimacy   Intimacy is commonly understood as being multifaceted (Clinebell & Clinebell, 1970; Mosier, 2006; Schaefer & Olson, 1981; Waring, 1981). However, couples may find it difficult to rebuild intimacy if they define intimacy too narrowly or rely on only one dimension of intimacy to sustain their relationship. For example, intimacy cannot be developed or maintained adequately when limited to just physical chemistry or sexual expression (Mosier, 2006). One couple in therapy defined intimacy in this one-dimensional way. Everything in their relationship seemed to rest on the quality of their sex life. When they had problems in their sexual relationship (their stated reason for coming to therapy), their whole relationship was a mess. Another couple with serious relationship problems seemed to be limited to intimacy on a spiritual level only. They reported sharing significant spiritual experiences together, but did not connect in other ways. This posed a significant obstacle in their relationship, which eventually ended in divorce after less than a year of marriage.

Differences in meaning (Popovic, 2005) and perception of intimacy (Greef & Malherbe, 2001) between partners may become obstructions to closeness and connection for some couples. Relationship partners can also have significant differences regarding the desired kinds of intimacy and desired level of intimacy (Schaefer & Olson, 1981; Weeks, 1995). These differences can constrain couples in their efforts to reestablish intimacy in their relationship. If these differences are not openly identified and discussed, couples may experience unmet expectations that contribute to loss of intimacy and create additional barriers to its recovery.

Individual Barriers

Although intimacy is often defined as an interpersonal process, there is also an individual, intrapsychic dimension to it (Aplerin, 2001, 2006). Certain individual struggles can create barriers that inhibit intimacy. Individuals have different capacities for intimacy (Aplerin, 2006), and not all people are able to have emotionally intimate relationships with others (Aplerin, 2001). When a therapist finds that a couple is having a hard time recovering or generating greater intimacy, he or she should consider the possibility that one or both partners may have individual issues that inhibit them from developing intimacy with their partner.

Fears of Intimacy   A couple's attempts to develop greater closeness and deeper connection can be undermined by a fear of intimacy. Individuals are often unaware of their fears regarding intimacy, and when too much closeness occurs, they may unknowingly interact in ways that push their partner away. Fears of closeness may prove to be a significant barrier to recovering intimacy for some couples (Martin & Ashby, 2004; Popovic, 2005; Weeks & Treat, 2001).

Fears of intimacy can originate in one's childhood and be related to poor separation or individuation or inadequate differentiation from one's family of origin (Alperin, 2006; Downey, 2001). Intimacy requires appropriate personal boundaries as well as adequate individuation (Popovic, 2005). Those who have not experienced sufficient separation or individuation may find the experience of intimacy to be threatening and anxiety provoking (Alperin, 2006).

A fear of intimacy can also arise from painful experiences in adulthood. Johnson, Makinen, and Millikin (2001) discussed the construct of attachment injuries, which are characterized by abandonment or by a betrayal of trust during a critical moment of need. An experience such as this may result in a loss of trust and inhibit vulnerability necessary for intimacy. If individuals have experienced attachment injuries in previous relationships, they may fear that new relationships will only lead to the same kind of hurt. Likewise, attachment injuries between partners in a current relationship may also prevent the rebuilding of intimacy.

Weeks and Treat (2001) described several fears related to intimacy. Although not an exhaustive list, the following discussion may help clinicians be aware of common intimacy-related fears.

Fear of Dependency. Sometimes partners feel that they must be emotionally self-sufficient and independent. In extreme cases, they may keep themselves constantly aloof from their partners, as if they do not need them at all. A fear of dependency may keep couples emotionally distant, ultimately leading partners to live relatively separate lives.

Fear of Feelings. Intimacy often involves the sharing of feelings with one's partner. Self-disclosure, an important part of intimacy, might include the sharing of personal thoughts, beliefs, and, especially, feelings. However, some partners have learned to fear the expression of feelings. They hide behind intellectualization, denial, or rigid beliefs of what is right.

Fear of Anger. Some people may suffer from a fear of anger. This can be manifested in two ways: (a) individuals may fear their own anger toward others, and (b) they may fear being the target of anger. Such individuals avoid getting too close in relationships, fearing that their partner's or their own hostility and aggression may come out in destructive ways.

Fear of Losing Control or Being Controlled. Healthy relationships include interdependence and mutual control. However, some partners are crippled by a fear of losing control or being controlled by the other. This type of fear has two levels of meaning. At one level, there may be the feeling that too much closeness will result in a loss of control in one's life. At a deeper intrapsychic level, losing control may mean feeling engulfed by one's partner. Those who fear losing control vigilantly keep their guard up, limiting the possibility of others getting to know them and hampering the development of intimacy.

Fear of Exposure. At the beginning of relationships, partners may limit what they choose to disclose to each other. As the relationship progresses, couples typically increase self-disclosure, which contributes to the development of intimacy. However, partners may stop at a surface level of disclosure due to a fear that exposing oneself will be too painful or will result in rejection. They may tell themselves things such as: "If they only knew who I really am or what I really did, they would never love me or want to be with me."

Fear of Emotional Vulnerability. Intimacy requires interpersonal vulnerability, which leaves partners susceptible to being hurt (Cordova & Scott, 2001). Many couples cannot recapture intimacy in their relationship because of lingering relationship wounds, either from the current or a past relationship. A lingering fear of being vulnerable may limit self-disclosure and inhibit the development of intimacy.

Fear of Abandonment or Rejection. The greater the emotional investment in a relationship, the deeper the pain experienced if the relationship ends. Individuals who have experienced the pain of rejection or abandonment in the past may become overly sensitive to getting too close in relationships. They may avoid close relationships altogether or keep their partners at a distance in order to protect themselves and avoid further pain (Alperin, 2001).

Maladaptive Cognitions and Unrealistic Expectations

Couples may also struggle to recapture intimacy because of maladaptive cognitions and unrealistic expectations regarding intimacy and their relationship (Popovic, 2005). These are often accompanied by negative emotions toward one's partner, which foster emotional distance and interfere with the recovery of intimacy. Dysfunctional beliefs may also lead to behaviors that diminish or block intimacy (Kayser & Himle, 1994).

Kayser and Himle (1994) described eight dysfunctional beliefs that may result in avoidant behaviors and interfere with the development of closeness and connection for couples (e.g., "If I become close to someone, he [or she] will leave me."). Other constraining beliefs may include "I'm not lovable." "My spouse can't meet my needs." "They won't change." These beliefs embody several maladaptive thought processes such as all-or-nothing thinking, unfounded assumptions, overgeneralizations, gender stereotyping, fortune telling, unrealistic expectations, and discounting the positive (see also Burns, 1980). They also may be connected to or give rise to some of the fears of intimacy described above. Beliefs such as these serve to constrain couples from moving forward and making changes in their relationships (Wright, Watson, & Bell, 1996).

In addition to constraining beliefs, couples may be hindered in their efforts to regain intimacy because of unrealistic relationship expectations or excessive demands (Kayser & Himle, 1994). When expectations are not met, frustration may set in, leading to emotional distance between partners. Spouses who are consistently told that their efforts are not good enough may give up, concluding that any effort will be criticized or discounted.

Frustration over unmet expectations or demands may be grounded in an excessive focus on one's own needs, to the minimization or exclusion of the needs of one's partner. Self-focus such as this inhibits the development of intimacy, which requires a mutual awareness of each other's needs and desires. Ironically, an excessive focus on getting one's own intimacy needs met may unintentionally undermine the development or rebuilding of intimacy for some couples.

Treatment Guidelines for Recovering Intimacy

Although the individual and relationship issues described above may limit couples' abilities to recover intimacy, there are effective ways in which therapists can help couples remove troublesome obstacles and rebuild closeness in their relationships. Helpful interventions related to fears of intimacy, cognitive distortions, unproductive expectations, communication problems, and desired types and levels of intimacy can be used by therapists to invite change and facilitate the restoration of intimacy for couples.

Therapists' efforts to work with couples on rebuilding intimacy are often hindered by individual barriers to intimacy. Therefore, Weeks and Treat (2001) argued that individual barriers must be removed first before working on interpersonal processes, such as communication. However, prior to addressing either individual or interpersonal barriers, the therapist must create an environment in which intimacy building can occur— one in which it is safe for clients to be emotionally vulnerable with each other (Fife, 2004).

Safety

Intimacy requires a degree of personal vulnerability (Martin & Ashby, 2004), and in order for couples to recover intimacy, they must (re)develop the capacity to be interpersonally vulnerable and supportive with each other. However, the personal vulnerability required for intimacy development may leave partners feeling sensitive to being hurt by the other (Mirgain & Cordova, 2007). Partners who are struggling to regain intimacy in their relationship have likely experienced a variety of painful interactions with each other in the past. As a consequence, they may not feel that it is safe to be vulnerable or intimate.

Part of the therapist's responsibility is to provide a safe, secure environment in which clients can take personal risks with increased vulnerability (Popovic, 2005). The clinician's empathic, patient, and caring interactions with clients will help establish this safe environment initially (Aplerin, 2006). Careful coaching and monitoring of partner interactions will also help them to open up and be emotionally vulnerable with each other without experiencing negative consequences. Although the therapist can help facilitate a safe environment, the source of safety must ultimately shift from the therapist to the clients (Fife, 2004). Therefore, the therapist's efforts must be directed toward shifting safety from him- or herself to the couple as soon as possible so that they can create a safe, open environment for each other.

Addressing Fears of Intimacy

In spite of their desire for intimacy, many couples have a difficult time increasing closeness. Certain fears related to intimacy may be formidable obstacles for some couples. If couples are not making progress in developing intimacy, Weeks and Treat (2001) suggested that the clinician consider assessing for fears of intimacy using the Intimacy-Fear Awareness technique (Weeks & Treat, 2001). This intervention is designed to invite clients to recognize and acknowledge possible intimacy-related fears.

As the therapist begins the Intimacy-Fear Awareness intervention, it may be helpful to point out that nearly everyone has some kind of fear of intimacy. Partners are then asked to think about what fears each brought to the relationship. Therapists may assist in this process by suggesting possible fears they have noticed in the couple or intimacy fears that are common in couples (see Fears of Intimacy section above). A thorough therapeutic examination will likely reveal one or more fears that can then be addressed.

As fears are identified, the therapist should help the couple work through each fear in therapy. Several interventions can help couples deal with their particular fears of intimacy. First, the therapist should normalize fears of intimacy. Letting couples know that others share their plight—and have successfully overcome it—can decrease anxiety and foster hope that change can occur. Utilizing enactments (see description below) and encouraging appropriate communication, therapists can invite partners to talk about their fears with each other. They can also share with each other what intimacy means to them and clarify the level or kinds of intimacy with which they are comfortable. Couples can evaluate their strengths as individuals and as a couple, as well as areas in which they would like to grow. An exercise such as this can unite a couple in deeper understanding and empathy for each other, thus facilitating greater intimacy.

Addressing Cognitive Distortions and Unrealistic Expectations

Often, couples' fears of intimacy are correlated with maladaptive thought process. When cognitive distortions and automatic thoughts are part of the barriers to intimacy, therapists may draw upon cognitive techniques and interventions to challenge clients' negative or distorted thoughts and help them recover closeness and connection. Cognitive interventions are typically applied from an individual perspective. However, it is important to remember that a couple is an interactional system, and the maladaptive thought processes are best understood and treated within the context of the relationship system (Weeks & Treat, 2001).

Clients are generally unaware of their thought processes. Therefore, therapists may begin by educating clients on common cognitive distortions and automatic thoughts and the negative emotional and interpersonal effects these can have (Weeks & Treat, 2001). Then clinicians can help clients identify the types of distortions and automatic thoughts they regularly experience. Once identified, a number of interventions can be employed to challenge maladaptive thought processes and constraining beliefs (Kayser & Himle, 1994; Popovic, 2005; Wright et al., 1996).

For example, clients can be taught to self-monitor and challenge their automatic thoughts. Once they are proficient at identifying their thoughts, efforts to challenge or change the thoughts in a positive direction can be implemented. One effective method for this is the Dysfunctional Thought Record (Dattilio, 2005). When a cognitive distortion or irrational thought is identified, clients are instructed to write down the situation, the automatic thought, the accompanying emotion, the cognitive distortion, and an alternative thought or response. Therapists then review the record with clients and provide guidance to improve the effectiveness and success of their efforts.

Another intervention is to have clients examine the evidence for a particular thought (Weeks & Treat, 2001). Therapists should help clients evaluate whether they know all the facts of a situation or whether the facts or behaviors of their partner point only in one direction. Partners may automatically attribute negative intentions to each other's actions and unnecessarily take offense. For example, one wife in therapy complained that when her husband came home from work, he did not come in immediately and ask her how she was doing or how her day went. Her conclusion was that he did not care about her, which was accompanied by feelings of sadness, loneliness, and anger. The therapist encouraged her to examine the situation and consider other possible meanings or reasons for her husband's behavior. In cases such as this, clinicians may also challenge partners' negative assumptions and beliefs about each other's intentions.

Many couples also experience frustration and emotional distance due to unmet expectations related to issues such as roles, responsibilities, parenting, finances, sex, and so forth. Sager (1976) articulated three types of expectations that each individual brings to relationships:

1. Expectations that the partner was clearly aware of and verbalized to the other partner.
2. Expectations that the partner was clearly aware of but did not verbalize to the other.
3. Expectations that the partner was or is not aware of and therefore could not be verbalized.

Therapists may invite couples to evaluate their expectations by reflecting on these three points. After careful, honest evaluation, couples should spend time discussing their expectations with each other. This helps clients clearly identify and own their expectations, modify unrealistic expectations, and learn to communicate and negotiate personal expectations.

Promoting Intimacy Through Communication

One of the most common and effective means of helping couples rebuild intimacy is through enhanced communication (Greenberg, James, & Conry, 1988; Weeks, Gambescia, & Jenkins, 2003). Couples must learn to break old patterns and establish new ways of communicating (Popovic, 2005). One method of helping clients improve communication is through increasing their awareness of destructive communication patterns that have developed. Therapists can educate clients about the circular nature of communication and help them gain an understanding of how each person participates in the harmful cycle.

In order to facilitate awareness and understanding, therapists begin by asking clients to describe their interactions. Subsequent questions should draw out information about clients' thoughts, feelings, and verbal or nonverbal behavior. Utilizing circular diagrams, therapists can draw out a couple's unique communication cycle (highlighting the thoughts, feelings, and behavior of each partner) and underscore the interconnected nature of their interactions. This should be followed by a discussion of what each can do differently so that communication brings them together, rather than pushing them apart.

For most couples, developing new communication patterns that build intimacy requires more than just an awareness or intellectual understanding of their ineffective ways of interacting. Therapy must also facilitate new ways of couples communicating in vivo, meaning through their lived experience with each other. An effective method of promoting intimacy through communication is the use of enactments, as described by Butler and colleagues (Butler, Davis, & Seedall, 2008; Butler & Gardner, 2003; Davis & Butler, 2004). Enactments are therapist-coached couple interactions designed to promote effective communication and greater intimacy. Enactments encourage cognitive and emotional self-disclosure, which when accompanied by compassionate listening and validation, facilitate mutual softening and greater intimacy (Greenberg et al., 1988; Waring, 1981; Weeks, 1995).

Davis and Butler (2004) provided a detailed clinical description of how to guide couples through successful enactments. Enactments emphasize both the speaker's and listener's roles, and a thorough description of each partner's responsibility is critical to the success of the intervention. The therapist may also ask the clients to move their chairs or shift sitting position so they can face each other and look each other in the eyes while communicating. The content for discussion should be carefully chosen and consistent with the couple's goals for therapy.

When describing the speaker's role, the therapist should emphasize the importance of emotional self-disclosure and avoiding accusations or criticism. However, self-disclosure alone is not sufficient for an effective enactment; careful, compassionate listening is also essential. "For the interaction to be experienced as intimate by the speaker, the speaker must also perceive the listener's responses as demonstrating understanding, acceptance, validation, and care (i.e., perceived partner responsiveness)" (Laurenceau et al., 2005, p. 315). Because of the importance of partner responsiveness, the listener's role should also be carefully explained and emphasized to clients. Snyder (2000) suggested that empathic listening requires one to set aside temporarily one's own perspective in order to focus on understanding the perspective and lived experience of the other. It entails "listening to the other and then reflecting the essential feelings, meanings, intentions, and desires of the other" (Snyder, 2000, p. 40). The listener should also be encouraged to seek correction and clarification from the speaker and to continue to reflect until it is clear that the speaking partner feels understood. Genuine, responsive listening leads to softening and is likely to be reciprocated between partners.

Butler and Gardner (2003) stressed that therapists should structure enactments in relation to the emotional reactivity and volatility of couples and their ability to sustain self-reliant couple dialogue. The authors present a five-stage developmental model to guide therapists in this process, which includes: shielded enactments, buffered enactments, face-to-face talk-turn enactments, episode enactments, and autonomous relationship enactments. Because enactments are used to promote self-reliant client interaction, the therapist generally stays engaged in the process but on the sideline as a coach. When necessary, the therapist may interrupt, point out what is going well, and offer suggestions for more effective sharing or listening. For couples who are emotionally reactive and cannot effectively communicate directly with each other, the initial communication is channeled through the therapist. As couples improve in their ability to speak and listen effectively, clinicians decrease personal involvement as a mediator and direct the clients to greater autonomous interaction. At the conclusion of the interaction, therapists should ask couples to reflect on the process by highlighting how they felt, what went well, what could be done better, and how they can utilize this process in communications outside of therapy.

Intimacy Exercises

In addition to addressing communication and barriers to intimacy, couples may benefit from additional exercises specifically designed to facilitate intimacy. Part of helping couples develop intimacy is to invite them to define what intimacy means and what behaviors will lead to greater feelings of intimacy in their relationship (Weeks, 1995). Some may have a difficult time articulating what intimacy means. Others may have a good idea of what it is and what they desire personally but may not know what it means to their partner. There are two exercises that may help couples assess their current level of intimacy, consider aspects of intimacy that are important to them, and identify helpful changes or improvements.

Exercise 1: Aspects of Intimacy   As discussed above, intimacy is a multifaceted phenomenon, and intimate interaction occurs in a number of dimensions. The Aspects of Intimacy handout (see Appendix A at the end of this chapter) provides a helpful framework for a therapeutic discussion of intimacy that emphasizes its multidimensional nature. Therapists can utilize the Aspects of Intimacy handout for a number of different purposes. It can be used to educate couples about the notion that intimacy is multidimensional and help them broaden their definition of intimacy beyond one particular dimension. It can also be used to facilitate an examination of their present level of intimacy and to understand the areas that are most important to them individually. Furthermore, it can help individuals develop a better understanding of their partner's definition of intimacy and changes they desire. Finally, it can be used to engage partners in a conversation of what they can do to build greater intimacy in their relationship.

Therapists can facilitate a discussion between partners in which they share their reflections with each other in an open, nondefensive way. Couples will likely find that some of their answers differ. In the areas that are different, therapists help clients seek to understand how the individual feels about that area of intimacy personally, why that particular aspect of intimacy is important to their partner, what changes he or she desires, and what behaviors can help bring about greater intimacy in these areas. Therapists should encourage couples to develop specific plans to strengthen intimacy in their relationship. Asking them to reflect on what has brought closeness for them in the past is a good place to start. They may find that they already have a number of intimacy-enhancing activities in their repertoire. Therapists may also brainstorm with clients and offer suggestions for additional behaviors that would enhance their intimacy or closeness. Some activities may target more than one aspect of intimacy at a time, thus building intimacy that is multidimensional. One couple in therapy found the idea of intimacy having multiple aspects to be very liberating. They embraced the definition of intimacy as an experience of connection, closeness, and sharing with each other in a variety of ways. It provided hope by helping the couple see that they had experienced closeness in ways that they had not previously defined as intimate. It also brought greater understand of what behaviors and experiences bring closeness and show love for each other.

Exercise 2: Intimacy Program   Another method of assessment and intervention for use with couples is the Intimacy Program (see Appendix B at the end of this chapter). Like the Aspects of Intimacy handout, the Intimacy Program has several purposes. It can be used to help couples (a) examine their present level of intimacy, (b) develop a better understanding of their partner's definition of intimacy and any desired changes, and (c) engage clients in conversations of what they can do to build greater intimacy in their relationship. The Intimacy Program begins by having partners independently fill out a worksheet designed to invite their reflection on several different constructs related to intimacy. The worksheet is used initially to explore partners' current evaluation of intimacy in their relationship. The couple's answers and evaluations serve as a framework for subsequent work in therapy. Because of the detailed nature of the worksheet, going through the Intimacy Program is likely to require multiple sessions.

The Intimacy Program begins with Sternberg's (1986, 1997) triangular theory of love, which emphasizes three components of love: commitment, intimacy, and passion. The clinician should note the similarities and discrepancies in the couple's answers. When there are discrepancies, the therapist needs to guide the couple toward an understanding of the other's desires and developing agreed upon behaviors that can help enrich those areas deemed to be lacking.

Therapists continue the Intimacy Program by reviewing the couple's answers regarding the seven components of intimate interaction (L'Abate, 1977, 1999). Couples should discuss their evaluation and ideas about each item so that they have a better understanding of the other person's views. Therapists should then facilitate a discussion of how to move from a conceptual understanding to behavioral application of their ideas about intimacy. In other words, what can the couple do to increase intimacy? Clinicians should help couples be accountable by following up on their progress in subsequent sessions. In addition, an affective component may be included by asking partners to describe how they felt when they experienced some of the intimacy behaviors (Weeks & Treat, 2001). Therapists may also ask clients to discuss their feelings toward their partner in light of the efforts they have made.

Clinicians may review with couples their ratings of the seven types of intimacy (Schaefer & Olson, 1981) and the eight facets of intimacy (Waring, 1984) in much the same way as the seven components of intimate interaction. Therapists should facilitate an open, nondefensive discussion of partners' answers and their ideas about the different types of intimacy. A major focus of the therapist's efforts should be on helping partners listen empathically to each other. As couples identify ways to rebuild intimacy and as they follow through on their commitments, they will experience greater closeness and connection in their relationship.

Homework Assignments   Out-of-session change is a critical aspect of client progress in therapy (Fife, 2004). Therefore, no matter what successes couples have with recovering intimacy during therapy sessions, clinicians must help clients continue to work and grow in between visits (Dattilio, 2005). The sections above describe several methods of encouraging out-of-session work for couples. Homework assignments should help clients identify mutually enjoyable activities that target specific facets of intimacy and promote closeness and connection in their relationship. Following through with assignments will help couples build on the gains experienced during therapy sessions and establish a level of independence and self-reliance that is essential to their continued growth beyond the successful completion of therapy. Therapists should be diligent in following up with clients on homework assignments and ask them to describe the outcomes of their efforts. In cases in which clients did not follow through with their assignments, therapists should help them examine what prevented completion of the assignment and ways in which these obstacles can be removed.

Time Together: Quality and Quantity

It is clear that relationship neglect will prevent couples from regaining lost or diminished intimacy. Couples must spend time together to nourish the relationship and build intimacy. There is no adequate substitute for time. As most would suspect, research indicates that quality time together positively affects intimacy (Emmers-Sommer, 2004). Quality time is defined as "focused, uninterrupted time with partners ... [and] should provide the opportunity for meaningful conversations and the chance to do worthwhile activities together" (Emmers-Sommer, 2004, p. 401). Some couples, however, have bought into the myth that quality time, but not necessarily quantity, is sufficient for building and maintaining close relationships. Research contradicts this assumption, showing that quantity is also critical, particularly in the case of relationship development or repair (Emmers-Sommer, 2004).

It appears that neither quantity nor quality time *alone* is sufficient. Both are critical for the development of intimacy. Therefore, couples *must* set aside the time necessary to (re)construct intimacy. One couple seen in therapy consistently failed to follow through on relationship-building assignments. When asked about this pattern, they replied that they just did not have time. Not surprisingly, they failed to experience the relationship growth that they desired from therapy. In order to recapture intimacy, couples must make spending time together a top priority. This may require adjusting work commitments, setting boundaries with friends and extended family, limiting time on the Internet or engaging in hobbies, or turning off the television.

Celebrating Successes

With all clinical efforts to help couples recover intimacy, it is important to help them see and acknowledge the efforts and successes they are experiencing. Efforts that remain unnoticed will have only a minimal (if any at all) positive effect on a couple's intimacy. However, successes that are recognized and celebrated will likely have a positive, reciprocal, and generative effect on couples' progress (Fife, 2004). Therapists may ask couples questions such as, "What were some experiences or times during the past week in which you felt close or connected?" Asking couples to elaborate on what they did that contributed to moments of closeness will help solidify the gains they are making (Fife, 2004; Wright et al., 1996). When working with couples on building intimacy, therapists often tell them that they will be asked about their experiences of closeness at the beginning of the next session. Knowing that they are expected to report back next week has the effect of focusing their attention and raising their awareness of times of closeness and sharing with their partner. Successful experiences with intimacy will create hope for future connection and closeness.

Conclusion

Couples often seek therapy for the purpose of eliminating their problems. However, as therapy progresses, it often expands to include intimacy enhancement and relationship building (Weeks, 1995). Whether it is a primary or secondary reason for couples seeking treatment, therapists' work with couples will often include developing, enhancing, or restoring intimacy. Regaining intimacy may be extremely challenging for some couples, given the possible neglect or damage that may have already occurred. Knowing common individual and relational barriers to recovering intimacy can help clinicians identify possible roadblocks that are hindering couples from rebuilding the closeness and connection they desire. Therapists can implement a variety of effective interventions to help couples reconstruct intimacy in their relationship and plan for continued growth beyond therapy. Therapists can also integrate ideas presented in this chapter to supplement their work with couples who seek treatment for other problems.

Appendix A: Aspects of Intimacy in Marriage

Review the list and identify the top two to five aspects of intimacy that are strengths for you as a couple. Also, note two or three areas in which you would like improvement or growth. Share your reflections with each other in an open, nondefensive way. In the areas where you both desire improvement, discuss specific steps that can be taken to increase closeness in your relationship. You will likely find that some of your answers differ. In those areas in which your partner wants improvement, seek to understand why that particular aspect of intimacy is important to him or her, what changes he or she desires, and what you can do to help intimacy grow. In areas where you are both satisfied, congratulate each other. Most successful relationships have a few (but certainly not all) core areas of intimacy that help keep the relationship strong. (Some items have been adapted from Schaefer and Olson [1981].)

Aspects of Intimacy Handout

Aesthetic Intimacy	Sharing experiences of beauty—music, nature, art, theater, dance, etc.
Communication Intimacy	Connecting through talking. Keeping communication channels open. Listening to and valuing your spouse's ideas. Being loving, compassionate, respectful, giving, truthful, and open in your communication.
Conflict Intimacy	Facing and struggling with differences together. Using resolution of conflict to grow closer together.
Creative Intimacy	Experiencing closeness through acts of creating together. Sharing expressions of love in creative ways.
Crisis Intimacy	Developing closeness in dealing with problems and pain. Standing together in tragedies. Responding together in a united way to pressures of life such as working through problems, raising a family, illness, aging, etc.
Emotional Intimacy	Feeling connected at an emotional level. Being in tune with each other's emotions; being able to share significant meanings and feelings with each other, including negative feelings.
Financial Intimacy	Working together to balance differing attitudes about money. Developing a unified plan for budgeting, spending, and saving. Having shared financial goals.
Forgiveness Intimacy	Apologizing to each other. Asking for forgiveness. Asking your spouse, "What can I do to be a better husband/wife?"
Friendship Intimacy	Feeling a close connection and regard for one another as friends.

Continued

Aspects of Intimacy Handout (*Continued*)

Humor Intimacy	Sharing through laughing together. Having jokes between the two of you that only you share. Making each other laugh. Enjoying the funny side of life.
Intellectual Intimacy	Experiencing closeness through sharing ideas. Feeling mutual respect for each other's intellectual capacities and viewpoints. Sharing mind-stretching experiences. Reading, discussing, studying together.
Parenting Intimacy	Sharing the responsibilities of raising children, including providing for their physical, emotional, and spiritual needs. Includes working together in teaching and disciplining them as well as loving them and worrying about their welfare.
Physical Intimacy	Closeness and sharing through physical touch. Experiencing your physical relationship (including sexual intimacy) with joy, fun, and a sense of becoming one. Being open and honest with each other in terms of desires and responses.
Recreational Intimacy	Experiencing closeness and connection through fun and play. Helping each other rejuvenate through stress-relieving and enjoyable recreation together.
Service Intimacy	Sharing in acts of service together. Growing closer as a couple as you experience the joy that comes from giving to others.
Spiritual Intimacy	Discovering and sharing values, religious views, spiritual feelings, meaning in life, etc.
Work Intimacy	Experiencing closeness through sharing common tasks, such as maintaining a house and yard, raising a family, earning a living, participating in community affairs, etc.
_____ Intimacy	Additional areas of intimacy in your relationship.

Appendix B: Intimacy Program

I. Sternberg's Triangle of Love (adapted from Sternberg [1986, 1997])

_____

_____

Do I desire a relationship that includes:

1. Commitment: Yes   No   My notion of commitment includes:

_____

2. Intimacy: Yes   No   My notion of intimacy includes:

_____

3. Passion: Yes   No   My notion of passion includes:

_____

_____

Assuming Yes on all of the above three, what level of intensity is important to you for each?

	Not Very Important		Somewhat Important		Very Important
1. Commitment	1	2	3	4	5
2. Intimacy	1	2	3	4	5
3. Passion	1	2	3	4	5

How do you express these three components of love in your relationship?

Commitment: _____

_____

Intimacy: _____

_____

Passion: _____

_____

What does your partner perceive that you contribute to the relationship?

Commitment: _____

_____

Intimacy: _____

_____

Passion: _____

_____

II. Seven Components of Intimate Interactions (adapted from L'Abate [1977])

Using the scale below, rate your present relationship on each component of intimate interaction.

Component of Intimacy	Low					High
1. Seeing the good: expressing appreciation, affection, and affirmation	1	2	3	4	5	6
2. Caring: concern about the other's welfare, happiness, needs, and feelings in a consistent and dependable way	1	2	3	4	5	6
3. Protectiveness: need to protect each other and the relationship	1	2	3	4	5	6
4. Enjoyment: being together and doing things together that are pleasurable	1	2	3	4	5	6
5. Responsibility: accepting responsibility for one's part in the relationship	1	2	3	4	5	6
6. Sharing hurt: sharing feelings of pain or suffering with each other	1	2	3	4	5	6
7. Forgiveness: achieved through an understanding of the other person's motivations, cherishing the goodwill that pervades the relationship	1	2	3	4	5	6

III. Seven Types of Intimacy (adapted from Schaefer and Olson [1981])

Using the scale below, rate your present relationship on each type of intimacy.

Type of Intimacy	Low					High
1. Emotional intimacy: experiencing a feeling of closeness	1	2	3	4	5	6

	Low				High	
2. Social intimacy: having common friends	1	2	3	4	5	6
3. Intellectual intimacy: sharing ideas	1	2	3	4	5	6
4. Sexual intimacy: sharing affection and sex	1	2	3	4	5	6
5. Recreational intimacy: doing pleasurable things together	1	2	3	4	5	6
6. Spiritual intimacy: having a similar sense regarding the meaning of life	1	2	3	4	5	6
7. Aesthetic intimacy: sharing the experience of beauty	1	2	3	4	5	6

IV. Eight Facets of Intimacy (adapted from Waring [1984])

Using the scale below, rate your present relationship on each facet of intimacy.

Variable of Intimacy	Low					High
1. Conflict Resolution: how effectively conflicts are resolved	1	2	3	4	5	6
2. Affection: feeling of emotional closeness	1	2	3	4	5	6
3. Cohesion: feeling of commitment to the relationship	1	2	3	4	5	6
4. Sexuality: degree to which sexual needs are met	1	2	3	4	5	6
5. Identity: your level of self-confidence and esteem as a couple	1	2	3	4	5	6
6. Compatibility: the degree to which you can work and play together comfortably	1	2	3	4	5	6
7. Expressiveness: sharing of thoughts, feelings, beliefs in the relationship; self-disclosure	1	2	3	4	5	6
8. Autonomy: success in gaining independence from your families of origin and your children	1	2	3	4	5	6

References

Alperin, R. M. (2001). Barriers to intimacy: An object relations perspective. *Psychoanalytic Psychology, 18*(1), 137–156.

Aplerin, R. M. (2006). Impediments to intimacy. *Clinical Social Work Journal, 34,* 559–572.

Burns, D. D. (1980). *Feeling good: The new mood therapy.* New York: New American Library.

Butler, M. H., Davis, S. D., & Seedall, R. B. (2008). Common pitfalls of beginning therapists utilizing enactments. *Journal of Marital and Family Therapy, 34,* 329–352.

Butler, M. H., & Gardner, B. C. (2003). Adapting enactments to couples reactivity: Five developmental stages. *Journal of Marital and Family Therapy, 29,* 311–327.

Clinebell, H. J., & Clinebell, C. H. (1970). *The intimate marriage.* New York: Harper and Row.

Cordova, J. V., & Scott, R. (2001). Intimacy: A behavioral interpretation. *Behavior Analyst, 24,* 75–86.

Dattilio, F. M. (2005). Couples. In N. Kazantzis, F. P. Deane, D. R. Ronan, & L. L'Abate (Eds.), *Using homework assignments in cognitive behavior therapy* (pp. 153–170). New York: Routledge.

Davis, S. D., & Butler, M. H. (2004). Enacting relationships in marriage and family therapy: A conceptual and operational definition of an enactment. *Journal of Marital and Family Therapy, 30,* 319–333.

Downey, L. (2001). Intimacy and the relational self. *Australian and New Zealand Journal of Family Therapy, 22*(3), 129–136.

Emmers-Sommer, T. (2004). The effect of communication quality and quantity indicators on intimacy and relational satisfaction. *Journal of Social and Personal Relationships, 21,* 399–411.

Fife, S. T. (2004). *A grounded theory of the therapist's perspective of therapeutic change for married couples in chronic conflict.* Unpublished doctoral dissertation, Brigham Young University.

Fife, S. T., Weeks, G. R., & Gambescia, N. (2008). Treating infidelity: An integrative approach. *Family Journal: Counseling and Therapy for Couples and Families, 16*(4), 316–323.

Gottman, J. M. (1994). *What predicts divorce: The relationship between marital processes and marital outcomes.* Hillsdale, NJ: Erlbaum.

Gottman, J. M., & Levinson, R. W., (1999). What predicts change in marital interaction over time? A study of alternative models. *Family Process, 38,* 143–158.

Gottman, J. M., & Levinson, R. W. (2002). A two-factor model for predicting when a couple will divorce: Exploratory analyses using 14-year longitudinal data. *Family Process, 41,* 83–96.

Greef, A. P., & Malherbe, H. L. (2001). Intimacy and marital satisfaction in spouses. *Journal of Sex and Marital Therapy, 27,* 247–257.

Greenberg, L. S., James, P. S., & Conry, R. F. (1988). Perceived change in couples therapy. *Journal of Family Psychology, 2,* 5–23.

Johnson, S. M., Makinen, J. A., & Millikin, J. W. (2001). Attachment injuries in couple relationships: A new perspective on impasses in couples therapy. *Journal of Marital and Family Therapy, 27,* 145–155.

Kayser, K., & Himle, D. P. (1994). Dysfunctional beliefs about intimacy. *Journal of Cognitive Psychotherapy, 8,* 127–140.

L'Abate, L. (1977). *Enrichment: Structural interventions with couples, families and groups.* Washington, DC: University Press of America.

L'Abate, L. (1999). Taking the bull by the horns: Beyond talk in psychological interventions. *Family Journal: Counseling and Therapy for Couples and Families, 7*(3), 206–220.

Laurenceau, J. P., Barrett, L. F., & Rovine, M. J. (2005). The interpersonal process model of intimacy in marriage: A daily-diary and multilevel modeling approach. *Journal of Family Psychology, 19*(2), 314–323.

Martin, J. L., & Ashby, J. S. (2004). Perfectionism and fear of intimacy: Implications for relationships. *Family Journal, 12,* 368–374.

Mirgain, S. A., & Cordova, J. V. (2007). Emotion skills and marital health: The association between observed and self-reported emotion skills, intimacy, and marital satisfaction. *Journal of Social and Clinical Psychology, 26*(9), 983–1009.

Mosier, W. (2006). Intimacy: The key to a healthy relationship. *Annals of the American Psychotherapy Association, 9*(1), 34–35.

Popovic, M. (2005). Intimacy and its relevance in human functioning. *Sexual and Relationship Therapy, 20,* 31–49.

Sager, C. (1976). *Marriage contracts and couples therapy: Hidden forces in intimate relationships.* New York: Brunner/Mazel.

Schaefer, M., & Olson, D. (1981). Assessment of intimacy: The PAIR inventory. *Journal of Marital and Family Therapy, 7,* 47–60.

Snyder, M. (2000). The loss and recovery of erotic intimacy in primary relationships: Narrative therapy and relationship enhancement therapy. *Family Journal, 8,* 37–46.

Sternberg, R. (1986). A triangular theory of love. *Psychological Review, 93*(2), 119–135.

Sternberg, R. (1997). Construct validation of a triangular theory of love. *European Journal of Social Psychology, 27,* 313–335.

Sullivan, H. S. (1953). *The interpersonal theory of psychiatry.* New York: Norton.

Waring, E. M. (1981). Facilitating marital intimacy through self-disclosure. *American Journal of Family Therapy, 9,* 33–42.

Waring, E. M. (1984). The measurement of marital intimacy. *Journal of Marital and Family Therapy, 10,* 185–192.

Weeks, G. R. (1995). Commitment and intimacy. In G. R. Weeks & L. Hof (Eds.), *Integrative solutions: Treating common problems in couples therapy* (pp. 21–54). New York: Brunner/Mazel.

Weeks, G. R., Gambescia, N., & Jenkins, R. E. (2003). *Treating infidelity: Therapeutic dilemmas and effective strategies.* New York: Norton.

Weeks, G. R., & Treat, S. (2001). *Couples in treatment: Techniques and approaches for effective practice* (2nd ed.). Philadelphia: Brunner/Routledge.

Wright, L. M., Watson, W. L., & Bell, J. M. (1996). *Beliefs: The heart of healing in families and illness.* New York: Basic Books.

CHAPTER 11

Internet Infidelity

Guidelines for Recovering Intimacy

KATHERINE M. HELM

Romantic relationships in the Western world often reflect the expectation that partners have an emotionally intimate connection with each other (Yarab, Sensibaugh, & Allgeier, 1998). Couples "fall in love with each other" and see this as a critical element for beginning and maintaining a romantic relationship together (Sternberg, 1988). Sternberg's Triangular Theory of Love describes the types of love: intimacy, passion, and commitment. He stated that relationships that stand the test of time have high levels of emotional intimacy and commitment. *Emotional intimacy* is a significant interpersonal and emotional connection between two individuals based on trust, love, understanding, and fidelity. The "rules" governing romantic relationships are often not communicated between partners; however, most couples believe that sexual fidelity is an automatically understood norm governing their relationships (Leiblum & Döring, 2002). In dating relationships, most individuals follow serial monogamy patterns where they are sexually faithful to each other while the relationship exists and then to their next romantic partners (King, 2008). Within the past 15 years the Internet has become an explosive force. This force shapes our communication patterns, increases our interpersonal accessibility, and augments sociocultural norms for accessing and processing information about a diverse array of topics (Cooper & Griffin-Shelley, 2002). Additionally, "a new sexual revolution has begun with the explosion of electronic technology, computers, and the rapid expansion of the Internet. These technologies are revolutionizing the ways in which we communicate, live our daily lives, establish communities, and work" (Jerome et al., 2000, as cited in Cooper & Griffin-Shelley, 2002, p. 407). This chapter will explore Internet infidelity as a threat to emotional intimacy in romantic relationships. Guidelines for recognizing Internet infidelity, specific treatment strategies, and implications for training will be reviewed.

Relationship Scripts and Couples' Contracts

Foundational to the development of romantic relationships is the concept of relationship scripts. Throughout childhood and into adulthood, we develop scripts or ideas about how we think our romantic relationships should proceed. These scripts include our rules, norms, values, and expectations. For example, most couples' scripts include the expectation of sexual fidelity (Whitty & Carr, 2005). Sex is supposed to be within a couple's committed relationship only. Romantic relationship scripts are powerful schemas that often heavily influence our feelings about our relationships. For example, if one partner's script reflects her expectation that her partner will share emotionally intimate data with her on a regular basis, while her partner does not have this expectation (and therefore does not share his or her emotional reactions), she is likely to be hurt, disappointed, and dissatisfied in the relationship. Couples are usually unaware of all of the "rules" and expectations in their scripts and therefore do not talk about it until one partner unknowingly breaks a "rule" of the other partner. Fitness (2001) finds that the key to defining betrayal lies in deciphering the couple's relationship script. Most couples do not have a script governing online romantic relationships because the notion of online relationships is still so new. This is supported in several survey studies that have found that when presented with a hypothetical scenario of a partner potentially cheating online, many participants were not convinced that this was "real" betrayal. Subsequent studies demonstrate that this attitude is rapidly changing. Whitty's (2005) later studies of Internet infidelity find participants viewing acts of cybersex as significant forms of emotional and sometimes sexual betrayal. A recent study by Whitty and Quigley (2008) investigated gender differences in attitudes about online and offline sexual and emotional infidelity. Their findings indicated that men found sexual infidelity more upsetting while women found emotional infidelity most disturbing. Interestingly, male and female participants did not assume that just because someone was having cybersex did not indicate one's being in love with his or her cybersex partners, nor did being in love (e.g., emotional infidelity) with someone online automatically mean there was a cybersexual relationship. These results speak to our conflicted attitudes about what infidelity actually is and how betrayals over the Internet only complicate our definition of infidelity. This underscores the importance of couples therapists assessing how the Internet impacts individual couples' scripts and that couples themselves should discuss their views with each other about developing relationships over the Internet.

In the treatment of Internet infidelity, clinicians can be helpful to their clients by expanding both their clients' and their own scripts to include discussions of appropriate and inappropriate (unacceptable) behavior over the Internet. This can go a long way in preventing hurtful boundary violations that threaten emotional intimacy between the couple.

The Attraction of the Internet

Cooper (1997) believes that the Internet is powered by the "Triple-A Engine." This "Triple-A Engine" accelerates and intensifies sexuality and the formation of romantic relationships online. The three components of the "Triple-A Engine" are: accessibility, affordability, and anonymity. His research defines these components in the following way:

Access: The Internet is available, convenient, and easy to use. Individuals can log in at work and at home. It is a virtual store that is open 24 hours a day, 7 days a week.

Affordability: Once an individual has a computer and an Internet connection, actual use of the Internet is inexpensive.

Anonymity: The belief (whether it is true or not) that one's identity is concealed online can have a powerful effect on sexual expression. "The use of the Internet increases the sense of freedom, willingness to experiment, pace of self-disclosure, as well as enhancing a person's ability to talk openly about their sexual questions, concerns, fantasies, and willingness to buy sexual materials online" (Branwyn, 1993, p. 785).

Cooper (1998) finds that the use of the Internet for sexual purposes can be classified in three broad categories: commercial aspects, positive connections, and negative patterns. It is now the norm for individuals to buy and sell things online and have their own personalized Web pages. Individuals also utilize the Internet to make social connections with people all over the world. For example, "the Internet can provide a sense of community and belongingness to those who are isolated (e.g., gays or lesbians, rape survivors, illness sufferers)" (Cooper & Griffin-Shelley, 2002, p. 8). In this way, the Internet can serve as an important form of social support for individuals who may not be able to access support from other sources. Another positive utility is the use of the Internet for information about mental, physical, and sexual health issues. Individuals can readily access important health information quickly, without having to physically leave their homes or consult health professionals for basic information.

There are some problematic issues associated with Internet use. Some negative influences of the Internet are Internet affairs, compulsive sexual behavior utilizing Internet adult sex sites, and those who compulsively use the Internet as a way to avoid coping with real-life problems. An individual can create a social identity online that is inconsistent with whom he or she really is (Atwood, 2005). Because of the availability, affordability, and accessibility of the Internet, individuals can easily become addicted. Although an in-depth discussion of sexually compulsive behavior over the Internet is beyond the scope of this chapter, a review of Internet pornography addictions will be provided. "Over half of all U.S. households (172 million) have Internet access while an estimated 20 to 33 percent of Internet users go online for sexual purposes. Most are male, about 35 years old, married with children, and well educated" (Dew & Chaney, 2005 as cited in Corley, 2006; p. 93; Cooper, McLoughlin, & Campbell, 2000). Some (Cooper, Putnam, Planchon, & Boies, 1999; Cooper, Scherer, Boies, & Gordon, 1999; Cooper, Delmonicao, & Burg, 2000; Cooper, McLoughlin, & Campbell, 2000) estimate that as many as 17% become addicted to online sexual behaviors, although most people who access the Internet for sex are recreational (not compulsive) users (Cooper, Putnam et al., 1999; Cooper, Delmonicao, & Burg, 2000).

Addictions to the Internet are on the rise. In their study of 164 marriage and family therapists, Goldberg, Peterson, Rosen, and Sara (2008) found that clinicians are reporting sharp increases in the numbers of clients presenting with cybersex issues and addictions. Similar to other forms of addiction, obsessive Internet use significantly interferes with the development and maintenance of interpersonal relationships and social and occupational functioning. Although research that explores how Internet addictions impact the family system is in its infancy, early research suggests that Internet addictions negatively impact the entire family system (Goldberg et al., 2008).

Internet Infidelity

Infidelity is defined as a breach of faith occurring in multiple contexts, and any violation of the mutually agreed-upon rules or boundaries of a relationship (Wikipedia); or unfaithfulness; failure in loyalty; or failure in a moral obligation (*Webster's Dictionary*). Atwood (2005) estimates that 50–60% of married men and 45–55% of married women engage in extramarital sex at some time in their marriage. It has been noted that infidelity over the Internet is a growing trend and a new contributing factor to divorce (Whitty & Carr, 2005). One Web site (ashleymadison.com) is specifically designed for married people looking to begin an affair. All one needs to do is become a member, which guarantees exposure to like-minded individuals looking to explore romantic relationships outside of their marriages. In 2000 the *New York Times* reported that approximately one of four regular Internet users (21 million Americans) visited one of the 60,000 sex sites on the Web at least once a month (Egan, 2001). Cooper, Morahan-Martin, Maheu, & Mathy (2000) conducted a large-scale study (7,000 randomly selected visitors to msnbc.com) examining many different areas of cybersex. They found that 20% of the individuals in their sample engaged in some kind of online sexual activity; half of the individuals in the study believed that online sexual activity influenced their sexual relationships with their romantic partners, and approximately 13% of participants identified these effects as negative. Nearly two thirds of the people engaging in online sexual activity are married or in committed relationships and of the remaining one third, more than half are involved in a romantic or sexual relationship with a "nonvirtual partner"(Maheu & Subotnik, 2001). Additionally, 45% of female respondents viewed cybersex as infidelity, while only 40% of men did. Sixty percent of people who had already engaged in cybersex did not think that it violated their marriage vows. It is often the case that couples struggle with the question of "Is it cheating if there is no sexual contact?" Is "virtual cheating" a legitimate phenomenon?

Because the notion of affairs over the Internet is still so new, clinicians and spouses alike often question the legitimacy of calling certain behaviors "cheating" when the two involved individuals have not met in person. Erotic attractions to others are natural and normal. Within themselves, they do not constitute a breach of a couple's contract to remain faithful to each other; however, when these attractions are acted upon, this is generally considered to be unfaithful behavior. Maheu and Subotnik (2001) believe an important part of determining whether or not infidelity exists in relation to the Internet has to do with exploring intent. If one's intent begins or becomes intimate, erotic, or secretive, this constitutes Internet infidelity. They state that "Cyber-infidelity occurs when a partner in a committed relationship uses the computer or the Internet to violate promises, vows, or agreements concerning his or her sexual exclusivity" (p. 119). In their work, Atwood and Seifer (1997), Shaw (1997), and Lusterman (1998) have also explored and defined Internet infidelity as an infidelity that consists of taking energy of any sort (thoughts, feelings, and behaviors) outside the committed relationship in ways that damage interactions within the couple and negatively impact intimacy within the relationship. Shaw stated that anything that is deliberately hidden can create emotional distance from one's partner, and Lusterman discussed Internet infidelity as a breach of trust. He further reflected that along with the vow couples assume in remaining sexually exclusive, most couples expect to have a level of emotional intimacy not shared by others.

In their work on Internet infidelity, several researchers report that a spouse's discovery of intimate contact over the Internet by their partners brings about feelings of extreme hurt, betrayal, anger, loss of self-esteem, and a questioning of the foundation of the relationship (Atwood, 2005; Cooper, Delmonicao, & Burg, 2000; Lusterman, 2005; Maheu & Sabotnik, 2001; Reid & Gray, 2006). "When one partner shares an emotional connection with one participating cyber-friend on the Internet, they use a great deal of time thinking about each other and writing to each other. It is easy for them to become deeply involved with one another to the detriment of their own primary romantic relationships" (Atwood, 2005, p. 118). These relationships can quickly become emotionally intense. When the nonparticipating partner discovers his or her spouse's or partner's intimate connection with another person over the Internet, he or she often feels betrayed. Betrayed partners feel a profound sense of loss—the sense of specialness and emotional intimacy between themselves and their partners has been ruptured. These feelings are the same feelings reported by betrayed partners who are the victims of physical (as opposed to virtual) sexual affairs. There are far more similarities between Internet affairs and physical affairs than differences. The complicating factor with Internet infidelity is that betrayed partners often question whether they have a right to feel so hurt, given that their partners may not have engaged in sexual contact with the cyberspace friend.

Even emotional affairs can carry with them feelings of betrayal and hurt by the noninvolved partner. Emotional affairs can be defined as an intimate emotional connection with another individual (in heterosexual relationships this person is usually of the opposite sex) where one consistently shares information with the other that he or she does not share with his or her romantic partner (Buss & Shackelford, 1997; Drigotas, Safstrom, & Gentilia, 1999; Spring, 1996). This information is often about the problems being experienced in the romantic relationship. In this way, emotional affairs threaten the intimacy of the primary romantic relationship. They engender a sense of closeness, which ends up not being shared with one's romantic partner. Additionally, Maheu and Sabotnik (2001) stated that even though there is no sexual intimacy present, the emotional connection felt with this other individual outside of the romantic relationship can easily become romantic and plant seeds of eroticism. This can quickly become a slippery slope leading to sexual infidelity (Glass, 2000). Emotional affairs are easily developed online. Because the Internet allows individuals worldwide access to others who share common interests, values, and social needs, it is readily utilized as a tool to connect like-minded individuals. Glass (2000) states that "Secrecy, emotional attachment, and sexual intimacy (which can consist of flirting and innuendo), are the hallmarks of an online relationship which has crossed the line of platonic friendship and drifted into an emotional affair" (as cited in Maheu & Sabotnik, 2001, p. 111).

Reasons for Internet Infidelity

Individuals engage in online affairs for many of the same reasons an individual would engage in a face-to-face, physical affair. Having an affair is an escape from the problems of life and the work of the primary romantic relationship (Brown, 2001). Individuals engage in cyber-infidelity to cope with life transitions, deal with feelings of loneliness and stress, as a way to compensate for poor relationship and communication skills, to engage in the fantasy of his or her "ideal" versus "real" self, and to reinforce narcissistic beliefs about oneself (Cooper, Scherer et al., 1999; Shackelford & Buss, 1997). Cyber-affairs allow both involved individuals to project their ideal mates and perfect love relationships onto each other (Atwood, 2005). Maheu and Subotnik (2001) also found that people have cyber-relationships to cope with feelings of dissatisfaction with their existing relationships where they lack the skills or desire to make necessary changes. Cyber-affairs contribute to one's feeling appreciated and alive. They allow individuals to "test their worth" in the dating market with minimal risk of emotional exposure and sexually transmitted infections. Lastly, positive reinforcement from cyber-partners boosts self-esteem. These can be powerful stimuli. Because email can be sent in near real time; Maheu and Subotnik (2001, p. 26) state that "email and chat rooms seem to accelerate romance and seduction and frequent contacts change (and speed up) our perception of intimacy. For example, in normal time, dates might be spread out over a few weeks, but online, individuals can connect multiple times a day when they are just starting to get to know each other. The Internet allows for private access to cyber-partners day or night, which makes reinforcement nearly immediate."

Sometimes cyber-affairs begin innocently. Individuals with common interests (e.g., a child suffering from cancer, a hobby, etc.) begin chatting in a chat room to connect around these interests. However, these initially innocent relationships can cross the line between friendship and sexually intimacy, even if there is no physical contact. These contacts usually begin with flirting and compliments and can quickly grow into sexual innuendo and mutual masturbation (Leiblum & Döring, 2002). McKenna and Bargh (1998) discussed the relationship between individuals "trying on" different sexual identities as a first step in altering offline sexual behavior. This is often called cybersex. *Cybersex* is defined by Cooper and Griffin-Shelley (2002) as using the medium of the Internet to engage in sexually gratifying activities, such as looking at pictures, participating in sexual chat, or exchanging explicit sexual images or emails. The present chapter largely explores how cybersex is harmful to primary romantic relationships when one partner engages in these activities in secret or lies to a partner about his or her cybersexual behavior. There are, however, positive aspects of cybersex. For example, when couples consensually seek out sexual information on the Internet to enhance their sex lives, this can be beneficial to their relationship and enhance emotional and sexual intimacy.

Offline and online affairs share many similarities such as patterns of minimization, secrecy, and deception on the part of the engaged partner. Maheu and Sabotnik (2001) stated that cyber-affairs are easier to hide because contact can happen at work and home at multiple times during the day. Additionally, these affairs can be supported through legitimate uses of the computer ("Honey, I am going upstairs to pay bills."). Bowen (1978) found that infidelity can often be a misguided attempt to manage anxiety and cope with feelings of low self-esteem (Reid & Gray, 2006). With an online partner, emotional support and positive reinforcement are usually the basis for the relationship. Thus, the minimization of anxiety and the support of one's sense of self are easily met in these relationships. Online partners rarely demand that the bills be paid, the garbage be taken out, focus on one's shortcomings, or tell their partners about their disappointments in the relationship. This makes comparisons between the primary romantic relationship and the virtual one very difficult on the nonbetraying partner. The real-life partner always falls short of the virtual one.

Real-life partners find it extremely difficult to compete with a virtual partner in part because virtual partners often have lower intimacy demands than virtual ones. Intimacy involves honesty, trust, and self-disclosing one's vulnerabilities. It is an anxiety-ridden task that "requires the capacity to stay emotionally connected to significant others during anxious times, while taking a clear position for self, based on one's values, beliefs, and principles." However, "people engaging in virtual romance report astonishingly strong feelings of intimacy even though most have never met their online partners" (Schnarch, 1997; as cited in Maheu & Subotnik, 2001, p. 121). Clearly, individuals engaging in online affairs feel deeply connected to their online partners. Similarly, real-life partners feel wronged upon discovery of an online affair. This answers the question whether online affairs are real—absolutely!

Signs and Patterns of Internet Infidelity

Maheu and Subotnik (2001) have reviewed the signs of an Internet affair. They include:

> *Preoccupation and distance:* Partner is preoccupied with getting to the computer; he or she is emotionally distant; seems distracted.
> *Changing sleep schedule:* Partner uses the computer at odd times of the day or night; a corresponding sign is the desire to skip family activities and stay home on the computer.

Insistence upon more privacy: When the primary romantic partner (PRP) walks into the room, the computer is suddenly shut off or the screen is quickly minimized; the cyber-engaged partner (CEP) keeps the door closed when using the computer or complains when the PRP enters the room; spends increasing amounts of time on the computer; questions about online activity are met with irritability, jokes, sarcasm, or other noninformative answers. This is a more serious indicator of a secret Internet life.

Lying: Things do not add up but when the PRP directly questions specific events, expenses, or behaviors, the PRP receives answers that continue to raise questions; the CEP hesitates or stumbles with an explanation or looks away or gives other signs of avoiding the truth; lies include repeated promises that time at the computer will soon end but it does not. CEP appears to be stalling.

Overreacting: The CEP flies off the handle when the PRP questions his or her Internet activities. The CEP may also use anger to intimidate the PRP, which prevents any further confrontation. Drama is used to cover the truth or the threat of discovery, which is a variation of the lying response.

Stonewalling: Another form of lying, which includes the CEP's refusal to answer any questions about Internet use; gives short, noncommittal responses when questioned about the computer; avoids any discussion about his or her computer use.

Decreasing interest in responsibilities: Disinterred in shared relationship responsibilities (e.g., children's activities, household chores, hobbies). Could be due to partner's preoccupation with online fantasies.

Decreasing interest in PRP: There is a noticeable decrease in activities spent with the PRP. This is especially a problem if it is sudden. The CEP shows a decreased interest in making holiday or vacation plans or in long-term plans for large expenses or discussing retirement together. The CEP takes less opportunity to talk about work, events, extended family, or future goals.

Differing sexual contact: The CEP refuses to have sex or the CEP's normal sexual behavior (likes and dislikes) changes. The CEP appears preoccupied when having sex with the PRP; the PRP feels used during sex. The CEP requests trying different sexual behaviors not previously discussed. The CEP speaks to the PRP differently during sex.

Signs of sexual activity without PRP: The CEP wears "easy access clothing" while in the computer room, making masturbation easier to hide. The PRP notices the CEP gets aroused or excited when approaching or at the computer.

Sudden changes in appearance.
New expenses (e.g., credit card).

Cooper, Putnam, Planchon, and Bois (1999a) find that there are various types of cyber-relationships. They divide cybersex users into three categories: recreational users, "at-risk" users, and sexually compulsive users. Cybersexual relationships are focused on sex and sexual experiences. This is in contrast to earlier chapter discussions on emotional affairs, which center around the development of romantic relationships online. Both cybersex and emotional infidelity can be considered types of Internet infidelity. According to Cooper, Putnam et al. (1999), *recreational users* access online sexual connections out of curiosity and for the purposes of occasional sexual pleasure. *Sexually compulsive users* spent at least 11 hours per week online engaged in cybersex activities. *At-risk persons* are those who have no prior history of online sexual online yet when afforded the opportunity would spend substantial time and energy online engaged in cybersex activities.

Although sexually compulsive behavior is rare, the rapid expansion of pornography over the Internet has significantly contributed to the growing numbers of individuals (usually but not always male) who are addicted to online pornography (Delmonico, Griffin, & Carnes, 2002). Greenfield and Orzack (2002, p. 133) stated that "There is little agreement among the psychiatric and psychological communities with regard to compulsive sexual behavior and even less when it comes to the Internet as a mediating or enabling factor." However, they found that clinicians are reporting an alarming increase in the numbers of clients struggling with Internet pornography addictions. The issue is complicated by cybersex users' adamant denial that their online sexual behavior is detrimental to their primary romantic relationships and families. Schneider (2002) refers to compulsive cybersex behaviors as the "new pink elephant" in the living room because oftentimes partners and families go to great lengths to minimize the impact the CEP's compulsive Internet behavior has on the family.

Effects of Cybersex and Internet Infidelity on the Relationship

Internet infidelity readily takes a toll on the primary romantic relationship. Even before the CEP's indiscretions are discovered, negative effects can be seen. Some effects such as time away from one's PRP and family, loss of physical and emotional intimacy, loss of trust, a breach of the couple contract, an erosion of the specialness of the primary romantic relationship, and a loss of self-esteem and identity for the betrayed partner have already been reviewed. Other consequences such as the betrayed partner becoming physically violent toward the CEP, the normalization of sexually dysfunctional acts (e.g., violence during sex), and feelings of shame, humiliation, abandonment, isolation, devastation, and anger—sometimes on the part of both partners—can be experienced as effects of Internet infidelity (Schneider, 2002). Similar to the discovery of a face-to-face physical affair, online affairs and cybersex often disrupt the sexual relationship within the primary romantic relationship. In Schneider's (2002) study of cybersex addicts, two thirds of the 94 respondents (68%) described sexual problems in the couple relationship, usually coinciding with the beginning of the cybersex activities. She further reported that 52% of the cybersex users had decreased interest in relational sex as had one third of the spouses. In approximately 18%, both partners had decreased interest. Only 32% of the couples were still interested in each other sexually.

In situations where Internet infidelity is cybersex (not relationally) focused, PRPs are often repelled by the pornographic images their partners are using to achieve sexual gratification. Reid and Gray (2006) cited other harmful effects on relationships as being distorted views of sexual intimacy; decreased emotional, spiritual, and physical intimacy; decreased sensitivity, tenderness, and kindness; financial instability and possible job loss; and strained communications and conflicts between partners as other harmful effects of cybersex. PRP's struggle to understand "why am I not good enough?" or ask themselves "what did I do to make this happen?" As a function of Internet infidelity, PRPs often question the primary relationship identity (i.e., we are not who I thought we were; you are not who I thought you were; and who am I now?). In reaction to the discovery of Internet infidelity, the PRP may initially try to have sex more often with the CEP, even to the point of engaging in sexual behaviors he or she is not comfortable with as a way of luring his or her partner away from the Internet (Schneider, 2002). The PRP may make promises to stop; however, because of the reinforcing nature of the Internet affairs, many CEPs find it difficult to stop engaging with their online partners. As a result, CEPs tend to lie about their online sexual activities, and PRPs may become hypervigilant of their partner's computer use. Each of these behaviors contributes to the emotional distancing of the couple from each other.

When infidelity occurs online, betrayed partners often have to justify to themselves whether or not they should feel infidelity has occurred and whether or not they should be as hurt and angry about it as they are. Obviously, psychotherapy can be helpful in guiding the PRP through this questioning process. Betrayed partners may question if they even want to stay in the relationship. Schneider (2002) reviewed the stages a PRP may go through when their partners are engaging in Internet infidelity. They include:

Stage 1: Ignorance/Denial: The PRP believes the CEP's denials, explanations, and promises while ignoring his or her own feelings of doubt and concern. The PRP may blame him- or herself for sexual problems that may be present.

Stage 2: Shock/Discovery of the Cybersex Activities: The PRP either accidentally or as a result of deliberate investigation discovers the betrayal. Gone are the PRP's ignorance and denial. Feelings of shock, anger, pain, hopelessness, confusion, and shame ensue. Even after discovery by the PRP, the CEP, despite repeated promises to stop his or her behavior, often does not. Cybersex users are often embarrassed and sometimes feel remorseful, which leads them to want to try to protect their PRP from the pain of the full evidence of their cybersex behavior. At this stage the CEP can also react with anger and denial ("I am not cheating. You are making a big deal out of nothing."). The PRP may begin to buy into this statement and question him- or herself.

Stage 3: Problem-Solving Attempts: The PRP may begin to take action that may be perceived by the CEP as trying to control him or her. The PRP may obsessively monitor the CEP's computer usage, asking for full disclosure after every use. The PRP may react by purchasing software to block certain sites and by thinking about his or her partner's cybersex use constantly. Finally, the PRP may engage in "snooping" behavior where he or she spends a great deal of time looking for evidence of cybersex behavior.

The literature on Internet affairs and cybersex clearly demonstrates that these experiences are traumatic for PRPs. They are no less traumatic and damaging because the infidelity occurred on the Internet. Internet infidelity is still a significant breach of trust and faithfulness regardless of whether sexual contact occurred. Additionally, when a CEP is discovered to have an addiction to the Internet for sexual purposes, this further complicates the treatment of couples seeking psychotherapy.

Treatment Guidelines for Recovering Intimacy From Internet Infidelity

Many couples consider psychotherapy when they are at a crisis point in their relationship. Frequently, one or both members of the couple are considering ending the relationship and none of their individual and combined problem-solving strategies have worked. There has been a great deal of research on effective psychotherapeutic interventions for couples (Brown, 2001; Gottman, 1999; Nelson, Piercy, & Sprenkle, 2005) from multiple theoretical perspectives; however, empirical study of the treatment of Internet infidelity is new. Hertlein and Webster (2008) recently reviewed some of the existing studies that examined ways in which technology impacts relationships negatively. Their findings demonstrated that men who meet people online to date are more likely than women to transfer these behaviors offline, that secretive cybersex behavior negatively impacts couples and can be a factor in separation or divorce, that Internet infidelity had a high degree of emotional involvement, and that partners who found their spouse or partner engaging in an online relationship feel hurt, angry, and betrayed and experience a loss of self-esteem. Nelson et al. (2005) studied Internet infidelity using a multiphase Delphi methodology to identify and explore critical issues, interventions, and gender differences in the treatment of Internet infidelity. Three vignettes were developed representing different types (degrees) of Internet infidelity based on the clinical experiences of 78 randomly selected expert clinicians. A sample of eight clinicians was interviewed regarding their evaluations and clinical judgments for each vignette. They were asked to identify (a) the critical issues that need to be addressed by therapists when working with the couple or family in the vignette, (b) what interventions he or she would use to address these critical issues in therapy, and (c) if the genders of the participants were changed within the vignette, how might his or her treatment approach change. The authors hypothesized that experts would believe that special expertise was required to work with Internet infidelity cases, as suggested by the research of Cooper, Scherer et al. (1999), Schnarch (1997), and Shaw (1997). Contrary to earlier research, Nelson et al. (2005) found that in their study the treatment of Internet infidelity did not require special clinical expertise. Clinician respondents seemed to feel that Internet infidelity was simply another type of infidelity and therefore a breach of intimacy, trust, and the couple's contract. This finding did not vary by vignette, even though each vignette presented differing levels of boundary violations from flirting to sexual innuendo to sexual contact. Nelson et al. found that "Apparently the context through which the infidelity developed, as well as the level of involvement, is seen as more 'symptomatic' issues of the underlying problem" (2005, p. 188). Below are some treatment guidelines for couples therapists to help their clients cope with Internet infidelity. Some of them are specific to online infidelity, whereas others are general models for treating infidelity.

It is critical that couples therapy begins with a thorough assessment of the presenting (and often hidden) issue(s). Couples therapists need to ask specifically about Internet use within the home. With regard to Internet infidelity, Greenfield and Orzack (2002) suggested that clinicians should assess the following: (a) Does this behavior interfere with the major spheres of daily living (e.g., work, kids, school, health, social and family relationships, etc.)? and (b) What is the context in which the behavior occurs? For example, a clinician must evaluate whether or not an individual's use of the Internet for sexual stimulation is the core issue (e.g., sexually compulsive behavior) or whether his or her use of the Internet in this way is symptomatic of sexual or emotional problems between the couple. Assessment of the impact online sexual behavior has on a couple is difficult because many CEPs do not believe that online flirting, sexual innuendo, masturbating, or developing close relationships with online partners negatively impacts their primary romantic relationship (Cooper, Delmonicao, & Burg, 2000; Greenfield & Orzack, 2002; Reid & Gray, 2006). Therefore, an important part of couples therapy would be in dealing with the CEP's denial of the betrayal, simply because it occurred over the Internet and not in person.

Further assessment should consist of determining if couples can commit to a course of couples therapy and if they can commit to staying in the relationship while the work of couples therapy proceeds. Obviously, these commitments change over time and clinicians' assessment of their clients' commitment to the process is ongoing. Maheu and Subotnik (2001) also suggested that the emotional connection to the CEP's virtual lover be explored. Specifically, is the CEP willing to end the online affair? If so, what demonstrations of good faith is the CEP willing to put forth? If the CEP has developed a close emotional attachment to his or her online partner, the CEP will grieve the loss of the relationship. If this grieving process is hidden from the PRP, this can inhibit healing and cause more distrust. Additionally, secretive grieving on the part of the CEP increases the likelihood that he or she will continue the affair. Most couples therapists do not support engaging a couple in the process of psychotherapy if one partner refuses to end his or her affair.

Bowenian family therapy has been utilized with couples to help them understand their family of origin patterns as an underlying dynamic to their current issues, as well as the multigenerational transmission of infidelity (Moultrup, 1990). This theory believes that our first models of relationships came from our families of origin (FOO). Additionally, this is where relationship scripts are developed. Helping couples understand how their patterns of relating to each other developed (by exploring each person's family of origin's dynamics) can often provide couples with insight regarding their current issues. For example, it is frequently the case that one or both partners saw evidence of infidelity in their FOOs. FOO infidelity is often shrouded in shame and secrecy. In these cases, messages transmitted to children are usually, "Do as I say (infidelity is wrong) and not as I do." Couples should understand how their history, current stressors, communication patterns, and unmet emotional needs contributed to the current breach of intimacy.

Emotionally focused therapy (Greenberg & Johnson, 1988) views adult love relationships through attachment theory (Bowlby, 1989). Briefly, attachment theory examines the emotional attachments we form to our primary caregivers as infants and children. It states that human beings need emotional attachments to survive. These attachments can be secure (where one feels consistently safe and loved, even if the attachment figure is not present), anxious (where one is consistently worried that the attachment figure will leave them; relationships are consistently distressed), or avoidant (an individual avoids interpersonal attachments) (Ainsworth, 1989). This theory states that we carry these attachments forward into our adult love relationships and sometimes unknowingly act out potentially unhealthy relationship patterns based on our early experiences with attachment relationships. For example, a child whose parent was emotionally unavailable to him or her may have abandonment issues in which she chronically fears being left. Therefore, in adult relationships, she fears deep emotional attachment to others. As a result she may destruct relationships so that the other person will leave (or she will leave) before a deep emotional attachment occurs where she can be hurt. Attachment theory can be used to help clinicians understand why an affair occurred (e.g., how an individual sought emotional connection with another to get his or her emotional needs met) and how the affair breached the couple's emotional bond with each other. Johnson (2002) summarized the goals of emotion-focused couples therapy as: (a) expanding constricted emotional responses that prime negative interaction patterns, (b) restructuring interactions so that partners become more accessible and responsive to each other, and (c) fostering positive cycles of comfort, caring, and bonding. She stated that "Therapists focus on emotion because it potently organizes key responses to intimate others, acts as an internal compass focusing people on their primary needs and goals, and primes key meaning schemas about the nature of self and others" (p. 21).

A significant part of successful couples therapy is managing the anxiety inside the room while continuing to do the work of therapy (Pittman & Wagers, 1995). Obviously, clinicians need to provide the couple with a safe environment in which to explore painful issues. This is done, in part, by not choosing sides, challenging partners equally on their relationship's disruptive behaviors, providing partners with needed validation of their feelings and need to be heard and understood, and finally, by informing couples of the process of couples therapy (i.e., informed consent). For example, I explain to couples that sometimes things get worse before they get better when working on the painful issue of infidelity. Additionally, the successful treatment of infidelity usually involves the betraying partner accepting responsibility for the intimacy breach and making clear and consistent demonstrations that he or she is trustworthy and will not do it again. Along the same continuum, the betrayed partner usually has to forgive and allow for closure so that the couple can move forward. These processes take a great deal of time and cannot be rushed by the couple or the therapist. Although healing is possible for many couples, not all couples are able to heal fully from infidelity.

Maheu and Subotnik (2001) suggested that the path to recovery from Internet infidelity includes four basic steps. Couples tend to cycle through these steps several times. Couples therapy can help couples understand and cope with the recovery process. The steps are:

1. *Coping with Emotions:* Learning to tolerate and manage strong emotional responses (rage, anxiety, depression, pain) while remaining connected to each other. Schnarch (1997, p. 18) believes this to be critical to the development of intimacy.
2. *Searching for Understanding:* Couples cannot get to this most critical step until they are able to reduce their emotional reactivity and think more clearly. This step involves improving communication skills, finding the reasons for the affair, looking at stresses and family history, and reaching an understanding about the infidelity.
3. *Reconstructing the Relationship:* This step helps the couple clarify what relationship they need. The emphasis is on correcting the cause(s) of the infidelity, looking at history, identifying individual needs, renewing their promise of fidelity, finding caring ways to relate to each other, and learning skills that bring them closer together and allow them ways to trust again.
4. *Finding Closure:* This last step puts closure on the cyber-affair through an apology, symbols that signify the end, and an agreement for the future of the relationship.

In the treatment of infidelity, Brown (2001) and Weiss (1975) discussed the betrayed partner's "obsessiveness" as a common and normal response to coping with a partner's infidelity. Weiss has deemed this coping mechanism "obsessive review." Obsessiveness is the ruminative thought process about the affair and causes the PRP a great deal of distress. Brown described this as the second stage of dealing with betrayal following shock. PRPs ruminate about why the affair occurred, what happened (sexual acts, the degree of emotional connectedness of their partner to the online partner, etc.) during the affair, if the affair is continuing, and questions about what this means for the relationship. Both describe this as a cognitive coping mechanism, which helps to defend the betrayed partner against emotional pain. Clinicians understand that this is a normal part of dealing with infidelity; however, if the PRP remains stuck in obsessive review, couples therapy will not be successful. The task then of the therapy is to validate the PRP's feelings and help him or her move through obsessive review. Behavioral strategies for decreasing obsessive review (OR) include relaxation strategies, limiting obsessive thoughts about the affair to a certain time of day and a specific period of time (e.g., 20–30 minutes), distraction strategies, journaling, physical exercise, and a gradual decrease in the amount of time for the OR (Brown, 2001; Maheu & Subotnik, 2001; Weiss, 1975). These strategies both validate the PRP's need to obsess and also help him or her move through the process. Therapy can also help the CEP cope with the PRP's OR and help educate him or her about how to answer the partner's questions about the affair and how to tolerate the OR.

Unlike face-to-face affairs, Internet affairs are detailed in online interactions sometimes accessible by the PRP. There are differing thoughts about how many of the details of an affair should be revealed to the PRP. Some experts feel that discussing the details are extremely important as a show of good faith by the betraying partner, while others feel that doing so causes more damage and prevents the clinician from getting to the "real" treatment issues (Brown, 2001; Maheu & Subotnik, 2001). Clinicians should use their best judgment regarding this issue, especially given that with online affairs, PRPs can access exactly what was said by the CEP to the online partner. In this way interventions will be twofold. Clinicians should consider, first, getting the CEP to agree to show the PRP the online interactions (knowing that this will be very painful for both partners) as a show of good faith, which can also combat some of the PRP's OR. Second, the PRP should agree to decrease his or her investigative behavior into their partner's online interactions. These interventions work in tandem with each other. Clinicians should be aware that partners' agreement to do these things takes time and commitment to the process of healing. However, this can go a long way toward reestablishing trust in the relationship.

Finally, clinicians can suggest some behavioral strategies for dealing with Internet infidelity. It is important to gain both partners' agreement when implementing these strategies and not to immediately suggest them. Another way of rebuilding trust in the relationship can be for the couple (together) to purchase computer monitoring or blocking software as well as moving the computer to a public place (family room) (Reid & Gray, 2006). Suggesting this too early in the therapeutic process could serve to alienate the CEP. These strategies are helpful for the PRP's OR, as an attempt for the CEP to accept accountability and make amends for hurting the partner.

A Word About Internet Sexual Compulsions

The treatment of sexually compulsive Internet behavior is well beyond the scope of this chapter; however, clinicians need to assess for it when conducting couples psychotherapy. Greenfield and Orzack (2002) stressed the importance of exploring the role online sexual behavior plays in the client's life in addition to the level of impairment or distress caused by the behavior. For example, evaluating how many hours a client spends online engaged in sexual activities, whether this behavior impacts his or her work performance (surfing sexual sites at work), the degree of impairment of sexual relationship with one's partner, and the amount of conflict this behavior is causing in a client's primary relationships should be part of the assessment. They suggested detailed self-monitoring on the part of clients in addition to an exploration of any triggers (e.g., stress, conflict) that precede online sexual behavior. Finally, clinicians should assess if their clients are engaged in any illegal sexual activity over the Internet (e.g., viewing child pornography sites). Sexually compulsive behaviors can easily go undiagnosed because clinicians fail to assess for them during routine intake interviews. The treatment of sexually compulsive behavior is similar to the treatment of other addictive behaviors; however, because the Internet is readily accessible and reinforcement is immediate, treating sexual addictions fueled by the Internet is a distinct challenge.

Implications for Training and Clinical Practice

Because the idea of infidelity committed through the computer is still so new, clinicians are not trained to assess for it in their work with clients. Additionally, couples who deal with their partners' boundary violations over the Internet still question their own emotional responses to "typed words." This response may be echoed by the CEP ("It's just words. Why are you upset over nothing?"). Clearly, there is confusion about this new form of infidelity, which has significant implications for training clinicians. Turkle (1995) underscored the importance of clinicians' recognition of the complexity of online interactions. She believes that it is possible to help clients use the Internet relationally in appropriate ways. From their study of Internet infidelity, Nelson et al. (2005) outlined several implications for training and clinical practice. They found:

1. There is no one "right way" of conducting therapy for those engaged in Internet infidelity. More research is needed to determine "right" interventions
2. Because the Internet increases one's chances of connecting with like-minded people, Internet infidelity cases could be more insidious to committed relationships as Internet partners may have an appeal that is greater than the "traditional" affair partner. Therapists will need to be particularly vigilant of the power and attraction that Internet relationships have upon spouses who have strayed.
3. Therapists can help their clients define for themselves what their definition of infidelity is as well as what needs the Internet affair relationship was meeting for the CEP. Therapists can help the PRP explore his or her role in the affair. Additionally, what insights were gained from the breach in intimacy?
4. Because affairs are overwhelming and emotionally draining, it is important for clinicians to foster a sense of hope in their clients.
5. Clearly, the arrival of the Internet challenges therapists to become even more efficient in helping couples to develop boundaries

around their relationship. The Internet is often an unchartered area. The Internet can be used in positive ways, so clinicians should assess how the Internet impacts each couple's relationship.

6. Partners should be encouraged to share information with each other about chat rooms they visit and any online friendships that develop and then monitor the amount of time spent with individuals over the Internet versus real-live relationships.

Finally, as with all affairs, clinicians should remember that Internet infidelity is often a symptom of deeper problems in the relationship. Breaches of trust are often reflective of unresolved issues within the couple and within each individual as partners. Regardless of how it is theoretically implemented, couples therapy requires a high degree of emotional connection and interaction on the part of the therapist with their couples clients. Clinicians, therefore, need to examine their beliefs about marital infidelity, sexual behavior over the Internet, their values, and their own romantic scripts (Nelson et al., 2005). Obviously, a clinician's beliefs regarding these issues will impact their therapeutic interventions with their couples clients.

Summary of Treatment Guidelines

1. Clinicians should explore their own feelings and biases about affairs and specifically Internet affairs. Hertlein and Piercy (2008) found that clinicians' biases significantly impact the assessment and treatment of Internet infidelity issues.

2. Do a thorough assessment of presenting (and sometimes hidden) treatment issues. Specifically ask about Internet use and misuse within the home.

3. If an Internet affair is discovered by one partner, assess both partners' feelings about it. Assess how long it has been going on and how much it interferes with the couple's, family's, and CEP's social or occupational functioning.

4. If it is determined that the Internet affair is actually reflective of an Internet addiction, individual therapy for the addiction is recommended either separate from or in addition to couples therapy.

5. Determine the couple's commitment to treatment and to staying in the relationship.

6. Strongly encourage the CEP to stop the affair. It is a clinician's choice to proceed or suspend treatment if the CEP refuses to discontinue his or her affair during therapy. Continuation of treatment with the couple is not usually recommended if the affair continues.

7. Determine which theoretical orientation to use in the conceptualization and treatment of the couple. Bowenian family systems

therapy and emotion-focused therapy have frequently been utilized in couples' treatment. There is currently no specific empirically validated treatment for Internet infidelity. Cognitive behavioral therapy is frequently used in the treatment of addictions.

8. Frequently process the anxiety and tension both in and outside of the session. Teach the couple constructive ways to handle these emotions and improve communication skills with each other. Traditional forms of couples therapy have focused on improving couples' communication skills.

9. It is important to maintain a balanced perspective when working with couples. Therapists should make sure that both partners have a chance to be heard and validated (when appropriate). Perspective taking (i.e., learning to see and feel things from one's partner's perspective) is often a foundational strategy in couples therapy.

10. Deal with the betrayed partner's "obsessive review" of the affair details.

11. Successful treatment of Internet infidelity involves the CEP accepting responsibility for the intimacy breach and making clear and consistent demonstrations that he or she is trustworthy and will not do it again. A CEP who does not show remorse may not be motivated to stay in the primary relationship or in couples therapy. Behavioral strategies may be employed to help rebuild trust (e.g., moving the computer to a public place in the house; purchasing blocking software).

12. Help the couple clarify what they need and want. This involves determining the causes of the infidelity. Help the couple find caring ways of relating to each other to bring them closer together.

13. Help the couple find closure from the Internet affair.

Case Study: Carin and David

Carin and David (names are pseudonyms) have been living together for 4 years. They are a Caucasian couple in their their late 30s. Carin was referred to me through her insurance company. She called my office requesting couples therapy for herself and David, her partner of 5 years. Over the phone she explains that she has had it with his addiction to pornography and has told David that if he does not agree to counseling, she would end their relationship. When Carin and David come in for their session, Carin is obviously angry at David and describes herself as being at her "wits end." David appears sullen and disconnected from Carin. He states that he does not understand what the big deal is. He admits to regularly looking at Internet pornography and believes it to be a "guy thing." David states that he loves Carin and has never cheated on her with another woman.

He estimates his weekly Internet pornography activities to be about three times a week. Carin states that she knows he spends several hours a day online. Carin says, "I have known for about 3 years that David has been disconnected from me and each year it's gotten worse. We rarely fight and enjoy each other's company, but he has been increasingly distracted for some time now. My first husband was a raging alcoholic, so in some ways I am used to relationships with some severe problems. That's probably why I have put up with it for so long. But, David rarely touches me. He seems preoccupied all of the time. We've started fighting more and he is irritable when I keep him out all day and away from the computer. I have become obsessed with checking his computer and have found that he has down-loaded thousands and thousands of Internet pornography pictures which I find disgusting and unacceptable."

"I have been telling myself that it's not a big deal. They're just pictures but I have to admit that it makes me so angry! I feel like I've become a detective because I am checking his computer for porn evidence all of the time. I even think about what he's doing at home while I am at work because he is out of work right now."

David tells you that he has been a good boyfriend. He feels like he has been supportive of Carin since they have been together. He states, "Yes, she caught me doing porn. I don't do it nearly as much as she thinks I do. I really don't see the problem. I am not cheating on her with another woman. I would never do that. I seriously think she's just overreacting. I would never hurt her on purpose. It's just something I need to do to de-stress. It's totally harmless. I've done it for years. I even told her about it when we had been dating about 6 months. Well, she actually caught me doing it but I didn't want her to think that I wasn't attracted to her. I care about her but dragging me here is not the answer. Please tell her that this is just what guys do!"

In conducting an initial assessment of this couple's issues, I found that Carin and David love each other very much. Both of them appear to be committed to their relationship, but David is not at all happy about being dragged into couples therapy. He says, "To keep her from nagging me, I will give it a try. But I don't really see anything wrong. She's just stressed out at work and it's having an impact on our relationship." Both Carin and David come from families where at least one of their parents abused drugs or alcohol and their parents were highly critical of them both. Although they both communicate with their families, neither of them is close to their parents.

David agrees to try to limit his computer use to three times a week. After being confronted with his account of how much he uses the computer, he agreed that Carin's assessment might be a bit more accurate than his.

I used a Bowenian family systems approach to help them understand their multigenerational patterns of substance abuse, enabling (Carin), family criticism, and in David's case (infidelity), his mother regularly cheated on his father. Emotion-focused therapy was used to understand their patterns of attachment. For example, Carin was parentified from an early age. She often took care of her parents when they got drunk. She never felt connected to her parents or worthy of their love. She has deep emotional scars from their abandonment of her. She is attracted to romantic partners she has to take care of. David has similar self-esteem issues as Carin. He always felt like a failure growing up because he never was able to accomplish anything on his own. His father got him his first job and he worked there for 20 years. He quit the job to go to school full time and finish his college degree, but he was never able to find a job on his own. Both Carin and David struggle with anxiety issues. Cognitive behavioral therapy was employed to explore their negative thought patterns about themselves and their relationship and to deal with their high levels of social anxiety. We also spent some time learning how to express anger appropriately toward each other. Carin and David rarely fought; however, because they both avoid conflict, they have a great deal of anger built up toward each other.

During my ongoing evaluation of this couple, I found that David has a pornography addiction. He is not emotionally attached to any of the women he visits online. In fact, he does not even know their names. David shows a great deal of shame regarding his discussions of his Internet pornography use but he still does not believe he is an addict. He was not able to keep his commitment to limit his online activities to three times a week, which prompted him to take a closer look at his behavior. He has agreed to move the desktop computer to the living room as a sign of good faith to Carin. Since moving the computer, he is often irritable and angry at Carin.

Carin often expresses her feelings of hopelessness and anger at herself for "choosing another addict." After working with this couple for six sessions, their communication skills have improved, as well as their ability to be honest with each other. Carin understands that David has an addiction and that treatment will take time. David is more willing to admit that he has more of a problem than he thought, but he is unwilling to say that he has an addiction. Both of them are more clear about the individual and couples work they will need to do to heal their relationship and themselves. Carin has agreed to stop attacking David's character. She frequently would call him a "spoiled little boy who can't do anything right." She would also ridicule him for not being able to find a job. She now recognizes how her overt hostility toward David complicates his feelings of failure and use of porn as a coping strategy. David is working to see things from Carin's perspective, although he struggles with recognizing the full impact of his addiction on their relationship and on himself. He is now willing to accept that his behavior hurts her.

The focus of treatment had been to help this couple explore their hurtful behaviors toward each other as well as David's breaches of trust and betrayal. David has begun to see why Internet pornography is so attractive to him. He does not feel like a failure when engaging in porn activities, and no one has any expectations of him. He also admits that he might be more proactive in finding a job if he did not spend so much time online.

I referred David to a therapist who specializes in Internet addictions. Carin also has her own individual therapist. Currently, Carin and David are focusing on their own individual issues. For both of them this includes an exploration of their FOO patterns of betrayal. Carin is exploring how her enabling behavior was inadvertently reinforcing David's addiction. Carin has been able to cut down on her "obsessive review" behaviors because she is able to talk to David more honestly about her feelings concerning his porn use, and he makes honest attempts to listen to her. I continue to see this couple once a month to maintain treatment gains. They have agreed to come back for weekly sessions after working on their individual treatment issues.

Conclusion

Internet infidelity is a new area of study within the psychological literature. Although in its infancy, it is critical that couples therapists incorporate an assessment of Internet use within a couple's relationship into their work with couples. Individuals who engage in secretive cybersex or Internet affairs create a breach of emotional intimacy in their primary romantic relationships, which is not easily healed. Therapists working with couples need to thoroughly assess how technology, including the Internet, text messaging, and cell phones, enhance or detract from their couples' relationships. These new technologies can be easily misused and represent an entirely new area in which physical and emotional boundary violations can occur. Additionally, these technologies provide romantic partners with a specific documented record of emotional breaches, which are often brought into the therapy session as "proof" of an emotional breach. Couples therapists need to consider how they will deal with this "proof" in sessions and share this with their clients before beginning therapy. This is a new but essential area of assessment for couples therapists. Finally, therapists need to examine their own biases and values regarding Internet infidelity and cybersex behaviors. Clearly, these attitudes impact therapists' evaluations, interventions, and relationships with their clients. This chapter was intended as an introduction to the topic of Internet infidelity. Its aim was to provide couples therapists with some useful interventions and strategies to use with couples presenting with Internet infidelity issues.

References

Ainsworth, M. D. S. (1989). Attachments beyond infancy. *American Psychologist, 44*, 709–716.

Atwood, J. D. (2005). Cyber-affairs: "What's the big deal?" Therapeutic considerations. In F. P. Piercy, K. M. Hertlein, & J. L. Wetchler (Eds.), *Handbook of the clinical treatment of infidelity* (pp. 117–134). New York: Haworth Press.

Atwood, J. D., & Seifer, M. (1997). Extramarital affairs and constructed meaning: A social constructionist therapeutic approach. *American Journal of Family Therapy, 25*(1), 55–75.

Branwyn, G. (1993). Compu-sex: Erotic for cybernauts. *South Atlantic Quarterly, 92*(4), 779–791.

Brown, E. M. (2001). *Patterns of infidelity and their treatment.* Philadelphia: Brunner-Routledge.

Bowen, M. (1978). *Family therapy in clinical practice.* New York: Jason Aronson.

Bowlby, J. (1989). *A secure base: Parent-child attachment and healthy human development.* New York: Basic Books.

Buss, D. M., & Shackleford, T. K. (1997). Susceptibility to infidelity in the first year of marriage. *Journal of Research in Personality, 31*, 193–221.

Cooper, A. (1997). The Internet and sexuality: Into the new millennium. *Journal of Sex Education and Therapy, 22*, 5–6.

Cooper, A. (1998). Sexuality and the Internet: Surfing its way into the new millennium. *CyberPsychology and Behavior, 1*(2), 24–28.

Cooper, A., Delmonicao, D., & Burg, R. (2000). Cybersex users and abusers: New findings and implications. *Sexual Addiction and Compulsivity: Journal of Treatment and Prevention, 1–2*, 5–30.

Cooper, A., & Griffin-Shelley, E. (2002). Introduction. The Internet: The next sexual revolution. In A. Cooper (Ed.), *Sex and the Internet: A guidebook for clinicians.* New York: Brunner-Routledge.

Cooper, A., McLoughlin, I. P., & Campbell, K. M. (2000). Sexuality in cyberspace: Update for the 21st century. *CyberPsychology and Behavior, 3*(4), 521–536.

Cooper, A., Morharan-Martin, J. Maheu, M. M. & Mathy, R.M. (2001). Random sampling of user demographics related to cybersex and other online sexual activity. Unpublished manuscript.

Cooper, A., Putnam, D. E., Planchon, L. A., & Boies, S. C. (1999). Online sexual compulsivity. *Sexual Addiction and Compulsivity: The Journal of Treatment and Prevention, 6*(2), 79–104.

Cooper, A., Scherer, C. R., Boies, S. C., & Gordon, B. L. (1999). Sexuality on the Internet: From sexual exploration to pathological expression. *Professional Psychology, 30*(2), 154–164.

Corley, D. M. (2006). Online infidelity. Brochure for the American Association for Marriage and Family Therapy. (Originally published in *Clinical Update in Family Therapy*, March–April, 2006)

Delmonico, D. L., Griffin, E., & Carnes, P. J. (2002). Treating online compulsive sexual behavior: When cybersex is the drug of choice. In A. Cooper (Ed.), *Sex and the Internet: A guidebook for clinicians* (pp. 147–167). New York: Brunner-Routledge.

Dew, B. J., & Chaney, N. P. (2005). The relationship among sexual compulsivity, internalized homophobia, and HIV at-risk sexual behavior in gay and bisexual users of Internet chat rooms. *Sexual Addiction and Compulsivity, 12,* 259–273.

Drigotas, S. M., Safstrom, C. A., & Gentilia, T. (1999). An investment model prediction of dating infidelity. *Journal of Personality and Social Psychology, 77*(3), 509–524.

Eagan, T. (2000). Wall Street meets pornography [Electronic verson]. New York Times. Retrieved from http://www.nytimes.com/2000/10/23/technology/23PORN.html?pagewanted=all

Fitness, J. (2001). Betrayal, rejection, revenge, and forgiveness: An interpersonal script approach. In M. Leary (Ed.), *Interpersonal rejection* (pp. 73–103). New York: Oxford University Press.

Glass, S. (2000). *Avoiding the slippery slope of infidelity.* Paper presented at Smart Marriages Conference for Coalition for Marriage and Family Counselors and Educators, Denver, Colorado.

Goldberg, P. D., Peterson, B. D., Rosen, K. H., & Sara, M. L. (2008). Cybersex: The impact of a contemporary problem on the practices of marriage and family therapists. *Journal of Marital and Family Therapy, 34*(4), 469–480.

Gottman, J. M. (1999). *The marriage clinic: A scientifically based marital therapy.* New York: Norton.

Greenberg, L.S. and Johnson, S. (1988). Emotion focused therapy for couples. Guilford, New York, N.Y.

Greenfield, D., & Orzack, M. (2002). The electronic bedroom: Clinical assessment of online sexual problems and Internet-enabled sexual behavior. In A. Cooper (Ed.), *Sex and the Internet: A guidebook for clinicians* (pp. 129–145). New York: Brunner-Routledge.

Hertlein, K. M., & Piercy, F. P. (2008). Therapists' assessment and treatment of Internet infidelity cases. *Journal of Marital and Family Therapy, 34*(4), 481–497.

Hertlein, K. M., & Webster, M. (2008). Technology, relationships, and problems: A research synthesis. *Journal of Marital and Family Therapy, 34*(4), 445–460.

Jerome, L. W., DeLeon, P. H., James, L. C., Folen, R., Earles, J., & Gedney, J. J. (2000). The coming of age of telecommunication in psychological research and practice. *American Psychologist, 55*(4), 407–421.

Johnson, S. M. (1988). *Emotional couples therapy from trauma survivors: Strengthening attachment bonds.* New York: Guildford.

Johnson, S. M. (1996). *The practice of emotionally focused marital therapy: Creating connection.* New York: Brunner-Routledge.

King, B. M. (2008). *Human sexuality today,* 5th ed. Upper Saddle River, NJ: Prentice-Hall.

Leiblum, S., & Döring, N. (2002). Internet sexuality: Known risks and fresh chances for women. In A. Cooper (Ed.), *Sex and the Internet: A guidebook for clinicians* (pp. 19–45). New York: Brunner-Routledge.

Lusterman, D. (1998). *Infidelity: A survival guide.* New York: MJF Books.

Lusterman, D. (2005). Marital infidelity: The Effect of delayed traumatic reaction. In F. P. Piercy, K. M. Hertlein, & J. L. Wetchler (Eds.), *Handbook of the clinical treatment of infidelity* (pp.71–82). New York: Haworth Press.

Maheu, M. M., & Subotnik, R. B. (2001). *Infidelity on the Internet: Virtual relationships and real betrayal.* Naperville, IL: Sourcebooks.

McKenna, K., & Bargh, J. (1998). Coming out in the age of the Internet: Identity "demarginalization" from virtual group participation. *Journal of Personality and Social Psychology, 75*(3), 681–694.

Moultrup, D. J. (1990). *Husbands, wives, and lovers: The emotional system of the extramarital affair.* New York: Guilford.

Nelson, T., Piercy, F. P., & Sprenkle, D. H. (2005). Internet infidelity: A multi-phase Delphi study. In F. P. Piercy, K. M. Hertlein, & J. L. Wetchler (Eds.), *Handbook of clinical treatment of infidelity.* New York: Haworth Press.

Pittman, F., & Wagers, T. P. (1995). Crises of infidelity. In N. Jacobson & A. Gurman (Eds.), *Handbook of couple therapy.* New York: Guilford.

Reid, R. C., & Gray, D. (2006). *Confronting your spouse's pornography problem.* Sandy, UT: Silverleaf Press.

Schnarch, D. (1997). Sex, intimacy, and the Internet. *Journal of Sex Education and Therapy, 22,* 15–20.

Schneider, J. P. (2002). The new "elephant in the living room": Effects of compulsive cybersex behaviors on the spouse. In A. Cooper (Ed.), *Sex and the Internet: A guidebook for clinicians* (pp. 169–186). New York: Brunner-Routledge.

Shackleford, T. K., & Buss, D. M. (1997). Spousal esteem. *Journal of Family Psychology, 11,* 478–488.

Shaw, J. (1997). Treatment rationale for Internet infidelity. *Journal of Sex Education and Therapy, 22*(1), 29–34.

Spring, J. A. (1996). *After the affair: Healing the pain and rebuilding the trust when a partner has been unfaithful.* New York: HarperCollins.

Sternberg, R. J. (1988). *The triangle of love: Intimacy, passion, and commitment.* New York: Basic Books.

Turkle, S. (1995). *Life on the screen.* New York: Simon and Schuster.

Weiss, R. (1975). *Marital separation.* New York: Basic Books.

Whitty, M. T. (2005). The "realness" of cyber-cheating: Men's and women's representations of unfaithful Internet relationships. *Social Science Computer Review, 23*(1), 57–67.

Whitty, M. T., & Carr, A. N. (2005). Taking the good with the bad: Applying Klein's work to further our understandings of cyber-cheating. In F. P. Piercy, K. M. Hertlein, & J. L. Wetchler (Eds.), *Handbook of the clinical treatment of infidelity* (pp. 103–116). New York: Haworth Press.

Whitty, M. T., & Quigley, L-L. (2008). Emotional and sexual infidelity offline and in cyberspace. *Journal of Marital and Family Therapy, 34*(4), 461–468.

Yarab, P. E., Sensibaugh, C. C., & Allgeier, R. E. (1998). More than just sex: Gender differences in the incidence of self-defined unfaithful behavior in heterosexual dating relationships. *Journal of Psychology and Human Sexuality, 10*(2), 45–57.

CHAPTER 12

Financial Infidelity and Intimacy Recovery

BYRON WALLER

In today's troubled economic environment, the impact of finances on relationships has increased tremendously. Financial fidelity has always been an important part of any relationship, and any financial misstep can affect the foundation of a relationship. If there are financial issues in a relationship, they will become more significant. The end result of any financial dishonesty in relationships is increased relational conflicts and major challenges. In a relationship survey conducted by Harris Interactive in 2005, 29% of individuals in committed relationships between the ages of 35 and 55 reported that they have been dishonest with their partner about spending. However, 24% report that financial honesty is more important than honesty about sexual fidelity. In addition, unsatisfied partners are reportedly two to four times more likely to be financially dishonest (Lawyers.com, 2005). Despite the many dishonesty issues in relationships, more than 7 of 10 surveyed reported that trust, the cornerstone for intimacy, is essential to have a successful relationship (Lawyers.com, 2005). These statistics are a sign of the growing trend toward issues that deal with financial *cheating* or *financial infidelity* with individuals and relationships.

Fidelity is expected in any marriage or committed relationship because relationships are built on the qualities of honesty, integrity, respect, love, and intimacy. However, as we know, infidelities often occur within these relationships. When we think about infidelity, we tend to think of only sexual infidelity as a breaking of the agreements of the relationship, although other forms of infidelity may be as influential, such as emotional infidelity, romantic friendships, and even virtual-Internet infidelity. Financial *cheating* erodes the foundation and trust in relationships and is a leading factor toward relationship destruction. Steinisch (2008) suggested that finances are one of the leading issues that create disagreement between couples and ranks as the first or second most argued issue for couples. As money and financial issues grow in significance, their effect on couples also increases. One of the most significant issues is *financial infidelity*. Financial infidelity is the act of financial deception a partner commits within a relationship. The behaviors that demonstrate financial infidelity are secretive acts of spending money, possessing credit and credit cards, holding secret accounts or stashes of money, borrowing money, or otherwise incurring debt unknown to one's spouse, partner, or significant other (Wikipedia, 2008b). Eaker Weil, in her book *Financial Infidelity*, suggested that financial infidelity occurs whenever you keep a secret about money; whether it is "how you spend it, or how you save it, or how it makes you feel when you or your partner uses it in any particular way" (2008, p. 6). It is also viewed as the money secrets we keep from our significant others. These money secrets may range from harmless and eccentric to painful and destructive (MacDonald, 2008). Financial infidelity strips away trust and destroys intimacy. It weakens the foundation of these relationships where recovery from this destructive force could be very difficult. This chapter will define financial infidelity and intimacy and explore several major reasons for the impact of financial infidelity on individuals and relationships. The chapter will also present some suggestions from financial professionals and clinicians to manage financial infidelity. It will also address how a relationship could recover trust and intimacy from financial infidelity by using two well-known models and present a case study discussion with the prominent model used to recover and rebuild trusting relationships after financial infidelity.

Definition of Financial Infidelity

Financial infidelity can be as devastating as any other form of infidelity. In fact, financial and sexual infidelities are often the primary causes of divorce (Loeffler, 2006). Financial infidelity is a form of cheating sometimes so subtle that one may be cheating unintentionally and without knowing it (Max, 2008). However, financial infidelity primarily is an intentional and conscious decision that one or both partners make that may result in a loss of intimacy and trust in the relationship. This form of infidelity leaves the affected party feeling "let down," cheated, betrayed, and deceived. Weston (2008) suggested that money conflicts provide a view of underlying issues within the relationship. This form of cheating is a problem beyond the financial value because it is not just what you are hiding but why you are hiding it (Loeffler, 2006).

When financial infidelity is evident in a relationship, it is usually a sign of other relationship issues. The existence of financial infidelity demonstrates that the relationship needs work and may be at risk for other problems. If these financial reasons persist, they may lead to other major relationship challenges such as addictions and divorce. Financial infidelity is similar to all other forms of infidelity in that it can create major barriers, especially as money and finances continue to grow in influence on the function and intimacy of personal partnerships and relationships. However, financial infidelity directly impacts couples in areas of their security and livelihood, one of the most sensitive areas especially considering our present economic troubles. Financial disagreements are common in all relationships. When conflicts persist, they can produce separation and undermine the closeness and the foundation of the connection.

Definition of Intimacy

Intimacy refers to the ability and the decision to be close, loving, and vulnerable toward someone else. It is the closeness of the relationship. There are several forms of intimacy: emotional intimacy, mental or intellectual intimacy, spiritual intimacy, recreational intimacy, sexual intimacy, and financial intimacy. Emotional intimacy is the closeness in the relationship when sharing feelings. It occurs when one person knows what another is feeling, they convey feelings to each other, and express concern and understanding of their feelings to each other. Mental or intellectual intimacy occurs when there is mutual understanding about all the important issues in the relationship. It involves understanding, planning, and goal setting together. Spiritual intimacy involves sharing religious beliefs and observing religious practice together. Shared spiritual experiences can unite the couple's attitudes and goals. Recreational intimacy involves enjoying activities together. Sexual intimacy involves frequency, satisfaction, enjoyment, and open communication about sex. Finally, financial intimacy involves discussing thoughts, feelings, and beliefs about finances and an ability to share the finances itself (Hagey & Brewer, 2008). Financial intimacy is often overlooked in relationships, and communication about money and finances usually does not happen before relationships become serious or committed (Lawyers.com, 2005). The lack of financial intimacy can lead to financial infidelity. All forms of intimacy involve a process that includes qualities such as mutual trust, tenderness, acceptance, caring, forgiveness, apologies, appropriate boundaries, interdependence, and open communication (Hagey & Brewer, 2008). Communication about finances provides an opportunity for the couple to understand how one's culture, past experiences, family, and personal beliefs shape financial decision making and behaviors of his or her partner. The result of a discussion can eliminate the deceptive and secretive financial act of betrayal or financial infidelity and give the opportunity to improve or change the environment of the relationship.

A major ingredient for intimacy is communication. Communication includes both the transmittal and reception of information. Communication is the process that allows intimacy to grow over time between two people. Each person must be able to express information in his or her way to the other and listen to whether the other person receives the message he or she intended. However, most individuals assume that the other person received the message intended. When it is received as the transmitter intended, it creates an atmosphere of communication and intimacy. In order to achieve this, each person must take the risk to become vulnerable to trust the other and to inject all the components needed for intimacy such as trust and love. Even if intimacy is initially found, it can be very difficult to maintain. Direct and constant communication is needed to establish intimacy in relationships.

All relationships are built on trust and communication. When trust disappears, it breaks the bond and destroys the relationship, and communication is avoided. Financial infidelity is an issue that can break away the bond, whether the relationship is strong or weakened with other stressors. Whenever there is a betrayal or deception, there is a loss of trust, a sense of anger, questioning of the safety of the relationship, and an abandonment of intimacy. Spring (1996) identified nine psychological losses as a result of a sexual infidelity. They are: loss of identity; sense of specialness; self-respect for forfeiting values; self-respect for not acknowledging you were wronged; control over thoughts; sense of order; religious faith; connection with others; and sense of purpose. These losses impact the person and the relationship. The loss experienced with financial infidelity is similar to sexual unfaithfulness and may be a sign of deeper relationship issues (Eaker Weil, 2008).

Financial infidelity produces a harmful consequence that destroys trust, ruins safety, and cuts off the opportunity of intimacy within the relationship. Bennett (2008) added that financial infidelity not only destroys trust but also proposed that it ruins opportunities to achieve increased intimacy, self-knowledge, respect for differences, safety to work through differences, and deeper more intimate topics. When opportunities to achieve intimacy are not used and financial infidelity results, it can lead to deeper emotional pain. The emotional pain is the loss of trust, honesty, and caring as well as the positive view that the other person has one's best interest in mind and at heart. The emotional pain is also the realization that now the person must pay attention to his or her own protection, a duty one has put in the hands of the partner or did not feel that he or she had to be aware of, but now has to give attention. And finally, the person now knows that he or she is not as close to the other person as once thought and no longer can be completely open and vulnerable to the other person because of the knowledge that the other person has hurt him or her and has the potential to do it again. These realizations come from betrayal, which is destructive to the bond between individuals and destroys the foundation of trust in the relationship. Financial infidelity not only crushes trust in the relationships, it also undermines opportunities to have intimacy.

Reasons for Financial Infidelity

Discussing and understanding the financial agreements of the partnership can prevent possible financial secretive behaviors. The discussion about finances can provide some mutual understanding of what, how, and why the partner feels, acts, and thinks about money. Each partner has unique experiences that influence his or her financial decisions and the ability to trust the partner about finances. What a person thinks about money may provide insight into his or her financial background and how the person may behave with money. There are many reasons for financial infidelity, but they seem to revolve around two major themes: personal challenges and relational issues. Personal challenges are issues that the person brings into a relationship. They are lessons learned from past experiences, from the observation of parents, from familial circumstances, and other financial experiences the person has internalized. The result of this internalization is that the person believes and behaves certain ways around money and finances. An example of a personal challenge might be the fears a person has about being financially honest or trusting or even the ability to become financially vulnerable. These personal features may interfere with the person's ability to share him- or herself with another. There are many factors that contribute to financial infidelity, but addressing all of them is beyond the scope of this chapter. A list of personal reasons for financial infidelity may include poverty, emotional deprivation, fear of a divorce, secret projects, addiction problems, discomfort with honesty, fear of punishment, compulsion to lie, lack of or excess of entitlement, minimal trust, lack of communication, low self-worth, lack of fulfillment, relief from emotional stress, identity problems, low self-esteem, control issues, insecurity, and desire for an emotional high (Ambrose, 2008; Hickman, 2008). This list highlights some of the ways personal factors can impact financial infidelity, and it provides an overview of the issues that can be used to better understand the financial infidelity problem of a partner after it has been identified.

Relational issues are the second major theme that impacts financial infidelity. These issues are the problems couples encounter as they attempt to deal with financial matters with another person. The relationship impacts how and why the couple interacts about money. Siegel (1990) suggested that money conflicts provide insight into the relationship dynamics of power, mutual respect, and trust and illustrates commitment, control, closeness, and affection. The relational issues are the personal challenges that impact how one person relates to another. Each partner brings his or her own personal issues to the relationship, and together they create the financial atmosphere for the couple. An example of this process is seen in Max (2008), who provided an illustration of when a friend shared that she cheated because she "learned everything from my mother" and other friends did it "just for the thrill of it." Addressing these financial relational issues become paramount in a relationship to avoid financial problems and potentially financial infidelity.

Below is a nonexhaustive list of relational issues that can impact financial infidelity, which can also be used to issue financial relationship issues: early childhood experiences, learned from parents, early family issues, lack of trust in spouse, reluctance to share with a spouse, feeling that the spouse does not believe you are entitled to buy things for yourself, inability to problem solve together about money matters, different money styles, and dealing with unresolved power and control issues (Ambrose, 2008; Hickman, 2008). Financial infidelity may have its source in a variety of areas and at many different levels. One thing that seems clear, however, is that finances impacts individuals differently. Financial infidelity cannot and should not be minimized in any relationship because money has different meanings to different people. It is necessary to examine the differences as to how financial infidelity might impact others. Several of the major reasons for financial infidelity will be explored in the sections that follow. The focus will be on the personal themes and how they affect relationship issues. The personal theme includes financial infidelity and the self, gender, and addiction.

Financial Infidelity as an Extension of the Self

Money is as important and valuable as the meaning the individual attaches to it. Money is, for some individuals, an extension of themselves, an expression of their self-esteem, an example of their past experiences, familial values and parental training, and the basis of their future success and safety; while for others, money is to be used to get what they need to survive and live. For the former, money appears connected to their identity and self-worth, and money is seen as very valuable; while for the latter, the meaning of money is not as connected to their identity and the value placed on money is not as significant. Financial infidelity could influence both of these individuals. One area of difference is when an individual places more value in the meaning and the use of money than his or her partner.

This creates a potential problem for the couple. Therefore, the impact of financial infidelity may be different for individuals based on their view and value of their finances. Financial infidelity can be very individualized and personal, and each couple needs to discuss these financial differences to future financial issues.

Some individuals reported cheating financially to avoid dealing with other issues in the relationship. For example, a husband realizes that his wife does not pay attention to him unless he is perfectly dressed. This stirs up personal issues for him and problems within the relationship. So in order to gain some attention from his wife, he constantly purchases clothing or shops to manage his personal feelings. He avoids communicating with her about his desire for attention, interaction, and intimacy. The environment becomes ready for financial infidelity. Stern (2007) called this the "gaslight effect." This is where one partner is lying with the aid of financial infidelity to alter the perception of the other partner and make the financial infidelity acceptable. The husband's buying of clothes becomes a manipulative effort to change the reality of the wife and does not confront the lack of attention he feels, nor does it bring to light the obvious lack of communication. If this type financial infidelity persists, it may serve as a signal of a major relationship problem and a buying or spending addiction may become evident.

Financial Infidelity and Gender

Financial infidelity impacts all individuals differently, but it also seems to influence men and women in special ways. Men and women tend to spend and manage money differently and therefore differ in how they commit infidelity. Men tend to hide income, while women tend to hide excess spending (Pawlik-Kienlen, 2007). Both are guilty of financial infidelity by hiding purchases or credit card statements and may be putting money into secret accounts. Whether the financial deception is small or large, money can come between couples (Jayson, 2008) and interfere with connection and intimacy. According to the Harris Interactive survey (Lawyers.com, 2005), women are more likely than men to cheat financially. Oftentimes one of women's financial roles is to manage the household budget, which allows them to pay cash for their secret items (Jones, 2006). Women are more likely to commit financial infidelity because of other personal or relationship issues. These relationship issues range from fear of their spouse, desire for financial freedom, power struggles with the partner, or just buying items for the children or the household. In fact, *knipl* is a Yiddish word that describes how women hide a little stash of money over the years or save the extra grocery money in case they or their family encounter some hardship (MacDonald, 2008). In our present economic world, women earn more than in the past, but still earn less than men on average. One survey (Lawyers.com, 2005) found that women are contributing more money to their family's income, but the major financial decisions are still made by men, which promotes resentment and leads to financial infidelity for women. As a result, many women may also want more financial involvement and decision making with their money. In order for this to happen, an adjustment must be made within the relationship; however, in some relationships it may not be possible to make these adjustments without assistance from a professional (MacDonald, 2008). When these issues are not addressed, the outcome can be financial infidelity and other relationship problems.

Men also commit financial infidelity. For example, they may avoid discussing finances with their wife to protect their position of financial power and freedom. In many relationships in the United States, men earn more money than women, and therefore believe they should make the financial decisions. Men primarily make the financial investments (Lawyers.com, 2005) and they sometimes avoid discussing financial problems to protect their partners from the financial stressors and pressures that come with money management (MacDonald, 2008). This in itself is not a problem. The problem may be not including their partner in the decisions. Rather than communicating with their partners to make a financial decision or to share their position of financial power and freedom, some men may commit financial infidelity, using money for bigger and more expensive purchases. Men sometimes commit financial infidelity in their attempts to protect their partners from financial realities or secretly hide money to surprise a partner for a birthday, anniversary, or for a vacation, but secretive hiding can lead to use for personal reasons (MacDonald, 2008). A recent television commercial shows a couple purchasing insurance. At the checkout, the cashier lists "RV insurance, motorcycle insurance, boat insurance, ATV insurance," and as the wife watches, she says, "We don't have any of those," to which the husband replies, "I do, huh, we do," looking embarrassed and squeamish. The cashier yells out, "Surprise!" as she sheepishly processes the items. Men commit financial infidelity just like women, but it may look different.

There are clear gender role and power issues related to financial expectations within relationships. These differences are most evident for both parties when role reversals are taken into account (Rochen, Suizzo, McKelly, & Scaringi, 2008). The gender expectations for the couple begin on the first date when the check comes. Who will pay the bill? If the male pays for it, this may set a traditional gender expectation for the couple; if the female pays for it, this may set a nontraditional expectation for the relationship. If they decide to split the bill, this too sets a precedent for the relationship and groundwork for financial agreement. Traditional gender roles would dictate that the male should pay for the meal. Generally, the best way to deal with gender role expectations is to discuss them and come to some level of agreement within the relationship. Even when some discussion has taken place, an amount of flexibility must be maintained (Rochen et al., 2008).

Many couples and relationships are dealing with gender role reversal (Rochen et al., 2008). The times have changed traditional roles for many couples. No longer are men always considered the breadwinners. In many cases, with the advancement of women in the labor market, women now earn more income than men (Lawyers.com, 2005) and may bring home more than their partners. Therefore, the traditional view of male–female relationships may not exist in some relationships. In some cases, men are becoming "stay at home dads" and take care of the home (Rochen et al., 2008). This has changed the dynamics within relationships and has produced more role reversals for couples. Some couples handle this revision seamlessly, while others struggle through the process. Dowd (2005), Voss (2007), and Williams (2007) document some of the challenges from role reversals within relationships. In these role reversals, the feelings of ambivalence and the power struggle centered on money and the financial decisions for both men and women (Jones, 2006). Eaker Weil (2008) provided suggestions for women and men who need to learn to manage various issues related to meeting each other's needs. Each member of the relationship may need something unique in order to deal with different approaches and perceptions. When role reversals occur, it is necessary for each member of the relationship to feel like an equal partner within a balanced relationship. Gender beliefs and characteristics are deeply ingrained in each person and within society. Therefore, it is necessary for the couple to address the issue of sharing power, influence, and money within their relationship. This is a difficult dance to navigate when money and feelings are involved. However, it is clearly possible when both partners work to maintain their partnership within the relationship, even when the roles are reversed. Financial infidelity is just one of the symptoms that may occur when the dance and direction are not balanced.

Financial Infidelity and Addiction

When the financial infidelity begins to impact the family's financial stability and threatens the individual's social, emotional, and occupation life, concerns about financial addictions become evident. Addiction as a reason for financial infidelity is more than just acting out as it involves the need to get that biochemical feeling of connection. Eaker Weil (2008) proposed that the behaviors that stimulate the feelings can easily become addictive and follow the same process of the addiction from self-medication to preoccupation to creating rituals for the high, and then to compulsion. The term addiction is used to "describe a recurring compulsion by an individual to engage in some specific activity, despite harmful consequences to the individual's health, mental state or social life" (Wikipedia, 2008a), and many individuals may be caught in an addictive process. The addictive behaviors of financial infidelity can include secretive gambling, both at casinos and on the Internet, binge spending, credit card debt, pornography and Internet pornography, or hoarding of money and things (Eaker Weil, 2008). These addictive financial risk-taking behaviors negatively affect the relationship and are becoming a leading cause of financial problems for families (Eaker Weil, 2008; Frieswick, 2008).

Financial infidelity is not a pathological problem in itself, but it presents the possibility of developing into one, especially if it goes without professional assistance. Financial behaviors and compulsions provide insight into a person's ways of managing relational and personal conflicts and internal challenges. When these ways of dealing with financial challenges become habits, they can develop into a disorder. Although the ideas related to financial infidelity are more recent, financial addictions have been around for a long time. The disorder oniomania is referred to as an "impulsive–control disorder not otherwise specified," using the *Diagnostic and Statistical Manual of Mental Disorder* (APA, 2000), and was first described more than 80 years ago (Hatfield & Chang, 2008). In fact, other countries such as Spain and England have been studying the phenomenon extensively (Rodriguez-Villarino, Gonzalez-Lorenzo, Fernandez-Gonzalez, Lameiras-Fernandez, & Foltz, 2006; Ureta, 2007). In the United States, it is believed that as many as 8.9% of our population may have this disorder, and the numbers are growing each day (Ridgway, Kukar-Kinney, & Monroe, 2008).

Oniomania is also called compulsive buying, spending, shopping or "shopoholism" and is defined as a maladaptive preoccupation with buying or shopping impulses or behavior. It includes frequent intrusive preoccupation or impulses with buying items that the person does not need or cannot afford or shopping for longer periods of time than the person intended. These behaviors are experienced as irresistible, intrusive, or senseless (Hatfield & Chang, 2008). The symptoms and reasons for such a disorder are similar to financial cheating, but more severe. The symptoms for compulsive buying or shopping are viewed as a cycle of negative emotions. The cycle begins with an emotional event such as anger and stress, which leads to buying something. After purchasing, the person regrets or feels guilty about buying the item. In order to cope with these feelings, the person purchases something else, which continues the emotional and behavior cycle. We know that shopoholism begins at an early age, usually with children who experience neglect by their parents, have low self-esteem, experience feelings of loneliness, depend on things for emotional support to cover feelings of early deprivation and affection, are unable to deal with everyday problems especially those that alter their self-esteem, and use buying to repress other areas of life challenge (Ridgway et al., 2008).

The disorder is connected to a variety of early experiences of emotional deprivation in childhood. They include an inability to tolerate negative feelings, the need to fill an internal void, excitement seeking, excessive dependency, approval seeking, perfectionism, the need to maintain a perfect image, general impulsiveness and compulsiveness, and the need to gain control (Benson, 2000; DeSarbo & Edwards, 1996; Faber, O'Guinn, & Krych, 1987). It represents a search for self in people whose identity is neither firmly felt nor dependable. Going shopping can be a source of self-definition, self-expression, creativity, and even healing for these individuals (Lewandowski & Ackerman, 2006). Although some of these same symptoms describe experiences a person dealing with financial infidelity may experience, those with the disorder have more of the symptoms described above and have more severe obsessions and compulsions to think and act to buy or shop.

Benson and Gengler (2004) addressed treatment for compulsive buying. They suggested that American culture impacts buying addictions and that there are particular ways to treat the disorder. Benson's (2008) Stopping Overshopping program offers a multifaceted approach to treat the disorder. Her treatment focused on issues such as recognizing impulses as they arise; tolerating impulses without acting on them; separating who they are from what they have; finding healthier ways to meet their needs; and reclaiming their power, freedom, and self-esteem. In the same way, Black (2007) recommended treatment interventions that focus on breaking the cycle of shopoholism. He suggested that the person admit he or she is a compulsive spender; eliminate checkbooks and credit cards; shop with someone for accountability; and find meaningful other ways to use time (Hatfield & Chang, 2008).

In order for recovery to occur, behavior change and consistent support are needed. This support can be found in a Debtor's Anonymous, a 12-step program or through a Recovery Connection, a support group for compulsive spenders. These programs are ideal to help individuals manage financial addiction within a group setting; for individuals dealing with financial infidelity, these treatment interventions may not be appropriate because they are geared toward pathological buying and spending and deception within relationships. Other recovery methods are recommended for financial infidelity, such as bibliotherapy, marital counseling, or individual therapy.

Financial Infidelity and Recovery

There are two areas of recovery recommendations. The first is through financial and relational professional counselors and clinicians. From the financial professional perspectives, Osteen and Neal (n.d.) from Oklahoma State University Cooperative Extension Service offered strategies to deal with money issues. They suggested that couples talk about it; develop a system of handling money; create ways to better handle money; and offer tips for talking about money. Osteen and Neal also addressed financial issues based on their survey on money and marriage. Sixty percent of the respondents reported fighting about money with their spouses. They recommended certain strategies to prevent financial issues from ruining a marriage or relationship. They recommend: (a) hold meetings to discuss money in a quiet, neutral place after discussing ground rules; (b) commit to discussing financial secrets openly; (c) share values and attitudes about money; (d) have each person separately write down his or her short- and long-term financial goals; (e) develop a budget that takes into account each person's goals; (f) determine what account system would be best; (g) agree on what to teach your children about money; and (h) be realistic about the money agreement.

Steinisch (2008) provided tips for couples to achieve "financial harmony." She states that "communication is the key" and gives five keys to financial harmony. They are: (a) explore each partner's "money personality" based on his or her upbringing, education, and personal experience; (b) discuss the nuts and bolts of long- and short-term goals; (c) if problems arise, ask why and what each person wants; (d) consider the timing of the discussion before sitting down to talk; and (e) agree on how both partners will allocate their income. Although these are clear practical suggestions to manage financial problems, they fail to address the deeper issues related to the broken trust, the feeling of betrayal and hurt, and the process in building these important ingredients back into the relationship. What is missing is a comprehensive clinical viewpoint to manage these significant issues.

There are many clinical treatment programs designed to help couples recover from deception and infidelity. This chapter will focus on only two treatment strategies: rebuilding after sexual infidelity and recovering after financial infidelity. Spring (1996) developed a clinical process to recover intimacy after infidelity. These steps and strategies are similar to recovery after a financial affair, since the two infidelities are so similar (Eaker Weil, 2008). She proposed that the clinician facilitate the expression of four feeling states to create an "intimacy map" that can lead the couple back to intimacy. She stated that this process may take months or even years before intimacy is recovered and described the four feeling states of denial, anger, guilt, and sadness. The couple needs to struggle through these states and commit themselves to recovery from the affair. The treatment continues by developing new ways to relate to each other. She acknowledged that the intimacy map for each couple would look different, but that there are four basic intimacy locations: (a) a willingness for each person to take responsibility for one's own feelings, thoughts, and actions; (b) a willingness to give each partner space to become known by the other partner; (c) a willingness to be known by expressing what is true about the experience; and (d) a willingness to keep agreements.

Spring also provided eight strategies for using the intimacy map to rebuild the relationship. These eight strategies are: identify the meaning of the affair and accept responsibility for it; say goodbye to the intrusive lover; earn trust or communicate what you need to trust again; talk in ways to allow your partner to hear you and understand your pain and listen in ways that encourage your partner to be open and vulnerable; recognize how you may have been damaged by early life experiences and how you can keep them from contaminating your relationship; manage your differences and dissatisfaction so you can stay attached when you do not feel it; become sexually intimate again; and forgive your partner and yourself. These tools can help the couple rebuild after a devastating deception and betrayal. Financial infidelity is both a deception and betrayal, and rebuilding a relationship afterward takes effort and focus.

Eaker Weil (2008) developed a model to manage both the financial and emotional issues related to rebuilding a relationship after an act or acts of financial cheating. She provided a seven-step process in order to rebuild the emotional, financial, and relational connection between the couple to reestablish the relationship and recover from the infidelity. The steps are negotiated through her proposed eight stages of relationships: euphoria; magical thinking; the power struggle; transition; breaking up; making up; reromanticizing; and real and lasting love. Counselors and therapists recognize that financial infidelity is as devastating as sexual infidelity. Therefore, a similar process is required in these cases to rebuild the trust, commitment, and safety within the relationship (Eaker Weil, 2008). She uses the language of the "Smart Heart Dialogue," derived from Hendrix's (1988) "Imago Therapy." The approach focuses on using dialogue to stabilize and rebuild the attachment language and experience within the couple's relationship by promoting safe, open communication, empathy, and self-honesty. The process is worked through slowly and carefully to allow the couple to deal with the issues that promoted the infidelity while restoring the safety, intimacy, and trust between the couple. She offers seven steps to resolve financial infidelity. A detailed review of the steps recommended by Eaker Weil is necessary to comprehend the infidelity, break away from it, and build a relationship that remains open, loving, and trusting.

Step 1: Calculate the cost—what is the balance sheet of your relationship? The first step helps the couple to review their financial and emotional balance sheet. This will aid them in identifying and treating their relationship issues. The method to calculate the cost is to explore the influence of magical thinking on the relationship. Magical thinking is the "nonscientific reasoning an individual may rely on to 'wish' situations into being or to practice denial when faced with unpleasant scenarios" (Eaker Weil, 2008, p. 58). She believes that these kinds of thoughts lead to emotional disconnection within the couple. This disconnection also can lead to sexual as well as financial infidelity. She has developed several exercises to assist the couple to identify and change magical thinking.

Step 2: Examine your power dynamic—if money is power, is there balance in your relationship? The second step of the approach examines the power struggles that relate to their financial behaviors. The couple is helped to investigate the roles and dynamics of each partner in the relationship and his or her values associated with money. The primary skill is learning how to fight fairly as the couple discusses the issues related to money and finances. The rules and skills of fair fighting are provided to help the couple create a safe space to express, validate, and heal within the process and to express anger and other emotions. The overall goal is for each partner to feel understood in order to develop a resolution to some of issues addressed. After the fight, the couple agrees to implement the negotiated financial behaviors to balance the power dynamics and to "stretch" themselves for their partner.

Step 3: Divest yourself of the past—understanding your inherited money history. The role money plays in our lives was learned from how our grandparents, parents, and role models handled their finances. This step examines the couple's money history idea by using Hendrix's (1988) Imago Therapy to develop a financial imago. A family "moneygram" is used to identify how the legacies of our family "money tree" impact our view, values, and behavior toward money. Practice exercises and dialogue skills are provided to help develop a contract for financial fidelity.

Step 4: Break up with your money—letting go of money's emotional hold. This step helps the couple to determine whether either partner is having an "affair" with money. The couple needs to address the question whether the relationship, money, or the partner is more important. It encourages an examination of pursuer and distancer, attachment styles to money, and what triangles money might have created within the relationship.

Step 5: Define the currency of your relationship—working toward a "free" exchange of love and intimacy. The fifth step begins to assist the couple to redefine and refinance both money and intimacy. Each person learns how to fully experience his or her emotional connection and understand how the emotional disconnection within the relationship leads to financial infidelity. The initial move is to acknowledge their personal and shared values and let go of emotions that hinder their ability to reconnect with the partner in a new way. These new processes of reconnection produce positive change within the relationship and keep the value and control of money in its appropriate place. Activities and exercises are offered to practice the process of reconnection through Smart Heart dialogue and a contract for fidelity.

Step 6: Refinance your relationship—reorganizing your priorities to reclaim lasting love. Now that emotional and financial reconnection has been reestablished, the next step is to solidify the progress in the relationship that has been experienced. This is accomplished by reducing negative interactions and increasing positive ones by following John Gottman's (1995) scientifically founded ratio, where five positives are needed for every one negative to change the context of a relationship. After the reestablishment of the positive nature of the relationship through the use of the Smart Heart techniques, the couple begins to reromanticize each other and move toward sexual intimacy.

Step 7: Invest in your future—the ongoing work of maintaining your relationship. In the final step, Eaker Weil (2008) reviews the use of the Smart Heart skills and dialogues so that the couple can maintain the safe, trusting communication learned about money and emotional connection. Guidelines are provided to prepare the couple to protect against the reemergence of financial infidelity by being aware of the time needed to maintain the growth, by reviewing the triggers that promote financial infidelity, and by following the rules for financial fidelity.

Financial Infidelity and the Case Study

Brad and Sara (names are pseudonyms) have been married for 26 years and have 4 children (25, 24, 20, and 14 years old). Brad is a licensed clinical social worker and Sara is a high school teacher. They are both in their early 50s and have come to counseling because Brad stated that he is "fed up with the money problems." He indicated that they have had financial troubles since they got married. "I am tired of going to our checking account and finding that we have no money and several checks have already bounced.

There is no more money to pay bills, I cannot take on another job, and we are stuck in financial problems. This happens every time Sara goes shopping with her friends." Sara says that "we would not have this problem if he made more money. I deserve to have some of the things in life that I want and as my husband, he is supposed to provide it for me. I have raised his four children, maintained his household, and work hard to contribute to the household budget, and I should get some things that I want in life." This is the first time the couple has come to counseling, and they are now separated and contemplating a divorce.

They stated that they met each other after college at a church function. They were very attracted to each other and spent "every waking moment together" since they were both newly "graduated and jobless." Brad was first to find a position and get his first apartment that was not "near a college campus." Sara would stay at his apartment while he was at work. She would clean the apartment and have meals ready for Brad when he returned. She graduated from a prestigious college and developed friendships with many of the students, graduates, and their families. Although not wealthy, Sara's family did not push her to find employment quickly, but allowed her time to enjoy her life a little before having to "become an adult." They paid her bills and her student loans while she became ready for a job. While getting ready for a job, she would frequently stay overnight with Brad, and then clean and decorate his apartment.

After a year of dating, Brad and Sara decided to get married and start a family. Throughout this time, Sara would work periodically as a substitute teacher. Because she was a very good teacher with an excellent reputation, she could find a school to work at anytime she wanted. She would use her money to buy things for herself, the children, the house, and Brad. Brad worked as a social worker at a community agency and paid all of the bills from his personal checking account. After their third child, Sara decided to work full time in the business world. She was initially very successful and was able to look and dress the part with very expensive items. They opened a joint account and each of them would put their checks into the account and pay bills from that account. Occasionally, they would be charged fees for insufficient funds because they did not often communicate about funds being used. It was Brad's responsibility to balance the account and pay the bills. However, after several years, Sara longed to change jobs and return to the classroom. During this time, Brad was finishing his graduate degree, working as a social worker, and helping to raise the children. When Sara had to attend meetings and conferences in and out of town, he would take full responsibility for the children and household. During these conferences and meetings, Sara would go shopping with her friends and buy things she wanted without telling Brad. Brad would take on part-time jobs to pay off the debt. Several years past and Sara found that she was pregnant with their fourth child. After the baby was born, they agreed that Sara should be closer to the children and she decided to return to the classroom as a schoolteacher. Brad supported this decision, but was concerned about the debt they had accumulated because of her shopping and spending sprees.

Step 1

In the initial sessions, the background information and the presenting issues were gathered. The therapist also focused on financial issues they presented. Following the model, the therapist dealt with the "magical thinking" to get an idea of the emotional and financial balance sheet of the couple. Brad announced that he was tired of talking about this issue with his wife both calmly and loudly. He believed that "talking about it again and again and expecting for her to change is just crazy. I have talked to her in every way. I have opened my own account. I have even offered to let her pay the bills, but nothing improves. The only thing she understands is action and I have made them after many years of trying to talk and communicate about this issue with her. I have taken on extra jobs to keep her happy and she continues to want more. I am fed up, that's why I left."

Sara said that Brad is "supposed to take care of me as his wife. He promised when we got married that he would do it when things were good or bad. I have taken care of him, four children, and the house, and now it is my turn to be taken care of. He needs to figure out how to pay the bills. It is his role and responsibility." Sara said that "Brad is always gone either at school or work and I am left here at home with the kids. I get lonely sometimes and my friends are there for me. We all hang out together, go shopping, and have a good time. My friends' husbands are able to afford for their wives' to go shopping without a complaint, why can't I!"

Brad and Sara are emotionally and financially disconnected. Through the use of the Smart Heart dialogue, the therapist helped them to create a safe place to talk about the thoughts about money and their relationship. The financial balance sheet exercise helped them to begin the process. Also, the process of creating a budget brought several areas of misunderstandings to light. Sara thought that Brad had more discretionary money available for spending for the family. When he would not give her extra money, she would get angry and "buy what I needed anyway." Brad would begin to set another budget to plan ahead and created a "just in case fund" to pay for unexpected expenses.

Brad's magical thinking was that he expected Sara to be able to discipline herself without consistent communication about their financial situation. He also believes that he alone can manage and solve their relationship problems. On the other hand, Sara believes that buying things allows her to connect with others and not feel so lonely. She did not see how it pushes Brad farther and farther away from her. She also magically thinks that she is not responsible for the financial care of her family. She has abandoned this area. They have continued to be sexually engaged with each other throughout these conflicts; however, their frequency of sexual activity has decreased. Sara began to "hang out" with her friends more and more during these times and shopping more.

The couple completed the Money Tree exercise, which asked them to list their 5-year goals as they seemed to dream big without limits of money or responsibilities. Sara enjoyed this exercise and was easily able to identify big dreams for them, but found it difficult to identify 5-year goals. Brad was able to come up with the 5-year goals, but they were realistically attainable and lacked imagination and expansiveness.

As a couple, they were able to come up with their individual core values and even identify some that they shared. This further mended some misunderstandings, helped them to create a safe place through their communication, and they began to experience some connection on several levels. They also examined how these money conflicts influenced their intimacy and sexual activity. They saw how each of them would move toward something else during these times; Brad to work and Sara to her friends and shopping.

Step 2

When addressing this step, both Brad and Sara stated that they felt controlled by the other. Although they tend to adhere to traditional gender roles, Sara expressed that "Brad controls all of the money and makes all of the financial decisions, most of the time without me. I have no influence over his time or his money. I feel totally controlled on one hand and all on my own on the other. So, I exercise some of my own influence by buying some things that I want, and it makes me feel good with my friends." Brad does not seem to enjoy the idea that he is the one in control of everything. He said that he would rather share the load, "because it gets very heavy and stressful sometimes, but I am supposed to be the man and take responsibility for my family and the money. So I do what I have to do by making a budget and setting limits for Sara."

Teaching Brad and Sara how to fight fair proved to be a challenge. Brad was the most expressive and he had to learn to lower his tone and to listen to Sara's point of view. So they practiced responsive listening skills while sitting close together. He practiced detaching from his emotions. For Sara, fighting fair was different with Brad. She would not express some of her emotions and when she did it was more personal toward Brad for what he was not doing. Therefore, the therapist focused on requiring the use of "*I*" statements rather than "*you*" statements and to be honest but not hurtful. The most helpful act was to learn to reach out to each other in a loving way by touching and practice emotional connection. This was initially difficult for both to do, but they practiced the behaviors in session.

Step 3

In the past, Brad and Sara talked about their family histories and were familiar with the role of money in their family and relationships. Although each of them was from a middle-class background, they viewed money differently. Brad talked about how his family struggled after his parents divorced and how his mother worked two jobs while attending college and taking care of the family. Money was "tight" but they were able to make it until she graduated with her degree and became a professional. She rationed the money and kept a budget that allowed for them to manage their lives. His father maintained contact with the children, but was not financially helpful to the family. Brad learned from his mother that you work hard for money and when you need more, you take on another job, and when that does not work, you ration and budget your money even tighter. He did not have the opportunity to enjoy money and what it could bring; he just experienced the process of earning it.

On the other hand, Sara's parents were professionals and money was more readily available. As the only girl, Sara was given money to spend and when she wanted more, she received it. Her only frustration occurred when her parents said no to her. She would ask them even more until they gave in to her requests. Sara's parents were very generous with money and things. She often received gifts and money for each holiday and sometimes just because the parents wanted to celebrate. When a child, Sara would receive more than her brothers and would feel as if she deserved it, even when it took away from their resources. Her mom initially was a stay at home mom until the children went to school, then she worked as a teacher. Her dad was a successful insurance salesman. Sara learned that money was an object to be used for happiness, and when you needed more, you ask for it until you get it from your supporters.

In session, the couple worked on understanding each of their financial imagos through exercises and identified their top 10 financial transitions and the corresponding stresses. The therapist used these exercises to initiate the Smart Heart dialogue in order to help than explore what they say to each other during these conflicts and what they really mean. They began to notice the impact their families' money legacies, money tree memories, and the emotional triggers have on their financial patterns and decisions. They began to discuss and develop new ways to respond emotionally to these conflicts and changes.

Step 4

In order to "break up with money," Brad and Sara had to confront the pursuer–distancer dynamic in their relationship. They were able to recognize how both of them had been pursuing and distancing themselves from each other through money availability and money limiting phases. They examined their attachment to money. Brad realized that he was avoidantly attached to money, which allowed him to be self-sufficient and to have no reaction to the money issues. He sees how his experience with his mother and seeing her struggle to manage the family's budget with limited resources and how she "put her head to the grindstone" and just worked things out without emotions and without support affected him. He would triangulate with working more in order to avoid dealing with Sara's emotional responses to him and the lack of money. The more she became resentful and demanding, the more he would turn toward work to avoid the conflict.

Sara was anxiously attached to money, which connected her to feelings of emotional distress and resentment toward Brad for not having enough. She recognizes how her mother was similar to her in that she would obsess about how to make and spend money. Her mother grew up poor and looked for financial security, and therefore chose to marry a man she believed would provide her with financial security. Sara did the same as her mother; however, Brad did not earn enough money for her to feel financially secure and therefore she would begin to experience anxiety about not having the money. She would then triangulate with spending and friends to ease the emotional distress.

In session, they spoke of a time when they rarely saw each other. Brad was working and going to school, while Sara was working, caring for the children, and hanging out with her friends. The only time they would see each other was in bed. They would occasionally talk about their day, mechanically have sex, or go to bed in silence. The passion, intimacy, and connection felt absent from their relationship. The needs of their children were the only concerns that brought them together. Therefore, Brad and Sara agreed to practice the Brush with Death exercise to help them to reconnect with one another. They thought, "Maybe this is what our relationship needed." They remained separated throughout the remainder of the sessions.

Step 5

Since they have been separated Brad and Sara have committed themselves to being honest with themselves and to each other about their finances. They began to explore their separate core values as they relate to money.

Brad's core value surrounding money is "work hard for it and manage it so it won't have to manage you." The underlying message with Brad was that he should work and earn money and use it as necessary to live, not so much for enjoyment. Sara's, on the other hand, was to have "others help her to get it, enjoy it, and get more." Her underlying message was that "others should help me to use money for fun, connection, and security."

The challenge for this couple is to help them to let go of their fears, greed, envy, and self-destructive impulses. When discussing exercises of going back to their partner in a new way, each experienced several real questions as to whether or not they wanted to return. They each felt that their differences in valuing money were so extreme, and they were not sure if they would be able or were willing to make the necessary changes. It was too soon to try to reconnect. In this step, the process of reconnection is the major goal. They both agreed to fully participate in the reconnection exercises because they both felt that no matter what happened to the relationship, it was necessary to learn to "put money in its place and not allow it to control their relationship." They completed the "Creating a shared financial relationship vision" exercise and were able to identify areas of shared agreement and vision.

Step 6

In this and the following step, the focus of the sessions turned to rebuilding the connection and the romantic relationship. Since some level of intimacy has been returned to the relationship from being empathic, caring, and open, the emphasis of the sessions was to make the relationship stronger and more intimate. Brad and Sara agreed to work on reconnecting in their relationship. The Brush with Death exercise helped them to experience missing each other and sharing their thoughts and feelings. They practiced having positive interactions, as recommended by Gottman (1995). They began dating and conducted the Trading Places exercise to help them to become more sensitive to one another. Sara planned an outing for her and Brad and paid for the outing herself to practice giving within the relationship.

Brad could not wait to talk about the feelings of happiness and connection he felt for Sara when she did these things for him. He tried to connect to her in these experiences and felt positive about her. He felt more passion and romantic toward her. Although they were still separated, Brad said that he missed her and wanted to interact with her more. Sara said that she enjoyed these outings, although they were difficult for her to plan and execute for someone else. Even paying for these events was a challenge for her. These positive experiences helped the couple to begin to create a romantic and sexual vision.

Step 7

The final step for Brad and Sara was to invest in their future. Because of these exercises, Brad and Sara decided to move back together. They continued to work on maintaining their communication, especially around money and their emotional connection. In order to do this, Brad and Sara reviewed the different areas money impacted their relationship and explored ways they could become proactive in dealing with their differences. In addition, they focused on following the "Ten Commandments for Financial Fidelity" as they practiced the Smart Heart dialogue for real and lasting love.

Summary

This case study provided an example of using the seven steps to conquer financial infidelity. When Brad and Sara came to counseling, they were ready to go their separate ways and were caught in a process of emotional struggle. As a result of their participation, Brad and Sara left counseling feeling more together. They learned what the money and emotional issues were and learned how money impacted their relationship daily and on deeper levels. They went through the process and decided to stay together and to continue to work. At the end of the counseling sessions, they were reconnected emotionally and financially. They continued to experience more romance and intimacy and agreed to continue to follow the "Ten Commandments of Financial Fidelity."

Financial Infidelity and Conclusion

Although the attention given to financial infidelity is recent and growing, the impact of financial infidelity has been witnessed for some time. Conflicts with money and finances continue to grow and negatively affect relationships. When there is a lack of communication and other personal and relational issues, opportunities for financial disagreements arise and fester in other relationship and personal problems. Surveys show that when couples do not discuss finances early in their relationship it can lead to dissatisfaction, divorce, or some other relationship betrayal. Financial infidelity is cheating and deception with money within a relationship. Although there may be many reasons for financial infidelity, the impact of a financial betrayal results in a couple's experiencing a lack of connection and a loss of intimacy. Both personal and relational reasons are responsible for financial infidelity. Financial issues in a relationship must be addressed. If they are left unchecked, they will create the environment for deeper and more severe relationship problems. Financial infidelity and impulse control buying and spending can destroy the relationship if left untreated. Financial infidelity is a significant betrayal and requires outside help to resolve the hurt and pain and to recover the intimacy lost by the financial infidelity.

This chapter has provided a variety of suggestions to deal with the recovery from financial infidelity. Some practical advice has been given by financial professionals to better manage the specific finances and to improve money management. Clinicians have developed treatment strategies and models to help couples deal with the relational impact of financial mismanagement and cheating and to recover the lost intimacy. Clinicians focus on certain relationship skills such as improving communication, dealing with emotional pain, letting go of the hurt, forgiveness, and rebuilding the intimacy over time. Several models have been presented; however, Eaker Weil's model (2008) has been featured as it is tailored for the treatment of financial infidelity. Financial infidelity and other infidelities require clear and supportive assistance and the committed effort of the couple. If these elements are present, a couple can recover and rebuild a stronger and more closer and connected relationship.

References

Ambrose, E. (2008). Financial infidelity is pretty common. *Baltimore Sun.* Retrieved April 11, 2008, from http://www.baltimoresun.com/business/bal-bz.ym.ambrose12feb12,0,4743990.column

American Psychiatric Association (APA). (2000). Diagnostic and statistical manual of mental disorders. 4th ed., text revision. Washington, DC: Author.

Bennett, R. (2008). *Financial infidelity and financial intimacy.* Retrieved November 23, 2009, from http://www.passionsaving.com/financial-infidelity.html

Benson, A. (2000). *I shop therefore I am: Compulsive buying and the search for self.* New York: Jason Aronson.

Benson, A. (2008). *To buy or not to buy: Why we overshop and how to stop.* Boston: Trumpeter Books.

Benson, A., & Gengler, M. (2004). Treating compulsive buying. In R. Coombs (Ed.), *Addictive disorders: A practical handbook* (pp. 451–491). New York: Wiley.

Black, D. W. (2007). A review of compulsive buying disorder. *World Psychiatry, 6*(1), 14–18.

DeSarbo, W. S., & Edwards, E. A. (1996). Typologies of compulsive buying behavior: A constrained cluster-wise regression approach. *Journal of Consumer Psychology, 5,* 231–252.

Dowd, M. (2005, October 30). What's a modern girl to do? *New York Times Magazine.*

Eaker Weil, B. (2008). *Financial infidelity: Seven steps to conquering the #1 relationship wrecker.* New York: Hudson Street Press.

Faber, R. J., O'Guinn, T. C., & Krych, R. (1987). Compulsive consumption. *Advances in Consumer Research, 14,* 132–135.

Frieswick, K. (2008). *Financial infidelity: The marriage breaker. Secretly overspending from the family coffers can be deadly marital money conflict.* Retrieved August 27, 2008, from http://articles.moneycentral.msn.com/Investing/HomeMortgageSavings/TheMarriageBreaker.aspx

Gottman, J. (1995). *Why marriages succeed or fail ... and how you can make yours last*. New York: Simon and Schuster.

Hagey, D., & Brewer, A. L. (2008). *Increasing intimacy in marriage*. Retrieved November 23, 2009, from http://foreverfamilies.net/xml/articles/marital_intimacy.aspx

Hatfield, H., & Chang, L. (2008). *Shopping spree, or addiction? What happens when shopping spirals out of control, and in some cases, becomes an addiction?* Retrieved November 23, 2009, from http://www.webmd.com/mental-health/features/shopping-spree-addiction

Hendrix, H. (1988). *Getting the love you want: A guide for couples*. New York: Harper Perennial.

Hickman, M. (2008). Financial infidelity: The things we buy, the lies we tell. *The Independent* [online]. Retrieved November 23, 2009, from http://www.independent.co.uk/news/uk/this-britain/financial-infidelity-the-things-we-buy-the-lies-lies-we-tell-427923.html

Jayson, S. (2008). Money, fidelity go hand in handy. *USA Today* [online]. Retrieved March 11, 2008, from http://www.usatoday.com/news/health/2008-3-17-financial-infidelity_N.html

Jones, M. (2006, October). Financial infidelity: How money secrets can devastate your marriage. *Ebony* [online]. Retrieved November 23, 2009, from http://findarticles.com/p/articles/mi_m1077/is_12_61/ai_n16776732

Lawyers.com. (2005). *New survey finds common financial infidelity*. Retrieved November 23, 2009, from http://research.lawyers.com/New-Survey-Finds-Common-Financial-Infidelity.html

Lewandowski, G. W., & Ackerman, R. A. (2006, August). Something's missing: Need fulfillment and self-expression as predictors of susceptibility to infidelity. *Journal of Social Psychology, 146*(4), 389.

Loeffler, W. (2006). Relationship real life story—Financial infidelity. *Pittsburgh Tribune-Review* [online]. Retrieved August 27, 2008, from http://pittsburghtrib/news/rss/s_465720.html

MacDonald, J. (2008). *Are you guilty of financial infidelity?* Retrieved November 23, 2009, from http://www.bankrate.com/brm/news/pf/20080103_financial_infidelity_a2.asp

Max, S. (2008). *Financial infidelity. A type of cheating; you may be straying without knowing it*. Retrieved November 23, 2009, from http://www.tangomag.com/20072473

Osteen, S. R., & Neal, R. A. (n.d.). *Couples and money: Let's talk about it*. Oklahoma Cooperative Extension Service. Retrieved August 11, 2008, from http://pods.dasnr.okstate.edu/docushare/dsweb/Get/Document-168/T-4201_pod.pdf

Pawlik-Kienlen, L. (2007). *Financial infidelity in marriage: Why spouses lie about money and how to find financial compatibility*. Retrieved November 23, 2009, from http://behavioural-psychology.suite101.com/article.cfm/financial_infidelity_in_marriage

Ridgway, N. M., Kukar-Kinney, M., & Monroe, K. (2008). An expanded conceptualization and a new measure of compulsive buying. *Journal of Consumer Research, 35*(4), 350–406.

Rochen, A. B., Suizzo, M. A., McKelly, R. A., & Scaringi, V. (2008). I'm just providing for my family. *Psychology of Men and Masculinity, 9*(4), 193–206.

Rodriguez-Villarino, R., Gonzalez-Lorenzo, M., Fernandez-Gonzalez, A., Lameiras-Fernandez, M., & Foltz, M. L. (2006). Individual factors associated with buying addiction: An empirical study. *Addiction Research and Theory, 14*(5), 511–525.

Spring, J. A. (1996). *After the affair.* New York: HarperCollins.

Steinisch, M. (2008). *Couples and money: Achieve financial harmony and prosperity.* Retrieved November 23, 2009, from http://hffo.cuna.org/12433/article/732/html

Stern, R. (2007). *The gaslight effect.* New York: Bantam Dell.

Ureta, I. G. (2007). Addictive buying: Causes, processes, and symbolic meanings. Thematic analysis of a buying addict's diary. *Spanish Journal of Psychology, 10*(2), 408–422.

Voss, G. (2007, September). *The starter husband.* Retrieved November 23, 2009, from http://www.marieclaire.com/sex-love/relationship-issues/articles/starter-husband

Weston, L. P. (2008). *Financial infidelity is rampant.* Retrieved November 23, 2009, from http://articles.moneycentral.msn.com/CollegeAndFamily/LoveAndMoney/FinancialInfidelityIsRampant.aspx

Wikipedia. (2008a). *Addiction.* Retrieved November 23, 2009, from http://en.wikipedia.org/wiki/Addiction

Wikipedia. (2008b). Financial infidelity. Retrieved November 23, 2009, from http://en.wikipedia.org/wiki/Financial_infidelity

Williams, A. (2007, September 23). Putting money on the table: with rising incomes, young women discuss the pitfalls of "dating down." *New York Times.*

CHAPTER **13**

Interview With Brent Atkinson

Brent Atkinson, Ph.D., is the principal architect of *Pragmatic/Experiential Therapy for Couples*, an approach that translates new scientific findings about the brain into practical methods for improving relationships. Dr. Atkinson is author of *Developing Habits for Relationship Success* and *Emotional Intelligence in Couples Therapy: Advances From Neurobiology and the Science of Intimate Relationships*. He is director of postgraduate training at the Couples Research Institute in Geneva, Illinois, and holds a senior graduate faculty post at Northern Illinois University. Dr. Atkinson's pioneering work has been the subject of dozens of professional journal articles, and he has recently been featured in magazines and newspapers such as the *Oprah Magazine*, the *Washington Post*, *Cosmopolitan Magazine*, *Psychotherapy Networker*, and others.

Eds: What knowledge from neurobiology would be helpful for a couple who is trying to restore intimacy after a betrayal?

BA: Studies suggest that partners who demonstrate more interest in each other, engage in more acts of caring and consideration, notice more positive things about each other, and express more appreciations have relationships that are more intimate than do couples who do less of these things. However, recent brain studies suggest that intimacy-building behaviors like these are likely to impact relationships differently depending on the areas of the brain that drive them. The trick to restoring intimacy has to do with figuring out how to "turn on" the brain's intrinsic motivational states that automatically make us actually *feel* more interested in our partners, invested in our relationships, and desirous of increased levels of attention from our partners. In the brain, there's a big difference between caring actions that are driven by a principled decision to act (e.g., "It's the right thing to do," or "It's how a good partner should act") and caring actions that emanate from one of the brain's intrinsic motivational systems. The former will feel like work—the latter will not.

The brain mechanisms crucial to intimacy have been discovered largely through electrical stimulation studies. Nearly five decades ago, researchers began implanting electrodes deep within specific regions of patients' brains, then applying electrical pulses. Early researchers were stunned to see the moods, desires, and concerns of patients change dramatically. Stimulated individuals were temporarily transformed from calm experimental subjects into intensely angry, fearful, lustful, driven, lonely, playful, or compassionate individuals, depending upon which circuits of the brain were stimulated. Activation of the brain's specialized circuits transformed subjects' thinking, beliefs, perceptions, interpretations, and motivations within a few seconds.

A summary of the groundbreaking research leading to the discovery of the brain's executive operating systems can be found in neuroscientist Jaak Panksepp's book *Affective Neuroscience* (1998). Panksepp and his colleagues at Bowling Green State University have located *seven* motivational systems in the brain that can be reliably turned on through electrical stimulation. Depending upon the circuit stimulated, subjects experience motivation to fight, flee, or draw closer to each other. Mother nature has not left to chance the important task of forming intimate bonds. Four of the brain's seven executive operating systems make us feel interested in, invested in, loyal to, and more desirous of attention from our partners. Let's take a look at each of them.

Tenderness

BA: Each of us has a brain system that, when activated, produces spontaneous feelings of warmth, tenderness, and concern for others, thoughts about the welfare of others, and urges to act in nurturing ways toward others. When this state is active, a person will feel empathic toward others, and be naturally motivated to give emotional support.

From the beginning of their lives, humans and other mammals are protected by the activation of a neural operating system in their mothers' brains that produces the motivation to care for their offspring. Before the birth of their first child, women commonly worry about their future adequacy as mothers, but such doubts typically vanish, as if by magic, soon after the birth of the baby. This is because all mothers have a neural operating system that is preprogrammed to produce caring motivations and behaviors. They don't have to learn how to nurture their young. It happens naturally. This system produces feelings that humans call acceptance, nurturance, and love, the feelings of social solidarity and warmth. The initial clue that there was a preprogrammed intrinsic brain system for nurturance was the fact that transfusion of blood from a female rat that had just given birth could instigate maternal behaviors in a virgin female rat (Panksepp, 1998). This brain system is activated by neurochemicals such as oxytocin and prolactin, which rise precipitously just before a mother gives birth. Scientists have discovered that this neural circuit can be activated just as surely by the introducing oxytocin and prolactin directly into certain areas of the brain (Keverne & Kendrick, 1992; Pedersen, Ascher, Monroe, & Prange, 1982; Rosenblatt, 1992; Uvnas-Moberg, 1998). Virgin female rats treated with these chemicals fly into a flurry of caring behaviors, probably to the confusion of young pups nearby who are the unsuspecting recipients of the virgin's newfound maternal urges. Other studies show that instinctive maternal behaviors can also be blocked by giving new mothers drugs that prevent oxytocin from being absorbed (Van Leengoed, Kerker, & Swanson, 1987). Although the most dramatic activation of this brain system can be seen in new mothers, all humans, both men and women, have this neural operating system, waiting to be activated. Considerable evidence suggests that, across all mammalian species, this brain system is more vigorous in female brains than male brains (Berman, 1980; Panksepp, 1998).

Longing

BA: Normally activated by separation from important persons or circumstances, feelings associated with this neural operating system produce variations of loneliness, sadness, and disappointment. When this state is active, a person will experience a need for the interest, nurturing, support, or attention of others, and look forward to expressions of warmth, admiration, or fondness from them.

When this circuit is activated, humans experience feelings ranging from mild loneliness to intense separation distress. The effect is always to promote an urge for emotional contact with others. This neural circuit is particularly active in the younger members of all species, who must depend upon the protection of others for survival. However, there is an abundance of evidence that in healthy adults, the circuit remains active throughout life, providing the motivation for human contact. Nature's plan doesn't involve emotional self-sufficiency. Scores of longitudinal studies suggest that individuals who cut themselves off from the need for emotional comforting from others don't function as well as individuals who continue to experience a need for emotional comforting throughout their lives (Siegel, 1999). When soothing emotional contact is consistently available, individuals develop a sense of security that allows them to avoid wasting energy being overly vigilant to danger (Cozolino, 2002). Neuroscientists believe that this brain system is central to the forming of secure emotional bonds that buffer individuals against stresses throughout their lives (Panksepp, 2001). When the system is aroused, humans and animals seek reunion with others who help create the feeling of a "secure neurochemical base" within the brain (Nelson & Panksepp, 1998). As Panksepp put it, "social bonding involves the ability of organisms to experience separation distress when isolated from social support systems and to experience neurochemically mediated comfort when social contacts are reestablished" (1998, p. 274).

This brain system is calmed through the release of specific neurochemicals, the chief of which are the internal opioids such as endorphins and enkephalins (Panksepp, 1998). These neurochemicals are released though intimate social contact, especially direct physical contact (Keverne, Martensz, & Tuite, 1989; Montagu, 1978). When this brain system in animals is electrically stimulated, they emit "distress vocalizations" (DVs) which are identical to those emitted naturally by young animals who are separated from their mothers (Panksepp, Bean, Bishop, Vilberg, & Sahley, 1980). One of the easiest ways to reduce DVs in experimental animals is to put mirrors on the wall of the test chamber. The animals calm down when they believe they are not alone. The same effect can be observed when music is pumped into the test chamber. Music simulates the comfort of audiovocal contact with other animals (Panksepp et al., 1980). This may be one of the reasons why people love to listen to music—it keeps them company. Apparently, chickens have their favorites in "mood music," too, as evidence by a notably positive reaction to the 1980s Pink Floyd recording *The Final Cut* (Johnson, 2004).

This brain circuit can also be dramatically calmed through the administration of external opiates such as morphine or heroin (Carden & Hofer, 1990; Kalin, Shelton, & Barksdale, 1988; Panksepp, Herman, Conner, Bishop, & Scott, 1978). In fact, brain researchers hypothesize that one reason why certain people become addicted to external opiates such as morphine or heroin is because they are able to artificially induce feelings of comfort similar to those normally achieved by the socially induced release of endogenous opioids. This also explains why opiate addicts tend to socially isolate themselves except for when they need to find another fix, and opiate addiction is most common in environments where social isolation and alienation are endemic (Panksepp, 1998).

There are many experiments that have shown that the DVs have a powerful effect in activating the caretaking circuits of other animals, even if the DVs are tape recorded. Not all crying comes from this separation distress system—both humans and animals respond to pain, hunger, and irritation by crying, but these cries can be distinguished from separation-induced DVs on both neuroanatomical and neurochemical bases. Adult animals instinctively know the difference (Panksepp, 1998).

People vary considerably with regard to the degree to which they experience the activation of this brain system, and in their relative abilities to self-soothe and benefit from comfort offered by others. In recent years, compelling evidence has emerged suggesting that early experiences with caregivers can have a dramatic effect on such abilities (Cozolino, 2002; Fonagy & Target, 1997; Schore, 1994, 1996, 2001a, 2001b, 2001c; Siegel,

1999, 2001). All infants and young children readily experience and express distress when they are separated from desired people or objects. Investigations into early processes related to emotional attachment reveal that children whose parents fail to respond consistently in comforting ways learn to detach from their need for human contact, and that this detachment can persist throughout their lives. On the other hand, children who experience inconsistent, unpredictable parental comforting may experience a chronic activation of this brain system and develop into adults who are continually looking for the kind of comfort that they never got enough of as children.

When caregivers respond to the emotions of developing children in ways that help soothe negative states and amplify positive ones, children develop the ability to fully experience both positive and negative emotions, and their brains also learn how to soothe stressful states. These children develop secure attachments. Studies suggest that the brains of securely attached children develop differently from the brains of insecurely attached children, specifically in the orbital prefrontal cortex, the area of the brain most responsible for emotional regulation (Schore, 1994, 1996, 2001a, 2000b). Schore summarized this point:

> During the first and second years of life, the infant's affective experiences, especially those embedded in the relationship with the primary caregiver, elicit patterns of psychobiological alterations that influence the activity of subcortically produced trophic bioamines, peptides, and steroids that regulate the critical period growth and organization of the developing neocortex. Interactive attachment experiences of psychobiological attunement, stressful misattunement, and stress-regulating repair and reattunement that maximize positive and minimize negative affect are imprinted into the orbitofrontal cortex. ... During the critical period of maturation of this system, prolonged episodes of intense and unregulated interactive stress ... result in structurally defective systems that, under stress, inefficiently regulate subcortical mechanisms that mediate the physiological processes that underlie emotion. (1996, p. 59)

Play

BA: Activation of this brain system produces the urge to interact with others in spontaneous or playful ways. When it is active, a person feels like teasing, roughhousing, tickling, or getting an unpredictable reaction.

When I first read about the brain's intrinsic intimacy-generating systems, I was surprised to find that one of them is devoted exclusively to instigating *play*. It's easy to see why each of the brain's other executive operating systems survived the challenges of evolutionary time. The brain's "fight" system promotes self-protection, the "flight" system facilitates withdrawal from danger, the urge to care for others and the desire for closeness promotes secure attachment, and the desire for sexual contact promotes the passing of genes from generation to generation. But play? How does play enhance chances of survival? The play circuit appears to have an important role in facilitating social bonding (Johnson, 2004; Panksepp, 1998). When this circuit is active, internal opioids are released throughout the brain (Panksepp & Bishop, 1981; Vanderschuren, Niesink, & Van Ree, 1995; Vanderschuren, Stein, Wiegant, & Van Ree, 1997) and when released through nurturing contact serve the function of calming an active separation-distress circuit. Internal opioids are now believed to be one of the prime neurochemical movers in the construction and maintenance of social bonds (Panksepp, 1998). Experimental studies reveal that mammals consistently prefer to spend time with others in whose presence they have experienced high brain opioid activity (Agmo & Berenfeld, 1990; Panksepp, Neson, & Bekkedal, 1997).

When the PLAY circuit is electrically stimulated, individuals experience urges toward vigorous and spontaneous social interaction, often accompanied by a sense of joy. Panksepp (1998) uses words like *carefree* and *rambunctious* to describe the state of mind resulting from an activation of the play circuit in rats. There is evidence across mammalian species that females are somewhat more playful than males (Panksepp, 1998).

Sexual Desire

BA: When activated, this system produces feelings of sexual desire in humans, thoughts oriented toward sexual fulfillment, and urges to make sexual contact. Often, it occurs in tandem with playfulness.

Probably the most important finding about the neural operating system that produces sexual desire is that activation of this system in both men and women elevates oxytocin levels throughout the brain. In animal studies, it has been shown that free access to sexual gratification can lead to an enormous threefold elevation of oxytocin in some parts of the male brain (Panksepp, 1998). Oxytocin is centrally involved in activating the motivation to nurture and care for others. Increased sexual activity diminishes the tendency of male rats to kill the young in a territory that they have successfully invaded (Hausfater & Hrdy, 1984; Menella & Moltz, 1988). In fact, the administration of oxytocin to experimental animals reduces all forms of aggression (Panksepp, 1998). It has been documented that societies that are permissive of premarital sex are generally low in adult physical violence (Prescott, 1971). Neuroscientist Jaak Panksepp has written, "Considering the importance of oxytocin in sexual behavior and the mediation of mother–infant bonds, we must suspect that sexual interactions among consenting adults may neurophysiologically facilitate the consolidation of social attachments, thereby promoting the more nurturant forms of human love" (1998, p. 259).

It should be noted that, while activation of the sexual interest can lead to a parallel activation of tenderness and nurturing motivation, the reverse is also true. Activation of the nurture circuit also makes the activation of sexual interest more likely, especially in women. It is commonly thought that men can have sex without intimacy and that women are less likely to operate this way. Indeed, there are neurochemical reasons for this. Oxytocin plays a greater role in facilitating female sexual interest than male sexual interest. For men, sexual eagerness is mediated by the neuropeptide arginine-vasopressin, which is also known to have a role in the activation of aggression (Sachser, Lick, & Stanzel, 1994; Schurman, 1980). Perhaps this is why men are often experienced as more conquest-oriented in their sexuality. For men, oxytocin levels peak during ejaculation (Carter, 1992), which may be why women often enjoy the company of men most during the "afterglow" period following sex. Due to the release of oxytocin, men are most naturally motivated to act in nurturing ways after sex.

Taken together, these four brain systems are mother nature's way of ensuring that we develop the kind of strong intimate bonds that can calm our nervous systems and propel us to watch over and protect each other. These four brain systems are, in effect, the *engines of intimacy*. When these neural systems are operating freely, we experience feelings of tenderness, the longing for emotional contact, the desire for spontaneous and joyful interaction with others, and the ecstasy of sexual union.

However, just as the brain's self-protective circuits can misfire, so can these intimacy-producing circuits. When relationships are distressed, the circuits that move partners toward intimate bonds become dormant, leaving partners without the emotional connection that once sustained them. Without these powerful circuits active in their brains, attempts to connect are destined to fail. Caring acts become just that—caring *acts* rather than authentic expressions.

Eds: Can you talk about how PET-C (Pragmatic/Experiential Therapy for Couples) can help couples to rewire and recover intimacy?

BA: PET-C helps partners restore intimacy by helping each partner more fully connect with the brain's intimacy-producing states—longing, tenderness, playfulness, and sexual interest (Atkinson, 2001, 2005, 2006). When couples enter therapy, they are frequently involved in patterns in which the fight/flight mechanisms in each of their brains are mutually triggered. Two of the brain's seven executive operating systems are devoted to self-protection. When relationships are distressed, these automatic self-protective mechanisms have usually taken over. The first task is to help each partner escape the pull of these brain systems when they get upset. This is no small task, and I've gone to some lengths to describe the methods we use to accomplish it (Atkinson, 1999, 2005).

But avoiding destructive interaction is only the beginning; it simply creates more possibility that the brain's intimacy states will become active. Once partners are acting more respectfully toward each other, sometimes they naturally experience an increase in feelings of longing, tenderness, playfulness, and sexual interest. But they frequently don't unless they give conscious attention to the task. It is here that popular admonitions such as "give more attention to your relationship," "show more interest," and "do more thoughtful and considerate things" often fall short. Attempts to increase in such actions will often fizzle out after a period of time and/or will often not have their intended effect unless they are motivated by genuine feelings which emanate from the brains intimacy states.

Rather than focusing on increasing acts of interest and/or consideration, PET-C helps each partner examine what may be blocking full and regular activation the natural desire for attention and nurturing, genuine interest in the emotional and physical well-being of one's partner, playfulness and sexual interest. Once blocks are located and resolved, interest in each other and urges to care for and nurture each other flow naturally from the internal states.

In PET-C, we conceptualize activation blocks as being on three levels:

Level I blocks are fairly easy to resolve, because they involve circumstances and schedules. In spite of good intentions, partners often find that their lives don't prompt or allow time for intimate feelings to surface. Partners experiencing Level I blocks find that if they simply pay more attention to building in time and reminders that help them "get into the mood, they easily experience tenderness, desire for closeness, playfulness and sexual interest." We use a variety of exercises to stimulate the intimacy states in this manner (Atkinson, 2005, 2006).

Level II blocks are somewhat complex, involving attitudes, beliefs, or assumptions that keep partners from wanting more full activation of the intimacy states. These attitudes, beliefs, or assumptions are often amenable to change once they are consciously examined. The examination process is often an ongoing time thing. The therapist gives clients tools that allow them to develop internal relationships between their "core self" and the "parts" of them that carry outmoded attitudes, beliefs, and assumptions (Schwartz, 1995). Gradually, clients learn how to *accompany* and calm the internal parts (brain states) that create anxiety when the client moves toward more intimacy. Example: One therapist helped a wife realize that her limited interest in sex was related to an assumption that it's wrong for a woman to ask for what she wants sexually. Once the client identified the part of herself who believed this and felt uncomfortable taking an active role during lovemaking, she found that she was able to separate herself from this part of her and offer assurances that gradually had the effect of calming her anxiety.

Many clients find that once Level I and II blocks are resolved, feelings of tenderness, desire for contact, playfulness, and sexual interest return naturally. However, some clients require further intervention.

Level III activation blocks are often experienced by individuals who have had experiences earlier in life that created a chronic over- or understimulation of the intimacy states. Examples include sexual trauma and less-than-optimal attachment-related experiences. The distinguishing feature of Level III blocks is longevity. Often, individuals experiencing such blocks have experienced low or exaggerated need for closeness with others most of their lives. The origins of the lack of desire for emotional connection are typically rooted in early affective experiences with emotionally distant caregivers. For such people, feelings of longing for nurturing are consistently unmet, the circuits in their brains that produce the longing for emotional contact go dormant. Ironically, such individuals are often paired with mates who have unusually high levels of need for emotional contact, typically traceable to early attachment experiences in which sometimes nurturing was available and other times it vanished. Level III intervention with couples such as these involves an ironic twist, illustrated in the following excerpt:

> Loretta was dying for more emotional understanding and support from Jack, and Jack wasn't really wanting emotional comforting from Loretta. Yet my main strategy was to connect Jack with his emotional need (which he didn't really want) and ask Loretta to delay getting support even longer (which she had been wanting all their married life). Experience working with the internal nurturing and longing states of individual partners has taught me that a person cannot respond very well with nurturing unless they have experienced the comfort of someone else in response to their own emotional need. (Atkinson, 2005, p. 53)

With Level III intervention, the therapist helps a client like Jack recognize when the faint edge or beginning of a desire for nurturing attention can be detected, then follows that edge, allowing it to deepen. Gradually, such clients allow feelings to surface while in the presence of their partners and develop the ability to relax and "take in" nurturing responses of their partners. In contrast, the therapist will help a client like Loretta develop more ability to self-soothe, as well as cultivate additional relationships which can serve as sources of support. The goal is to help this type of client learn how to avoid overwhelming their partners with emotional need, so that the partners are able to provide meaningful emotional contact.

Eds: Can you describe mirror neurons and how they may impact couples in recovery?

BA: When relationships are going well, the intimacy states are naturally active—and the feelings they produce are contagious. When one person is feeling sad, tender, playful, or lustful, it's easy for the other to feel something similar. For example, Panksepp has found that distress cries of young animals automatically activate the caretaking circuits of nearby adult animals. UCLA researcher Marco Iacoboni (2008, 2009) believes that this may be because of "mirror neurons" recently discovered in various areas of the brain. Mirror neurons allow us to feel what another person is experiencing. This is why we cry at the movies when we sense the emotions of the characters, even though we don't know them. Mirror neurons help our brains re-create the feelings inside of ourselves, allowing us to be powerfully affected by others.

Often, people who want more intimacy from their partners fail to capitalize on the advantages that mirror neurons offer. The logic behind mirror neurons is this: If you want your partner to feel more tender, playful, sexually interested, or desirous of emotional closeness, rather than complaining to your partner about the lack of what you want, get yourself more fully into the particular feeling state you'd like to get from your partner, then let your partner *feel* you for a while. Don't pressure your partner into responding immediately, and don't give up if your partner doesn't respond right away.

BA: Here's an excerpt from a story of one of my clients showing how a woman used mirror neurons to get more of what she wanted from her partner:

> I remember the look on Loretta's face the day I posed a simple question to her: "When you're feeling disconnected or lonely, why do you always try to get sympathy from Jack?" She looked at me as though I had lobsters crawling out of my ears. "You've been telling us for months that we need more emotional support from each other! Now you're saying I shouldn't expect that?" Anticipating her response, I smiled and teased her, repeating her words in a play-mocking tone back to her. She smiled immediately, recognizing that I was trying to get a rise out of her, and quipped, "Okay, smart ass, where the hell are you going with this?" I replied, "What I mean, Loretta, is that you always use the same approach to connect with Jack, when there are several avenues available to you." I went on to explain that she seems to forget all about her strong suit— playfulness. When she was feeling lonely or upset, would it be possible for her to make an internal shift and connect with her playfulness as a means of making contact with

Jack? Loretta looked confused, and sat silent, frowning for a few moments. Gradually, her expression changed, and she then told me about a time she remembered when she did exactly that. It was one of those days when everything that could go wrong was indeed going wrong. She rushed to her car after work thinking that she couldn't wait to vent to Jack when she got home. But on the way home, she got so sick of herself that she realized what she really needed was to just forget about the whole damned day and do something to take her mind off of it. When she got home the first thing she did was pinch Jack in the ass. Jack responded by tackling her, and they romped gleefully with each other for 15 minutes until they were laughing so hard that Loretta had to stop because she thought she was going to pee her pants! Loretta admitted that this was probably better than any kind of serious, supportive conversation they might have had. As it turned out, she did confide in Jack later in the evening, and at that moment, he was able to be sympathetic. What happened? Loretta had connected with Jack in a different way. (Atkinson, 2005, pp. 60–61)

Without even realizing it, Loretta had tripped Jack's mirror neurons and he couldn't help but respond!

References

Agmo, A., & Berenfeld, R. (1990). Reinforcing properties of ejaculation in the male rat: Role of opiates and dopamine. *Behavioral Neuroscience, 107*, 812–818.

Atkinson, B. (1999). The emotional imperative. *Family Therapy Networker, 23*(4), 22–33.

Atkinson, B. (2001). Brain to brain: New ways to help couples avoid relapse. *Psychotherapy Networker, 26*(5), 38–45, 64.

Atkinson, B. (2005). *Emotional intelligence in couples therapy: Advances from neurobiology and the science of intimate relationships.* New York: Norton.

Atkinson, B. (2006). *Developing habits for relationship success.* Electronic Workbook for Couples. Geneva, IL: Couples Research Institute.

Berman, P. W. (1980). Are women more responsive than men to the young? A review of developmental and situational variables. *Psychological Review, 88*, 668–695.

Carden, S. W., & Hofer, M. A. (1990). Independence of benzodiazepine and opiate actions in the suppression of isolation distress in rat pups. *Behavioral Neuroscience, 104*, 160–166. *Psychology, 14*, 42–58.

Carter, C. S. (1992). Oxytocin and sexual behavior. *Neuroscience and Biobehavioral Reviews, 16*, 131–144.

Cozolino, L (2002). The *neuroscience of psychotherapy: Building and rebuilding the human brain.* New York: Norton.

Fonagy, P., & Target, M. (1997). Attachment and reflective function: Their role in self-organization. *Development and Psychopathology, 9,* 679–700.

Hausfater, G., & Hrdy, S. B. (Eds.). (1984). *Infanticide: Comparative and evolutionary perspectives.* New York: Aldine.

Iacoboni, M. (2008). *Mirroring people: The new science of how we connect with others.* New York: Farrar, Straus and Giroux.

Iacoboni, M. (2009). Imitation, empathy, and mirror neurons. *Annual Review of Psychology, 60,* 653–670.

Johnson, S. (2004). *Mind wide open: Your brain and the neuroscience of everyday life.* New York: Scribner.

Kalin, N. H., Shelton, S. W., & Barksdale, C. M. (1988). Opiate modulation of separation-induced distress in non-human primates. *Brain Research, 440,* 285–292.

Keverne, E. B., & Kendrick, K. M. (1992). Oxytocin facilitation of maternal behavior in sheep. *Annals of the New York Academy of Sciences, 652,* 83–101.

Keverne, E. B., Martensz, N., & Tuite, B. (1989). B-Endorphin concentrations in CSF of monkeys are influenced by grooming relationships. *Psychoneuroendocrinology, 14,* 155–161.

Menella, J. A., & Moltz, H. (1988). Infanticide in rats: Male strategy and female counter-strategy. *Physiolology & Behavior, 42,* 19–28.

Montagu, A. (1978). *Touching: The human significance of the skin.* New York: Harper and Row.

Nelson, E. E., & Panksepp, J. (1998). Brain substrates of infant-mother attachment: Contributions of opioids, oxytocin, norepinephrine. *Neuroscience and Biobehavioral Reviews, 22*(3), 437–452.

Panksepp, J. (1998). *Affective neuroscience.* New York: Oxford University Press.

Panksepp, J. (2001). The long-term psychobiological consequences of infant emotions: Prescriptions for the twenty-first century. *Infant Mental Health Journal, 22*(1–2), 132–173.

Panksepp, J., Bean, N. J., Bishop, P., Vilberg, T., & Sahley, T. L. (1980). Opioid blockade and social comfort in chicks. *Pharmacology, Biochemistry and Behavior, 13,* 673–683.

Panksepp, J., & Bishop, P. (1981). An autoradiographic map of the (^{3}H) diprenorphine binding in rat brain: Effects of social interaction. *Brain Research Bulletin, 7,* 405–410.

Panksepp, J., Herman, B., Conner, R., Bishop, P., & Scott, J. P. (1978). The biology of social attachments: Opiates alleviate separation distress. *Biological Psychiatry, 13*(5), 607–617.

Panksepp, J., Neson, E., & Bekkedal, M. (1997). Brain systems for the mediation of social separation-distress and social-reward: Evolutionary antecedents and neuropeptide intermediaries. *Annals of the New York Academy Science, 807,* 78–100.

Pedersen, C. A., Ascher, J. A., Monroe, Y. L., & Prange, A. J. (1982). Oxytocin induces maternal behavior in virgin female rats. *Science, 216,* 648–649.

Prescott, J. W. (1971). Early somatosensory deprivation as an ontogentic process in the abnormal development of brain and behavior. In E. I. Goldsmith & J. Mody-Jankowski (Eds.), *Proceedings of the Second Conference on Experimental Medicine and Surgery in Primates* (pp. 356–375). Basel: Karger.

Rosenblatt, J. (1992). Hormone-behavioral relations in the regulation of parental behavior. In J. B. Becker, S. M. Breedlove, & D. Crews (Eds.), *Behavioral endocrinology* (pp. 219–259). Cambridge, MA: MIT Press.

Sachser, N., Lick, C., & Stanzel, K. (1994). The environment, hormones, and aggressive behaviour: A 5-year-study in guinea pigs. *Psychoneuroendocrinology, 19,* 697–707.

Schore, A. N. (1994). *Affect regulation and the origin of self.* Hillsdale, NJ: Erlbaum.

Schore, A. N. (1996). The experience-dependent maturation of a regulatory system in the orbital prefrontal cortex and the origin of developmental psychopathology. *Development and Psychopathology, 8,* 59–87.

Schore, A. N. (2001a). Effects of a secure attachment relationship on right brain development, affect regulation, and infant mental health. *Infant Mental Health Journal, 22*(1–2), 7–66.

Schore, A. N. (2001b). The effects of early relational trauma on right brain development, affect regulation, and infant mental health. *Infant Mental Health Journal, 22*(1–2), 201–269.

Schore, A. N. (2001c). Contributions from the decade of the brain to infant mental health: An overview. *Infant Mental Health Journal, 22*(1–2), 1–6.

Schurman, T. (1980). Hormonal correlates of agonistic behavior in adult male rats. In P. S. McConnell, G. J. Boer, H. J. Romijin, N. E. van de Poll, & M. A. Corner (Eds.), *Adaptive capabilities of the nervous system* (pp. 415–420). Amsterdam: Elsevier/North Holland.

Schwartz, R. (1995). *Internal family systems therapy.* New York: Guilford.

Siegel, D. (1999). *The developing mind: Toward a neurobiology of interpersonal experience.* New York: Guilford.

Siegel, D. J. (2001). Toward an interpersonal neurobiology of the developing mind: Attachment relationship, "mindsight," and neural integration. *Infant Mental Health Journal, 22*(1–2), 67–94.

Uvnas-Moberg, K. (1998). Oxytocin may mediate the benefits of positive social interaction and emotions. *Psychoneuroendocrinology, 23*(8), 819–835.

Vanderschuren, L. J. M. J., Niesink, R. J. M., & Van Ree, J. M. (1997). The neurobiology of social play behavior in rats. *Neuroscience and Biobeahvioral Reviews, 21*(3), 309–326.

Vanderschuren, L. J. M. J., Stein, E. A., Wiegant, V. M., & Van Ree, J. M. (1995). Social play alters regional brain opioid receptor binding in juvenile rats. *Brain Research, 680,* 148–156.

Van Leengoed, E., Kerker, E., & Swanson, H. H. (1987). Inhibition of post-partum maternal behavior in the rat by infusion of an oxytocin antagonist into the cerebral ventricles. *Journal of Endocrinology, 112,* 275–282.

CHAPTER **14**

Recovering Intimacy With Regard to Health, Work, and Friendship Issues

MAUREEN DUFFY

Definition and Description of Intimacy

One of the difficulties in thinking and writing about the recovery of intimacy is our collective vagueness in understanding what we mean by intimacy in the first place. What is it that we have lost when we have "lost" intimacy, and what is it that we are hoping to recover when we attend to increasing intimacy in our own relationships and in the relationships of couples with whom we work? In couples, is intimacy synonymous with sexual intimacy, is it emotional connectedness, is it the yearning to be known by one's partner in a fuller way than in other relationships, is it a skill set that allows couples to repair inevitable ruptures in their relationships, is it a capacity that an individual has for closeness or is it something that resides in the in-between of the relationship between the two partners, or is it some alchemy of all of these elements and more?

In his work with couples using neurobiological and emotional intelligence frameworks, Atkinson (2005) focused on activating a sense of "longing" for the other and referred to "longing" as an internal state influenced by neurobiological brain states. Atkinson stated that "in successful relationships, partners champion each other's dreams, and make every effort possible for each other to realize their deepest hopes and longings. This process is central to creating shared meaning" (p. 286). Weingarten (1992) also spoke about shared meanings and identified these as central to the experience of intimacy. She defined intimacy as an interactional, dynamic relational activity, rather than as a state of being. Weingarten described intimacy as "occurring when people share meaning or co-create meaning and they are able to coordinate their actions to reflect their mutual meaning-making" (p. 47).

Sperry, Carlson, and Peluso (2006) identified intimacy as a systemic dimension of the couple relationship, together with two other dimensions: power and boundaries. They described the intimacy dimension as the partners' "need for and fear of closeness and caring" (p. 22), reminding us that longing and yearning for emotional connection can also come with a concomitant anxiety and fear of it. Page, Nisan, Eckstein, and Ane (2008) indicated that "two key aspects of intimate interaction are self-disclosure and partner responsiveness or warmth" (p. 83), emphasizing the activities necessary for partners to do in order to experience intimacy.

Intimacy requires both a desire for emotional connection and a set of behaviors coordinated between partners designed to achieve it. The desire for emotional connection with one's partner is neurobiologically mediated (Atkinson, 2005; Schore, 2003a, 2003b; Sperry, 2002; Sperry et al., 2006). Similarly, Johnson (2003a, 2003b) identified the need for closeness and connection with significant others as innate and the absence of such connection as intrinsically traumatizing. In essence, attachment and connection to our partners is basic, and it matters profoundly whether the connection between partners is mutual and reliable.

In order for people to be successful in intimate relationships, Atkinson stated that "they must become more concerned about how they respond to the upsetting things that their partners say or do than they are about the upsetting things their partners are saying or doing" (2005, p. 6). In other words, to achieve intimacy, one must practice emotional self-regulation and become more concerned about one's own behaviors and reactions than about the behaviors and reactions of one's partners. The activities required to achieve and maintain intimacy with one's partner are skill sets of behaviors that can be learned and practiced (Atkinson, 2005; Gottman, 1999; Johnson, 2003a, 2003b; Schnarch, 2002). Thus, intimacy can best be understood as a combination of the emotional desire and practical skill set required to engage in repair behaviors following the rupture of attunement or emotional connection within a love relationship.

The language used to describe intimacy in couples' relationships is usually evocative but not always clear enough for clinicians to identify key elements that can be translated into concrete and achievable therapeutic goals. In this chapter, based on research and clinical evidence, a primary goal will be to unpack the meaning of couples' intimacy in ways that can be understood and translated into clinical practice by couples therapists, irrespective of their theoretical and clinical models. The research and clinical evidence presented in this chapter will be gathered from the general research and clinical literature on couples therapy and also from the specific research and clinical literature on the reciprocal effects of health, work, and friendship on intimacy in the context of couples' relationships.

Table 14.1 summarizes the research and clinical-based evidence used to identify key elements descriptive of intimacy within couples' relationships. The strength of evidence represented by each research study, analysis, and clinical application of existing research literature varies. That limitation notwithstanding, the table provides clinicians with a useful evidence-based tool for understanding and assessing the presence or absence of core elements of intimacy in the relationships of couples who come to them often desperate for help. The table also illustrates that the evidence-based descriptors and language used to identify key elements of intimacy within couples' relationships is somewhat imprecise and that the meanings of some of the descriptions and categories could be interpreted in multiple ways. In addition, some of the descriptors and categories overlap.

The core elements of intimacy within couples' relationships are not listed in any rank order because of the absence of levels of evidence or strength in their identification. However, the fact that these elements of intimacy are drawn from the research and clinical evidence suggests that couples therapists can more confidently use these elements as aspects of assessment of intimacy in couples' relationships and as the focus of therapeutic intervention and change. It is not suggested that every element listed here must be present in a couple's relationship for it to be assessed as intimate. A couple's relationship must contain some of these elements for it to be intimate, from both the insider experience of being in a couple's relationship and from the outsider observations of the couple by a competent therapist. In spite of the lack of levels of evidence or strength, the preponderance of the evidence does gravitate toward relationship repair skills as critical in maintaining intimacy. A summary of the core elements of intimacy would include:

- Being in a committed relationship,
- Relational awareness,
- Authenticity,
- Mutuality and mutual understanding,
- Mutual support,
- Emotional closeness,
- Mutual responsiveness and warmth,
- Trust,
- Sharing confidences,
- Self-disclosure,
- Decreasing marital tension or conflict,

Table 14.1 Evidence-Based Core Elements of Intimacy Within Couples' Relationships

Core Elements	Research Evidence	Clinical Evidence
Being in a committed relationship	Gottman (1999); Gottman & Silver (1999); Kiecolt-Glaser & Newton (2001)	Atkinson (2005); Ornish (1998)
Relational awareness	Atkinson (2005); Kayser, Watson, & Andrade (2007)	Atkinson (2005); Gottman (1999)
Authenticity	Kayser, Watson, & Andrade (2007)	
Mutuality and mutual understanding	Heller & Wood (1998); Kayser, Watson, & Andrade (2007)	
Mutual support	Gerson et al. (2006)	
Emotional closeness	Atkinson (2005); Johnson & Greenberg (1985); Sperry (2002); Timmerman (1991)	Atkinson (2005); Johnson (2003b); Sperry, Carlson, & Peluso (2006)
Mutual responsiveness and warmth	Kayser, Watson, & Andrade (2007); Page, Nisan, Eckstein, & Ane (2008)	
Trust	Timmerman (1991)	
Sharing confidences	Weihs, Enright, & Simmens (2008)	
Self-disclosure	Mikulciner & Nachson (1991); Page, Nisan, Eckstein, & Ane (2008); Timmerman (1991); Weihs, Enright, & Simmens, (2008)	Carlson & Sperry (1999)
Decreasing marital tension and/or conflict	Coyne (2001); Gerson et al. (2006); Gottman (1999); Kiecolt-Glaser et al. (2005); Kiecolt-Glaser & Newton (2001)	Atkinson (2005); Gottman (1999); Gottman & Silver (1999)
Improving marital quality	Rohrbaugh, Shoham, & Coyne (2006)	
Increasing positive perceptions of relationship	Ray (2004)	

Table 14.1 Evidence-Based Core Elements of Intimacy Within Couples' Relationships
(*Continued*)

Core Elements	Research Evidence	Clinical Evidence
Sexuality and sexual relating	Elliott & Umberson (2008)	Schnarch (2002)
Creating shared meanings		Weingarten (1992)
Relationship repair skills	Gottman (1999); Johnson (2003b); Johnson & Greenberg (1985); Schore (2003a, 2003b)	Carlson & Sperry (1999); Schore (2003a, 2003b)

- Improving marital quality,
- Increasing positive perceptions of relationship,
- Sexuality and sexual relating,
- Creating shared meanings,
- Relationship repair skills,

How Intimacy Is "Lost" or "Cools"

If we regard intimacy as a combination of an internal state heavily influenced by neurobiological underpinnings related to early attachment experiences and as a set of behaviors and activities engaged in by a couple over time during their relationship, then the cooling of intimacy can be related to (a) neurobiological processes or (b) to behaviors, actions, or omission of behaviors or actions, or (c) to a combination of these. This view of intimacy includes acknowledgment of the underlying neurobiological substrata upon which the capacity to emotionally connect with another rests (Bowlby, 1969; Johnson, 2003a, 2003b; Schore, 2003a, 2003b) as well as understanding the specific behaviors in which couples engage (Gottman, 1999) that either promote or inhibit emotional connection and overall relationship satisfaction.

For couples therapists it should be axiomatic that disruptions and periodic difficulties in relationships are normal and expected and not, in and of themselves, indicative of serious relationship problems. The presence of relationship ruptures and difficulties in couples therapy should immediately direct the attention of the therapist to how effective the couple is in their attempts at conflict resolution and to the level of distress exhibited by each member of the couple when such relationship ruptures occur. Distance and closeness in couples' relationships are primarily affected by the attachment history of each partner as it expresses itself in neurobiological reactions to threat and conflict in the relationship (Schore, 2003a, 2003b) and through the habits the couple has developed to manage closeness, distance, conflict, and reconciliation. This combination of neurobiological substrata and interactional patterns or habits of relating have particular implications for the health of partners in a couple relationship, for their responses to the demands of work at both the workplace and at home, and in their personal and external friendship patterns. Each of these three areas will be explored separately.

Health and the Cooling of Intimacy

There is a long history of research findings that suggests that marriage improves the health of individual partners, in particular, of husbands (Kiecolt-Glaser & Newton, 2001) and that, overall, improved health and lower risk of death from all causes confer a "marriage benefit." Whether married or not, health and the quality of intimacy in couples relationships are uniquely correlated. Ornish (1998) stated:

> Love and intimacy are at a root of what makes us sick and what makes us well, what causes sadness and what brings happiness, what makes us suffer and what leads to healing. If a new drug had the same impact, virtually every doctor in the country would be recommending it for their patients. It would be malpractice not to prescribe it—yet, with few exceptions, we doctors do not learn much about the healing power of love, intimacy, and transformation in our medical training. Rather, these ideas are often ignored or even denigrated. (p. 3)

Participating together as a couple in health-promoting behaviors like physical activity and the planning and preparation of healthy meals can enhance intimacy when such behaviors support a mutually shared goal of living healthy lives. There appears to be a bidirectional correlation between health and intimacy insofar as the quality and experience of intimacy can affect the health status of the individual partners in a couple. Likewise, the health status of one or both partners affects the quality and experience of intimacy.

Intimacy and Its Effects on Health

Abundant research evidence suggests that the quality and experience of intimacy within a committed couples' relationship affects the health status of the individual partners. Within marriage, wound healing is impacted by marital tension. Wounds heal more slowly when marital tension is high (Kiecolt-Glaser et al., 2005). Marital tension has also been demonstrated to affect the release of stress hormones and increase blood pressure and heart rate (Kiecolt-Glaser & Newton, 2001). Patients with congestive heart failure whose interactions with their spouses were assessed as more negative were 1.8 times as likely to die within 4 years as those whose marital interactions were assessed as less negative (Coyne, 2001). In a follow-up study (Rohrbaugh, Shoham, & Coyne, 2006), marital quality predicted mortality over an 8-year period for a group of heart failure patients and did so more powerfully than examination of individual risk and protective factors. For women, dissatisfaction with one's marriage was correlated with greater perception of pain and disability among a mixed-gendered sample of chronic back pain patients (Ray, 2004).

In the case of cancer, Kayser, Watson, and Andrade (2007), in their qualitative research study, found that cancer is very much a "we-disease" and that coping with the cancer of a partner is contingent upon the quality of the couple's relationship awareness, communication, warmth, and responsiveness. Depending on the quality of intimacy, couples coped with the cancer of one of the partners either through a pattern of mutual responsiveness or disengaged avoidance. In powerful but preliminary research findings, confiding in one's husband, an indicator of marital closeness, was protective against the progression of breast cancer and was predictive of decreased mortality (Weihs, Enright, & Simmens, 2008). While these data are striking, Gottman and Silver (1999) provided a summative, overarching reason for attending to the maintenance and recovery of intimacy in relationships. They stated that individuals in successful marriages will live an average of 4 years longer than those not involved in such positive relationships. To paraphrase Ornish (1998), if there were a medicine that would increase our productive lifespan by 4 years, most of us would be in line demanding it and its generic name would be an intimate relationship.

Health Status, Illness Intrusiveness, and Effects on Intimacy

Although the quality of intimacy within a couple's relationship has both global and specific effects on health, as described above, the health status of individual partners within a couple's relationship also has effects on intimacy. Illness intrusiveness refers to the degree that the presence of disease or illness impacts daily functioning and the activities of daily life, including sex and intimate communications. A good example of the direct impact of illness on sexual intimacy comes from the research of Moore and Seeney (2007) who found that gross motor impairment associated with Parkinson's disease had a direct effect on reducing the frequency of sexual intimacy and resulted in self-blame on the part of the partner with Parkinson's. The authors suggested that therapists need to understand the impact of Parkinson's disease on sexuality and help to educate couples that reduced frequency of sexual intimacy within this context is normal.

The illness intrusiveness theoretical framework (Devins et al., 1983, 1990) provides one of the more comprehensive frameworks for understanding the impact of illness in major areas of life functioning, including intimacy. This framework suggests that the presence of illness disrupts and compromises the quality of daily life in significant life domains in those with life-threatening conditions. Significant life domains include the daily activities of living, the nurturing of important relationships, paying attention to one's personal and professional development, and promoting emotional and sexual intimacy. The illness intrusiveness model also suggests that the magnitude of illness intrusiveness is mediated by other social, psychological, and contextual factors such as perceptions of illness intrusiveness, financial and educational status, caregiver burden, and social support networks. The illness intrusiveness framework supports the examination of the effects of illness from a couple's and family's perspective. Since demands on caregivers in couple relationships where one partner is ill can range from mild to extreme, it makes the most sense to examine the impact of illness from an interactional, couple and family perspective rather than from an individual perspective. When chronic or life-threatening illnesses occur, life changes dramatically for the partner in an intimate relationship. In the presence of chronic or life-threatening illness, intimacy may increase, it may decrease, or it may oscillate between increased closeness and increased distance.

Binik, Chowanec, and Devins (1990) found that the greater the degree of perceived illness intrusiveness, the greater the negative impact on marital adjustment and individual well-being of both partners when one partner was suffering from end-stage renal disease. Twenty-five years later, Devins, Bezjak, Mah, Loblaw, and Gotowiec (2005), in their study of illness intrusiveness in 656 persons with one of six common cancers, concluded that the illness intrusiveness theoretical framework was supported for persons with cancer and provided a basis for continuing research and therapeutic interventions.

In summary, behavioral health research suggests that any of the following or a combination thereof can result in the "cooling off" of intimacy in couples' relationships impacted by illnesses and by the demands of care giving to ill partners:

- Marital tension and conflict,
- Lack of relational awareness,
- Lack of mutual responsiveness and warmth,
- Inadequate information about the health condition given to either the patient, the partner, or both,
- Uncertainty and doubt about one's attractiveness to the other,
- Concerns about becoming a burden to the other,
- Exhaustion and fatigue on the part of the patient, the partner/caregiver, or both,
- Patient or partner's resentment of the illness, or resentment of the "trappings" and signifiers of illness (e.g., bedpans, walkers, syringes, medication bottles, prescriptions, etc.),

- Decreased sexual desire due to depression, medications, or both,
- Impact of loss of time on capacity to connect emotionally.

Work and the Cooling of Intimacy

Work–life balance may be an interesting metaphor to signify an aspirational state, but its reification as an ideal may be more related to the world of fantasy than to the world of reality. The "life" part of the work–life balance distinction suggests that outside of employment, there is something other than work. When you eliminate housework, the work of childcare, the work of personal grooming and health maintenance, and the work of maintaining friendships, intimate relationships, and family relationships, there is precious little time left for activities that we do not typically consider "work." In a nutshell, the "life" part of work–life balance is itself filled with activities that require various forms of effort and work.

Sociologist Arlie Russell Hochschild's (1983) classic work on "the managed heart" has much to say to therapists who work with couples. She was among the first to point out that the management of emotions is work, and that people engage in complex processes of generating and expressing emotions that are socially expected within given situations. For example, modern couples often want to have dual careers, children, and enriching lives and opportunities for those children. If a couple manages to attain those goals and then finds that maintaining all of the dimensions of their desired life is exhausting and may not be sustainable, they may experience cognitive and emotional dissonance. Their actual experiences and emotions are at odds with the socially expected experiences and emotions for a couple who has achieved such success, thereby only compounding their conflict. Another example is one of those taken-for-granted assumptions by most of us, including couples therapists, that home is an escape from work and that most people are happy to "get home" after work and to get away from the pressures of the workplace. For some couples this may be the case, but for other couples, the exact opposite may be the case. Feeling good at home may be the taken-for-granted expectation, but feeling stressed out and overwhelmed may be the emotional reality for many partners in couples' relationships.

In dual income and dual career couples, Hochschild's (1997) idea of escape into work is immensely interesting. With this concept, Hochschild turns the idea of work–life and work–family balance on its head by suggesting, as a result of her research, that for many in couples' relationships, especially those with children, the guilt over long hours away from home and the work of home become so demanding that couples seek refuge and escape in work, thereby creating an Orwellian context in which home is work and work is home or sanctuary. She then added the "third shift" to the by-now overused construct of the "second shift" (Hochschild & Machung,

2003) and suggested that the work of the "third shift" is the work of rees-tablishing emotional connection at home.

Hochschild's (1983, 1997) classic and continuing research about emo-tion, work, and home can offer important insights for family therapists. In all three domains or major sites of contemporary life—namely, work, home, and emotional expression and attachment—the demands of work are huge and complex. The workplace has its own set of expectations and obligations that are determined by the nature of the job and the work set-ting. The flexibility of these workplace expectations and obligations var-ies greatly with the nature of the job and organization. While, for some, home does represent rest and sanctuary, it does not for all. For many, home represents just another set of fairly unyielding obligations that cannot eas-ily be ignored. Housework, childcare, and financial management are all essential instrumental activities of living that take continuous effort and fairly sizable amounts of time. In addition, the continuing nature of the work of home, and its repetitiveness, can present a more unyielding and unsatisfying set of work obligations than those of some workplaces where projects have more finite beginning and endpoints. Each site of work—the workplace, home, and the work of emotion—generates some measure of discontinuous experiences and expectations. The cumulative effect of the experience of work in these major domains of life can be both sustaining and exhausting, complicating the effect of work on intimacy.

In this section, the idea of "work" has been expanded to include the activities and obligations to which couples must attend in the home and in managing the intimate relationships of family life, both with part-ners and spouses and with children. So what this means for the average couple is that one or both must shoulder the responsibilities and obliga-tions of paid employment, then they must shoulder the obligations and responsibilities of managing a household and children, if there are any, and in the midst of both these sets of "work" responsibilities, the couple must also manage the responsibilities and obligations of doing the emo-tional work of maintaining intimate relationships. For therapists who work with couples, work is best understood as consisting of three types: namely, paid employment that may or may not be outside of the home; running and managing a household and children and their activities, if there are any; and, finally, the emotional work that the couple must do to maintain connection and intimacy. Understood in this way, work repre-sents a huge set of responsibilities and obligations that must be continu-ously and effectively fulfilled by couples. That many, if not most, couples are ill-prepared for the personal and professional dimensions of work in their lives and that they are shocked and exhausted by its demands should come as no surprise. These demands only increase in times of economic downturn.

Work-related factors influencing the cooling off of intimacy are:

- Fatigue and exhaustion,
- Lack of time,
- Too many physical and mental demands at home, including child-care, housework, and financial management,
- Preoccupation with work obligations,
- Preoccupation with home obligations,
- Preoccupation with concerns about money,
- Managing the emotional demands and obligations of work, home, and relationships with partner and children,
- Inadequate support networks of family, paid help, or both,
- Doing the emotional work required to remain connected with one's partner,
- Inadequate recreation and "play" time,
- Insufficient rest and sleep.

Friendship and Intimacy

At the theoretical level, friendship can lead to the cooling off of a particular aspect of intimacy if partners develop habits of relating that emphasize companionship without the elements of sexual relating and sexual intimacy. Such platonic couples may share emotional connectedness without sexual connectedness and thereby miss out on an important aspect of intimacy.

Conversely, friendship and the positive affect states that are usually produced by friendship can be extremely important, in what Gottman, Driver, and Tabares (2002) referred to as the "sound marital house." Therefore, in their therapy with couples, they actively focus on helping couples to develop patterns of shared interest and meaning that are designed to promote friendship states in couples. Likewise, Atkinson (2005) has developed a series of activities designed to help partners build friendships as a way of activating positive internal neurobiological states that are positively triggered by thoughts and presence of their partner. Self-disclosure, mutual responsiveness and warmth, and sharing confidences are all central aspects of human friendship. They are also evidence-based aspects of intimacy within couples' relationships.

The best evidence points toward the importance of promoting friendship and companionable activities within a couple's relationship as a way of building intimacy. However, other kinds of friendship activities outside the primary couple relationship may get in the way of intimacy for the couple and actually work against its development. For example, in most couples' relationships, time is a scarce resource, especially after factoring in the demands of work on three fronts, as described above. So picture a partner in a couple's relationship spending an hour, or perhaps longer, talking on the telephone with a friend or two on most weeknight evenings. The content of the phone conversations may be mundane and related to shared interests or benign gossip and the intent of the partner in spending time on the phone may be simply to keep up with friends. The net effect on the couple's relationship, however, may be quite dramatic in that the partner not involved in the phone conversations may feel left out or even emotionally abandoned, and, at the least, the regular phone conversations leave less time for the couple to spend enhancing their own sense of shared connection and intimacy.

With the dramatic increase in Web 2.0 interactive social networking applications like Facebook and LinkedIn, relationship partners may sit alone at their computers touching base with friends all over the country and the world in their off hours. Many employers block social networking applications and therefore the only time that many people can participate in them is on their own time—again using time, a scarce relationship resource, to virtually connect with others while ignoring their primary partner a few feet away in the same physical space. With Facebook utilization increasing at an annual rate of around 153% (Techtree News Staff, 2008), it is hard to imagine the problem of left out partners getting smaller. And even if both partners are clicking away on social network applications with others, they are not connecting with each other and that is what represents a threat to intimacy over time.

Although online activities and connecting with friends and acquaintances through email and through Web 2.0 social networking applications seem to represent the greatest threat to intimacy in terms of engaging in friendship-directed activities that do not include one's partner, there are other "live" as opposed to "virtual" ways that outside friendships can get in the way of enhancing intimacy with one's partner or spouse in a couple's relationship. Work is a setting in which people may be grouped together in situations that demand high levels of interaction and collaboration to accomplish projects and to meet deadlines. In those kinds of work settings, it is not unusual for people to develop a sense of camaraderie or esprit de corps during which they might share personal stories or personal information, including information about any difficulties they may be having on the home front. A coworker may then become a confidante, and one who is not one's partner triangulates the flow of intimate communication that should ordinarily flow directly between the two partners. The coworker confidante thus becomes a threat to intimacy and even to the stability of the couple's relationship. In the same way, the partner who is frequently out with drinking or sporting buddies or who spends significant time exercising or working out or even meditating with friends cheats his or her primary partner of the time and attention that intimate partners require to do the work of relationship building and maintenance.

Factors relating to friendship influencing the cooling off of intimacy are:

- Given the limited resource of time, spending excess time on the telephone with friends at the expense of one's primary relationship.
- Given the limited resource of time, spending excess time engaged in emailing friends and on social networking applications with friends at the expense of one's primary relationship.
- Developing workplace confidante(s) through whom intimate communication is channeled and triangulated rather than being shared directly between partners.
- Given the limited resource of time, spending excess time with drinking or sporting buddies or exercise and work-out partners at the expense of one's primary relationship.
- Involvement with friends at the expense of one's primary relationship and to a degree that leaves one's partner feeling emotionally abandoned.

Strategies and Interventions for Recovering Intimacy

Best practices are increasingly evidence based so that we can more confidently answer the question, as therapists, of why we are doing or not doing something in therapy. The treatment guidelines for recovering intimacy that follow must be carried out within the context of a therapeutic relationship that is experienced as safe by both partners. Earlier in the chapter intimacy was defined as a combination of an internal state heavily influenced by neurobiological underpinnings related to early attachment experiences and as a set of behaviors and activities engaged in by a couple over time during their relationship. We have understood the cooling of intimacy as related to (a) neurobiological processes or (b) to behaviors, actions, or omission of behaviors or actions, or (c) to a combination of these. Therefore, a therapist's interventions will be aimed at shifting individual internal affective states from neutral or negative to more positive and open to new understandings. Interventions will also be focused on helping couples to change their habitual patterns of interacting. Dealing with emotion will occupy an important role in these strategies and this kind of couples therapy. Defensiveness and avoidance of emotional vulnerability and expression are related to early attachment patterns, and therapists should therefore expect some clients to be anxious and avoidant at the prospect of engaging in emotional work. Based on the evidence, it is difficult to support therapeutic strategies that do not include at least some emotional work for couples who present with diminished intimacy. Many therapists who practice primarily from solution-focused, cognitive-behavioral, and structural-strategic models of therapy may want to reevaluate the reemerging importance of attachment schemas in the development and maintenance of intimacy patterns and their link to neurobiological substrata if they wish to grow as effective couples therapists. In addition, when dealing with couples who have been impacted by health, work, and friendship issues, therapists may want to review some of the significant findings related to the effects of health issues, work demands, and outside friendship patterns on the experience of intimacy. In this chapter, intimacy is clearly understood as a desirable state in and of itself and furthermore as a state desired by most couples, however lost they may be in their pursuit of it. The road to regaining intimacy follows a path that inevitably leads through facing and understanding the emotional vulnerability of oneself and of one's partner, caring about and respecting that vulnerability, and then identifying patterns of behavior change that couples can learn primarily in the service of repair of disruptions in the relationship once they occur.

Treatment Guidelines for Recovering Intimacy and for Including Health, Work, and Friendship Issues as Affecting Intimacy

Gottman (1999) stated that "every couple in their daily life together messes up communication, and every marriage has a 'dark side.' It seems that what may matter most is the ability to repair things when they go wrong" (p. 7). Viewing the ability to engage in mutual repair efforts when a relationship is distanced as the single most important aspect of recovering intimacy introduces an optimistic and hopeful note into our work with couples. Improving intimacy becomes largely a measure of how well couples can learn the skills for repairing relationship damage and how effectively they can put those skills into practice. The following treatment guidelines for recovering intimacy are based on the research and clinical evidence cited throughout this chapter.

1. Create a therapeutic safe zone in which both partners feel safe and secure. In obtaining a couple's history, in conducting an assessment, and in developing interventions, keep the couple at the center of your focus. Do not get sidetracked by descriptions of health, work, friendship, or other couples' issues; bring everything back to its impact on the couple and what they have tried to do about their difficulties.
2. Obtain an individual and couple history from each partner that includes information about:
   a. medical conditions and their perceived impact by each partner on individual and couples functioning; and a global assessment of illness intrusiveness.

   b. current work history and any past work history important to either partner; specific details about time spent out of the home at work; time spent at home on outside work; details of work involved in managing the household and caring for the home; details about childcare and children's activities, if children are present; strategies used by the couple to build and maintain intimacy and emotional closeness; information about division of labor; information about reconciliation and repair efforts when there has been a relationship rupture.

   c. time spent online for social purposes such as emailing friends and using Facebook or similar social networking applications; time spent individually with friends and on what activities; friendship roles of coworkers.

3. Openly discuss with the couple:

   a. medical issues and their impact on the couple's functioning and intimacy.

   b. the global and individual impact of work outside and inside the home on the couple's functioning and intimacy.

   c. the role of friendships in either enhancing or hurting intimacy.

4. Collaborate with the couple in the development of treatment goals and objectives and in development of a process to help the couple evaluate the degree of progress they are making toward achievement of their goals.

5. Provide the couple with a brief description and rationale about the importance of attachment schemas in shaping how they relate to each other and to other important people in their lives. Explain to the couple that their own physical and emotional responses to events and situations in their relationship are important clues to their attachment styles.

6. Discuss the importance of emotions in intimate relationships and emphasize the importance of emotional self-regulation.

7. Normalize relationship disruption, but intensify the significance of relationship repair efforts.

8. Encourage the sharing of experiences, feelings, and feeling states without evaluation of them. Encourage and help the couple to practice uncritical acceptance of the feelings and feeling states of the other. Encourage the use of gentle humor, empathy, and self-control and self-regulation of one's own emotions and affect states during repair efforts while avoiding criticism of the other.

9. Identify typical or characteristic patterns of attempts by couple at relationship repair and reconciliation. Find out whether one

partner usually initiates reconciliation or whether both partners participate in relationship repair efforts. Ask each partner to describe his or her understanding of how their pattern of relationship repair developed and their degree of satisfaction with it. If only one partner typically initiates relationship repair efforts, find out from the other partner what he or she might need to be able to begin to initiate "mending fences."

10. Have the couple give an example of a disagreement or conflict that they have been having trouble resolving. Assess the quality of repair efforts by each partner and assess the degree of either acceptance or criticism of the other's point of view and emotional state.

11. Provide examples of relationship repair strategies (e.g., apology, expressions of kindness and affection, gentle words, gentle touch, "you're more important to me than this argument," etc.) and encourage each partner to assume personal responsibility for relationship repair efforts.

12. Help the couple to promote a sense of "we-ness" or relational awareness by exchanging confidences and stories, by developing shared rituals, however brief, and by elaborating on the story of themselves as a couple, including the story of their unique health, work, and friendship challenges.

Case Example

Julie and John (names are pseudonyms) have been together for 22 years, 5 years before they were married and 17 years since. Early on in their marriage they were having trouble becoming pregnant and adopted a baby girl, Emily. Shortly afterward Julie conceived and had twin boys. Emily is now 12 and the twins are 10. Both Julie and John describe themselves and each other as overachievers. John has built up a successful special events planning and photography company that keeps him away from home fairly frequently several evenings a week and on the weekends. Julie has never really complained about John's unpredictable hours, viewing the success of his business as a family asset.

Julie, who was an art history major in college, works at a university-based museum four mornings a week. In the afternoons she takes primary responsibility for picking up the kids from school and chauffeuring them to their multiple after-school activities. Emily takes ballet and modern dance two afternoons a week and swims on her swim team five evenings a week. The twin boys are in scouts and on their school's soccer team. One of the boys has speech and reading problems and goes to a tutor and speech therapist once a week for special treatment.

Depending on his schedule, John helps with the drop-off and pick-up of the kids, but most of the responsibility falls on Julie's shoulders. Julie is proud of her design and aesthetic sensibility, so keeping her house attractive and clean is very important to her. She calls herself a "nester" and knows that she will give up sleep to do things to maintain her standards for the house. Julie does not know whether it is related to the many demands of her life or not, but she has developed irritable bowel syndrome (IBS). Recently, John has expressed exasperation at Julie because her condition has prevented her from accompanying him to business meetings to meet potential new clients. John has always relied on Julie to help make a good first impression with potential clients and to "seal the deal."

Between both their careers and the responsibilities of home and children, there is very little disposable time left for John and Julie. Emotional connection and other forms of intimacy have diminished. For years, Julie has assumed major responsibility for the childcare and home care in the relationship in addition to her work in acquisitions at the museum and has done so without much complaint or, indeed, resentment. The comments of her younger colleagues at the museum who marvel at how she manages all of the demands on her time have begun to make Julie rethink the arrangements between her and John, and she is beginning to feel resentful that John can focus mainly on his job without having to take primary responsibility for the other areas of family and home life. Julie has begun to ask John to get more involved in helping out with chauffeuring the kids and with being home a little more so that she can have some time to herself. John's response has been to ask why after all these years she is complaining now and points out that everything he does he does for her and the family.

Julie feels that while she is the overworked one, John has turned himself into the victim by claiming he is unappreciated for what he does because of her recent requests for more help and support from him. John's response has also been to immerse himself further in the work of his company and to avoid dialogue with Julie about her concerns. Instead, John has taken to having afternoon coffee with a contract employee of his whose marriage broke up a year ago and who tells John that Julie is being unreasonable just like his ex-wife. John also decided that he needed to exercise more in order to handle his stress, so he and his coworker have been meeting at the gym to work out together several late evenings a week after they finish work. Julie called a therapist and said she is tired of the situation and tired of always having to be the one to make nice to John and fix things up between them. She says the way the marriage is now she is not even allowed to complain and blames herself for quietly assuming so much responsibility over the years.

Treatment Strategies for Julie and John

Julie and John, like many dual career couples with children, are shouldering significant work obligations, both to their careers and to their families. As their children and careers have grown, so have their workloads both inside and outside of the home. On the plus side, each of their relationship styles is marked by a sense of commitment, task-orientedness, and willingness to assume a high degree of personal responsibility for carrying out work and family obligations. On the minus side, each demonstrates avoidance of actively confronting relationship issues like those related to division of household labor and the impact of Julie's IBS on John's expectations of Julie's ability to help him with new clients. John's recent practice of talking over his problems with a coworker and working out several nights a week indicates an avoidant attachment style. Julie's avoidant attachment style is indicated by her years of quietly shouldering an ever-increasing share of household and childcare labor without complaint and without addressing her concerns and needs directly with John. Both Julie and John, while displaying many individual and marital strengths, also display a remarkable absence of skill in addressing relationship and intimacy issues directly with each other. John has begun to further short circuit the likelihood of intimate communication with Julie by hanging out with a coworker and by sharing with him some of his marital problems.

The couples therapist working with John and Julie would be responsible for facilitating fairly lengthy and detailed conversations with them about the role of work in their lives, including the work of both career and home, while being highly supportive in order to avoid what would be a significant risk of premature termination, given their avoidant attachment styles. Because of their task orientedness, Julie and John would have a tendency to stay at the level of content in discussing issues that brought them to therapy, and the therapist would need to be careful to focus the therapeutic conversations on the effects of their work, health, and friendship issues on them as a couple and on how these issues have affected their level of emotional connection with each other. The didactic element of explaining attachment styles to them would probably be both helpful and anxiety reducing since the information would represent a content-level takeaway that they could take home, think about, and, ideally, act upon. The other content-level takeaway that would likewise be helpful and anxiety reducing for this couple would be the message that difficulties and disruptions are normal and inevitable in couples' relationships, but that what is more important is the work of repair and reconciliation. The therapist would need to work closely with Julie and John to help them develop goals directed toward the increase of shared communication and emotional intimacy. These are high achievers who avoid emotional communication. The vulnerability involved in such communication is likely to be anxiety provoking for the couple who will need the support of the therapist to be successful.

Specific therapeutic goals for John and Julie might include: increasing emotional communication, in particular, about the effects for each of them of their demanding careers and home workloads; developing practical strategies for greater mutual support; reevaluating the current division of labor in terms of equity, practicability, and skill; identifying and expressing hopes and needs for the other's presence, availability, and support; setting up communication strategies for noticing and responding to emotional distancing; and developing and practicing strategies for reconnecting after relationship ruptures or distancing, as is more likely in their case. To help them get started, the therapist will need to be quite active in providing examples and suggestions of the kinds of behaviors needed to increase emotional sharing. It will be up to the couple to decide which of the many possible intimacy-promoting behaviors will suit their individual and relationship styles best. Because of their avoidant and distancing styles, this couple will need follow-up at periodic intervals to reinforce and anchor new behaviors that are supportive of closeness and intimacy.

Concluding Note

In this chapter, research and clinical evidence has been gathered to identify core elements of intimacy. These core elements of intimacy can be used productively by couples therapists to both assess the presence or absence of these elements in couples' relationships and as a focus of therapeutic intervention and change. Additionally, the special topics of health, work, and friendship, and their potential effects on intimacy, have been explored from the perspective of available and useful research. Given that there are a number of core elements of intimacy, the weight of the evidence points to the development of relationship repair skills as crucial in both maintaining and recovering lost intimacy. Hence, treatment guidelines for recovering intimacy have been organized around the critical significance of the development of relationship repair skills while including other core elements of intimacy as aspects of couples' relationship repair efforts.

References

Atkinson, B. J. (2005). *Emotional intelligence in couples therapy: Advances from neurobiology and the science of intimate relationships.* New York: Norton.

Binik, Y. M., Chowanec, G. D., & Devins, G. M. (1990). Marital role strain, illness intrusiveness, and their impact on marital and individual adjustment in end-stage renal disease. *Psychology and Health, 4,* 245–257.

Bowlby, J. (1969). *Attachment and loss: Vol. 1 Attachment.* New York: Basic Books.

Carlson, J., & Sperry, L. (Eds.). (1999). *The intimate couple.* Philadelphia: Brunner/ Mazel.

Coyne, J. C. (2001). Prognostic importance of marital quality for survival of congestive heart failure. *American Journal of Cardiology, 88,* 526–529.

Devins, G. M., Bezjak, A., Mah, K., Loblaw, A., & Gotowiec, A. P. (2005). Context moderates illness-induced lifestyle disruptions across life domains: A test of the illness intrusiveness theoretical framework in six common cancers. *Psycho-Oncology, 15,* 221–233.

Devins, G. M., Binik, Y. M., Hutchinson, T. A., Hollomby, D. J., Barré, P. E., & Guttmann, R. D. (1983). The emotional impact of end-stage renal disease: Importance of patients' perceptions of intrusiveness and control. *International Journal of Psychiatry in Medicine, 13,* 327–343.

Devins, G. M., Mandin, H., Hons, R. B., Burgess, E. D., Klassen, J., Taub, K. et al. (1990). Illness intrusiveness and quality of life in end-stage renal disease: Comparison and stability across treatment modalities. *Health Psychology, 9,* 117–142.

Elliott, S., & Umberson, D. (2008). The performance of desire: Gender and sexual negotiation in long-term marriages. *Journal of Marriage and Family, 70,* 391–406.

Gerson, M. J., Gerson, C. D., Awad, R. A., Dancey, C., Poitras, P., Porcelli, P. et al. (2006). An international study of irritable bowel syndrome: Family relationships and mind-body attributions. *Social Sciences and Medicine, 62,* 2838–2847.

Gottman, J. M. (1999). *The marriage clinic: A scientifically based marital therapy.* New York: Norton.

Gottman, J. M., Driver, J., & Tabares, A. (2002). Building the sound marital house: An empirically derived couple therapy. In A. S. Gurman & N. S. Jacobson (Eds.), *Clinical handbook of couple therapy* (3rd ed., pp. 373–399). New York: Guilford.

Gottman, J. M., & Silver, N. (1999). *The seven principles for making marriage work.* New York: Crown.

Heller, P., & Wood, B. (1998). The process of intimacy: Similarity, understanding and gender. *Journal of Marital and Family Therapy, 24,* 273–288.

Hochschild, A. R. (1983). *The managed heart: Commercialization of human feeling.* Berkeley: University of California Press.

Hochschild, A. R. (1997). *The time bind: When work becomes home and home becomes work.* New York: Metropolitan Books.

Hochschild, A. R., & Machung, A. (2003). *The second shift: Working parents and the revolution at home* (updated ed.). New York: Penguin.

Johnson, S. M. (2003a). Introduction to attachment: A therapist's guide to primary relationships and their renewal. In S. M. Johnson & V. E. Whiffen (Eds.), *Attachment processes in couple and family therapy* (pp. 3–17). New York: Guilford.

Johnson, S. M. (2003b). Attachment theory: A guide for couple therapy. In S. M. Johnson & V. E. Whiffen (Eds.), *Attachment processes in couple and family therapy* (pp. 103–123). New York: Guilford.

Johnson, S. M., & Greenberg, L. S. (1985). The differential effects of experiential and problem solving interventions in resolving marital conflicts. *Journal of Consulting and Clinical Psychology, 53,* 175–184.

Kayser, K., Watson, L. E., & Andrade, J. T. (2007). Cancer as a "we-disease": Examining the process of coping from a relational perspective. *Families, Systems, and Health, 25,* 404.

Kiecolt-Glaser, J. K., Loving T. J., Stowell, J. R., Malarkey, W. B., Lemeshow, S., Dickinson S. L. et al. (2005). Hostile marital interactions, proinflammatory cytokine production, and wound healing. *Archives of General Psychiatry, 62,* 1377–1384.

Kiecolt-Glaser, J. K., & Newton, T. L. (2001). Marriage and health: His and hers. *Psychological Bulletin, 127,* 472–503.

Mikulciner, M., & Nachson, O. (1991). Attachment styles and patterns of self-disclosure. *Journal of Personality and Social Psychology, 61,* 321–332.

Moore, K. A., & Seeney, F. (2007). Biopsychosocial predictors of depressive mood in people with Parkinson's disease. *Behavioral Medicine, 33,* 29–37.

Ornish, D. (1998). *Love and survival: Eight pathways to intimacy and health.* New York: Harper Perennial.

Page, L. J., Nisan, L., Eckstein, D., & Ane, P. (2008). The intimacy task inventory: Taking a relationship snapshot. *Family Journal, 16,* 83–86.

Ray, O. (2004). How the mind hurts and heals the body. *American Psychologist, 59,* 29–40.

Rohrbaugh, M. J., Shoham, V., & Coyne, J. C. (2006). Effect of marital quality on eight-year survival of patients with heart failure. *American Journal of Cardiology, 98,* 1069–1072.

Schnarch, D. (2002). *Resurrecting sex: Solving sexual problems and revolutionizing your relationship.* New York: Quill.

Schore, A. N. (2003a). *Affect dysregulation and disorders of the self.* New York: Norton.

Schore, A. N. (2003b). *Affect regulation and the repair of the self.* New York: Norton.

Sperry, L. (2002). The relevance of the biological dimension and biopsychosocial therapy in maintaining and enhancing close relationships. In J. Harvey & A. Wenzel (Eds.), *A clinician's guide to maintaining and enhancing close relationships* (pp. 313–320). Mahwah, NJ: Erlbaum.

Sperry, L., Carlson, J., & Peluso, P. R. (2006). *Couples therapy: Integrating theory and technique* (2nd ed.). Denver: Love Publishing.

Techtree News Staff. (2008, August 13). *Facebook: Largest, fastest growing social network.* Retrieved November 23, 2009, from http://www.techtree.com/India/News/Facebook_Largest_Fastest_Growing_Social_Network/551-92134-643.html

Timmerman, G. M. (1991). A concept analysis of intimacy. *Issues in Mental Health Nursing, 12,* 19–30.

Weihs, K. L., Enright, T. M., & Simmens, S. J. (2008). Close relationships and emotional processing predict decreased mortality in women with breast cancer: preliminary evidence. *Psychosomatic Medicine, 70,* 117–124.

Weingarten, K. (1992). A consideration of intimate and non-intimate interactions in therapy. *Family Process, 31,* 45–59.

CHAPTER 15

Context and Culture in Intimate Partner Infidelity

Co-Constructing Preferred Couple Narratives

J. MARIA BERMÚDEZ and MICHELE L. PARKER

Depending on how infidelity is defined, estimates indicate that 20–60% of men and 12–40% of women living in the United States participate in extrarelational sex at some point in their marriages (Atwood & Seifer, 1997; Laumann, Gagnon, Michael, & Michaels, 1994). The shame and social stigma associated with infidelity make it a challenging phenomenon to study. Additionally, couple therapists may insist on disclosure and refuse to work with a couple when one of the partners is actively involved in an affair. In addition to the multitude of treatment approaches suggested by clinicians and researchers (Atkins, Baucom, Eldrigde, & Christensen, 2005; Gordon, Baucom, & Snyder, 2004; Martell & Prince, 2005; Pittman & Wagers, 2005; Zola, 2007), there is currently a substantial amount of research on predictors and effects of infidelity. For example, intrapersonal variables and qualities of relationships shown to affect the likelihood of infidelity include education level, personality traits, income level, and relationship satisfaction (Treas & Giesen, 2000). Documented effects of infidelity may include psychological distress, intimate partner violence, or fear of relationship dissolution (Atwood & Seifer, 1997; Buunk, 1997; Drigotas, Safstrom, & Gentilia, 1999). However, there has yet to be any efficacious research related to a particular clinical approach for infidelity (Atkins et al., 2005), with a noticeable lack of attention dedicated to cultural and contextual factors.

There is a notable gap in the clinical literature related to the cultural influences on experiences of infidelity. Regardless of the clinical approach, problem-solving interventions have expressed a Eurocentric focus, which seeks to identify pathology (Ledesma, 2007). Such approaches often polarize the couple by identifying one member as an "offender" and the other as a "victim." Effective clinical work with couples who have experienced infidelity results from a focus on the *couple's* unique experience, as opposed to a problem-oriented, deficit model, which may produce counterproductive results (Atwood & Seifer, 1997). With this in mind, a narrative therapy approach is especially useful in helping individuals deconstruct their own experience of infidelity (Parker, Berger, & Campbell, 2010). Deconstruction and reconstruction can be especially helpful when considering the complexity of assessing and working with infidelity from a cross-cultural perspective.

The objective in this chapter is threefold: (a) to offer an alternative view to the dominant discourse of intimate partner infidelity, (b) to discuss how cultural and contextual factors intersect with the various meanings associated with experiencing infidelity, and (c) to offer a strength-based, narrative approach for therapists working with clients who present with intimate partner infidelity as a clinical concern. Narrative therapy (NT) is offered as a vehicle for deconstructing a couple's experience of infidelity as well as helping them co-construct a preferred narrative about their *new* relationship. The co-construction process that occurs enables a couple to contextualize the meanings associated with infidelity. Over the course of therapy the clients then restory a preferred narrative, which enables them to move forward in a positive manner. Included are questions to help illustrate a deconstruction and restorying process using a lens of intersectionality (culture, gender, socioeconomic status, and gender).

The Dominant Discourse of Infidelity

Relational infidelity, affairs, and extramarital sex are widely considered among researchers and clinicians to be the most detrimental experiences a relationship can endure. Specifically, clients seeking therapy for relational infidelity may also be concerned about acquiring HIV/AIDS or sexually transmitted illnesses, coping with depression and other forms of psychological distress, as well as intimate partner violence (Buunk, 1997; Drigotas et al., 1999). Although we do acknowledge that the effects of infidelity can be difficult and disruptive to the integrity of the intimate partner's bond and relational stability, a problematized view of infidelity is pervasive throughout social, scholarly, and clinical discourses. It is important to assess the dominant discourse that prevents a couple from disentangling themselves from its web. Freedman and Combs (2002) note that therapists have a responsibility "to cultivate a growing awareness of the dominant stories in our society, and to develop ways of collaboratively examining the effects of those stories" (p. 316).

The complexity and stigma associated with infidelity suggest clients may not immediately disclose their extrarelational infidelity, if they disclose it at all. The current dominant discourse may impose a prescribed script by shaming or silencing the voices of clients and their experiences (Parker et al., in press). This silencing is compounded when practitioners and scholars struggle to arrive at a consensus toward an agreed upon definition or treatment approach for infidelity (Allen et al., 2005). However, the complexity of the experience suggests infidelity cannot be examined in such a simplistic or linear fashion (Blow & Hartnett, 2005). Multiple definitions pose a challenge for researchers who try to draw conclusions. However, a single definition of infidelity is problematic and may promote the exclusion of cross-cultural and contextual factors, which personalize the clients' unique experiences. Consistent with a social constructionist perspective, we will review various definitions from the literature that allow for contextual variations based on couples' meanings and experiences.

Blow and Hartnett (2005) defined infidelity as "a sexual and/or emotional act engaged in by one person within a committed relationship, where such an act occurs outside the primary relationship and constitutes a breach of trust and/or violation of agreed-upon norms (overt and covert) by one or both individuals in that relationship" (pp. 191–192). Additionally, Drigotas and colleagues (1999) described infidelity as involving a violation of relationship norms about appropriate interactions with another person that typically results in feelings of jealousy or rivalry. Such definitions provide a therapeutic foundation, but the discrepancy of the prevalence and definitions of infidelity may be associated with limitations in clinical efficacy. As noted above, infidelity researchers and clinicians use definitions that do not allow for multiple conceptualizations, which can vary based on an individual's contextual influences. By offering only a problematized version, we may hinder clients' ability to examine the multitude of feelings and reactions associated with experiences of infidelity, which may prevent them from moving forward from the experience in a positive manner.

Infidelity From Contextual Perspectives

Various contextual factors are important to consider when assessing infidelity from a multicultural perspective. We specifically address culture, gender, sexuality, and socioeconomic status (SES), but there are many others that should be considered within a cultural and contextual framework (i.e., physical challenges or disabilities, age, life stage, religion, educational level, country of origin, rural vs. urban, regional differences, and language differences). Although we present the following contextual factors separately, they do not operate in isolation. Instead, we highlight intersectionality as a lens to examine the ways in which such factors intersect to influence clients' unique experiences of intimate partner infidelity. Kimberlé Crenshaw (2006) defined intersectionality as "the recognition of the many strands that make up identity" (p. 204). Additionally, Newman (2007) stated that it is the intersections of race, class, gender, and sexuality that help us understand the complexity of who we are and how we interact with one another. While some of these contextual factors may be more punctuated than others, it is the confluence of these factors, and many others, that shapes our experiences in the world.

Cultural Influences

Culture shapes individuals' social behavior, expression of distress, and communication patterns and provides the structure and meaning to all life experiences, influencing identity, beliefs, and values (Ledesma, 2007). One's cultural values and beliefs influence the development of identity, which specifies what is important and what is unimportant (Ledesma, 2007). Despite the recent interest in "treating" infidelity, there is a surprising gap in the literature related to cultural influences on client's perceptions and experiences of infidelity. When attempting to work in the most ethical and culturally competent manner, understanding cultural influences is vital, specifically when working with clients whose culture differs from your own. Equally important is the understanding of how the dominant culture shapes our narratives about ourselves and our relationships. The dominant culture informs one's personal story or "narratives." Through this socialization, each member of the couple constructs a reality or script about commitment, which affects the rules for conduct within the relationship. The ways in which this shaping process is related to views and definitions of infidelity are still unknown.

Penn, Hernandez, and Bermúdez (1997) examined infidelity from a cross-cultural perspective and defined infidelity as a partner's violation of relationship norms about extramarital sex. We add to this definition by suggesting that in a broader sense, infidelity is defined as the betrayal of the agreement for sexual or intimate conduct outside the primary intimate relationship, especially if exclusivity was part of the original relational "contract." Within these definitions, we must take into account the range of differences from which people from various cultures and ethnicities interpret the experience of infidelity. To begin the deconstruction process, therapy may begin by asking the couple or each individual to define intimate partner infidelity. We cannot assume a shared meaning or definition or predict that a client's definition will be consistent with others from a similar cultural background.

Every couple is an intercultural couple; however, not all couples who seek therapy will espouse a Eurocentric, heteronormative, white, middle-class bias, as do many therapists. In addition to value-laden personal beliefs, clinical models and approaches also impose particular biases and assumptions, which, in turn, affect the therapist's approach to infidelity in therapy. Zola (2007) stated that "the universally taught approach that complete honesty and the sharing of details is the only way to rebuild a relationship after an affair, seems ethnocentric destined to blame one partner, reinforces flawed assumptions, and neglects contextual factors like gender, power, social support, culture, and religion" (p. 27). Additionally, a therapist should carefully assess the conditions for which the couple sought therapy. There is still a strong stigma and shame associated with therapy, and therapists cannot assume that clients are there freely to discuss their issues. Thus, while we might espouse a belief that all couples have their unique culture, even if they have many similar contextual factors (race, class, sexuality, religion, education, etc.), there still may be differences in how they view infidelity.

When we think from a cross-cultural perspective, there is an endless continuum for the prevalence and perceptions of infidelity across cultures, and such variances have clinical implications in working with multicultural and cross-cultural clients. Penn and colleagues (1997) discussed clinical issues from the perspective of three main ethnic minority groups in the United States—African Americans, Hispanic Americans, and Asian Americans—offering religion as a lens to assess cultural values imbedded in beliefs about infidelity. While discussing the cultural nuances of these minority groups is useful, it is essential that therapists also value *within* group differences inherent in all groups. Additionally, Bermúdez (1997) cautioned therapists to be aware of how their stereotypes and cultural biases affect their work with clients, especially with clients from cultural groups different from their own. Therapists who are not culturally aware are likely to fall into two traps.

One trap is a therapist's natural response to rely on stereotypes to guide his or her work. For example, Latino and Arabic men are often perceived as less likely to be sexually exclusive with their wives. Additionally, some cultural groups are hypersexualized or sexually objectified, such as African American men and women, Latino men, and Asian women. On the other hand, others are rarely thought of in a sexualized manner, such as with Native Americans, fundamental religious group members (excluding Mormon men), elderly adults, or people with physical handicaps or challenges. Such stereotypes are harmful and can make clinical progress almost impossible.

The other cultural trap in therapy involves the use of your own cultural framework as the normative reference point. A common reference is the idea that sexual intercourse is for adults in a heterosexual, legal marriage, and sexual exclusivity is a lifelong expectation. Therapists often struggle to work with couples who do not fit this prescribed, heteronormative standard. Efforts to guard against these cultural traps include continuing a multicultural education, seeking peer consultation, and increasing personal self-awareness and cultural consciousness. In both of the cultural traps mentioned above, therapists run the risk of failing to provide culturally responsive therapy, which may result in unintended harm to clients.

Gender Influences

The social construction of gender continues to shape women's and men's interpretation of infidelity. It is highly probable that there are more similarities than differences (as with most cultural groups), but because people are socialized to "do gender" differently (West & Zimmerman, 1987), gender differences are continually emphasized in the literature related to infidelity. Specifically, studies continue to find that women show greater distress when their partner engages in emotional infidelity, whereas men displayed greater distress when their partner engages in sex outside the primary relationship (Cann, Mangum, & Wells, 2001; Whitty & Quigley, 2008). These findings dichotomize gendered responses by reinforcing the stereotype that men are "naturally" more sexual and women are "naturally" more emotional.

It is also suggested that women and men have different reasons for engaging in extrarelational intimacy (Staheli, 1995). Due to male privilege, men hold more power in society and therefore display more power in relationships. Thus, individuals in more powerful job positions, with higher incomes, and powerful social positions are also more likely to engage in extrarelational intimacy (Staheli, 1995). Employment status and gender have also interacted to affect infidelity processes. Traditionally, the majority of women (approximately 80%) have worked in the home to care for children preschool age or younger. Currently, more than 50% of women are employed full or part time during this stage (Teachman, Polonko, & Scanzoni, 1999). Because more women are in the workforce, women have more power in romantic relationships. Participation in the labor force has also provided women greater access to alternative partners, increasing the likelihood of infidelity (South, Trent, & Shen, 2001). Therefore, the same patterns seen for men in high-powered, high-status positions are starting to emerge for women in similar positions. Power, autonomy, and access to alternative partners are other factors that perhaps transcend gender.

Gender has also been identified as a factor in shaping one's perceptions of those engaged in extrarelational infidelity. It is a generally accepted belief that in most "*machista*" cultures, marital infidelity is more acceptable for men. These cultures are those that espouse strong patriarchal views such as Latin American, Middle Eastern, Asian, and many European cultures. However, for women from these cultures who participate in an extramarital affair, the assumptions are made that they will feel greater guilt, be perceived as being more responsible for the event, and have acted with greater intent than men (Mongeau, Hale, & Alles, 1994). Penn and colleagues (1997) further highlighted the ways in which religion and gender shape perceptions of infidelity. For instance, Christian and Islamic cultures condemn sex outside of marriage; however, women continue to be disparately severely punished for being unfaithful to their spouses, whether or not the accusations are legitimate. Negative outcomes can result in being ousted from a community, being labeled as "damaged" and a whore, being stoned, raped, beaten, or murdered. Women who run the risk of these severe outcomes often live in strict, patriarchal societies or subcultures or are in relationships with misogynistic men.

Sexuality Influences

Another confounding issue when assessing infidelity from a cross-cultural perspective is that people from dominant groups determine what is normative for a society (Goodman, 2001; Tatum, 1997). When others do not fit in to the normative perspective, those from the subordinate groups are thought of as deviant or pathological. Notably, this happens in same gendered or sex relationships, polyamorous individuals, and "swinging" couples, to name only a few. Working from an ethnocentric standpoint is inevitable given that our clinical models, theories, research, and training programs have a strong Eurocentric, heteronormative bias.

Variations due to sexual identity and orientation also affect how individuals interpret extrarelational intimacy. The relational norms expected by members of gay and lesbian partnerships are often marginalized by the dominant script imposed by Western, heterosexual values. Overwhelmingly, a heteronormative bias abounds in scholarly, clinical, and mainstream literature that addresses the topic. Same sex, queer couples, and heterosexual couples have varying degrees of tolerance and acceptance of extrarelational intimacy. Martell and Prince (2005) suggested incorporating the relational context with nonmonogamous partners by agreeing on particular parameters for sexual conduct, the degree of disclosure, and amending the original parameters if one partner becomes uncomfortable. Whether or not the couple is heterosexual, therapists must obtain a thorough history describing a couple's expectations for primacy in the relationship prior to their union. As well, changes in expectations due to changes in life-cycle transitions, circumstances, or other factors should be assessed. It is also beneficial to include a genogram and to assess the cultural, contextual, life stage, and family of origin issues that created the space for infidelity to occur.

People who are considered sexual minorities do not differ significantly from those of heterosexual clients when experiencing the effects of infidelity; however, relational "infidelity" may be defined differently among gay or lesbian couples. In gay and lesbian relationships, sex outside the relationship may not automatically be considered an affair. Couples in same-sex relationships may maintain relationships with former lovers long after the relationship has ended due to the social barriers that prevent gay, lesbian, bisexual, and transgendered or queer individuals from having an expansive social network. Blasband and Peplau (1985) found that nonmonogamous partners did not experience a reduction in relationship satisfaction compared to those who practiced monogamy. It is particularly important for therapists to recognize the difference between acts considered to be infidelity versus nonmonogamy (Martell & Prince, 2005). Although the terms are often used interchangeably, they are not the same.

Couples therapists often implicitly operate from a therapeutic perspective valuing legal marriage as the ideal template for intimate relationships. This heteronormative bias often has negative repercussions for couples in nonheterosexual relationships. In regard to infidelity, definitions are influenced by religious teachings, which are then reinforced by the legal system restricting sexual behavior to marriage (Atwood & Seifer, 1997). Stated differently, gay and lesbian partnerships in therapy are often held to the values of a societal discourse that does not recognize their relationship. As such, therapists must take the stance of exploration and be aware of their own personal heterosexist assumptions. One of these assumptions may be that once a romantic relationship has terminated, former lovers should no longer be closely involved in each other's lives. Triangles are common among lesbians (Goodrich, Ellman, Rampage, & Halstead, 1990), and maintaining close relationships with former partners is sometimes necessary for decreasing the intensity of anger and stress and maintaining a sense of community and social support. While these former relationships may cause conflict with emotional and psychological intimacy being dispersed in multiple relationships, therapists should not pathologize a client's relationship with former partners, even though it may cause conflict in the current relationship. Goodrich et al. (1990) also observed that traditional constructs in family therapy such as triangles, fusion, and boundaries have a heterosexist bias, and applications of these to lesbian relationships will result in a pathologized and impoverished description.

Socioeconomic Status

As mentioned above, SES has a direct effect on how infidelity is experienced and how it will be addressed in a clinical setting. Cross-culturally, men have more economic freedom, power, and control and are more often socially sanctioned to having discrete encounters of infidelity. However, as women gain higher social status, education, employment opportunities, and financial stability, they are more likely to experience infidelity in ways that would not have been possible in past generations. Additionally, most often there is a bias that one has to be married in order for infidelity to be considered a real threat. This has consequences for ethnic groups of lower SES who may not legally marry. For example, it is common for many poor immigrant Latinos to not be legally married or married in the church (which for many Latino(a) Catholics is more important and binding). They would still consider themselves "married," but not in a socially legitimate manner. Clinically, this informal marriage presents challenges for couples therapists working with Latino couples. This is a slippery slope for the couple who is "married," but not officially, and therefore not as restricted to outside sexual relationships. Again, one must be mindful that higher SES Latinos will not fit this scenario. The higher their SES, the more likely they are to have a legal, religious marriage and therefore to define extramarital infidelity as any sex outside of marriage. Although not related to SES, this perception of what constitutes a legitimate union and a legitimate affair also applies to same-sex relationships, given that most are unable to marry legally or marry in their religious centers or places of worship.

Another factor to consider is the SES of the therapist. Most often, couple therapists and counselors have middle- to upper-class status, regardless of the SES they had in their family of origin. These social class biases also affect how therapists work with couples from cultural backgrounds different from their own. Bermúdez (1997) urged that therapists need to be aware of their own biases when working with clients who they perceive to come from cultural backgrounds different from their own. It has been suggested that therapists explore their beliefs related to infidelity through self-assessment and reflection with a colleague prior to treating couples (Parker et al., in press).

As noted earlier, intersectionality is a useful and necessary lens when assessing how culture affects individual's experiences with infidelity. As a case in point, consider the contextual differences of two Mexican women: one with white privilege, legal residential status, who is college educated, a lesbian, from an upper-class background, and who does not rigidly adhere to religious values, and the other who is a Latina with dark skin, an illegal status, who does not have a high education, who is from a working-class background, has a religious background, and depends on her husband financially. Although both have the same nationality and gender, each woman will interpret and experience infidelity in different ways due to contextual differences. Further, the gender of the person engaging in extrarelational intimacy also affects the way each partner and family members interpret the infidelity. It is imperative that therapists proceed accordingly.

The contextual factors mentioned above only begin to scratch the surface, and, as previously mentioned, it is far more important to assess the intersectionality of these factors in order to fully understand the complexity of the clients' experience of infidelity from a cross-cultural perspective. Therefore, we offer here a strength-based and creative approach to help deconstruct a couple's experience of infidelity and co-construct a preferred narrative.

Narrative Therapy as a Clinical Approach to Infidelity

One of the primary assumptions of NT is that people, through the course of their lives, internalize problematic beliefs about themselves or others that have the potential to deny them from experiencing preferred narratives (Freedman & Combs, 1996; White, 1995; White & Epston, 1990). This internalized script of the problematic, dominant narrative is significant given that our lives are affected by the internal, contextual, and interpersonal factors that shape our identities and relationships (Parker, Bermúdez, & Neustifter, 2007). With the use of externalizing conversations (White, 1995) and deconstructive questioning, therapists can help loosen the power of the dominant, problematic narratives. Ultimately, clients are able to redefine and restory a preferred relationship and course of action. This preferred way may be informed by their relational dynamics, culture and contextual influences, interpersonal or internal conflicts, family-of-origin patterns, gender scripts, notions of masculinity and femininity, and emotional reactivity. This strength-based approach serves to generate unique outcomes in relation to a couple's problem-saturated story (White & Epston, 1990). An NT approach helps clients explicitly discuss the influences of infidelity on their sense of self and their relationship. The goal of this approach is to help clients co-construct a preferred narrative that will move the relationship, or sense of self, forward in a positive manner, regardless of the relational outcome.

NT is useful for working with ethnically and culturally diverse clients, as relationships are central to the construction of meaning, and identity (collectivistic) and collaborative forms of communication are valued (Bermúdez, Keeling, & Stone Carlson, 2009). Narrative therapy has been applied to diverse populations, and empirical studies are beginning to emerge. Keeling and Nielson (2005) found support for the use of NT and nontraditional treatment delivery for Asian Indian women. Additionally, Keeling and Bermúdez (2006) suggested that the externalization of problems through art and sculpture was helpful by: (1) enabling clients to express emotional intensity, (2) increasing awareness of unique outcomes when the problem was not present or dominant, (3) recovering a sense of personal agency, (4) blaming the problem instead of themselves, and (5) altering their relationship with the problem in a way in which the person was dominant instead of the problem. With this in mind, however, we must be sensitive toward our clients' responses to this approach, which will provide clues as to what constitutes culturally responsive and competent therapy.

It is our assertion that by empowering couples to deconstruct the dominant discourse of infidelity and experience an alternative narrative consistent with their relationship goals, they will have the freedom to express themselves more fully and experience greater depth in their relationship. Below we present components of NT and offer examples for using this approach to co-construct a preferred narrative around experiences of intimate partner infidelity. We will also discuss the role of the therapist and offer illustrative questions based on Freedman and Combs's (1996) work.

Role of the Therapist

A social constructionist perspective has challenged the role of the therapist as an expert on clients' mental instability and psychological health (McNamee, 2004). Through the use of NT, a therapist becomes a collaborative, co-constructor of reality, as well as an expert on facilitating the clinical process. Always mindful that the clients are the experts on their own lives, such a stance is contrary to other approaches, which advocate for the therapist-as-expert role. We assert that therapists have generally accepted the negative social construction of infidelity as a threat from which a marriage must be protected (Atwood & Seifer, 1997). This view has led therapists to approach infidelity from a problem-oriented, deficit model, which may produce counterproductive results. In contrast, therapists who have an unassuming, not-knowing stance (Anderson & Goolishian, 1988) create a space for clients to share their perspectives and experiences related to the infidelity working from a nonjudgmental and collaborative approach.

Additionally, therapists and supervisors need to unpack personal narratives related to infidelity. Either in self-reflection or peer supervision, Parker and colleagues (in press) offered therapists deconstruction questions that can help the clients and the therapist deconstruct the meanings associated with the extrarelational infidelity. Therapists who carefully examine their own personal experience, gender roles, and theoretical orientations (and we add culture, race, class, gender, and sexuality) will be better situated to understand their personal contribution to each couple's story (Glass, 2002). Although it is important to be aware of current research related to infidelity and treatment with couples, it is equally necessary not to be restricted by the literature. We have previously cautioned against a therapist-imposed script related to infidelity. It is worth restating that therapist neutrality is not consistent with an NT approach. We advocate that therapists assess their own assumptions and beliefs about infidelity from a cross-cultural perspective. This type of self-reflection enables therapists to identify the ways in which she or he influences the clinical process.

Deconstructive Listening

The following is an integration of the work of White and Epston (1990), Freedman and Combs (1996), and our own work in applying NT with client concerns related to infidelity or extrarelational intimacy (Bermúdez, 1997; Parker et al., in press). Most commonly, the beginning phase of therapy involves the deconstructive process. As the therapist is deconstructing the client's meanings and experiences surrounding infidelity, the contextual factors feeding life to the problem become apparent and provide clues as to which factors will help them reconstruct a preferred narrative. The therapist begins to deconstruct the dominant or problem-saturated story. Deconstruction is the first phase to accomplish the following goals: (a) loosening the grip of restrictive stories, (b) examining the various possible meanings, (c) looking for gaps in understanding, and (d) asking the client to fill in the details. As the story is shared, the therapist can interrupt at intervals to summarize his or her sense of what the clients are saying.

Subjectively, deconstructing the meanings and experiences of infidelity offers individuals and couples a wider range of definitions and experiences than those imposed by the dominant discourse (Parker et al., in press). Deconstructive listening allows one to determine other possible meanings of the experience by engaging in a process of listening and questioning by the therapist (Freedman & Combs, 1996). This process of NT may be especially challenging for strength-based therapists, given the nature of these questions is to focus more intentionally on the client's problematic beliefs, feelings, and practices (Freedman & Combs, 1996).

Externalizing the Problem

Externalizing the problem is one of the hallmarks of narrative therapy. Although this process may not be used by all narrative therapists, it is a tool for depathologizing individuals and placing the problem outside of the person in order to increase one's sense of agency over the problem. In essence, the problem becomes the problem, instead of the individuals being the problem. It is essential for the couples to name "the problem." In the case of a couple or individual discussing infidelity as a clinical concern, examples of such names will typically be a variation of one of the following: "the infidelity," "the mistrust," "the rift," "the intruder," "the distance." In sum, an externalization process can be defined as follows: (a) persons objectify and personify the problem or an experience they believe to be oppressive; (b) it enables one to see the problem as separate from the person; (c) the problem becomes the problem, and then the person's relationship with the problem becomes the problem; (d) it is an attitude or an outlook, as opposed to a technique; (e) when the problem is external, the couple (or individual) can take responsibility for how they interacted to it and allowed it to influence their lives. The externalization process can help decrease feelings of blame, shame, and anger and help the couple join forces to defeat the power of the problem. In the case of infidelity, giving the problem a name can help the couple begin to understand its *life* and its *coercive tactics* to undermine a couple's relationship.

Externalization and the deconstruction process are intricately related. By using the client's language to describe the problem, the problem can be modified so that it is objectified and personified. The couple can then face it in a different way. Additionally, narrative questions are generative in that they are used to generate experience, rather than gather information. Below we offer deconstruction questions in the context of infidelity. Deconstruction questions focus on the history of the person's relationship with the problem, contextual influences, effects or results, interrelationship with other beliefs and practices, and tactics or strategies. These questions are asked within the context of an externalizing conversation.

Examples of Deconstruction or Externalizing Questions

- When did X (the name of the problem) become a problem in your relationship?
- Have you made any conclusions about your relationship because of X's influence?
- Do you think there is anything related to your culture or gender scripts that would give more life to X? How did you learn these beliefs?
- If you were not a man (or woman), how would your experience of infidelity be different?
- How has your interactions with your partner changed since X have has become a part of your life?
- Do you think X has always interfered with your sense of connection and commitment in your relationship, or has there been a time when it wasn't this way? Can you describe that time to me?
- If your ways of connecting was different before, what were the factors that helped X evolve and develop to create the distance between the two of you? Were any of these factors related to your culture or gender? Were any of these factors related to your social status?
- What effects does X have in your relationship when it is not in control of your relationship or how you treat or perceive each other?
- Does X ever try to convince you into thinking that you are no longer in love, friends, or compatible, committed or attracted to each other? How does X do it?
- When you think about X now, what emotions and thoughts does it evoke in you both? Were any of those thoughts or feelings present at another point in time in your lives?

Reconstructing a Preferred Narrative

Helping couples co-construct a preferred narrative about their experience with the problem is one of the most exciting parts of NT. The reconstruction of a preferred story begins with discussion of a unique outcome. We are able to ask clients to talk about what their current relationship means to them, what feelings emerge as they discuss the new possibilities, and what important memories are triggered that they have forgotten, perhaps from before the infidelity occurred. The preferred narrative or unique outcome is how they experience their relationship when the problem is not present. This would be how they experience their relationship outside the influence of the infidelity. The therapist can also ask about events that do not fit with problem-saturated stories, such as referring to the times or places when the new experience might have occurred. For example, if a couple begins to refer back to a time when they felt distant and resentful, or when they begin to remember the feelings prior, during, or after the infidelity, the therapist can ask them to remember a time when they were there for each other and felt the feelings that brought them close to each other. Specifically, it is important to ask questions that track actions, behaviors, interactions, thoughts, and awareness, and then link the unique outcome with the present and extend the story into the future. By amplifying the unique outcomes, the therapist is able to help the couple experience the relationship in a more satisfying way.

The externalizing conversation helps people identify previously neglected, but vital, aspects of lived experience. Similar to *exceptions* in solution-focused therapy (deShazer, 1988), these aspects are referred to as *unique outcomes,* which are aspects of one's life that cannot be predicted or will emerge by solely focusing on the dominant story. The therapist works toward widening the space for unique outcomes that have occurred. This process is accomplished through the use of questions about hypothetical experiences, multiple points of view, and oriented toward their future. By externalizing or personifying the problem, a space is created for new stories and experiences to emerge. It is the therapist's role to punctuate each new experience, or unique outcome, which will eventually lead to the co-construction of a preferred narrative.

Questions Creating the Space for Unique Outcomes
- When was the last time that X could have hijacked your positive communication with each other and you didn't let it? What did you do to prevent it from happening?
- It seems like you are really beaten down by X's influence in your relationship, but was there a moment during the week that you felt more hopeful?

- If you would have been able to turn toward each other during the series of losses in your life, do you think you would have been as vulnerable to the infidelity?
- If you were to discover without a doubt that your partner is on the computer doing his work, as opposed to being in communication with his ex-lover, how would that knowledge change things for you (i.e., thoughts, feelings, actions, and reactions)?
- If your parents were (are) still alive, what would they think about how your have dealt with this crisis in your marriage? What positive trait did they know about you that you had forgotten was an important resource?
- Which friends would be the most supportive of you getting a divorce? Which ones would be the most supportive of you staying together? What does one group see in you that the other one doesn't?
- When your relationship with your ex-lover was consuming you, how did this experience fit with your perceptions of yourself prior to the affair?

Amplifying the New Story (Thickening the Plot)

New experiences or a new way of thinking or being needs reinforcement to strengthen it or keep it alive. In the case of infidelity, these new actions, interactions, thoughts, and feelings decrease the ability for infidelity to have life. The preferred story is amplified by asking detailed questions that invite people to slow down an event or an experience and honor the efforts in maintaining the new experience. It is helpful to ask questions related to time (past, present, or future), actual or hypothetical. Additionally, questions about the context can anchor a couple's story to a particular place and situation. Such questions can invite them to extend their new narrative into new places and new situations, which helps solidify the changes made in therapy.

Questions to Amplify the Preferred Narrative

- Can you each describe the first step you took to rescue your relationship from the side effects of X? What was the second most important step? How did those steps lead you to where you are now?
- When you talk to him (her) now, what are the physical signs that he (she) is really listening to what you are saying? How are you responding to him (her) differently because of it?
- If I were to observe you in your home now, what would be the signs that you are getting along and that the influence of X is no longer creating distance?
- Who would have predicted that you would have turned things around? What would have lead them to predict it?

- If you were to continue on this path, how do you envision your lives together 1 year from now? What about 5 years from now? What about 10 or 20 years from now?
- How is your reaction to her (him) different now as opposed to before? How are you different because of it?
- Is your new way of resolving your conflict consistent with the values of your culture?
- What does this mean to you that your partner was able to recommit to your marriage? What personality traits or characteristics does it show?
- What do you think motivated you to take that first step? How were you able to do it? How did you overcome the temptation not to do it?
- What is it about your relationship now that gives you hope?
- Has there been anything that you learned from this experience of overcoming the effects of infidelity that could be important to other parts of your life?
- Has there been anything from this experience of overcoming the effects of infidelity that has taught you something new about yourself?
- As you reflect on this phase of your relationship, what do you now know that X (name of problem) didn't want you to know?

Spreading the News of Difference

Identifying and recruiting a wider audience are essential for strengthening a preferred perspective or story (White & Epson, 1990). As significant others begin to view the relationship differently, a reciprocal process occurs, which reinforces the preferred narrative. As others learn about the couple's new experience, they will reinforce the changes, thereby helping to strengthen the preferred narrative for the couple. This strengthening is important given the tenuous nature of the new narrative. As the couple involves others in their new narrative, they begin to free themselves from the constraints of the old story that tried to pull them apart. This new, preferred narrative will need the support of others to grow stronger, especially if those loved ones were aware of the couple's relational problems or acts of infidelity or betrayal.

If significant others are not aware of this new process in the couple's life, they will continue to generate the old problematic narrative of "the couple is in trouble" and continue to give life to the outdated dominant discourse about the couple. In essence, the couple has moved into a preferred narrative, but their family and friends, if still unaware of the positive changes, will continue to give life to the old narrative, which may creep back into the couple's or individuals' life. Spreading the *news of difference* is important to extend the new narrative's life into the future and to give it strength and momentum to continue to strengthen. Sharing experiences of a renewed relationship with significant others (i.e., friends, coworkers, family members, etc.) will also help the couple simultaneously challenge any residual, stubborn internalized problematic messages about their relationship.

White and Epston (1990) suggested circulating the new experience of their relationship or their preferred narrative through letters, documents, and ceremonies. Creating a ceremony or ritual in therapy, using an altar or shrine made by the client (Bermúdez & Bermúdez, 2002), can be a creative way to perform a ritual to punctuate the desired relational outcome. A ceremony, for example, can create an experience that enables couples to experience their lives and themselves in new ways as they focus on previously neglected and unstoried aspects of their experience. Nonetheless, as we consider cultural differences, it is important for therapists to note that some may feel their experiences in their relationship to be too personal, sacred, or private to share with others. The couple's public or private nature or the intersections of the contextual factors mentioned above (i.e., culture, class, gender, and sexuality) will influence the level of comfort with disclosing any intricacies of their relationship, whether positive or negative. It is imperative for therapists to be mindful of these preferences and to support the clients' private stance if that is consistent with their beliefs.

Conclusion

More research is needed on the interrelationship between culture and infidelity. In this chapter, we have highlighted intersectionality as a lens to examine the ways in which contextual and cultural factors such as culture, gender, SES, and sexuality intersect to influence clients' unique experiences of intimate partner infidelity. We assert that effective clinical work with couples who have experienced infidelity results from a focus on the *couple's* unique experience, as opposed to a problem-oriented, deficit model, which may produce counterproductive results (Atwood & Seifer, 1997). Narrative therapy was offered as a vehicle for deconstructing a couple's experience of infidelity from an intersectionality perspective, as well as helping them co-construct a preferred narrative that will increase the vitality of their *new* relationship.

References

Allen, E., Atkins, D., Baucom, D., Snyder, D., Gordon, K., & Glass, S. (2005). Intrapersonal, interpersonal, and contextual factors in engaging in and responding to extramarital involvement. *Clinical Psychology: Science and Practice, 12*, 101–130.

Anderson, H., & Goolishian, H. (1988). Human systems as linguistic systems: Preliminary and evolving ideas about the implications for clinical theory. *Family Process, 27*, 371–393.

Atkins, D. C., Baucom, D. H., Eldridge, K. A., & Christensen, A. (2005). Infidelity and behavioral couple therapy: Optimism in the face of betrayal. *Journal of Counseling and Clinical Psychology, 73*(1), 144–150.

Atwood, J., & Seifer, M. (1997). Extramarital affairs and constructed meanings: A social constructionist therapeutic approach. *American Journal of Family Therapy, 25*(1), 55–75.

Bermúdez, J. M. (1997). Experiential tasks and therapist bias awareness. *Contemporary Family Therapy, 19*(2), 253–267.

Bermúdez, J. M., & Bermúdez, S. (2002). The therapeutic use of altar-making. *Journal of Family Psychotherapy, 13*(3–4), 329–347.

Bermúdez, J. M., Keeling, M., & Stone Carlson, T. (2009). Using art to co-create preferred problem-solving narratives with Latino couples. In M. Rastogi & V. Thomas (Eds.), *Couple therapy with ethnic minorities*. Thousand Oaks, CA: Sage.

Blasband, D., & Peplau, L. (1985). Sexual exclusivity versus openness in gay couples. *Archives of Sexual Behavior, 14*(5), 395–412.

Blow, A. J., & Hartnett, K. (2005). Infidelity in committed relationships: A methodological review. *Journal of Marital and Family Therapy, 31*(2), 183–216.

Buunk, B. P. (1997). Personality, birth order and attachment styles as related to various types of jealousy. *Personality and Individual Differences, 23*, 997–1006.

Cann, A., Mangum, J., & Wells, M. (2001). Distress in response to relationship infidelity: The roles of gender and attitudes about relationship. *Journal of Sex Research, 38*(3), 185–190.

Crenshaw, K. (2006). Mapping the margins: Intersectionality, identity politics, and violence against women of color. In I. Grewal & C. Kaplan (Eds.), *An introduction to women's studies: Gender in a transnational world* (2nd Edition) (pp. 200–206). New York: McGraw-Hill.

deShazer, S. (1988). *Clues: Investigating solutions in brief therapy*. New York: Norton.

Drigotas, S. M., Safstrom, C. A., & Gentilia, T. (1999). An investment model prediction of dating infidelity. *Journal of Personality and Social Psychology, 77*, 509–524.

Freedman, J., & Combs, G. (1996). *Narrative therapy: The social construction of preferred realities*. New York: Norton.

Freedman, J., & Combs, G. (2002). Narrative couple therapy. In A. Gurman & N. Jacobson (Eds.), *Clinical handbook of couple therapy* (pp. 308–334). New York: Guilford.

Glass, S. (2002). Couple therapy after the trauma of infidelity. In A. Gurman & N. Jacobson (Eds.), *Clinical handbook of couple therapy* (pp. 488–507). New York: Guilford.

Goodman, J. (2001). *Promoting diversity and social justice: Educating people from privileged groups*. Thousand Oaks, CA: Sage.

Goodrich, T. J., Ellman, B., Rampage, C., & Halstead, K. (1990). The lesbian couple. In M. P. Mirkin (Ed.), *The social and political contexts of family therapy* (pp. 159–178). Needham Heights, MA: Allyn and Bacon.

Gordon, K. C., Baucom, D. H., & Snyder, D. K. (2004). An integrative intervention for promoting recovery from extramarital affairs. *Journal of Marital and Family Therapy, 30*, 1–12.

Keeling, M. L., & Bermúdez, J. M. (2006). Externalizing problems through art and writing: Experiences of process and helpfulness. *Journal of Marital and Family Therapy, 32*(4), 405–419.

Keeling, M. L., & Nielson, R. (2005). Indian women's experience of a narrative therapy intervention using art and writing. *Contemporary Family Therapy, 27*, 435–452.

Laumann, E. O., Gagnon, J. H., Michael, R. T., & Michaels, S. (1994). *The social organization of sexuality: Sexual practices in the United States.* Chicago: University of Chicago Press.

Ledesma, R. (2007). American Indian and Alaska Native children: A legacy of suffering, survival, and strength. In N. Cohen, T. Tran, & S. Rhee (Eds.), *Multicultural approaches in caring for children, youth, and families* (pp. 114–147). Boston: Pearson.

Martell, C. R., & Prince, S. E. (2005). Treating infidelity in same-sex couples. *Journal of Clinical Psychology: In Session, 61*(11), 1429–1438.

McNamee, S. (2004). Social construction as practical theory: Lessons for practice and reflection in psychotherapy. In D. Pare & G. Larner (Eds.), *Collaborative practice in psychology and therapy* (pp. 9–21). New York: Haworth.

Mongeau, P., Hale, J., & Alles, M. (1994). An experimental investigation of accounts and attributions following sexual infidelity. *Communication Monographs, 61*, 326–344.

Newman, D. (2007). *Identities and inequalities: Exploring the intersections of race, class, gender, and sexuality.* New York: McGraw-Hill.

Parker, M. L., Berger, A. T., & Campbell, K. (2010). Deconstructing couples' experiences with infidelity. *Journal of Couple and Relationship Therapy.*

Parker, M. L., Bermúdez, J. M., & Neustifter, R. (2007). Kite in Flight: Identity and empowerment of adolescent girls in dating relationships. *Journal of Feminist Family Therapy, 19*(4), 1–20.

Penn, C. D., Hernandez, S. L., & Bermúdez, J. M. (1997). Using a cross-cultural perspective to understand infidelity in couples therapy. *American Journal of Family Therapy, 25*(2), 169–185.

Pittman, F. S., & Wagers, T. P. (2005). Teaching fidelity. *Journal of Clinical Psychology: In Session, 61*(11), 1407–1419.

South, S., Trent, K., & Shen, Y. (2001). Changing partners: Toward a macrostructural-theory of marital dissolution. *Journal of Marriage and Family, 63*(3), 743–754.

Staheli, L. (1995). *Affair-proof your marriage: Understanding, preventing, and surviving an affair.* New York: Cliff Street Books.

Tatum, B. (1997). *Why are all the black kids sitting together in the cafeteria? And other conversations about race.* New York: Basic Books.

Teachman, J., Polonko, K., & Scanzoni, J. (1999). Demography and families. In M. Sussman, S. Steinmetz, & G. Peterson (Eds.), *Handbook of marriage and the family* (pp. 39–76). New York: Plenum.

Treas, J., & Giesen, D. (2000). Sexual infidelity among married and cohabiting Americans. *Journal of Marriage and the Family, 62*, 48–60.

West, C., & Zimmerman, D. (1987). Doing gender. *Gender and Society, 1*(2), 125–151.

White, M. (1995). *Re-authoring lives: Interviews and essays.* Adelaide, South Australia: Dulwich Centre Publications.

White, M., & Epston, D. (1990). *Narrative means to therapeutic ends.* New York: Norton.

Whitty, M., & Quigley, L. (2008). Emotional and sexual infidelity offline and in cyberspace. *Journal of Marital and Family Therapy, 34*(4), 461–468.

Zola, M. F. (2007). Beyond infidelity-related impasse: An integrated, systemic approach to couples therapy. *Journal of Systemic Therapies, 26*(2), 24–41.

CHAPTER **16**
Interview With Harville Hendrix

Harville Hendrix, Ph.D., couples therapist, clinical pastoral counselor, lecturer, and teacher, authored the international best seller, *Getting the Love You Want: A Guide for Couples* and co-created with his wife, Helen LaKelly Hunt, Imago Relationship Therapy, a couples theory and process practiced by over 2,000 imago therapists in 30 countries. His work has been featured 17 times on the *Oprah Winfrey Show*.

Eds: Can couples really get the love (and keep the love) they have always wanted?

HH: Yes, definitely, if they meet certain conditions. The imago premise is that the unconscious purpose of intimate partnership/marriage is to finish childhood. To finish childhood means two things: healing and growing. To heal one must get unmet needs from childhood met in one's intimate relationship. This heals the childhood wounds. To grow means to complete one's passage through the developmental stages. This means becoming an adult. To achieve healing, each partner must become a good surrogate parent to his or her partner, meeting needs not met in childhood. Since our own childhood wounding disinclines us to behave in a way that meets our partner's emotional and physical needs, this means we have to stretch into new behaviors relevant to our partner's needs. Stretching into those new behaviors propels us through the developmental stage where we were arrested, furthering our developmental growth and thus putting us on the path to adulthood. Since all childhood wounding whether from intrusion or neglect results from caretaker failure to be "present" in an attuned way to child, all healing in adulthood intimate relationships requires the development of the capacity to be "present" to one's partner. If couples are willing to become a resource for each other's healing, and thereby stretching into growing through their developmental stages by acquiring the skill of "presence," they can get and keep the love they want.

Eds: What are the important ingredients that couples can learn from you to help restore intimacy to their relationship?

HH: In my view, there are four important ingredients for restoring intimacy and they operationalize the healing and growing process referred to in the preceding question. (1) To become present to your partner is a precondition of intimacy. To become present requires a transformation of consciousness in which one discovers the "otherness" of the partner—to get it, that your partner is "not you." This is called differentiation. (2) Becoming present and intimate requires learning a new way to talk, namely shifting conversation from an exchange of parallel monologues to dialogue. Dialogue creates equality, safety, and connection. (3) Dialogical conversation replaces judgment—the destroyer of intimacy—with curiosity which ensures safety and deepens connection. To ensure safety and sustain connection, and thus intimacy, all negativity must be eliminated since negativity stimulates anxiety and thus activates defenses=danger. (4) To sustain and deepen connection and intimacy, all judgment (negativity) must be replaced with acceptance, appreciation, and partner advocacy. This is the path to love.

Eds: Do we focus too much on giving love? What about receiving love?

HH: In the Imago process, we see giving and receiving as an oscillation between polarities that needs to be kept in balance. Paradoxically, most partners complain because they are not receiving the love they want and at the same time are not giving the love their partner wants. So the first swing of the polarity is mutually to stretch into meeting each other's needs, to move from victim to being a healing resource for each other. This stretching heals and evokes growth. However, this shift toward giving creates anxiety in each partner, evoking a defense against receiving the love they want. This defense is rooted in the pain of ruptured intimacy between caretaker and child, a pain housed in implicit memory. It is unconsciously reactivated in adult intimate relationships to prevent the recurrence of that pain. To move this pain from implicit to explicit memory, to make what seems eternally present clearly a relic from the past, one must stretch to receive the love offered, hold it in consciousness, tolerate the anxiety until it recedes, and then integrate it into consciousness and the self, thus achieving growth toward wholeness. Because of what appears to be cultural bias against receiving, receiving love seems more challenging than giving love and is often neglected by therapists as an essential pole in the dynamic balance of giving and receiving.

CHAPTER 17

Restoring Intimacy With African American Couples

SHEA DUNHAM and CYRUS MARCELLUS ELLIS

Intimacy, for the African American couple, is not just "squishy" feelings between two people that can lead to sex, love, and possibly marriage. Because of the harsh realities of discrimination and oppression, intimacy needs to include the ability to create a safe haven, a shelter from the storm of indignities and injuries that many African Americans face on a daily basis. Trust, love, acceptance, fidelity, and commitment are soul food for the soul mate. Intimacy includes not only the ability to love one's partner but also to love their "blackness."

While there are certainly many commonalities between African American men and women, what they need and want in a relationship may be slightly different. African American men tend to focus on the companionship and emotional support aspects of marriage, and African American women tend to focus on security and the instrumental (two people to pay the bills, parent, and handle other responsibilities) aspects of marriage (Patterson, 1998). Black men want a "ride or die chick"—a woman who is going to be there every step of the way. She is there even when he disappoints her, when he does not live up to expectations, and the only way she will not be there is if she physically cannot be and the only way she cannot physically be there is if she ceases to exist. African American women are willing to be there every step of the way as long as her man does not commit a transgression specifically against her. Black women want "a do-right man." She wants her husband to be dependable, responsible, monogamous, and honest about self and with self. She wants her mate to be close and connected to her, but she also wants to see him being close to others like their children, friends, and family. Connection to extended kin is important. Trust, demonstrated in different ways (i.e., commitment, fidelity, and follow through with stated promises), is key to African American men and women.

Perhaps the need to test these trusts is part of the struggle between African American men and women. How can a man really know that his mate is a dependable partner unless he first violates her trust and then waits to see if she stays and supports him? How can he see if she is really willing to stick around unless he is at his lowest point? How can a woman know if she really has a "do-right man" unless she is hypervigilant and watches to see if he puts her welfare and the welfare of their family above all else?

In this chapter a review of the unique challenges, based on the history of slavery, racism and sexism, and internalized stereotypes or discrimination, will be presented to help clinicians understand the distinctive sociocultural factors that influence African American couples. African American marriages can benefit by assisting couples in analyzing the challenges they grapple with that affect their love relationship (Collins, 2005). In addition, interventions designed or redesigned to increase intimacy and take into account the challenges and strengths of African American couples will be presented.

The State of the Union

When looking at the state of opposite-sex unions in the United States and making recommendations to support and improve those unions, one has to take into consideration the rate of occurrence, quality, and stability of marriage. Over the past four decades African Americans have experienced significant changes related to the institution of marriage. According to the 2006 U.S. Census, between 1970 and 2000, the percentage of African Americans who decided to marry in their lifetime declined from 64 to 55% among men and from 72 to 58% among women (Tuker, Subramanian, & James, 2004). Although divorce rates may be high for Americans in general, they are even higher for African Americans. After 10 years of marriage 32% of white women have ended their marriage compared to 47% of African American women (Bramlett & Mosher, 2002). In summary, African American men and women are less likely to get married, less likely to see marriage as a lifelong commitment, and are less likely to identify benefits associated with marriage compared to white men and women (Bulanda & Brown, 2007).

This higher risk of relationship dissolution could be accounted for by poorer marital quality, but there is little research looking at what specifically accounts for marital quality in African American couples (Bulanda & Brown, 2007). Despite the fact that there are 10.3 million married African Americans in the United States (U.S. Census Bureau, 2006), there have been few studies aimed at understanding African American marriage and divorce rates (Bulanda & Brown, 2007; Hairston, 2000; Orbuch, Veroff, Hassan, & Horrocks, 2002). Researchers have suggested that the differential rates of marriage and divorce between African American and white couples could be accounted for by socioeconomic status, education, culture, values, or the history of discrimination in the United States (Bulanda & Brown, 2007; Hairston, 2000; Trent & South, 2003). However, contrary to popular hypotheses, several studies have found that the higher perceived divorce risk and lower marital commitment among African American couples cannot be attributed to racial differences in socioeconomic and demographic predictors of marital quality (Bulanda & Brown, 2007; Orbuch et al., 2002; Trent & South, 2003; Tuker et al., 2004), and few studies have looked in depth at the other hypotheses.

Research on African American marriage has begun to turn away from demographic and socioeconomic explanations of marital dissolution and turn toward exploring group norms and sociocultural hypotheses. "Past research has given little focus to specific cultural factors, beyond the structural, in terms of their role in explaining differential rates of quality and stability among Black and White marriages. In terms of divorce rates, these meanings are important to understanding the nature of racial differences" (Hairston, 2000, p. 20). African American couples may attach a unique meaning to marriage, conflict, and emotion due to different culture, historical backgrounds, and experiences in the United States (Bulanda & Brown, 2007; Dunham, 2008; Hairston, 2000; Trent & South, 2003). Differences in marital dissolution and quality would be better understood by assessing racial differences in marital experiences and identifying how predictors of marital quality may differ for racial groups (Amato & Rogers, 1997; Bulanda & Brown, 2007; Dunham, 2008; Orbuch et al., 2002; Raley, Durden, & Wildsmith, 2004; Trent & South, 2003).

Barriers to Intimacy

The history of African Americans in the United States has influenced every aspect of their lives, including the institution of marriage (Pinderhughes, 2002). Couples' relationships and family bonds were often severed by the rules of particular slave masters and the sale of slaves. In some states it was illegal for African Americans to marry, and after the abolishment of slavery, migration to Northern states to find jobs interrupted kinship networks (Pinderhughes, 2002). The unique history and obstacles of African Americans in the United States create distinct challenges to their marital relationships. For example, internalized stereotypes about race, gender, and sexuality may be a barrier to trust, commitment, and flexibility in African American couples.

Racism

Discrimination and oppression did not end with abolishment of slavery, the passage of civil rights legislation, and the movement of more black families into the middle class. Even the election of the first African American president will not erase practices of discrimination; in fact, the achievement of having the first African American in the highest office in the United States may obscure the ongoing oppression of the black community and increase the tendency to blame the victims. Whites and blacks alike fall into the trap of obscuring the role of discrimination in the everyday lives of African Americans and are especially loathe to admit how racism is also complicated by sexism (Collins, 2005; hooks, 1995; Pinderhughes, 2002).

Although there are commonalities in experiences for both African American men and women, there are also gender-specific experiences (Boyd-Franklin, 2003; Boyd-Franklin & Franklin, 1998; Collins, 2006; Franklin & Boyd-Franklin, 2000; hooks, 1995). The effects of the interplay between racism and sexism painfully emerge in the dynamics of African American couples (Boyd-Franklin & Franklin, 1998). Whether or not people are ready and willing to discuss the effects of racism on their relationship, there is evidence that suggests that couples who face experiences of racism and discrimination are more likely to report verbal and physical aggression than positive communication patterns (La Taillade, Baucom, & Jacobson, 2000 as cited in Boyd-Franklin, Kelly, & Durham, 2008). Internalizing experiences of racism and discrimination also have a negative effect on trust and marital satisfaction (Kelly & Floyd, 2001, 2006).

Sexism

The gender war affects European American couples, but for African American couples there is the added dimension of the pain and deleterious effects of racism. African Americans have a unique history in the United States and have different experiences than other groups, so their views of typical gender roles may also be different. In the United States African American men and women have been subjected to oppression through the vessels of slavery and racism (Boyd-Franklin, 2003). Caricatures of African American "men as irresponsible, undependable, abusive, and exploitive, or of women as evil, domineering, and suspicious, filter into the expectations that each partner has of the other and become the source for marital problems" (Pinderhughes, 2002, p. 274).

African American men and women both experience the "invisibility syndrome." For men it is defined as a "paradoxical process in which

African American men, because of their high visibility, are perceived with fear and distrust and are more often ignored or avoided by White society" (Boyd-Franklin, 2003, p. 88). African American men become visible in white society when they are viewed as being threatening, challenging, or dangerous (Boyd-Franklin, 2003; Littlefield, 2003). African American women experience a different kind of invisibility based on the combination of racism and sexism. African American women have to deal with the same issues or conflicts in life that many other women face (e.g., wife, mother, and domestic goddess). The difference is the additional pressure of racism.

African American Men   African American men live "within the veil" (DuBois, 1903). W. E. B. DuBois wrote and spoke of this unique characteristic for black men because he recognized that in a society based on gender roles, black men will have to contend with an overarching question: Are we Negro or are we American? DuBois terms the aforementioned phenomenon "double-consciousness," which is the sense of looking at one's self through the eyes of others, the measuring of your soul by the contemptuous and pitiful lens of a world that holds the black phenotype in disdain.

White and Cones (1999) underscored the socialization of African American men that are rooted in three primary arenas: (a) establishing a strong self-concept, (b) establishing goals and strategies to achieve their goals, and (c) and creating a set of standards and values to be used as guides for their overall behavior and standard of living. In past times the method many African American men used to develop a strong sense of self, goal setting, and personal morality came from within the African American community and the example of the men in their communities. In more recent times the ability to be exposed to the same ethic that was demonstrated many years ago is complicated by the onslaught of cultural attacks by various media.

What connotation emerges when discussing the black male phenotype? Are they gangsters, roughnecks, or B-Boyz, as made popular by the medium of rap music and music videos? Do black men seek to define their overall self and thereby strategize for their future based on these false impressions of who they are and what they are supposed to be? Simply put, do they understand the relative nature of our society attempting to alter the internal development of black men by asserting the premise that one type of black man is preferable to another type of black man?

Examine for a moment the 1990s television show *Family Matters*. Jaleel White was one of the stars on the show who played the character Steve Erkel. He was a young African American male who was portrayed as goofy, awkward, and a bit nerdy. His daily interactions and mannerism were seen as incongruent with the black phenotype promoted and imprinted in our psyches. Over the course of the show, he developed and created his alter ego, Stephan. Stephan was cool, calm, and collected, but not as smart as Steve. Stephan had confidence, a degree of arrogance, and a certain swagger; all the things a black man is said to possess. Steve created this alter ego to contend with his negative responses to the community. His interests as Steve were viewed as incongruent with the interests of cool and hip young black people. His ability to attract the woman who won his heart was filtered through whether or not she could receive cultural feedback that would be considered valuable. White and Cones (1999, p. 132) recognized this manner of development by demonstrating that African American men, implicitly or explicitly, most likely choose their way of being from three clusters of reference: (a) traditional Euro-American values, (b) African American values, or (c) and those that represent the "renegade" street culture. The television example of Steve versus Stephan demonstrates that societal themes are present in everyday society and can provoke one to seek a remedy to gain a sense of identity, formulate goals and methods to provide remediation to the internal confusion concerning how the black man will obtain his self-identity, reconcile his personal strivings to be seen as a man, and contend with the assaults on his physical representation, intellect, and ability to demonstrate his love.

Slavery and the consequent discrimination and negation of the African American male marginalized black men in the role as financial supporter, protector, and head of the household (Hill, 2002; Pinderhughes, 2002). Patterson (1998) has commented that one of the most demoralizing lingering effects of slavery was the obliteration of family roles, especially those of men as husbands and fathers, and these lingering effects have left wounds in the relationships of African American men and women. For example, the names of slave fathers of children were often not listed on birth records and parentage was only associated with the mother (Pinderhughes, 2002). The role of the father was not legally recognized for black men.

Although African American men are important, whether their role is legally recognized or not, they still get much of their identity from their social world rather than from their family. Their social world includes groups such as other African American men in their social network and the mainstream media (Brewer, 1998). From the social world African American men receive messages that masculinity is important (Levant, Majors, & Kelley, 1998; Pinderhughes, 2002) and that they cannot show weakness because they risk the possibility of being rejected from their peer group (Boyd-Franklin, 2003). If their masculinity is compromised, they can feel powerless in other areas of their lives (Pinderhughes, 2002). The focus on masculinity and power can negatively impact African American marriages (Taylor, Tucker, & Mitchell-Kernan, 1999).

Although African American men, at times, have not had the financial, cultural, and legal access to fulfill many of the traditional gender roles, they still live in a society where men, regardless of race, are expected to fill those roles if they are "real men" (Hill, 2002; Pinderhughes, 2002). African American men may be more egalitarian in their roles as husbands (e.g., sharing decision making, finances, household chores), but that does not mean they like or accept having to be more egalitarian (Clarkwest, 2007; Hill, 2002; Pinderhughes, 2002). Some African Americans have internalized the "gender rules" but cannot live within the context of these expectations when sociopolitical factors make this impossible (Clarkwest, 2007; Collins, 2006).

African American Women   African American women, unlike many white women, are expected to be leaders of their households, to fulfill the financial provider role (because there are more unskilled jobs open to them than men), and be strong (Hill, 2002; Pinderhughes, 2002). In addition, it is perceived that black women should compensate for the societal injuries that black men face in society, and this responsibility has been a source of relational tension (Pinderhughes, 2002). The messages received by black women are that they need to be competent, raise the children, work, be self-reliant, and believe in their own capabilities and strengths (Boyd-Franklin, 2003). African American women may place African American men in one or more of six categories: (a) absent father, (b) transient male relationship, (c) weak or dysfunctional father, (d) egalitarian marriage, (e) strong or authoritarian father, or (f) abusive male-female relationship (Boyd-Franklin, 2003, p. 91). This view impacts their ability to view relationships with African American men as committed relationship material; instead they may view men as "no good" and "unreliable." African American women with negative early observed experiences often "don't know how to have a positive relationship with a man" (Boyd-Franklin, 2003, p. 91).

Love and Sexuality

Love and sexuality have both always been very personal and political topics. Who people choose to love and have sex with can be a private, romantic, and special choice. In addition, who people choose and their ability to choose also have sociopolitical implications. Although the laws of the United States at times have discounted African Americans as citizens, segregated them, and restricted their rights to marry, black sexuality is a form of black power that others have very little control over (West, 1999). The prowess and sexual appetites of African Americans have been mythologized and simultaneously seen as taboo to discuss within both white and black America. West (1999) believes that an open discussion about black sexuality between and within these communities is essential for improved race relations in the United States.

> This demythologizing of black sexuality is crucial for black America, because much of black self-hatred and self-contempt has to do with the refusal of many black Americans to love their own black bodies— especially their black noses, hips, lips, and hair. Just as many white Americans view black sexuality with disgust, so [too] do many black Americans—but for very different reasons and with very different results ... fear is best sustained by convincing them that their bodies are ugly, their intellect is inherently underdeveloped, their culture is less civilized and their future warrants less concern than that of other peoples. Two hundred and forty-four years of slavery and nearly a century of institutionalized terrorism in the form of segregation, lynchings and second-class citizenship in America were aimed at precisely this devaluation of black people ... this dehumanizing endeavor has left its toll in the psychic scars and personal wounds now inscribed in the souls of black folk. These scars and wounds are clearly etched on the canvas of black sexuality. (West, 1999, p. 516)

Patterson (1998) contended that African American men have viewed their treatment by the majority culture as castrating and emasculating. In reaction, sexual domination has come to symbolize masculinity and freedom. Famous African American analysts such as bell hooks, Cornel West, and Patricia Hill Collins have argued that equating black masculinity with hypersexuality colludes with the very racism and sexism that emasculates African American men. In fact, they stated that it is not the sexual and physical domination of African American women that will lead to more power and freedom—it is the love ethic that will lead to better gender relations in the African American community and is a form of rebellion against oppression (Collins, 2005; hooks, 1995; West, 1995). It is loving oneself and loving other African Americans in a committed, loving, and respectful relationship that is the true form of rebellion and resistance against oppression.

Love, versus dating or having sex, in the African American community is the height of rebellion in a society that degrades and demeans blackness (Collins, 2005). To love another in a committed, trusting relationship puts, as bell hooks (1995) stated, "loving blackness as political resistance" into action. Similar to what feminists refer to as "the personal as political," choosing to love blackness through loving, trusting, and committing to an African American partner is an act of defiance rather than an act of submission to societal expectations (as some might see marriage).

For heterosexual African American men, *choosing to love and committing to a heterosexual relationship with a black woman is a rebellious act.*

By choosing to love women whom society has so demonized, black men exhibit a form of "strength" in resisting their depictions as hustlers, bad boys, and criminals. For heterosexual African American women, demanding that their black male sexual partners respect them for who they are constitutes a rebellious act in a society that stigmatizes black women as unworthy of love (Collins, 2005, p. 250).

Stereotypes

Sexual attitudes and behaviors are burdened with many stereotypes for African Americans, which can put a burden on couples who are simply looking to be intimate with each other. The stereotypes of blacks is that they are sexual deviants, when in reality they tend to be more conservative when it comes to sexual variation (e.g., types of sex, sexual positions, communication about sex) than some other groups (Sinclair, 1999). Males are stereotyped as promiscuous, oversexed studs, having innate knowledge of sexuality, untrustworthy, and incapable of commitment (Pinderhughes, 2002). Sexual acts tend to be intercourse and genital focused, and other forms of sex tend not to be seen as "real sex." Stereotypes, lack of sexual knowledge, inability to discuss sexual values and attitudes, and a restricted view of what constitutes real sex can all be problematic in creating satisfying sex lives.

In addition, the meaning of sex and what it is used to symbolize can be problematic. In a society that does not usually value African American men, they can prove their worth through their sexual conquests and the number of children they create. Sexual conquests are seen as a definition of a man's manhood and success. For some African American men, sex is about whether you can "run game" and "close the deal." When a man talks a woman into bed it is a way of showing how intelligent and clever he can be. How much can he get with putting out the least effort? "Running game" puts women in their place and shows them that they are not as strong as they think—it shows they have weakness and, relatively speaking, the man has control and power. Getting a woman into bed levels the playing field—she may have more opportunities, more education, and more money, but once a man gets her into bed then he has more power. Because sex may be defined as just sex for a man and as love for a woman, once a woman has sex, she is on the hook. The man has a connection to her that is more important to the woman and has a different meaning than it does for the stereotypical male. For men, sex with women is like another job and it is a way that he can feel on top. Men who run games are getting a lot of perks (e.g., uncommitted sex, attention, financial gifts). They are getting more than they are giving. Sex with many women can symbolize status, and in a world where African American men do not have much status it can give them a sense of self-worth and importance. In the hip-hop culture a strong man is not shown as a man who can "close the deal" on a job; it is the man who can talk the girl into his car. The more women he has in his car, the more his status increases.

For African American women, sex may be a way to be connected to men while minimizing her vulnerability. Sex and love may be separated to show that she does not need a man. African American women are supposed to be self-sufficient, independent, and strong. There is a tension between being taught that you do not need a man and wanting a man to prove that she is "woman enough" to get and keep a man. African American women are faced with two options—wanting to be self-sufficient and independent and wanting a man. By the time a woman has mastered her education and career, it is a difficult transition to share one's life and decision making with a man. Once she does form a relationship a man is sometimes treated like another purse—you carry it for a while and it feels good, but you will never let it be known that you need or desire it. A purse is an accessory; not a necessity. Needing and desiring a man in some ways makes a woman seem weak. African American women are sometimes afraid that they are just a conquest for a man, that they will be taken advantage of, or that the only man that will stay around is one that they do not want to keep.

As for most couples, it may helpful to discuss with African American couples the stereotypes about men and women related to sex, to help them become more comfortable communicating what increases their sexual satisfaction, to provide sex education when appropriate, and to discuss expectations around fidelity as well as the meaning of sex and how it influences their view of their own masculinity or femininity. In addition, clinicians should help couples explore how sex may be attached to power in their relationship and power within society. Sex can be used as a form of intimacy, a form of power, or a form of aggression.

Strategies and Interventions for Recovering Intimacy

There are few therapeutic models specifically researched for effectiveness with African American couples. The suggested interventions discussed here are based on an integration of aspects of research-based models of couples therapy and guidelines suggested for work with African Americans. Several ideas from Gottman's (1999) Relational House Theory (i.e., fondness and admiration, honoring dreams and expectations, overcoming gridlock, being open to influence, creating a sense of we-ness), Johnson's (2004) Emotionally Focused Therapy (i.e., softening, normalizing the attachment bond, and creating a safe space to be vulnerable), and ideas from the popular book *The Five Love Languages: How to Express Heartfelt Commitment to Your Mate* (Chapman, 1995) were altered in a way to be more culturally relevant to African American couples.

Interventions focused on decreasing spousal dissimilarity may be of particular importance for African Americans. Spousal dissimilarity may lead to greater conflict and divorce for African American couples (Clarkwest, 2007). Incompatibility in sexual attitudes (Patterson, 1998), in expectations regarding spousal roles (Franklin, 1984), and in religiosity (Lawson & Thompson, 1995) have been cited as dissimilarities related to divorce in African American couples.

Some basic guidelines for working with African American clients, no matter what models and interventions are used, are: (a) orient the couple to the therapy process, (b) do not assume familiarity with clients in the first session, (c) address the issue of racism and its effects in their lives, (d) join with the couple before gathering sensitive information, (e) maintain a broad definition of family when assessing the couples structure and roles, (f) assess and intervene multisystemically, (g) use a problem-solving focus in treatment, (h) include discussions of spirituality or religion and if appropriate consult spiritual or religious leaders, (i) use scriptural references or metaphors, and (j) acknowledge strengths, resources, and successes (Bean, Perry, & Bedell, 2002). Be willing to discuss some of the statistics about African American marriage and divorce, but first discuss that racism and economic marginalization have placed undue burdens on African American couple relationships that often are not experienced by white couples (Boyd-Franklin, 2003; Boyd-Franklin & Franklin, 1998; Boyd-Franklin, Kelly, & Durham, 2008; Franklin, 2004; Kelly, 2003; Kelly & Floyd, 2001, 2006; La Taillade, 2000).

The Great Invitation of Marriage

The last three verses of Matthew 11 are called the Great Invitation. It is Jesus Christ's invitation to people to believe in him and in exchange for the light burden that he is asking (belief in him and doing God's will), he will help believers carry the heavy burdens of life.

A yoke, in those times, was a piece of wood that was fashioned to fit farm animals to help them carry heavy loads. The more skillfully the yoke was made to fit a certain animal, the less it irritated the animal and the more helpful the piece of wood was to the hard work the animal had to do.

Spouses can offer each other the Great Invitation of Marriage. This invitation is an offer to help carry the burden of life with a partner in exchange for a light burden—faith, commitment, and fidelity. In exchange for this yoke a spouse will in return offer respite from the chaos of life, shelter from oppression, and partnership in the defense against discrimination. A spouse cannot stop the hardships of life from happening, but he or she, through love and support, can help lighten the burden. It is not that marriage does not carry with it any responsibilities or is never wearisome, but within the context of a promise to love, heal, and find peace, these toils take on a meaning of spiritual productivity and purpose. Marriage may be a burden at times, but it is a burden that allows one to carry a much heavier load. It is a burden that makes all other burdens bearable, and it will be a light yoke as long as people believe, respect, and honor their vows.

Clinicians can have a discussion with spouses about what they thought the "burden" of marriage would be, based on their internalized personal experiences and stereotypes about marriage. For African American couples, clinicians should discuss the effect that racism and sexism have had on their view of marriage and how these messages may make it scary to pursue. Marriage clinicians can explore questions such as: What does it mean for African American men and women to humble themselves, submit to one another, be monogamous, and offer to carry the burdens of a partner? How would it feel to truly trust that a partner had faith in the relationship and was willing to accept the invitation of marriage? What is it that each partner likes, loves, and admires about the other that will help them face the burdens of life? What strengths do each of them possess and what strengths do they possess as a couple that will help them fulfill the marital commitment?

The marital commitment should be placed in the context of the larger kinship network that tends to be so important for African Americans. For example, in Clarkwest's (2007) study, African American newlyweds tended to focus on negotiating relationships with their families of origin rather than focusing on how to be a couple independent of their families: "The couples are more focused on negotiating their 'connecteness' than 'separateness'" (p. 123). Gottman and Silver (1999), in the research-based *Seven Principles for Making Marriage Work*, discuss creating a sense of "We-ness" for the couple in the context of their family of origin, but perhaps the better description for African Americans would be to help them focus on creating a We-ness within the context of an Us-ness. "We" are a couple within the context of "Us" as an extended kinship network. So, the Great Invitation to Marriage, in some ways, is extended to the partner and his or her family as well.

Creating a Safe Haven

The ache for the home lives in all of us, the safe place where we can go as we are and not be questioned.

—**Maya Angelou**

In a harsh world where African American men and women feel like they have to be better than their white counterparts, African American couples may not have much energy or motivation to give extra time and attention to their personal relationships (Lawson & Thompson, 1995). In a life filled with visible and invisible struggles, the last place a person wants to exert great effort is at home. Paradoxically, if one does put forth time and energy into his or her home life and marriage, that person can become a safe haven from the inequities and pains experienced in the outside world. Marriage can provide a context for creating and maintaining African Americans' sense of personal well-being (Billingsley, 1992; Cahida, Verhoff, & Leber, 1998).

Home should be a safe place where people can recharge from the effects of overt and covert racism (Clark, Anderson, Clark, & Williams, 1999). Home often represents a safe place where African Americans can feel safe from the "microaggressions" of being part of an oppressed minority in the United States (Franklin & Boyd-Franklin, 2000). A safe home also provides a place where a person is no longer invisible. Couples that lack a safe home are at risk for disharmony and problems (Burton, Winn, Stevenson, & Clark, 2004).

The African American home can serve as a "safe haven," a place where a person can feel validated, important, and as if he or she has a voice. A home that is a safe haven will allow each partner to feel heard, both spouses give input into decisions, and each spouse has areas of expertise that are recognized in the home. Although a safe haven is a place to commiserate over discrimination and racism, it is not the focus of their marriage. When they walk out the door they put on their "black suit," but when they come home they are just "Bill" and "Patricia." Each partner can relate and identify with the black suit because they both have to wear the same suit when they walk out the door. In the house, they do not have to wear that facade, but they can empathize and help heal the wounds that come with it.

Home is where you should reveal vulnerabilities that are ordinarily hidden to the outside world. However, home is often where people project their stresses because it is safe. Bill may not yell at his boss about getting passed over for a deserved promotion for the third time because he is afraid of losing his job, but he can go home and yell at his wife, Patricia, because she has made a decision without consulting with him. The injuries of feeling powerless in the outside world can compound the feelings of powerless one might sometimes feel in a marriage in a way that nonoppressed groups do not have to deal with. A lot of people may at times feel powerless in their marriages, but that is not magnified by the oppression outside the home. A key point to having a safe home is that it serves as a place where one can receive a "greater sense of acceptance and legitimacy" (Franklin & Boyd-Franklin, 2000, p. 39). Feeling accepted will help decrease feelings of invisibility and increase a sense of validation. Counselors can encourage African Americans to acknowledge verbally that their home is a safe place where they can feel accepted. This is where they can gather with their partner or other African Americans as part of the self-healing process that is intended to reduce the effect of psychic injuries due to oppressive environments (Franklin & Boyd-Franklin, 2000).

There are several things that couples can do to ensure that their home is a safe haven. First, start with identifying when they already feel safe and what each one of them does to help create a feeling of safety. Examples may be if a couple has alone time every night when they talk about the day's events, when they plan together how they will handle a problem, or when they cuddle or have sex. Second, a clinician can teach specific skills that will increase a person's sense of safety. For example, when a couple wants to discuss a problem, teaching them a soft start up (devoid of criticism or contempt and shows appreciation for the partner) rather than a harsh start up (starting a conversation with criticism) may help them feel safer (Gottman, 1999). Third, the therapist can help clients be comfortable expressing vulnerability to one's partner and accepting vulnerability from a partner (Johnson, 2004). Fourth, clients need to learn to forgive themselves and their partners for making mistakes in life and in the relationship. Spirituality and prayer can serve as a vehicle for finding forgiveness (Gottman, 1999).

Into-Me-See: Making Oneself and Spouse Visible

Part of feeling invisible in the outside world is only being seen for the stereotyped, demonized aspects of oneself. Clients may not have much control over whether they are recognized, rewarded, and validated in larger society, but a couple can do specific visibility interventions to at least make them feel seen at home and in their marriage. Helping oneself and one's spouse feel seen and important can be an incredibly intimate act.

The invisibility syndrome for African Americans has a negative impact within the relationship. The trials and tribulations of African Americans remain in the collective memory and add to an already ingrained view of inadequacy, low self-esteem, and feelings of inferiority (Hopson & Powell Hopson, 1994). This results in an inner struggle for many African Americans and impacts their personal identity (Franklin & Boyd-Franklin, 2000) and how they will interact interpersonally. There are several things a counselor can do to decrease the risk for disharmony within their intimate relationships. First, counselors have to be trained not to view couples as separate, independent units who are not connected to their family, extended family, and history (Boyd-Franklin et al., 2008). Second, counselors have to make sure that ethnic identity is integrated into every theory or model used to work with the couple. Keeping ethnic identity as a constant companion during treatment will decrease the possibility of the invisibility syndrome creeping into another area of the couple's life.

Not all African American couples will present with issues of invisibility as the reason for seeking counseling. However, it is the responsibility of the counselor to discuss issues that may pose a problem in the couple's attempt to adjust to the struggles they may face throughout life as individuals and as a couple within their cultural context (Wyatt, 1999). Acknowledging issues such as the invisibility syndrome and healthy cultural suspicion of mental health services (Boyd-Franklin, 2003) can help strengthen the therapeutic alliance. Third, counselors need to investigate interventions chosen to work with African American couples because many interventions are created by and evaluated in therapy for whites. Interventions that acknowledge different cultural perspectives help promote change by encouraging trust and self-disclosure. This is important for African Americans because traditional counseling viewpoints reflect cultural racism (Brown & Landrum-Brown, 1995, as cited in Yeh, 1999) and, therefore, during the counseling process feelings of invisibility may be reinforced (Franklin & Boyd-Franklin, 2000).

There are several things that clinicians and spouses can discuss to help them feel more visible within their marriage and recognized for each individual's strengths. Interventions aimed at recognition, rewards, validation, legitimacy, respect, dignity, and identity make people visible (Franklin & Boyd-Franklin, 2000). Clinicians need to discuss the topic of invisibility with their clients and help them recognize how instances of invisibility may create problems within their relationship. In addition, clients can identify what coping mechanisms they use to survive in a "white world" and the strategies they use in their marriage in order to identify which coping strategies are helpful or hurtful in one or both contexts. Although the therapist should be sympathetic and assist the couple with empathizing with each other, these processes should not be used to excuse harmful behaviors toward each other (Boyd-Franklin & Franklin, 1998). There is a difference between understanding and excusing.

There are also specific interventions clients can be directed to do within sessions and outside sessions. One way to help clients feel recognized and rewarded is to have the spouses tell how they appreciate each other, what each contributes to the relationship and household, and how those things uplift the couple or family. Nurturing a couple's fondness and admiration for each other is one of Gottman's (1999) principles for a successful marriage. For African American couples these conversations should be particularly focused on what they do not receive fondness and admiration for in the larger world. Although words are a great form of recognition, awards and certificates are also excellent ways to provide recognition and validation. Clients can create awards or certificates to recognize and validate aspects of their partner or the relationship that they enjoy or these can be created to focus on an area that each spouse has not received recognition for in the outside world. For example, an African American parent may not be recognized by a school until his or her child gets into trouble, despite the fact that the parent has been an active participant in the child's education (e.g., attending parent–teacher conferences, attending field trips, attending parent–teacher association meetings). The spouse could create a dedicated parent certificate for the other spouse to recognize his or her invisible contributions.

In addition, Franklin and Boyd-Franklin (2000) suggested finding ways to do sanity checks and creating support groups as ways to combat invisibility. Sanity checks are ways that African American men and women substantiate mistreatment and racism. Twenty- to 30-minute stress-reducing conversations at the end of the day can serve as sanity checks. These types of conversations should focus on what happened that day in order to help partners manage the stresses of life that are not caused by the marriage (Gottman & Silver, 1999). Keeping outside stresses from overwhelming one's marriage is key to keeping the relationship strong (Gottman & Silver, 1999). The spouses should pick a time when they both can talk and show interest in the conversation. Each partner should take turns being the complainer (about half the time each). During the other person's complaining time, the listener should not give unsolicited advice, should show interest, communicate understanding, make sure to take the spouse's side (this is not the time to point out the error of his or her ways), express an "us against them" attitude, express affection for the spouse (verbally and physically), and validate the complainer's emotions.

Reinterpreting the Five Love Languages for African American Couples

I've learned that people will forget what you said, people will forget what you did, but people will never forget how you made them feel.

—**Maya Angelou**

Author Gary Chapman (1995) wrote the best-selling book *The Five Love Languages: How to Express Heartfelt Commitment to Your Mate.* In this book the author introduces the idea that keeping their partners "emotional love tank" full is key to maintaining a happy and satisfied marriage (Chapman, 1995, p. 24). The five love languages include: words of affirmation, quality time, receiving gifts, acts of service, and physical touch. Words of affirmation are words that are used to build one's spouse up. Quality time is making sure that your spouse is the focus during conversations or during shared activities. Receiving gifts is the physical act of showing one's spouse "Hey, you were on my mind"; it is a symbol of love. Acts of service are those acts that a spouse knows will bring joy to his or her partner. And finally physical touch is a way to express love by hugging, holding, kissing, or sexual intercourse. In essence it is the physical contact that fills their emotional love tank.

Understanding which of these is a partner's primary love language helps keep each person's emotional love tank full. Like grades of gasoline, different engines need different octane-rated gasoline for optimum performance. Car engines can run on any of the octane levels, but if one uses the wrong grade, over time it can produce engine knock, which jeopardizes the quality of performance and longevity of the engine. Understanding the five love languages and zeroing in on one's partner's primary love language can result in meeting your spouse's emotional needs, increasing the quality of the relationship, and increasing the likelihood of longevity. "We must be willing to learn our spouse's primary love language if we are to be effective communicators of love" (Chapman, 1995, p. 14). Chapman's love languages may be more helpful for African Americans if they are infused with a cultural perspective and reinterpreted for African Americans.

Words of Value   Words of value are a reinterpretation of words of affirmation. Words of value are more than words to build up one's spouse. Instead words of value convey that sense of worth to one's partner. If the world rejects you, it does not matter because you are valued by your partner and family. Words of value, like words of affirmation, convey encouragement and are meant to inspire with a conscious effort to not "nag" in between words of value. Words of value show flexibility, respect, and self-lessens. For African American men words of value secure the relationship because they show that their spouse is not looking for a better deal but really happy and satisfied with his or her current purchase. Words of affirmation are more global, whereas words of value are specific of your worth to your spouse and family.

Acts of Sacrifice   Chapman defined quality time as "giving someone your undivided attention" (1995, p. 55), and "quality conversation—sympathetic dialogue where two individuals are sharing their experiences, thoughts, feelings, and desires in a friendly, uninterrupted context" (p. 61). Quality time is an experience of deep connection, but it is important to acknowledge that sometimes a spouse may appreciate the willingness of a partner to sacrifice time even without quality of time. For example, a husband may want his wife to watch the game with him, even though it is not an activity they both enjoy. Acts of sacrifice include spending time together without resentment or an expectation of quid pro quo. During this time the wife sits close to her spouse and listens to her husband berate the other team. From the husband's view, this is quality time that is not necessarily pouring into her love tank; however, their love tank is filled by bring the couple closer together.

The Gift of Commitment and Interdependence   Receiving gifts is the act of giving one's mate tangible objects in order to express fondness and love. This love language supports the fundamental act of giving and the joy that is received from that gift. Chapman (1995) added that one's "physical presence" is a gift as well and it should be view as such. Among couples, received gifts are important; however, this differs for African American men and women, which I will call "more than receiving gifts." For many African American women received gifts are appreciated; however, many would like to include receiving the gift of commitment. The "gift of commitment" is an act of giving one's self to one's mate. This can be done through marriage or just the simple act of being faithful, honest, and loyal. Although this cannot always be measured through materials, it can be measured by living up to verbalized expectations and most important by following through with promises. For African American men the gift of interdependence is a key gift that can secure his place within the relationship, therefore increasing satisfaction. The gift of interdependence is an act by African American women through which they have a sense of self and are not totally dependent on their mates (McElroy, 2002). The key to being interdependent is that although women are capable of making their own decisions, consulting their mate is a priority for them. This is done when the woman seeks her husband's view on important matters and reinforces his role as the man in her life (McElroy, 2002). Due to the history of racism and oppression African American men often feel as if they are ignored in the outside world (Boyd-Franklin, 2003). Therefore, within intimate relationships it is important that the man feels as if he is valuable and has something to offer.

Unconditional Acts of Love   An act of service is actually doing something that would be pleasing to one's mate without obligation (Chapman, 1995). This includes doing things that may be different from traditional role socialization. In African American culture "unconditional acts of love" encompass acts of services in the general sense. Unconditional acts of love support respect, equality, and companionship. This is accomplished by creating a friendship that is open to new experiences and autonomy within the relationship (Pinderhughes, 2002). This means that "for better or for worse" you will continue to do acts of service despite how you may feel about your mate in the moment. Everything that is done within the relationship is love affirming.

Acts of Vulnerability and Intimacy   One of Chapman's five love languages is physical touch, which is bodily contact with one's partner (Chapman,

1995). This can be accomplished through hugging, kissing, caressing, or sex. Physical touch is a way to let spouses know that they are loved and thought about. Physical touch is important for African Americans, but the purpose of touch is particularly important. It is not touch itself that is so important, it is using touch to convey vulnerability and increasing intimacy. For African American couples touch may be especially important for expressing and accepting vulnerability. However, vulnerability and intimacy can also be expressed through self-disclosure and dependence on others.

Because of life's road blocks and the need to physically and emotionally protect oneself from the outside world, it may be difficult for African Americans to accept being vulnerable, accept other people's vulnerability, and depend on others. Vulnerability may be confused with weakness. Struggling with vulnerability can cause conflicts in communication and interactions (Johnson, 2004). Distress due to past (hurt from past relationships and events) and current stressors (hurt from current relationships and events) makes it more likely that partners will feel defenseless and try to conceal their vulnerabilities from their partner and themselves (Johnson, 2004). Proficiency at hiding one's vulnerabilities protects people, but it also hinders intimacy formation. Those who are well protected become distressed when faced with vulnerability and requests for intimacy. "Experiencing such feelings becomes problematic and/or foreign to them" (Johnson, 2004, p. 141).

Clinicians can use strategies from models such as Emotionally Focused Couples Therapy (Johnson, 2004) to help African American couples become more comfortable with vulnerability and intimacy touch combined with self-disclosure of dreams and aspirations, things that each partner is not proud of, and discussing things that scare each person, all aspects of vulnerability. A partner needs to learn how to accept these self-disclosures without judgment. A spouse should learn to be comfortable with being uncomfortable—building trust that the partner will be accepting. These acts may be verbal or physical, but the commonality is the act of taking a risk to show their soft side or risk showing the people how much they love and care about them.

Chapman (1995) believes that the five love languages are predicated on the fact that couples basically have all of the needed skills, but couples need to hone how they express these by identifying the best way to express feelings for a partner to receive them. However, not all couples come to the table being basically secure in the relationship and skillful in expressing their love. African Americans may be more afraid than other couples to express their vulnerability because they have had to be strong and endure injuries from the outside world and have not always been allowed to seek solace in their closest relationships through the different love languages. In fact, these languages have been distorted by people in the past (e.g., forcing women to have sex, forcing men and women to spend time and serve others against their will, giving gifts as a way to make up for atrocities). The fears and obstacles to being vulnerable and intimate may need to be discussed and deconstructed before African Americans are comfortable letting down their guard.

References

Amato, P. R., & Rogers, J. (1997). A longitudinal study of marital problems and subsequent divorce. *Journal of Marriage and the Family, 59*(3), 612–624.

Bean, R. A., Perry, B. J., & Bedell, T. M. (2002). Developing culturally competent marriage and family therapists: Treatment guidelines for non-African-American therapists working with African-American families. *Journal of Marital and Family Therapy, 28*(2), 153–164.

Billingsley, A. (1992). *Climbing Jacob's ladder: The enduring legacy of African American families.* New York: Simon and Schuster.

Boyd-Franklin, N. (2003). *Black families in therapy: Understanding the African American experience* (2nd ed.). New York: Guilford.

Boyd-Franklin, N., & Franklin, A. J. (1998). African American couples in therapy. In M. McGoldrick (Ed.), *Re-visioning family therapy: Race, culture, and gender in clinical practice* (pp. 268–281). New York: Guilford.

Boyd-Franklin, N., Kelly, S., & Durham, J. (2008). African American couples in therapy. In A. S. Gurman (Ed.), *Clinical handbook of couple therapy* (4th ed., pp. 681–697). New York: Guilford.

Bramlett, M. D., & Mosher, W. D. (2002). Cohabitation, marriage, divorce, and remarriage in the United States. National Center for Health Statistics. *Vital Health Stat, 23*(22).

Brewer, A. (1998, December). The relationships among gender role conflict, depression, hopelessness, and marital satisfaction in a sample of African-American men. *Dissertation Abstracts International, 59.*

Bulanda, J. R., & Brown, S. L. (2007). Race-ethnic differences in marital quality and divorce. *Social Science Research, 36*(3), 945–967.

Burton, L. M., Winn, D., Stevenson, H., & Clark, S. L. (2004). Working with African American clients: Considering the "homeplace" in marriage and family therapy practices. *Journal of Marital and Family Therapy, 30*(4), 397–410.

Chadiha, L. A., Veroff, J., & Leber, D. (1998). Newlywed's narrative theme: Meaning in the first year of marriage for African American and white couples. *Journal of Comparative Family Studies, 29*, 115–130.

Chapman, G. (1995). *The five love languages: How to express heartfelt commitment to your mate.* Chicago: Northfield.

Clark, R., Anderson, N. B., Clark, V. R., & Williams, D. R. (1999). Racism as a stressor for African Americans: A biopsychosocial model. *American Psychologist, 54*(10), 805–816.

Clarkwest, A. (2007). Spousal dissimilarity, race, and marital dissolution. *Journal of Marriage and Family, 69*(3), 639–653.

Collins, P. H. (2005). *Black sexual politics: African Americans, gender, and the new racism.* New York: Routledge.

DuBois, W. E. B. (1903). *The souls of black folk.* Cambridge: University Press.

Dunham, S. M. (2008). *Emotional skillfulness in marriage African American marriage: Intimacy as a mediator of the relationship between emotional skillfulness and marital satisfaction.* Ph.D. dissertation, University of Akron–Ohio.

Franklin, A. J., & Boyd-Franklin, N. (2000). Invisibility syndrome: A clinical model of the effects of racism on African-American males. *American Journal of Orthopsychiatry, 70*(1), 33–41.

Franklin, A. J. (2004). *From brotherhood to manhood: How Blackmen rescue their relationships and dreams from the invisibility syndrome.* Hoboken, NJ: Wiley.

Gottman, J. M. (1999). *The marriage clinic: A scientifically-based marital therapy.* New York: W.W. Norton.

Gottman, J. M., & Silver, N. (1999). *The seven principles for making marriage work: A practical guide from the country's foremost relationship expert.* New York: Three Rivers.

Hairston, R. E. (2000). *Predicting marital satisfaction among African American couples.* Psy.D. dissertation, Seattle Pacific University–Washington. Retrieved June 11, 2007, from ProQuest Digital Dissertations database. Publication No. AAT 9991030. http://proquest.umi.com

Hill, S. A. (2002). Teaching and doing gender in African American families. *Sex Roles 47* (11/12), 493–506.

Hooks, B. (1995). *Killing rage: Ending racism.* New York: Holt.

Hopson, S. D., & Powell-Hopson, D. (1994). *Friends, lovers, and soul mates: A guide to better relationships between black men and women.* New York: Simon and Schuster.

Johnson, S. M. (2004). *The practice of emotionally focused marital therapy: Creating the connection* (2nd ed.). New York: Brunner/Routledge.

Kelly, S., & Floyd, F. (2001). The effects of negative racial stereotypes and Afrocentricity on Black couple relationships. *Journal of Family Psychology, 15*(1), 110–123.

Kelly, S., & Floyd, F. (2006). Impact of racial perspectives and contextual variables on marital trust and adjustment for African American couples. *Journal of Family Psychology, 20*(1), 79–87.

LaTaillade, J. J. (2006). Considerations for treatment of African American couple relationships. *Journal of Cognitive Psychotherapy: An International Quarterly, 4,* 341–358.

Lawson, E. J., & Thompson, A. (1995). Black men make sense of marital distress and divorce: An exploratory study. *Family Relations, 44,* 211–218.

Levant, R., Majors, R., & Kelley, M. (1998). Masculinity ideology among young African American and European American women and men in different regions of the United States. *Cultural Diversity and Mental Health, 4*(3), 227–236.

Littlefield, M. (2003). Gender role identity and stress in African American women. *Journal of Human Behavior in the Social Environment, 8*(4), 93-104.

McElroy, J. (2002). *Trophy man: The surprising secrets of black women who marry well.* New York: Fireside.

Orbuch, T. L., Veroff, J., Hassan, H., & Horrocks, J. (2002). Who will divorce: A 14 year longitudinal study of black couples and white couples. *Journal of Social and Personal Relationships, 19*(2), 179–202.

Patterson, O. (1999). *Rituals of blood: Consequences of slavery in two American centuries*. NY: Basic Civitas.

Pinderhughes, E. B. (2002). African American marriage in the 20th century. *Family Process, 41*(2), 269–282.

Raley, R. K., Durden, T. E., & Wildsmith, E. (2004). Understanding Mexican-American marriage patterns using a life-course approach. *Social Science Quarterly, 85*(4), 872–890.

Sinclair Intimacy Institute (1999). *The better sex video series for black couples: volume I*. Chapel Hill, NC: Townsend Enterprises.

Taylor P. L., Tucker, M. B., & Mitchell-Kernan, C. (1999 Dec) Ethnic variations in perceptions of men's provider role. *Psychology of Women Quarterly, 23*, 741–761.

Trent, T., & South, S. J. (2003). Spousal alternatives and marital relations. *Journal of Family Issues, 24*(6), 787–810.

Tuker, M. T., Subramanian, K. S., & James, D. A. (2004). Diversity in African American families trends and projections. In M. Coleman & L. Ganong (Eds.), *Handbook of contemporary families: Considering the past, contemplating the future* (pp. 352–369). Thousand Oaks, CA: Sage.

U.S. Bureau of the Census. (2006, June 12). *Marital status of the population 15 years old and over, by sex and race: 1950 to present*. Table MS-1. Retrieved November 30, 2009, from http://www.census.gov/population/socdemo/hh-fam/ms1.pdf

West, C. (1999). On black sexuality. In C. West (Ed.). *The Cornel West reader*. New York:*Civitas* Books. (pp. 514–520).

White, J. L. & Cones, J. H. (1999). *Black man emerging: Facing the past and seizing a future in America*. New York: Routledge.

Wyatt, G. E. (1999). Beyond invisibility of African American males: The effects on women and families. *Counseling Psychologist, 27*(6), 802–809.

Yeh, C. J. (1999). Invisibility and self-construal in African American men: Implications for training and practice. *Counseling Psychologist, 27*(6), 810–819.

CHAPTER 18

Recovering Intimacy With Latino Couples

Cultural, Religious, and Gender Considerations

ROBERT L. SMITH and R. ESTEBAN MONTILLA

When visiting the Shamu show at Sea World, one cannot help but think about the powerful connection between this killer whale and humans. Certainly, it would be too pretentious to imply that this kind of human–animal relationship is a demonstration of intimacy. However, even in these interactions one can identify key elements of intimacy such as trust, passion, loyalty, closeness, respect, love, and social commitment.

Cultural Considerations

Intimacy, among Latino couples from a collectivistic culture, perhaps is the ultimate lifelong need and the goal of most human interactions. Members of collectivistic societies invest considerable time and effort in seeking the beauty of a harmonious life, possibly obtained through empowering relationships and intimate connections. Intimacy is a kind of close interaction and a process of expressing oneself, characterized by the corporal, social, psychological, and spiritual integration of two or more people. Intimacy is also considered the definitive measure of total well-being. However, when working with Latino couples it is important to keep in mind that intimacy is a construct with multicultural and multidimensional implications that requires the consideration of the contextual setting and present circumstances. In collectivistic societies, developing and maintaining intimate relationships perhaps constitutes the primary reason to exist (Marshall,

2008). In essence, the assumption is that human beings are designed to be connected with themselves, others, and nature, and that people strive to be in an intimate relationship at each dimension of their existence. However, depending on the context, individuals from a collectivistic culture conceptualize, experience, and express intimacy with varying intensity and style (Seki, Matsumoto, & Imahori, 2002). Intimacy can be expressed corporally, socially, psychologically, emotionally, and spiritually.

Corporal intimacy refers to the holistic need to be touched, embraced, and caressed by another human being. The brain requires social interaction and corporal intimacy to the degree that healthy development and functioning are only possible through mutual interactions with others' brains (Emde, 1988; Gusnard & Raichle, 2001; Siegel, 2007). Corporal intimacy can be expressed in many different ways such as physical closeness, nonsexual touch (handshaking, social kissing, embracing, handholding, and dancing), and sexual touch. Spatial proximity or physical closeness is of capital importance with Latino couples from a collectivistic society where people tend to sit very close, converse at a very short distance, speak at arm's length, eat close to one another, and in some cases sleep as a group in small places (Montilla & Medina, 2005). Although there are clear boundaries concerning people in authority and hierarchies, the need to be close seems universal among members of collectivistic societies. This spatial proximity is also a way to express loyalty and respect. Nonsexual touch such as handshaking and social kissing represents more than a cultural and socially desirable custom. In many cases, it is the appropriate way of closing a deal, making a contract, or expressing solidarity. In addition to markers of intimacy, embracing and hugging suggest friendship, affection, and commitment. Hugs often express positive and negative emotions such as happiness, joy, excitement, sadness, and sorrow. In addition, the act of hugging can be seen as a religious custom that conveys respect and reverence.

The importance of touch is widely recognized among people from collectivistic societies. For example, in a study conducted by Jourard (1966), couples were observed in casual conversations in coffee shops for a period of 1 hour. During this period of time couples in San Juan, Puerto Rico, touched on 180 occasions, in France couples touched 110 times, in Gainesville, Florida, couples touched only twice, and in London, England, couples did not touch at all. Morreale, Spitzberg, and Barge (2001) cited more recent studies that rendered similar results. Human touch and physical closeness are so prevalent in collectivistic cultures that isolation is viewed as punishment.

Sexual touch is another way to express love, closeness, and belonging. Sexual touch as a way to procreate, recreate, or relate evolves across the lifespan. Among collectivistic societies, the procreational dimension of sex is viewed as an existential responsibility toward the preservation of the human species and maintaining the family name. Procreation is so important for people in these societies that not having children suggests signs of abnormality. In some collectivistic cultures, such as the ancient Hebrews, not being able to have children was a sign of being under the punishment of the deity. The pressure to have children comes from many different fronts, including parents, grandparents, relatives, community, as well as cultural expectations. The emphasis on procreation is so heavily emphasized that it is still common today to see families in these societies with eight or more children. The second function of sex is connected to recreation or pleasure. People engage in sexual touch to have fun and experience the joy of being close together. The third function of sex is relational. Sexual touch can be the vehicle to strengthen a romantic relationship and promote interpersonal sharing. The procreational, recreational, and relational function of sexual touch may be experienced simultaneously; however, in certain situations only one dimension is present, possible, or more relevant. The level of intimacy seems to be stronger or higher when these dimensions are combined.

Social intimacy refers to the level of closeness with family members, friends, coworkers, or classmates. The type and quality of interpersonal relationships people develop and maintain depend on many factors, including biology, psychology, and social context. In collectivistic cultures, the social context is often the predominant factor that determines how close an interpersonal connection is going to be. In collectivistic societies, the level of social intelligence or ability to relate in meaningful ways hinges on the person's capacity to be aware of self and others' emotions, understand cultural context, respect people's space, read people's motivations, interpret people's behavior, realize the importance of mutual engagement, recognize social status, and practice effective intercultural communication.

Most human beings function better when they are in healthy connections with others (Prager, 1995). People with meaningful relationships tend to have a stronger immune system, sharper cognitive abilities, healthier physical condition, possess a more positive attitude and outlook on life, and tend to be more psychologically stable (Haber, 1994; Uchino, Cacioppo, & Kiecolt-Glaser, 1996). The collective group tends to provide members with emotional, spiritual, informational, and instrumental support, which is given via mutual encouragement, empathic listening, companionship while exploring existential dilemmas, sheltering from the storms of life, giving wise guidance, empowering advocacy, and directing help with particular needs (Forsyth, 2006).

Among member of collectivist societies, the measure of success is viewed by how well a person relates and connects with others. In that context, social intimacy implies that people make a conscious effort to form, nourish, and strengthen lasting, positive, and impactful interpersonal relationships across their lifespans (Rook, 1984). In fact, for joiners, as opposed to loners, survival depends on the inclusion and active participation as a member within a group (Caporael, 2001; Marsh & Morris, 1988).

Social intimacy also implies taking responsibility for one's own behavior and for balancing the satisfaction of personal needs with the needs of the group and those of the community (Moemeka, 1998). In addition, social intimacy involves coming together to work toward achieving goals set by the group and individual. The recognition of interdependence and the value of cooperation lead people to embrace the commitment to initiate communal activities that give meaning to the group, strengthen their relationships, and satisfy their needs. This kind of social intimacy demands communication patterns that consider the motivations, intentions, thoughts, feelings and the nature of each person (*we, us*) participating in the collective project.

Social intimacy is connected to self-worth, as people with a strong sense of belonging and membership within a particular group tend to report a higher level of self-esteem (Crocker, Luhtamen, Blaine, & Broadmax, 1994; Crocker & Major, 1989). Social motives such as the need for affiliation, intimacy, and power might explain the reason most people from collectivistic societies excel when they clearly identify with a particular group (Geen, 1995). The need for affiliation, a biological, psychological, social, and spiritual longing, is what moves most people to actively seek membership within a group or community. The need for affection, inclusion in a group, and connection with others also stresses the importance of forming caring, warm, and sustaining relationships across the lifespan in order to enjoy life fully and experience total well-being. People also have a need for power or sense of being an important member of the group. To realize this need, people must feel as if they have a role in the collective as either organizers or keepers of the group's processes. The road to this kind of social intimacy is not without blocks as there are many barriers, including fear of rejection by others, shame, distrust, suspicion, social anxiety, shyness, and disloyalty (Asendorpf & Meier, 1993; Vertue, 2003). Albrecht (2005) proposed five steps toward increasing the level of social intimacy. The first step involves being aware of the social context in which the dialogue and engagement is taking place. The second step involves conveying a presence that is warm, respectful, humble, as well as confident. The next step highlights the importance of being truthful and honest in the interpersonal relationship. The fourth step involves using effective communication skills when expressing thoughts and emotions by each member of the relationship. The last step refers to empathy in the sense of appreciating, respecting, and having solidarity with other's realities and needs.

Psychological intimacy refers to the depth of sharing ideas, thoughts, motivations, emotions, and feelings with a spirit of respect and mutual acceptance. The vehicle for this shared experience is the accurate and honest dialogue that takes place within the relationship. This dialogue through verbal and nonverbal communication offers the opportunity to explore freely the heart, mind, and soul of the people involved in the relationship. Psychological intimacy is connected to physical, mental, and social well-being.

Cognitive or intellectual intimacy refers to the level of closeness by which intimate thoughts, ideas, and beliefs are shared openly and without reserve. A trustful and caring atmosphere paves the way for this kind of intimacy. Cognitive intimacy also implies the suspension of judgment, mutual acceptance, and consistent affirmation by both members of the relationship. When individuals perceive they are being heard without interruption or condemnation, they tend to self-disclose more and present themselves in a more authentic way. Therefore, cognitive intimacy requires transparency and trustfulness from the people involved in the social interaction. Respect is a fundamental principle that needs to be observed at this level of intimacy, since intellectual communication is founded on the fundamental need to be understood and supported. Although people's worldview and ideas may be challenged, confronting these paradigms should be viewed as a process with gradual steps to allow the other person to grow slowly as new ideas are embraced. A sudden challenge might become confusing and provoke unfavorable reactions. Mutual respect and acceptance do not imply simply agreeing or sanctioning the ideas shared, but understanding the intellectual, emotional, and spiritual meaning behind the thoughts that were communicated. The level of cognitive intimacy and connection is greater when the emotional components are also taken into consideration.

Emotional or affectional intimacy refers to the level of closeness that invites the sharing of deep emotions and feelings. This kind of intimacy requires an environment where solidarity and loyalty anchor the relationship. Once created, this environment gives people permission to share their inner beings and most intimate dreams. Emotional intimacy is connected to good mental health, life-giving relationships, and healthy human development (Gross, 2000; Prager, 1995). Emotions are biological and universal givens that also serve as survival mechanisms central to experiencing life in meaningful and enriching ways. In addition, emotions and feelings are the most important means of communication and vital tools for establishing relationships. Although the language of feelings can be intimidating and threatening, it allows people to connect at a deeper level and promotes mutual understanding. People who are able to communicate and express their feelings and emotions are often more willing to step outside themselves and consider the other's position (Montilla & Medina, 2005).

Spiritual intimacy refers to the coming together of people who are joined by a common quest: the search for ultimate concern, the need for transcendence, and the making or finding of existential meaning. As people come together to explore and discuss these concerns, they expect to experience mutual respect, encouragement and support, hopeful observations, nonjudgmental listening, empowering reflections, and warm hospitality. Spiritual intimacy is connected to mental, emotional, and social well-being. People who consider their search for wholeness a priority in their lives tend to live longer and experience healthier and happier lives.

Religious Considerations

There are two Greek words to describe the religious experience: *religare* and *relegare*. *Religare* implies the process of reconnecting people with themselves, nature, universe, and deity. This meaning is perhaps the most common as it is easy to measure, referring to concrete and external ways people use to connect with their religion. Generally, this term entails the practice of rituals such as prayer, meditation, communal or individual worship, readings of sacred books, religious pilgrimage, participation of sacraments, communal good deeds, practical hospitality, and other tangible religious customs. *Relegare* means to read again or to review what is happening within us. This particular definition speaks of the internal spiritual or religious experience that is difficult to describe and measure. This kind of religious phenomenon is very personal as it deals with the struggles of the inner soul. In this context, it refers to the sharing with others our own pilgrimage toward the inner soul. People from collectivist societies tend to understand religion in these two inseparable meanings. It is difficult to understand a dualistic view of the religious experience where religion and spirituality are often seen as two different things. In collective societies, religion and spirituality are more commonly understood as two aspects of the same phenomenon. Spiritual people are recognized by the horizontal relationships they develop and maintain with others and nature. In this sense, a person with deep religious experiences is an individual who relates well with others. In collectivistic societies, people who experience a profound intimacy with their neighbors could be seen as individuals with a deep sense of spirituality and religious. This implies that when spiritual intimacy and religious beliefs coincide a mutual concern for others and the universe is also present.

The formalities of religion are expansive, often involving sharing thoughts, feelings, and beliefs of a deep spiritual nature. The coming together involves exploring and discussing moral values, the meaning of existence, life after death, the nature of one's own relationship with that which we transcend, spiritual longings, the mystery of life, ways to serve and show compassion, advocacy for a better world where justice and peace reign, and the pilgrimage toward wholeness. This intimacy, influenced by religion, may also imply spending time together to appreciate the beauty of life, nature, and people. As a religious experience, this aesthetic intimacy might involve listening to music together, visiting museums, or simply walking while enjoying nature and the beauty of the universe.

Gender Considerations

Gender considerations are important when working with individuals, couples, and families. However, it is also important to consider culture, economics, history, family status, occupation, family of origin, opportunity, tradition, acculturation, personality, intelligence, knowledge, and a multitude of other factors when examining gender. It is true that we are in large part made up of where we have been and where we are going. It is the past, present, and future (sense of hope) that significantly influence the emotions, thoughts, and behaviors of both men and women. These factors make every man and woman unique as an individual and as a person within one's culture.

However, there is not a denial of a prevalence of thought regarding Latino men and women as related to intimacy and marriage. Male and female roles have often been prescribed within traditional Latino families. The concept of hierarchy has influenced the roles of males and females, resulting in the identification of a level of power and authority with older men gaining the most respect within the family. McGoldrick, Giorgano, and Pearce (1996) viewed this hierarchy as part of a Latino culture that has included male dominance and female submission explained by *machismo* and *marianismo*. Falicov (1998) provided a balance when discussing the concept of *machismo* by including the male's dedication to his children and devotion to the female, especially to one's mother. It is this devotion to children and the parental love that often helps keep a Latino couple together, even with the existence of infidelity (Falicov, 1998). The concept of *marianismo* has been more difficult to understand by counselors as it infers a submissive, self-sacrificing, long-suffering female with a strong religious background. Duffey (2000) pointed out that traditionally, Hispanic women have assumed their place and position by providing nurturance and care for their husbands and children. It is therefore important to understand and respect the traditional intergenerational roles and hierarchies often found within the Latino culture. Yet, to say all Latino couples are characterized this way would be a huge stereotypical mistake. The level of acculturation and the changing dynamics of gender will greatly affect the Latino couple system. Gender roles are not static in both thought and action within a collectivistic society.

Recovering Intimacy

Infidelity transcends culture. Affairs are not unique to a particular group of individuals or culture. Infidelity crosses religion, gender, social status, income, race, age, and cultural boundaries. Strategies and interventions that might help Latino couples recover their intimacy may differ only slightly from those used when working with Anglo couples. However, it is important for counselors to be culturally aware and culturally sensitive when working with cases of infidelity.

In order for interventions to be successful when counseling Latino couples to recover intimacy after an affair, certain therapeutic conditions need to be present. If these conditions are not met during the counseling relationship, a sense of discomfort will prevail. In such cases the couple will discontinue counseling, experience minimal change, or experience harm to the relationship, despite which strategy or intervention was employed. These conditions transcend language differences, gender, culture, and ethnicity. Research findings support that a set of core conditions within the counseling relationship are essential if change is to take place (Carkhuff, 1969, 1971; Lambert & Cattani-Thompson, 1996; Rogers, 1957). The presence of these core conditions is necessary not only when counseling individuals but also when working with couples and families.

Counselors working with Latino couples who are in the process of repairing intimacy need to employ "the necessary and sufficient conditions of therapeutic personality change" identified by Rogers (1957). These conditions include empathy (understanding), congruency (genuineness), and unconditional positive regard (warmth). Empathy refers to the counselor's ability to experience a client's inner world. Congruency involves the integrity of the counselor to be authentic and honest. Unconditional positive regard is characterized by a nonjudgmental attitude that includes warmth and acceptance. Additional core conditions were added (Carkhuff, 1969, 1971) that included respect and immediacy. Today these conditions are considered essential when working with Latino families (Smith & Montilla, 2006). Respect is portrayed by the counselor's attitude that conveys a high regard of the worth of others, while immediacy involves sensitivity to the immediate experiences of the client. Successful counseling with Latino couples is characterized when the counselor exemplifies these conditions and when the couple exhibits these same conditions back to the counselor (Smith & Montilla, 2006).

With the above conditions present, there is an increased possibility that Latino couples will recover a sense of intimacy after an affair. However, when working with infidelity in the couple relationship the counselor also needs to be aware of his or her own values and assumptions, as well as those presented within the couple system and through their culture.

Transparency as a dimension of couple counseling has been a value and the dominant theme advocated by family therapists in the United States who work with infidelity cases. Having no secrets involving the infidelity is emphasized. The general belief is that at some moment within the course of therapy, the affair will be openly discussed. However, if the therapist becomes aware of the infidelity and the individual fails to come forward with this information during therapy, the therapist should discontinue treatment. This may result in a referral or involve individual counseling with members of the couple system. If the therapist uses this procedure, this information must be presented to the couple, verbally and in writing, before commencing therapy. This therapeutic stance identifies the couple system as the client and disallows secrets between the couple, or between individuals in the relationship and the therapist (Smith, 1991).

The underlying assumption of the above position is that disclosure of the affair will allow the couple to work through their problems and that intimacy will be restored. However, questions have surfaced regarding this position when working with couples from diverse cultures. Scheinkman (2005), born and raised in Latin America, identified several flaws with this practice, including a concern of leaving the couple with nowhere to turn, disrespecting self-determination, and essentially abandoning the couple when they are in most need of assistance. Scheinkman compared this policy to that of telling a bulimic that you cannot continue seeing him or her unless he or she stops binging before he or she is able to do so. Furthermore, cultural differences need to be considered when working with couples from outside the United States or couples who have recently moved to the states, but have strong cultural ties, beliefs, values, and experiences that are carried over from several generations. Perhaps an open description and discussion of the affair will be more damaging than helpful. Perhaps the shame and the possibility of creating a more unbearable situation need to be carefully considered. These are legitimate issues when working with Latino couples.

The above considerations indicate the wisdom of an awareness of the macro system surrounding both the counselor and the couple. Counseling from a macro systems perspective allows one to understand couples living in a collectivistic society. The identified issue, infidelity, is viewed through the lens of each individual in the couple system, helping the counselor understand the surrounding systems that affect the couple, including culture. Immediate everyday concerns such as poverty, opportunity (or lack of), repression, intergenerational influences (support and stress), family history, and health are considered.

Imber-Black (1998) stated that it is important for the therapist to be able to work with the ambiguities of secrets and affairs. Perhaps neither the therapist nor individuals in the couple system needs to be continuously reminded whether to tell or not tell. This flexibility by the therapist seems to be important when working with Latino couples recovering from an affair. In order to maintain this flexibility, therapists need to be aware of not only their own values, but also the values of the couple's culture. Researchers have emphasized the relevance of the personal values of the therapist and how they subsequently influence their methods of treatment (Aponte, 1985; Hecker, Trepper, Wetchler, & Fontaine, 1995; Stabb, Cox, & Harbe, 1997), particularly as related to issues of infidelity.

Latino couples recovering from loss of intimacy need assurance of confidentiality, allowing an open sharing of feelings such as guilt and shame. Under conditions of trust it is the couple who decides what is to be shared. The couple, and often the family, will also determine the time-line for sharing. The counselor also needs to be aware of when the timing seems right. Patience by all involved is important. The time and moment of sharing is gauged so the family can maintain a sense of dignity and respect, an important consideration within a collectivistic culture. After the affair is made public, the therapist needs to be aware of possible positive and negative consequences. The traditional belief has been that once the affair is in the open, it is time to repair, openly express feelings, admit guilt, stop the affair, and renew commitment, so the couple can embark on forgiveness and reconstruct the relationship. This theory, not fully researched, can have negative as well as positive consequences when working with diverse cultural systems. Potential consequences are the reasons why one should treat the disclosure of an affair with care when counseling Latino couples.

Waring (1988) identified four areas one can focus on in order to create an intimate relationship once the affair is in the open. Intimacy is first demonstrated through the couple's behavior. New behavior patterns such as stopping the abuse of alcohol or staying at home rather than spending time away from the family can restore stability within the couple system. These behavioral changes are usually welcomed by the female. The emotional aspect of intimacy involves feelings that partners have for each other. If those feelings have been shaken, it is the counselor's job to first allow the expression of feelings and eventually repair that part of the relationship. Once the couple's feelings are not imploding, solution-focused techniques can be used to facilitate intimacy. The cognitive aspect of creating a more intimate relationship involves a mental understanding of the affair, including what led up to the affair. During this time, self-disclosure is difficult for both individuals within the couple system. If the male is responsible for the affair, his partner will often find it difficult to understand why he would do this to her and their family. The male will often have difficulty articulating reasons that make sense to his partner. The attitudinal aspect of intimacy can be the most complicated when working with couples when an affair is presented. Counselors should expect a wide array of emotions and attitudes to surface. The focus should be on reaching a consensual attitude of commitment that will assist in the recovery of intimacy. By focusing on solutions, using solution-focused practices, common goals for the relationship are often established, including renewing the couple's commitment to the relationship.

As inferred above, when working to restore intimacy with Latino couples after an affair, a solution-focused approach is recommended. By concentrating on solutions, rather than the affair itself, the therapist may find more cooperation and participation, particularly by the male in the couple system. A discussion about the affair is not ignored or swept under the rug, rather it is put on hold until both partners trust and believe in the counseling process. In addition, the underlying concepts of solution-focused counseling seem to be acceptable with Latino families (Smith, Bakir, & Montilla, 2006). This approach emphasizes what has been working within the family system, including areas such as positive child rearing and supportive practices by extended family members. The following fundamentals associated with solution-focused therapy seem compatible with a collectivistic society:

- An emphasis and belief in the couple and family system to solve their problems,
- A belief in self-determination,
- A recognition that positive change is not only possible, but is inevitable,
- An emphasis on solutions, rather than rehashing problems and focusing on blame,
- A spirit of hope and the belief in positive change.

A solution-focused approach to repair a couple's intimacy when infidelity is present has great promise. However, it is essential to include within this approach core conditions of counseling identified as person-centered counseling. Concepts evolving from person-centered and solution-focused counseling must also be embedded within a multicultural template. This person-centered, solution-focused multicultural approach is one model of treatment to consider when attempting to restore intimacy after an affair. Additional concepts, thoughts, and considerations to keep in mind when restoring intimacy with Latino couples include:

- Consideration of the stage of acculturation of each individual in the couple system, family history, religion or spirituality, cognitions or expectations, and readiness to change and repair the relationship;
- Work systemically to build rapport and trust not only with the couple but also with their extended family and community;

- Identify the couple's level of commitment and readiness for intimacy;
- Observe and teach communication skills (both verbal and nonverbal);
- Identify outcome possibilities for the relationship, allowing the couple to define their outcome(s);
- Embrace the "we" collectivistic concept with Latino couples;
- Embrace the extended family and a family orientation concept by exploring intergenerational family influences including gender roles, power, and authority;
- Embrace the couple relationship and its importance as related to children and child rearing;
- Embrace the spiritual values of the family, including intergenerational history and its presence and importance within the couple system;
- Utilize humor and a sense of playfulness where appropriate.

In summary, this chapter examined the different expressions of intimacy within a collectivistic society. Intergenerational influences, religion and spirituality, gender, acculturation, and the importance of the extended family are emphasized when counseling Latino couples. Respect for the individual and one's culture is considered paramount. Respect is demonstrated through the use of core counseling conditions evolving from person-centered counseling. The principles of solution-focused counseling are considered appropriate and effective when working with Latino couples. Multicultural sensitivity is the necessary template when infusing person-centered and solution-focused counseling to assist Latino couples in their quest to recover intimacy. This person-centered, solution-focused multicultural model is recommended as an approach to restore intimacy within couple systems, particularly within a collectivistic culture. In closing, intimacy has been defined as that quality of a relationship characterized by emotional closeness, trust, self-disclosure, and reciprocity (Timmerman, 1991). As we observe Shamu at Sea World, it becomes evident that we *are* provided there with an example of several key elements of intimacy, including trust, passion, loyalty, closeness, respect, love, and social commitment.

References

Albrecht, K. (2005). *Social intelligence: The new science of success*. San Francisco: Pfeiffer.

Aponte, H. J. (1985). The negotiation of values in therapy. *Family Process, 24,* 323–338.

Asendorpf, J. B., & Meier, G. H. (1993). Personality effects on children's speech in everyday life: Sociability-mediated exposure and shyness-mediated reactivity in social situations. *Journal of Personality and Social Psychology, 64,* 1072–1083.

Caporael, L. R. (2001). Parts and wholes: The evolutionary importance of groups. In C. Sedikides & M. B. Brewer (Eds.), *Individual self, relational self, collective self* (pp. 241–258). New York: Psychology Press.

Carkhuff, R. (1969). *Helping and human relations* (vols. 1 & 2). New York: Holt, Rinehart and Winston.

Carkhuff, R. (1971). *The development of human resources.* New York: Holt, Rinehart and Winston.

Crocker, J., Luhtamen, R., Blaine, B., & Broadmax, S. (1994). Collective self-esteem and psychological wellbeing among white, black, and Asian college students. *Personality and Social Psychology Bulletin, 201,* 503–513.

Crocker, J., & Major, B. (1989). Social stigma and self-esteem: The self-protective properties of stigma. *Psychological Review, 96,* 608–630.

Duffey, T. (2000). The Hispanic couple in therapy. In M. F. Flores & G. Carey (Eds.), *Family therapy with Hispanics* (pp.). Boston: Allyn and Bacon.

Emde, R. N. (1988). Development terminable and interminable: Innate and motivational factors from infancy. *International Journal of Psychoanalysis, 69,* 23–42.

Falicov, C. J. (1998). *Latino families in therapy: A guide to multicultural practice.* New York: Guilford.

Forsyth, D. R. (2006). *Group dynamics.* Belmont, CA: Thomson Higher Education.

Geen, R. G. (1995). *Human motivation: A social psychological approach.* Pacific Grove, CA: Brooks/Cole.

Gross, J. J. (2000). *Cognition and emotion.* Washington, DC: Psychology Press.

Gusnard D. A., & Raichle M. E. (2001). Searching for a baseline: Functional imaging and the resting human brain. *Nature Reviews Neuroscience, 2*(10), 685–694.

Haber, D. (1994). *Health Promotion and Aging.* New York: Springer.

Hecker, L. L., Trepper, T. S., Wetchler, J. L., & Fontaine, K. L. (1995). The influence of therapist values, religiosity and gender in the initial assessment of sexual addiction by family therapists. *American Journal of Family Therapy, 23,* 261–272.

Imber-Black, E. (Ed.). (1998). *The secret lives of families: Truth telling, privacy, and reconciliation in a tell-all society.* New York: Bantam.

Jourard, S. M. (1966). An exploratory study of body-accessibility. *British Journal of Social and Clinical Psychology, 5*(3), 221–231.

Lambert, M., & Cattani-Thompson, K. (1996). Current findings regarding the effectiveness of counseling: Implications for practice. *Journal of Counseling and Development, 74,* 601–608.

Marsh, P., & Morris, D. (1988). *Tribes.* Layton, UT: Gibbs Smith.

Marshall, T. C. (2008). Cultural differences in intimacy: The influence of gender-role ideology and individualism-collectivism. *Journal of Social and Personal Relationships, 25*(1), 143–168.

McGoldrick, M., Giorgano, J., & Pearce, J. K. (Eds.). (1996). *Ethnicity and family therapy* (2nd ed.). New York: Guilford.

Moemeka, A. A. (1998). Communalism as a fundamental dimension of culture. *Journal of Communication, 48,* 118–141.

Montilla, R. E., & Medina, F. (2005). *Pastoral care and counseling with Latinos and Latinas.* Minneapolis: Fortress.

Morreale, S. P., Spitzberg, B. H., & Barge, J. K. (2001). *Human communication: Motivation, knowledge, and skills.* Belmont, CA: Wadsworth/Thomson Learning.

Prager, K. J. (1995). *The psychology of intimacy.* New York: Guilford.

Rogers, C. R. (1957). The necessary and sufficient conditions of therapeutic personality change. *Journal of Consulting Psychology, 21,* 93–103.

Rook, K. S. (1984). Promoting social bonding: Strategies for helping the lonely and social isolated. *American Psychologist, 39,* 1389–1407.

Scheinkman, M. (2005). Beyond the trauma of betrayal: Reconsidering affairs in couple therapy. *Family Process, 44,* 227–245.

Seki, K., Matsumoto, D., & Imahori, T. T. (2002). The conceptualization and expression of intimacy in Japan and the United States. *Journal of Cross-Cultural Psychology, 33,* 303.

Siegel, D. (2007). *The mindful brain: Reflection and attunement in the cultivation of well-being.* New York: Norton.

Smith, R. (1991). Ethical issues in marital and family therapy: Who is the client? *Family Psychologist, 7,* 16–17.

Smith, R., Bakir, N., & Montilla, E. (2006). Counseling and family therapy with Latino couples. In R. Smith & E. Montilla (Eds.), *Counseling and family therapy with Latino populations* (pp. 3–25). New York: Routledge.

Smith, R., & Montilla, E. (Eds.). (2006). *Counseling and family therapy with Latino populations.* New York: Routledge.

Stabb, S. D., Cox, D. L., & Harbe, J. L. (1997). Gender-related therapist attributions in couples therapy: A preliminary multiple case study investigation. *Journal of Marital and Family Therapy, 23,* 335–346.

Timmerman, G. M. (1991). A concept analysis of intimacy. *Issues in Mental Health Nursing, 12,* 19–30.

Uchino, B. N., Cacioppo, J. T., & Kiecok-Glaser, J. K. (1996). The relationship between social support and physiological processes: A review with emphasis on underlying mechanism and implications for health. *Psychological Bulletin, 119,* 488–531.

Vertue, F. M. (2003). From adaptive emotion to dysfunction: An attachment perspective on social anxiety disorder. *Personality and Social Psychology Review, 7,* 170–191.

Waring, E. M. (1988). *Enhancing marital intimacy through facilitating cognitive self-disclosure.* New York: Brunner/Mazel.

CHAPTER 19

Marital Satisfaction, Intimacy, *Enqing,* and Relationship Stressors Among Asians

KOK-MUN NG, PAUL R. PELUSO, and SHANNON D. SMITH

Formation and maintenance of the couple relationship is a universal human activity that occurs regardless of national, regional, or cultural factors. But how a couple acts and interacts with each other in the relationship do seem to be influenced by a variety of cultural factors. Indeed, many of the relationship maintaining behaviors are learned in the context of the family, which transmits cultural values and norms from generation to generation (Greenfield, Keller, Fuligni, & Maynard, 2003). Although the majority of human coupling experiences take place in non-Western cultures, the current bulk of research has focused on Western ideals and constructs of marriage (Chen & Li, 2007). Research on the Asian marital relationship and intimacy is needed to provide empirical data to guide clinicians' attempts to provide culturally informed and responsive services to Asian couples. The present chapter will address some of the most important marital factors, including marital satisfaction, intimacy, culture, and relationship stressors from an Asian perspective.

Marital Satisfaction

Perhaps one of the most salient variables related to intimacy in couples is marital satisfaction. Marital satisfaction is commonly defined as the extent to which individuals feel that their spouse or marital relationship fulfills their expectations (Lucas et al., 2008). Its primacy as an indicator of marital health has been studied over the past three decades. For example, several researchers have shown that a decline in marital satisfaction is strongly predictive of divorce, infidelity, and poor physical health (Keicolt-Glaser, McGuire, Robles, & Glaser 2002; Peluso, 2007; Sperry, Carlson, & Peluso, 2006). As a result, many couples counselors and researchers have sought to find methods for understanding and increasing couples' level of satisfaction both before and after a couple experiences difficulties (Sperry et al., 2006).

Although marital satisfaction appears to be a ubiquitous element of human relationships, there are a number of cultural and contextual factors associated with it. Recently, Lucas et al. (2008) investigated whether marital satisfaction was a universal construct or was culturally invariant. They surveyed 2,000 intact couples from four diverse cultures (United States, Britain, Turkey, and China), which allowed the researchers to see both the between-culture and within-culture elements of marital satisfaction. They found that marital satisfaction was a multidimensional construct that had both universal aspects (congruence between wives' and husbands' level of satisfaction across cultures) and specific cultural factors (differences between couples of each of the four cultures studied) associated with it. They found that the universal aspects were statistically stronger than the cultural factors, although the cultural differences were robust.

One explanation for the findings of Lucas et al. (2008) may be that while marital satisfaction is universal for pair bonding and relationship maintenance, the pathway toward achieving satisfaction has cultural elements that are unique, subtle, and often complex. In fact, several authors (Li & Chen, 2002; Lucas et al., 2008) have called for further study of couples relationships in non-Western cultures. The present study looks at some of these complex cultural factors related to Asian couples residing in the United States. We will begin by discussing the unique culture of Asian couples and families.

Asian Cultures

Culture is often seen as a complex construct that underlies many elements of human behavior. Greenfield and her colleagues (2003) defined culture and the process of its influence succinctly:

> We view culture as a socially interactive process of construction comprising two main components: shared activity (cultural practices) and shared meaning (cultural interpretation). Both components of cultural processes are cumulative in nature since they occur between, as well as within, generations. Meanings and activities not only accu-

mulate but also transform over both developmental time—across a single life cycle, and historical time—between generations. (p. 462)

As a result, parenting is the most important factor in the transmission of culture and cultural values to children (Keller et al., 2004). Strategies of parenting across cultures are oriented toward one of two goals: independence and interdependence. These goals are related to the cultural ideals of individualism and collectivism, respectively. In individualistic cultures (predominantly Western Europe and North America), children are socialized to be oriented toward their own self and self-interest. As a result, individual performance and competence are priorities for individualistic societies, which breeds competition among people. In collectivistic cultures (i.e., many Asian cultures), children are socialized to be other interested and to consider the common good when acting (Greenfield et al., 2003; Keller et al., 2004).

In many Asian cultures, the collectivistic approach is reflected by an orientation toward intergenerational harmony across the lifespan and obedience to the family of origin. According to Greenfield et al. (2003):

[M]any Asian cultural traditions, such as Confucianism, have valued family solidarity, respect, and commitment. … Recent studies of immigrant families within the United States have suggested that many Asian and Latin American families continue to emphasize the familial duty and obligation of their adolescents in a new society. Several ethnographies have indicated how such family obligation may even be heightened among immigrants, given parents' limited knowledge of American society and because many adolescents feel indebted to their parents for immigrating to a new society to provide their children with a better life. (p. 470)

In fact, as children get older, the caretaking roles are often reversed and the parents expect the children to take care of them in their old age. This can become a source of tension for a couple, particularly if there are issues between a spouse and his (or more likely her) in-laws. Yet, what accounts for the stability of these marriages and levels of satisfaction under such pressures? For answers to this, we turn to the Chinese cultural factor known as *enqing*.

Enqing

As in many Eastern cultures, in ancient Chinese society, arranged marriages were the norm, with parents choosing their child's mate. The preference of the individual was not an important factor, nor were feelings of romance or desire for the intended mate (Li & Chen, 2002). As a result, the definition of a healthy, successful marriage was focused more on the ability to produce offspring than it was to ensure the emotional satisfaction and well-being of the spouses. Despite dramatic shifts toward more Western ideas of individualism, which have also influenced the choice of one's mate, there are the emotional artifacts of these bygone customs inherent in many modern Eastern couples (Li & Chen, 2002). Indeed ideas such as intimacy and passion are often not as prevalent (Chen & Li, 2007). Invariably this leads to the question: What can account for the relative stability of these relationships when there is no a priori feelings of attraction or romantic love?

Although Western definitions of intimacy emphasize the sharing of deep feelings and personal experience, it is not so in many Asian cultures. In 1997 Li (as cited in Li & Chen, 2002) classified four basic elements commonly found in Asian (in particular, Chinese) couples' concept of affection: (a) feelings of gratitude, (b) admiration, (c) togetherness, and (d) compatibility. Interestingly, when he compared these with Western couples, Li found that while compatibility and togetherness are central to Western couples, gratitude and admiration are less so:

> Although some Chinese couples may not share feelings and thoughts with each other or consider each other confidants, they may still have a stable marital relationship. For Chinese couples a particular form of affection exists in a marriage that cannot be explained by the concept of intimacy. Chinese couples may be tied closely by *enqing*—the expression of feelings of gratitude and admiration. (Chen & Li, 2007, pp. 393–394)

Tang (1991, as cited in Li & Chen, 2002) defined the construct of *enqing* as inclusive of feelings of admiration and gratitude that "stem from conjugal love and role fulfillment, respectively" (Chen & Li, 2007, p. 395). Kim (2001, as cited in Chen & Li, 2007) described Confucianism's concept of *fen*, or place for people in society, as a way to understand the internal attitudes of many Eastern couples. *Fen* is a virtue that flows from each person's fulfillment of his or her duties and obligation to society. Complying with the principle of *fen* and fulfilling the required obligations and duties (such as in one's couple relationship) preserve harmony and social order (which are highly esteemed values in virtually all Asian or collectivistic cultures). Accordingly, *enqing* "originates from traditional values such as duty in marriage" (Chen & Li, 2007, p. 395). In other words, *enqing* goes beyond the cognitive and emotional dimensions of love and liking and taps into the communal and cultural dimensions of couplehood.

In addition to the enduring, traditional cultural aspects of *enqing* that explain the unique elements of many Eastern couples, there is also evidence that *enqing* may be a protective factor for marital stress. Li (1997, as cited in Li & Chen, 2002) interviewed Chinese couples about their marital affection and found that, in times of family stress (financial, illness, etc.), spouses expressed gratitude and appreciation (*enqing*) for what they perceived the other person did for the family during that time. Although other researchers (Kiecolt-Glaser et al., 2002) have described the negative effects of stress on marital relationships, Eastern couples who experience high levels of *enqing* have been shown to be *positively* impacted by the stress (Chen & Li, 2007; Li, 1997). This may be due in part to the fact that in many Eastern cultures, people are "generally willing to subordinate their personal goals, interests, and welfare for the sake of their families' existence, harmony, solidarity, glory, prosperity, and prolongation" (Chen & Li, 2007, p. 396). Couples who experience *enqing* are more likely to be more resilient and thus healthier, although they may not show the "classic" Western traits of intimacy and affection (Chen & Li, 2007).

Critical Relationship Stressors

Several associations regarding critical stressors have been noted in relationship to both marital affection and marital satisfaction. Critical stressors such as debilitating and chronic illnesses, infertility, infidelity, imprisonment, and long-term job-related travel have been shown to negatively impact marital relationships (e.g., Fekete, Stephens, Mickelson, & Druley, 2007; Gerstel & Gross, 1982; Peluso, 2007).

Marital dissatisfaction has also been linked to a variety of health issues (e.g., Hawkins & Booth, 2005). When a couple is faced with a chronic stressor or life-threatening illness, the extent to which marital partners feel that their emotional needs are being met is associated with each partner's psychological well-being and marital satisfaction (Fekete et al., 2007). It is unfortunate that individuals who are coping with a variety of chronic life stressors tend to lose support from others over time (Norris & Kaniasty, 1996), and deterioration in support tends to increase the struggle related to coping with chronic stressors.

Infidelity is a phenomenon in marriages that has a tendency to place significant stress on the relationship. Couples therapists tend to view extramarital affairs as one of the most damaging relationship events and one of the most difficult problems to treat (Wisman, Dixon, & Johnson, 1997). When infidelity occurs, it is typically viewed as a marital betrayal and is the most commonly cited reason for marital dissolution (Amato & Previti, 2003). Research on this topic involving Asians remains limited.

Interestingly, *enqing* has been shown to be a mediating factor when it comes to dealing with many stressors in a relationship among Asian couples. Chen and Li (2007) found that for family stressors, such as coping with aging parents, prolonged separation, and economic hardship, that high level of *enqing* may act as a buffer and enhance marital satisfaction. Seen through the lens of *enqing*, "family stresses provide an opportunity for one to appreciate what one's spouse does for the marriage and family" (Chen & Li, 2007, p. 409). Indeed, this is more indicative of a collectivistic cultural norm than an individualistic one. However, to date, only one large-scale research study has investigated this phenomenon (Chen & Li, 2007).

Globalization has provided many people the opportunity to work outside of the United States. As such, many Asian Americans, men and women, travel extensively between the United States and other countries on business. This social trend extends beyond the phenomenon of commuter marriages. Job-related extensive traveling has brought about many changes and challenges to these Asian families; for example, change of family pattern from having both parents at home to where one or both of the parents are away for an extended time, and stress to the marital relationship when a spouse or both partners travel frequently for an extended time (Wong, 2007). To date, research to investigate the effects of job-related travel on couple intimacy among Asians remains limited.

Acculturation and Multiethnic or Multiculture Relationships

Acculturation has been defined as a process of cultural learning and behavioral adaptation that takes place as exposure to a nonnative culture occurs (Berry, 1980, as cited in Barry, 2001). As such, this process can place varying degrees of stress on individuals and families (Miranda, Bilot, Peluso, Berman, & Van Meek, 2006). According to Berry (1997), there are four "options" for acculturation: *separation, marginalization, integration,* and *assimilation.* Each of these has different influences on individual and familial dynamics. Separation refers to the option of accepting the culture of origin while rejecting the new culture. Marginalization refers to the inability or unwillingness to identify either with the culture of origin or the host culture and is tied to the poorest coping indicators. Integration refers to biculturality, whereby the individual mixes the culture of origin with the host culture. This is linked to the most positive coping outcomes. Finally, assimilation refers to fully accepting the practices of the host culture while abandoning those of the culture of origin (Miranda et al., 2006).

Confusion due to acculturation (or lack thereof) can lead to isolation, despair, decreased academic performance, and severe forms of psychological distress. For immigrants, acculturation is an important factor that relates to personal orientation, the development of a perspective toward a dynamic cultural identity, and psychological well-being (Miranda et al., 2006). Very little research has examined the effects of acculturation on marital relationship in general and among Asians in particular.

More individuals in the United States are marrying outside their culture (Negy & Snyder, 2000). This is evidenced by an almost fourfold increase in the number of these marriages over the time span of the 1970s to 1990s

(U.S. Census, 1994). Although there is evidence to show that couples in interracial marriages have to work harder to achieve satisfaction than other couples, there are conflicting viewpoints about the relative stress level and marital satisfaction of these couples. According to Fu, Tora, and Kendall (2001), women in interracial couples tended to have lower levels of marital satisfaction than do men in these marriages. They suggested that it seems to have more of an effect on women who often have to balance the pressures of both families of origin, as well as their own current family, more so than men. In addition (and perhaps, in part, as a result), these couples have a higher divorce rate than couples who marry within their culture. Yet, Negy and Snyder (2000) found that mixed culture couples are not inherently more stressed than couples from the same cultural background. The only place where these couples reported more distress was in child rearing. This makes sense as child rearing is a place in the marriage where conflicting models of culture (particularly individualistic vs. collectivistic) can manifest themselves and can disproportionally affect women (Keller et al., 2004).

The level of acculturation may also account for some of the conflicting findings about mixed-culture couples. Acculturation can affect acceptance by family of origin and flexibility of gender roles, which can impact marital satisfaction. Indeed, Farver, Narang, and Bhadha (2002) found that parents who had a less integrated style of acculturation (separated or marginalized) reported higher family conflict than those who had an integrated or assimilated acculturation style. This would lead to interculture couples experiencing more stress and pressure from their family of origin. In Asian families who adopt more separate acculturation styles, this could be a significant burden. If the family of origin does not approve of the choice of spouse, or if the spouse does not understand the obligations of a more collectivistic culture, then the marriage may experience greater stress. However, for those Asian couples who are more integrated or assimilated, tolerance for the influence of other cultures by the family of origin (represented by a spouse of a child from another culture) may significantly decrease the stresses on the marriage and increase the level of marital satisfaction (Farver et al., 2002).

For Western counselors working with individuals from Asian populations, the level of acculturation is a crucial aspect in determining the influence of culture (e.g., collectivism, family loyalty, and *enqing*) on marital satisfaction and intimacy. This is particularly salient as the Western ideal of autonomy and assertiveness would be viewed as immature and an indication of lack of cultivation in East Asia (Zhou & Bankston, 1998). As a result, couples who are not acculturated (e.g., "separated") may not embrace a non-Asian counselor's well-meaning attempts at "individuation" or exhortation for free "expression of emotion." Furthermore, a counselor's discouragement of "enmeshment" of one spouse with his or her family of origin may be seen as wholly incompatible with their cultural ideals for individuals who may not be integrated into a Western (individualistic) culture. As a result, understanding the acculturation level of the members of a couple is a sine qua non before making any therapeutic interventions (Miranda et al., 2006).

Purpose of This Study

The purpose of the present study is to add to the existing literature on Asian couples and the unique cultural factors that impact their marital relationships and intimacy. Specifically, we will consider the interplay between marital cultural makeup, acculturation, intimacy, and *enqing* on Asian couples' marital satisfaction. We will also examine participants' experience with three relationship stressors (i.e., illness, separation due to job-related travel, infidelity) and what they have found to be useful in helping them regain the lost intimacy due to these stressors.

This study will investigate the predictive influences of several independent variables on the dependent variable of marital satisfaction: acculturation, cultural makeup of the marriage, intimacy, and *enqing*. It is hypothesized that these variables will significantly predict levels of marital satisfaction. In addition, an analysis of qualitative survey answers will be employed to gather information on the effects of stressors on marital intimacy and strategies used to regain lost intimacy.

Method

Participants

Ninety participants responded to an online survey. Of the 90, 6 were single and had not been married, 1 did not complete a substantial portion of the study, and 1 identified himself as Afro-American. These eight individuals were excluded from the study. The final sample size was 82 (21 males, 61 females). Participants' ages ranged from 21 to 59 years ($M = 36.02$, $SD = 8.58$). Two did not report age. Fifteen (18.3%) were born in the United States. In terms of nationality, 46 (56.1%) were Americans, 11 Indians, 8 Malaysians, 6 Chinese, 2 Japanese, 1 each Bangladeshi, Canadian, Filipino, Indonesian, Korean, Mongol, Pakistani, and Taiwanese. Culturally, 21 self-identified as Chinese, 14 as Indian, 7 as Filipino, 5 as Hmong, 5 as Japanese. Other cultural groups represented by three or less participants were Korean, Taiwanese, Vietnamese, Thai, Pakistani, Mongolian, Laotian, Malay, and Bengali. Four were interracial and identified as multicultural. Thirty-seven were Christians, 7 Buddhists, 10 Hindus, 2 Muslims, 2

Shamanists, and 1 Jehovah's Witness. One reported practicing a mixed of Buddhism and Christianity, while another practiced a mixed of Hinduism and Christianity. One reported being agnostic, and 19 had no religion. One did not report religious affiliation. Forty-seven (56.1%) of them had full-time employment (self-employed or worked for pay). Ten (12.2%) were part-time employed. Eleven (13.4%) were full-time students. Ten were full-time homemakers. Four were unemployed and one retired. Educationally, 42 (51.2%) had graduate level education, 23 (28.0%) had a bachelor's degree, 14 (17.0%) had some college, and three had high school or less. Fifty (61.0%) of them married within their own culture, and 31 (37.8%) did not. One did not provide this information.

Procedures

A web-based survey was developed to collect the present data in 2008. Electronic invitations to take part in the survey were mailed to student, staff, and faculty listed in the email directories of two mid-size universities, one in the southeastern United States, and the other in the western United States. Electronic invitations were also sent to personal contacts of the researchers who were of Asian descent.

Instruments

Marital satisfaction was measured by the 3-item Kansas Marital Satisfaction Scale (KMSS; Schumm et al., 1986). Respondents use a 7-point Likert-type scale (1 = extremely dissatisfied to 7 = extremely satisfied) to rate their agreement with three statements regarding their satisfaction with their marriage. Internal consistency coefficient of the measure was .97, a magnitude comparable to those reported for U.S. samples (Schumm et al., 1986). The scores on the three items were summed to create a possible composite score ranging from 3 to 21, with higher scores indicating greater marital satisfaction. The validity of the KMSS for Asian groups has been reported in the literature (e.g., Ng, Loy, Gudmunson, & Cheong, 2009).

The 32-item Marital Affection Inventory (MAI; Li & Chen, 2002) was used to measure the two key components of affectionate marital relationship: *feelings of intimacy* and *enqing*. The intimacy scale comprises eight *togetherness* items (e.g., "I feel close to my spouse") and eight *compatibility* items (e.g., "My spouse and I totally understand each other's needs"). The *enqing* scale comprises eight *gratitude* items (e.g., "I'll feel indebted if my spouse is not well treated") and eight *admiration* items (e.g., "I am especially proud to be my spouse's mate"). Respondents use a 6-point Likert-type scale (1 = strongly disagree to 6 = strongly agree) to endorse their agreement with the items. The internal consistency reliabilities for *enqing* and intimacy reported by Li and Chen were .83 and .97, respectively.

Reliability analyses of the MAI items showed that three items in *enq-ing* and two items in intimacy had low corrected item-to-total correlations in the present sample. They lowered the scales' internal consistencies. We decided to exclude them from the scales. Cronbach's alphas for the revised scales were .91 (*enqing*) and .96 (intimacy). Because the MAI was developed originally for use with Chinese and our sample comprised both Chinese and non-Chinese, we split the sample to further examine the subscales' reliability. Alphas for the revised *enqing* subscale for the Chinese and non-Chinese groups were .88 ($n = 30$) and .94 ($n = 52$), respectively. Alphas for the revised intimacy subscale for the two groups were .94 and .96, respectively.

Acculturation was measured by the East Asian Acculturation Measure (EAAM; Barry, 2001), a 29-item self-report questionnaire that contains four subscales: *assimilation, separation, integration,* and *marginalization.* The measure assesses respondents' social interaction and communication styles in various settings. Respondents use a 7-point Likert-type scale to rate their agreement with the items (1 = strongly disagree to 7 = strongly agree). Total score is computed by summing the reverse-scored and positively scored items. Higher scores indicate a higher level of acculturation. Item sample include "I feel comfortable around both Americans and Asians." We decided to use the total score instead of the four subscale scores in this study because the modest sample size precluded the use of large number of predictor variables.

We dropped an item, "I tell jokes both in English and in my native language (for example, Chinese, Japanese, and Korean)," from the study because it lowered the internal consistency of the total score. Cronbach's alpha for the revised EAAM in this study was .87. Because the EAAM was developed based on East Asians and our sample consisted of 18 individuals who could be classified as non–East Asian, we examined the reliability of the measure for East Asians as well as for non-East Asians. The alpha for the former was .86 ($n = 64$) and that for the latter was .90 ($n = 18$). The high alphas support the use of the EAAM for the study sample, although it included East Asians as well as non–East Asians.

Based on the above-reviewed literature on stressors that impact marital relationship, we included three sets of questions in order to explore participants' experiences with and perceptions of these stressors in relation to their experience of intimacy in their marriages. We predicated our questions on the following definition of intimacy, which includes (Waring, 1984):

1. The ease with which differences of opinion are resolved between the couple.
2. The degree to which feelings of emotional closeness are expressed by the couple.
3. A feeling of commitment to the marriage.

4. The degree to which sexual needs are communicated and fulfilled by the marriage.
5. The couple's level of self-confidence and self-esteem.
6. The degree to which the couple is able to work and play together comfortably.
7. The degree to which thoughts, beliefs, attitudes, and feelings are shared within the marriage as well as their level of self-disclosure.
8. The success with which the couple gains emotional independence and space from their families of origin.

The first question set concerned the experience of major illness. The questions were as follows:

1. Have you ever been inflicted with a major illness that you believe has negatively affected your marriage? (If this has happened more than once, respond to the following based on the medical incident that you believe has the most negative impact.)
2. How negative had/has this medical incident impacted the intimacy between you and your spouse? (Options: Not at all negative, mildly negative, moderately negative, and extremely negative.)
3. If this medical incident is causing or has caused a loss of intimacy in your marriage, what have you found to be useful in helping you regain the intimacy you lost?

The participants were then asked about their spouse's experience with a major illness with questions in similar fashion.

The second set of questions concerned participants' experience of physical separation from their spouse as a result of job-related traveling that they believed had negatively impacted their relationship. The questions were phrased similar to those in the first set. The last set of questions concerned the experience of infidelity, whether they were the party committing the infidelity or their spouse was the committing party. The format of the question set was similar to that of the previous question sets. Participants were told to respond to the questions according to their own definition of infidelity within a marriage.

Results

Preliminary Analyses

Data were screened and missing values for the study variables were replaced by the respective series means. Data on marital satisfaction, intimacy, and *enqing* required transformation because they did not conform to the assumption of linearity. A reflect-and-square-root transformation was used on intimacy and *enqing*, while a reflect-and-natural-log transformation was used on marital satisfaction. When interpreting reflected variables, the direction of the interpretation needs to be reversed.

Multivariate analysis of variance (MANOVA) was carried out to determine the effect of marital cultural makeup (married within culture vs. married outside of culture) on marital satisfaction, intimacy, *enqing*, and acculturation. MANOVA results indicated that marital cultural makeup significantly affected the combined variables (Wilks' λ = .869, $F(4, 76)$ = 2.875, p = .028, η^2 = .131). Analysis of variance results showed that only marital satisfaction differed for marital cultural makeup ($F(1, 79)$ = 3.848, p = .05, η^2 = .046). Although the effect size was small but nontrivial, individuals marrying within their culture reported higher levels of marital satisfaction (M = 4.03, SD = 1.43) compared to those married outside of their cultures (M = 4.21, SD = 1.65) (lower scores indicate higher levels of marital satisfaction).

Gender differences in the study variables were examined using nonparametric procedures because of the small number of men in the study. However, there were no significant differences between men and women on any of the study variables.

Table 19.1 presents the means, standard deviations, alphas, and intercorrelations of all the study variables. The statistically significant correlations among the variables showed that individuals with higher acculturation levels reported higher levels of marital satisfaction, intimacy, and *enqing*. Individuals who reported higher levels of marital satisfaction also reported higher levels of intimacy and *enqing*. Intimacy and *enqing* were highly correlated. The interactions between acculturation and intimacy and acculturation and *enqing* were not significantly related to marital satisfaction.

We performed a hierarchical regression to investigate the effects of intimacy and *enqing* on marital satisfaction, after controlling for participants' cultural makeup in their marriages as well as their acculturation levels. We decided to treat participants' marital cultural makeup and acculturation level as control variables because the former is a demographic variable and the latter an internal variable that had been found to be related to minority individuals' psychosocial adjustment in the United States (Miranda et al., 2006). We also further tested the interactional effects of acculturation and intimacy and *enqing* on marital satisfaction.

Effects of Intimacy and Enqing on Marital Satisfaction

Results from the hierarchy regression (Table 19.2) revealed that acculturation and marital cultural makeup combined to statistically significantly predict 13% of the variance in marital satisfaction (Step 1). Both these variables were significant predictors and shared relatively similar strength of

Table 19.1 Means, Standard Deviations, Alphas, and Intercorrelations of All Study Variables (*N* = 81)

Variable	M	SD	α	2	3	4	5	6	7
1. Marital cultural makeup[a]				.17	.22*	.06	.16	-.14	-.07
2. Acculturation	136.97	22.89	.87		-.25*	-.32*	-.36*	.23*	.13
3. Marital satisfaction[b]	1.45	.86	.97			.62**	.64**	.04	-.07
4. Intimacy[b]	4.10	1.51	.96				.82**	-.03	-.06
5. Enqing[b]	4.07	1.23	.92					-.12	-.16
6. Acculturation × Intimacy	-.30	1.17							.77**
7. Acculturation × Enqing	-.34	1.04							

Note: **$p < .001$. *$p < .05$.
[a] The variable was dummy coded: -1 = married within culture, 1 = married outside of culture.
[b] Variables were reflected when transformed. Interpretation needs to reverse the direction. Higher values indicate lower scores.

Table 19.2 Hierarchical Regression Analysis of Variables Predicting Marital Satisfaction

Variable	B	SEB	β	t	R^2	Adj. R^2	ΔR^2
			Step 1				
Acculturation	−.01	.00	−.29	−2.72*			
Marital cultural make-up	.23	.10	.27	2.48*	.13*	.11	
			Step 2				
Intimacy	.19	.08	.33	2.23*			
Enqing	.23	.11	.33	2.16*	.46	.43	.33**

Note: $* p < .05$. $** p < .001$. Marital satisfaction, intimacy, and *enqing* were reflected and transformed. Interpretation needs to reverse direction for these variables.

prediction as indicated by their β weights. Higher levels of marital satisfaction were predicted by higher levels of acculturation as well as being married to a spouse from the same culture.

Results in Step 2 in the regression revealed that intimacy and *enqing* both significantly predicted marital satisfaction. Intimacy and *enqing* explained 33% of the variance in marital satisfaction above and beyond that explained by acculturation and marital cultural makeup. The interactional terms between acculturation and intimacy and acculturation and *enqing* were found to be irrelevant for any additional variance in marital satisfaction (Step 3). Hence, they were not included in the reported regression model.

We conducted additional analyses to examine if intimacy and *enqing* predicted marital satisfaction differently between individuals who married within their culture ($n = 50$) and those who married outside of their culture ($n = 31$). Results for individuals who married within their own culture indicated that, after controlling for the effects of acculturation (β = -.29, t = -2.08, p = .04, R^2 = .08, adjusted R^2 = .06), intimacy (β = .30, t = 1.72. p = .09) and *enqing* (β = .35, t = 1.62, p = .06) combined to explain an additional 33.4% of the variance in marital satisfaction. When the β values were compared, *enqing* was a slightly stronger predictor than intimacy among individuals who married within culture.

For those who married outside of their culture, after controlling for the effects of acculturation (β = -.32, t = -1.81, p = .08, R^2 = .10, adjusted R^2 = .07), intimacy (β = .58, t = 1.86. p = .07) and *enqing* (β = .17, t = .54, p = .60) combined to explain an additional 42.6% of the variance in marital satisfaction. Although the R^2 change (F change = 12.139, p < .001) was significant for the regression model, only intimacy approached the conventional p value of .05. However, the β value indicated that intimacy was a much stronger predictor than *enqing* among individuals who married outside of their culture. This pattern differed from that found for those who married within their culture.

Critical Relationship Stressors

We further examined participants' experiences with several relationship stressors in relation to their experience of intimacy. Because only a few participants responded to this portion of the study, we only report the descriptive data and their textual responses to the open-ended questions. We were not able to compare these data to the quantitative data on acculturation, marital satisfaction, intimacy, and *enqing*.

Major Illness Four (4.9%; 1 male, 3 females) of the 82 participants indicated they had been inflicted with a major illness that they believed had negatively affected their marriage. Two of them indicated the illness had extremely negatively impacted their intimacy with their spouses, and two said it had not at all impacted them negatively. One person reported that "therapy and communication" help to regain the loss of intimacy. The other three persons did not provide any information on what they had found to be useful in helping them regain the lost intimacy.

Three of the 82 (3.7%; all females) participants indicated their spouses had been inflicted with a major illness that had affected their marriage. Two reported that the event had extremely negatively impacted their marriage, and one said it impacted the couple mildly negatively. Two of the participants reported the following to be helpful in their regaining of lost intimacy as it relates to illness suffered by spouse. One participant stated, "Physical intimacy has been replaced by closeness in other ways" but did not expand on what those other ways were. The other participant stated, "remembering how much he does for the family even through illness."

Separation Due to Job-Related Traveling Sixteen (19.5%, 11 females, 5 males) indicated they had experienced separation from their spouses for an extended time due to job-related traveling, which they believe had negatively affected their marriage. Three (18.8%) indicated the separation had a mild negative impact on their marriage, one (6.3%) indicated moderate negative impact, and nine (56.3%) said no negative impact was experienced. Three responses were unclear. Textual responses to job-related traveling affects on the marriage included the following. One participant stated, "One eight-month deployment to Iraq. It was early in our marriage and the separation anxiety made it very difficult for us to communicate." Four of the participants indicated that some type of communication (e.g., talking on the phone, getting together for brief moments when possible) was helpful toward regaining intimacy. Two of the participants stated that "having faith" and "praying" were also helpful toward regaining intimacy.

Infidelity Thirteen (15.9%) participants indicated they had committed infidelity, however they defined infidelity, in their current marriage. Nine (11.0%) said their spouses had committed infidelity. Among these participants, three had experienced infidelity committed by themselves as well as their spouses. Of the 13 (4 males, 9 females) who indicated they had committed infidelity in their current marriage, two (15.4%; 1 female, 1 male) indicated the infidelity event had a moderately negative impact on their marriages, four (30.7%; 2 females, 2 males) indicated a mildly negative impact, and five (38.5%; 4 females, 1 male) indicated no negative impact at all. Two did not respond to this question. Textual responses to intimacy lost as a result of infidelity were as follows. Two indicated their Christian faith helped them regain lost intimacy, while another indicated "understanding and forgiveness." Another indicated "spending more time with my spouse; distancing myself from events that would make me think of the other person."

Of the nine (7 females, 2 males) who indicated their current spouse had committed infidelity, six (66.7%; 5 females, 1 male) indicated the infidelity incident had an extremely negative impact on their marriages, one (female) indicated a moderately negative impact, one (male) indicated a mildly negative impact, and one did not respond to the question. Compared to when the respondents were the committing person, a higher percentage among those who experienced infidelity committed by their spouse reported the event having a greater negative impact. Textual responses from the participants indicated that their Christian faith was helpful toward regaining lost intimacy. Two other people had indicated the notion of recommitting (i.e., "second chance") to the marriage. One of them stated, "I had to readjust my thinking and decided that commitment and marriage was important to me." Finally, one participant indicated that "understanding, forgiveness, and love" were necessary to regain intimacy in a case of infidelity.

Discussion

The purpose of this chapter was to present an understanding of some of the unique cultural factors that impact Asian marital relationships as it relates to intimacy and marital satisfaction. The results of the survey showed that within Asian couple relationships the cultural factor known as *enqing* (feelings of respect, admiration, and gratitude toward one's spouse for what they do for the family) and intimacy are very strong predictors of marital satisfaction. At the same time, acculturation and culture of a respondent's spouse (Asian vs. non-Asian) also predicted marital satisfaction. *Enqing* had a stronger effect on marital satisfaction (as measured by the relative beta weights for the variables) than intimacy. This finding suggests that there are both general factors (intimacy) as well as some unique cultural factors (e.g., *enqing*) that are important to consider when working toward improving marital satisfaction. Our findings concur with Li and Chen's (2002) in terms of the relationship between marital satisfaction and intimacy and *enqing*. However, Li and Chen found that intimacy was a stronger predictor than *enqing*.

When we observed whether individuals had married within or outside the Asian culture, there was no difference with either *enqing* or intimacy, but significant differences were detected for marital satisfaction. So when the sample was split between couples who married within the Asian culture and outside the Asian culture, for those participants who married within the Asian culture, both *enqing* and intimacy were strong predictors of marital satisfaction. For those individuals who did *not* marry a spouse from within their culture, intimacy predicted marital satisfaction, but not *enqing*. This finding would suggest that while *enqing* is present in these Asian-to-non-Asian couples, it does not have the same effect on marital satisfaction. This may be due either to the fact that the spouse was not raised in a collectivistic-based culture and was simply not exposed to this cultural value, or it may be indicative of the participating spouse's (who was Asian) level of detachment from the traditional values of the Asian culture. While this might seem to be self-evident, given that the participating spouse had married outside of the Asian culture, several researchers (Greenfield et al., 2003; Keller et al., 2004) found that traditional cultural values often exert an indirect influence in relationships that are more "modern." It is here that perhaps an individual's level of acculturation with the new culture may be worth investigating. For example, an individual who is "assimilated" (and thus rejects the culture of origin) may not admit to feeling this exertion, while an individual who is "integrated" (and is at home in both cultures) may understand the traditional cultural forces and be able to better cope with them and place them in the proper context for his or her relationship (see Miranda et al., 2006).

Higher levels of acculturation were found to be related to higher levels of marital satisfaction. This concurs with existing findings that show higher levels of acculturation are related to better psychosocial adjustment (Miranda et al., 2006). Because we did not study the marital dyad, it was not possible to investigate the interactional effect of the partners' acculturation levels on their marital satisfaction. Future research should consider doing so.

The textual responses, although very limited in number, were helpful in illuminating the data collected. One prominent theme from the textual responses is that intimacy can be regained when lost due to illness, separation due to work, and infidelity. The manner in which couples achieve the renewed intimacy varied (e.g., personal faith, forgiveness, communication, recommitment to the relationship); but it is possible for couples to reestablish relationship intimacy. Another implication that can be drawn from the textual responses is that reestablishment of intimacy requires a recommitment to the relationship, and work is necessary to reach this end.

Among the three relationship stressors, infidelity committed by one's spouse seems to have the most negative impact. This reflects the literature on the severe impact of infidelity (Peluso, 2007). Although each relationship injury or stressor (infidelity, separation, illness) was painful in its own unique way, there is an indication that a recommitment to the relationship is something necessary to help overcome such injuries. What participants have reported to be useful in helping them regain the lost intimacy as a result of these relationship injuries reflects their use of cognitive, behavioral, and spiritual coping skills. It is interesting that one individual indicated use of a cognitive strategy that reflects the concept of *enqing* when the person's spouse had an illness—"remembering how much he does for the family even through illness." However, responses provided for the other two stressors did not seem to be related to *enqing*. Additional research is needed to learn how cultural values affect the types of coping skills couples use to help them regain intimacy and manage relationship stressors.

Implications for Practitioners

The implications of these findings for couples counselors who are working with Asian couples are clear. Specifically, couples counselors who want to help Asian clients should understand whether they married within the culture and then decide their strategy for helping the couple. If it is an Asian-based couple, counselors need to understand the influence of the cultural factors on the couple's marital satisfaction and intimacy. Deeply embedded in this is the construct of *enqing*—the deep respect and admiration that is centered around collectivist ideals related to fulfilling one's sense of duty that is centered around familial obligations. Tapping into the couple's mutual respect and admiration while working with them to rebuild intimacy would be a culturally sensitive strategy for couples counselors to bear in mind.

Enqing seems to play a lesser role in intercultural couples compared to Asian-based couples. However, for intercultural couples, couples counselors need to assess the relative importance of Asian cultural values in helping these couples work toward marriage and intimacy. For couples who have higher acculturation levels, couples counselors using Western couples counseling intervention may not need to adjust too much to fit the needs of their couples. However, couples who are less acculturated may require counselors to adjust their intervention accordingly.

In efforts to help Asian couples regain their lost intimacy, counselors need to explore with them what resources and strategies would be helpful for them in view of their cultural values and religion. It seems reasonable to expect that the impact of infidelity on Asians, especially on those who experience the betrayal, will be great compared to stress from illness and separation due to work-related travel. Hence, counselors need to be aware of the qualitative impact of a particular experience. Yet counselors need to remember that clients do have their own coping resources, which can and should be tapped into when empowering them.

Limitations of the Study

Interpretation of the findings in this study needs to keep several limitations in mind. First, intact couples were not surveyed. Only one member of the marital dyad responded to the survey, despite researchers' efforts to recruit couples to participate. This is a frequent issue that couples researchers report (Sperry et al., 2006), and future research replicating the degree to which *enqing*, intimacy, and marital satisfaction are related should take this into consideration.

Second, the present study had a low number of male participants. However, the female-dominated pool of participants did shed some light on the construct of *enqing*. Most studies of Asian populations find that *enqing* is a stronger factor for males than for females (Li & Chen, 2002). However, in the present study, there were no significant differences between men and women on *enqing*. In addition, the predominance of women participants, along with the overall strength of the finding for *enqing*, is an indication that this is a relatively robust phenomenon even among non–Chinese Asians. Future researchers should recruit intact couples and include more males.

Third, Asian cultures are immensely heterogeneous. Although most Asian cultures are considered collectivistic in comparison to most Western cultures, Asians differ in many cultural aspects such as religion and marriage practices. Future work should investigate how different Asian subcultures might express intimacy, *enqing*, and marital satisfaction differently. The sample size limitation in the present study precluded an investigation on this level.

Fourth, the small number of responses seriously limited the data on participants' experiences with the study relationship stressors. Researchers should consider conducting qualitative studies on Asian couples who had experienced these stressors in order to gain in-depth appreciation of their impact and what helped them regain their lost intimacy.

Conclusion

We examined the effects of marital cultural makeup, acculturation, intimacy, and *enqing* on Asian couples' marital satisfaction. We found that individuals who married within their culture and had higher acculturation levels also reported higher levels of marital satisfaction. Furthermore, intimacy and *enqing* predicted individuals' level of marital satisfaction. *Enqing* was a stronger predictor of marital satisfaction than intimacy among those who married within their culture, whereas *enqing* was not as relevant as intimacy in predicting marital satisfaction among those who married outside of their culture. Our findings corroborate earlier work, suggesting that satisfaction with one's marriage has both universal and specific cultural elements. Based on our findings, we recommend that couples counselor who are working with Asian couples who are experiencing a loss of intimacy and a lack of satisfaction should approach their clients from an informed perspective of collectivistic cultures, and that helping the couple to revive feelings of respect, admiration, and gratitude toward one's spouse for what they do for the family may be the most powerful way to restore intimacy and satisfaction.

References

Amato, P. R., & Previti, D. (2003). People's reasons for divorcing: Gender, social class, the life course, and adjustment. *Journal of Family Issues, 24,* 602–626.

Barry, D. T. (2001). Development of a new scale for measuring acculturation: The East Asian Acculturation Measure (EAAM). *Journal of Immigrant Health, 3,* 193–197.

Berry, J. (1997). Immigration, acculturation and adaptation. *Applied Psychology: An International Review, 46,* 5–68.

Chen, F., & Li, T. (2007). Marital *enqing*: An examination of its relationship to spousal contributions, sacrifices, and family stress in Chinese marriages. *Journal of Social Psychology, 147,* 393–412.

Farver, J. M., Narang, S. K., & Bhadha, B. R. (2002). East meets West: Ethnic identity, acculturation, and conflict in Asian Indian families. *Journal of Family Psychology, 16,* 338–350.

Fekete, E. M., Stephens, M. A. P., Mickelson, K. D., & Druley, J. A. (2007). Couples' support provision during illness: The role of perceived emotional responsiveness. *Families, Systems, and Health, 25,* 204–217.

Fu, X., Tora, J., & Kendall, H. (2001). Marital happiness and inter-racial marriage: A study in a multi-ethnic community in Hawaii. *Journal of Comparative Family Studies, 32,* 47–60.

Gerstel, N., & Gross, H. E. (1982). Commuter marriages: A review. *Marriage and Family Review, 5,* 71–93.

Greenfield, P. M., Keller, H., Fuligni, A., & Maynard, A. (2003). Cultural pathways through universal development. *Annual Review of Psychology, 54,* 461–490.

Hawkins, D. N., & Booth, A. (2005). Unhappily ever after: Effects of long-term, low quality marriages on well-being. *Social Forces, 84,* 445–465.

Keller, H., Lohaus, A., Kuensemueller, P., Abels, M., Yovsi, E., Voelker, S., et al. (2004). The bio-culture of parenting: Evidence from five cultural communities. *Parenting, Science and Practice, 4,* 25–50

Kiecolt-Glaser, J. K., McGuire, L., Robles, T. F., & Glaser, R. (2002). Psychoneuroimmunology: Psychological influences on immune function and health. *Journal of Consulting and Clinical Psychology, 70,* 537–547.

Kim, U. (2001, October). *Indigenous psychologies and the transactional model of science: A new paradigm for understanding psychological and cultural phenomena.* Paper presented at the international workshop on Scientific Advances in Indigenous Psychologies: Philosophical, Cultural, and Empirical Contributions, Taipei, Taiwan.

Li, T.-S., & Chen, F.-M. (2002). Affection in marriage: A study of marital *enqing* and intimacy in Taiwan. *Journal of Psychology in Chinese Societies, 3,* 37–59.

Lucas, T., Parkhill, M. R., Wendorf, C. A., Imamoglu, E. O., Weisfeld, C. C., Weisfeld, G E., et al. (2008). Cultural and evolutionary components of marital satisfaction: A multidimensional assessment of measurement invariance. *Journal of Cross-Cultural Psychology, 39,* 109–123.

Miranda, A. O., Bilot, J. M., Peluso P. R., Berman, K., & Van Meek, L. (2006). Latino families: The relevance of the connection among acculturation, family dynamics, and health for family counseling research and practice. *Family Journal: Counseling and Therapy for Couples and Families, 14,* 268–273.

Negy, C., & Snyder, D. K. (2000). Relationship satisfaction of Mexican- and non-Hispanic white-American interethnic couples: Issues of acculturation and clinical intervention. *Journal of Marital and Family Therapy, 26,* 293–304.

Ng, K. M., Loy, J. T.-C., Gudmunson, C. G., & Cheong, W. (2009). Gender differences in marital and life satisfaction among Chinese Malaysians. *Sex Roles, 60,* 33–43.

Norris, F. H., & Kaniasty, K. (1996). Received and perceived social support in times of stress: A test of the social support deterioration deterrence model. *Journal of Personality and Social Psychology, 71,* 498–511.

Peluso, P. R. (2007). *Infidelity: A practitioner's guide to working with couples in crisis.* New York: Routledge.

Schumm, W. R., Paff-Bergen, L. A., Hatch, R. C., Obiorah, F. C., Copeland, J. M., Meens, L. D., et al. (1986). Concurrent and discriminant validity of the Kansas Marital Satisfaction Scale. *Journal of Marriage and the Family, 48,* 381–387.

Sperry L., Carlson, J., & Peluso, P. R. (2006). *Couples therapy: Integrating theory, research, and practice* (2nd ed.). Denver: Love Publishers.

Tang, J. Y. (1991). Division of domestic labor in dual-earner families: A perspective of the nature of housework. *Research in Applied Psychology, 4,* 131–173. [In Chinese].

U.S. Bureau of Census. (1994). *Current population reports, population characteristics. P20-484, marital status and living arrangements.* Washington, DC: U.S. Government Printing Office.

Waring, E. M. (1984). The measurement of marital intimacy. *Journal of Marital and Family Therapy, 10,* 185–192.

Wisman, M. A., Dixon, A. E., & Johnson, B. (1997). Therapists' perspectives of couple problems and treatment issues in couples therapy. *Journal of Family Psychology, 11,* 361–366.

Wong, B. P. (2007). Immigration, globalization, and the Chinese American family. In J. E. Lansford, K. Deater-Deckard, & M. H. Bornstein (Eds.), *Immigrant families in contemporary society* (pp. 212–228). New York: Guilford.

Zhou, M., & Bankston, C. L. III. (1998). *Growing up American: How Vietnamese children adapt to life in the United States.* New York: Russell Sage Foundation.

CHAPTER 20

Interview With David Burns

David D. Burns, M.D., is the best-selling author of *Feeling Good: The New Mood Therapy* and numerous other books, articles, and research studies. He is adjunct professor of psychiatry and behavioral sciences at the School of Medicine, Stanford University.

Eds: Our own clinical observation in working with couples is that keeping their relationships alive and satisfying is probably the primary challenge for couples therapists today. Have you noticed this or a similar challenge in your work with couples?

DB: No, I have not noticed this in my work. I think the primary challenge for couples therapists is to find a treatment method that actually works. The outcome studies in this area have been universally disappointing. Treatment failure, I think, is the primary challenge for people working with troubled couples.

Eds: What do you find are the major reasons or causes why couples relationships are devitalized and less satisfying today?

DB: I am not aware of any evidence for changes in relationship satisfaction through the decades. Before you can speculate about the cause of a trend or finding, I tend to focus on the original research that made such a claim. In most cases, I find the research to be faulty, so there is no reliable finding to interpret. The media loves people to speculate about historical trends in depression and every other psychological problem, but I've never seen any valid research that showed such trends to exist. And when trends have been shown to exist, I am convinced that the theories mental health "experts" expound to interpret such trends tend to be false.

Eds: Could you say a bit more about the empathically challenged partner?

DB: To me, the key problem in troubled relationships is not a failure of empathy, but a problem of motivation. Empathy is important, and can be hard to learn, even for mental health professionals, but it is not, in my opinion, a primary causal factor of relationship problems. When you are angry and blaming the other person, you don't "want" to listen. So skill deficits are not the real problem, although mental health professionals want to believe they are central.

Eds: What can be done about low motivation? Can you help our readers understand this distinction with a brief example?

DB: There is a strong tendency not to want to get close to people we're at odds with. I call that problem Outcome Resistance. Outcome Resistance is a term I coined to refer to the idea that the patient might not want a positive treatment outcome, even if it could happen magically, suddenly, and without any effort. So if you're mad at someone and you're not feeling close to him or her, Outcome Resistance means that you might not *want* to be close to that person. Therapists who don't take this into account will run into a wall of resistance—and that seems to include most therapists most of the time.

In addition, if you do want to get close to someone you're not getting along with, you may not be willing to pay the price of intimacy. I call that problem Process Resistance. Process Resistance refers to the fact that you might *want* a positive result—in this case, a loving, joyous relationship—but you're not willing to pay the price of bringing that result about. Process Resistance and Outcome Resistance will be different for different kinds of problems, such as depression, anxiety disorders, habits and addictions, or relationship problems. As a result, there are four totally unrelated patterns of Outcome Resistance, and four additional completely different patterns of Process Resistance. These eight patterns represent a new way of thinking about, and reversing, the familiar and vexing problem of therapeutic resistance.

To illustrate Outcome and Process Resistance for relationship problem, I often ask participants in my workshops to think about one person they're not getting along with, someone they don't like. It could be someone who is hypercritical, or narcissistic exploitative, or who complains constantly, or who will not express his or her feelings, or who always has to be right, or controlling, or nasty, or who refuses to listen. Then I ask for a show of hands to see if they have thought of someone, and all the hands go up. Mine too!

Then I say, "Let's imagine there's a magic button on the desk in front of you. Now, if you press that magic button, that person who you're thinking of, the person who you resent and dislike, will suddenly and magically become your best friend in the whole world. How many of you are going to press that button?" In an audience of 200, three or four hands might go up, and there will be some giggling. Then I say, "That's an excellent example of Outcome Resistance for a relationship problem. Nearly all of you are choosing hostility and mistrust over love and joy. In other words, you are saying very clearly that you *want* a bad relationship with that person—that's the choice you just made."

I explain that I made the same choice. I was thinking of a colleague I don't like or trust, and I wouldn't want a close relationship with him. I'd prefer to keep my distance. So if you said, "Oh, David, you can use some wonderful communication skills to get close to him," I'd tell you I wasn't interested and that you're barking up the wrong tree. This is just human nature. There's no rule that says we have to have good relationships with everyone.

How about Process Resistance? Next, I invite the audience to do another thought experiment. Let's assume that you *did* want a close relationship with that person. What's the one thing you'd have to do, that you'd probably be unwilling to do, in order to bring that result about? The answer people quickly gravitate to is some version of this: First, you'd stop blaming the other person for the problem, and focus instead on pinpointing your own role in the problem. In addition, you'd have to pour all your energies into changing yourself instead of trying to get the other person to change.

The Process Resistance to resolving relationship problems is incredibly intense. To illustrate this, I ask the participants to answer this question from their heart of hearts: "Who, in your opinion, is more to blame for the problem you're having with that person? Who's the bigger jerk? Is it you, or the other person? ... How many say it's the other person?" Ninety-five percent of the hands go up, with more giggling.

Then I ask a final question: "What's the prognosis for helping someone who blames others and says the problem is always someone's else fault?" The answer is obvious—close to 0%. In fact, I don't know of any interpersonal tools powerful enough to help someone who blames others for their problems.

Hopefully these examples illustrate the nature of Outcome and Process Resistance for relationship problems. These patterns of Outcome and Process Resistance can be almost as intense for depression, anxiety, and addictions, but those patterns are entirely different. In my workshops I illustrate new Paradoxical Agenda Setting techniques that will help therapists accurately pinpoint the kinds of Outcome Resistance and Process Resistance that will get in the way for each patient they treat. In addition, I illustrate how to head each type of resistance off at the pass before you use any therapy techniques designed to help the patient change and grow. These Paradoxical Agenda Setting techniques have been extremely helpful and appear to have triggered an orbital jump in the effectiveness of our treatment of depression, anxiety, relationship problems, and addictions. However, the methods are somewhat sophisticated and challenging for therapists to learn. That's because many therapists—perhaps nearly all—seem to have a kind of narcissistic or codependent need to jump in and "help" patients without dealing with resistance or making their patients accountable. This is the most common cause of therapeutic failure. So learning these new resistance-melting techniques requires considerable technical training, but also a deep shift in the attitudes of the therapist, and the willingness to "let go" without the compulsive urge to chase the reluctant patient.

[Readers who are interested in learning more about these new approaches might want to attend one of Dr. Burns's workshops around the country or check out his latest relationship book, *Feeling Good Together*. For more information go to www.feelinggood.com]

CHAPTER 21

Intimacy and the Recovery of Intimacy in Religious and Faith-Based Relationships

JILL D. DUBA

The purpose of this chapter is to review how intimacy and the recovery of intimacy can be viewed within a religious context. Many self-help books have been written to help couples regain intimacy in their relationships, specifically from a Christian basis (Balswick & Balswick, 2006; Chapman 2003, 2007; Schnarch, 1997; Wheat & Wheat, 1997). However, counselors lack significant resources regarding how to integrate a couple's religious or faith perspective when helping them work through intimacy-related challenges. This chapter will serve to fill this particular gap in the professional literature. More specifically, it will provide a brief review of how intimacy is defined as well as a focus on (a) how intimacy is "lost" or "cools" within a religious framework; (b) guidelines for recovering intimacy; (c) clinical approaches for incorporating a couple's faith; and (d) a brief case example.

Intimacy Defined

Before describing what intimacy in relationships looks like, it is helpful to consider what factors are needed in a relationship for intimacy to be cultivated or formed. Rampage (1994) suggested three preconditions for marital intimacy, including (a) equality between partners, (b) empathy for each other's experience, and (c) a willingness to come together around action and meaning. Based on the suggestions of other authors, I would like to add a fourth prerequisite, namely the differentiation of self. Maintaining a

357

healthy self-concept and autonomy while simultaneously connecting with others sets up partners to experience and share genuine intimacy between each other (Patrick, Sells, Giordano, & Tollerud, 2007). Further, differentiation can be viewed from a religious lens, which I will propose later.

Intimacy is difficult to measure. It is a subjective experience measured by each individual partner's perception of the relationship interactions. Contributing to one's sense of closeness or intimacy toward another is that person's perceptions about the following relationship characteristics: its positive and confirming nature; degree of intensity, reciprocity, openness, and mutual collaboration; and validation of self and of the relationship. These perceptions may originate from the meaning a partner constructs from the interactions that either contribute to or negate one's feeling of intimacy toward his or her partner.

Many authors refer to intimacy as a dynamic process. First, it occurs over time. As partners begin to trust each other (and themselves), they are more inclined to share of themselves in deeper and unrestricted ways. Second, developing intimacy also requires an understanding of what the other partner needs, in terms of his or her ideal degree of intimacy, while also being able to accept this level of need if different from one's own. This, too, occurs over time as each partner changes and grows. Third, intimacy is most likely to be experienced when it is mutually shared (Heller & Wood, 1998). Both partners need to feel that the other is reciprocating on a similar level (Bagarozzi, 1997; Kenny & Acitelli, 1987). Reciprocating with self-disclosure, for example, has been found to be a significant factor in establishing intimacy (Waring & Chelune, 1983). Sharing of ideas and values, activities, and knowledge of each other also increase intimacy (Patrick et al., 2007). Finally, intimacy may best be viewed as multidimensional or the sum of various dimensions. That is, intimacy may be experienced on several dimensions: emotionally, sexually, psychologically, intellectually, spiritually, socially and recreationally, and physically. Still other dimensions of intimacy may include expressiveness, compatibility, conflict resolution, and autonomy. What is most important about this concept of multidimensional intimacy is not whether or how much couples experience intimacy in all dimensions, but rather that partners agree that they share a satisfying degree of intimacy in the dimensions that are important to them.

Marital Intimacy Within a Religious or Faith-Based Relationship

I have found Giblin's (1994) review of the Three C's (or the three factors essential to marital satisfaction) to be an appropriate springboard from which to address how intimacy emerges or is maintained. The Three C's include: (a) how couples communicate, (b) resolve conflict, and (c) how they express their commitment. In addition, I will illustrate how each task can be addressed through a religious lens.

The first of the Three C's includes communication. Healthy communication begets marital intimacy. Giblin (1994) suggested that "religious practice and related beliefs support honest, hopeful, humble self awareness in communication" (p. 54). Take for example a couple who subscribes to a humanistic belief system. Within this belief system, marital partners are within their rights to express individual autonomy and to define the marriage as they so wish. However, such "freedoms are maximized by open lines of communication during every stage of the agreement" (Koepsell & Mercurio-Riley, 2008, p. 170). In order to maintain intimacy throughout an ever changing relationship, effective communication for a humanistic couple is absolutely essential. A lack of communication may contribute to a degree of loss in intimacy between partners. On the other hand, a Christian couple will marry based on the belief that marriage was a gift from God or something created by God. In this case, intimacy may be established and strengthened based on communication between partners regarding how they can relate to each other in a way that puts God at the center of the relationship. Another more specific example might include working with a childless Hindu couple. According to Madathil and Sandhu (2008), childless Hindu women tend to feel guilty and blame themselves for the inability to conceive. A lack of open communication, whether it is based on respect for one's husband or out of fear, may leave such women feeling isolated and abandoned. Partners who are willing may strengthen their relationship by discussing how cultural expectations (including gender) and ideals of self-responsibility affect their relationship. Counselors are encouraged to teach and review healthy communication skills with couples and then ask questions about what issues they have consistently not discussed.

As mentioned previously, conflict resolution has been regarded as an important factor in how intimacy is experienced. Religious couples can rely on their belief systems in the wake of conflict and marital problems. For example, Buddhist partners who are in conflict with each other are expected to search within themselves for the role they played in constructing the conflict (Shaneman, 2008). This introspection can move partners from blaming to examining how their actions caused marital suffering. Christian couples, on the other hand, can rely on scripture to move them out of conflict or stalemate by practicing forgiveness, servanthood, and being a channel of God's grace and mercy through the gift of the Holy Spirit. (See the following Bible references to this concept: Col. 3:13–14; 1 John 1:9; Matt. 18:21–22, Rom. 5:5.) For religious couples facing conflict, various religious tenets can be used to help partners move from resistance to positions of forgiveness, other-based interest, and self-responsibility. Couples may be encouraged to rely on scripture (i.e., Koran, Torah, Bible) or the behaviors of religious leaders (i.e., Buddha, Muhammad) to direct their own attitudes and behaviors. (Readers are behooved to peruse the

360 • Jill D. Duba

professional literature on using forgiveness as a healing and conflict resolution mechanism in counseling religious couples. See Holeman, 2008.)

Finally, commitment plays a significant role in the establishment of
intimacy. If spouses feel safe with each other, mutual sharing is likely to
occur across the dimensions mentioned above (i.e., self-disclosure, sexuality, social, etc.). Further commitment between partners is supported
among many different religions. For example, in Catholicism, marriage
is considered a sacrament where a partner gives him- or herself to the
other exclusively in an act of irrevocable consent (Duba Onedera, 2008).
Catholic couples can be reminded of their moral commitment to each
other for life (with the exception of abuse being present in the relationship)
by rereading their vows or reviewing the Catholic catechism's teaching on
marriage (Catholic Church, 2003) to rejuvenate their relationship. Even
within a liberal Christian framework, couples are encouraged to try to
enhance their understanding of each other, while increasing communication before considering divorce or separation. Partners who have a degree
of confidence that their spouses are willing to "try" before throwing in
the towel may be more inclined to self-disclose, give, forgive, and hope for
change. Within the Buddhist religion, divorce is acceptable; however, the
marriage ceremony itself is a "celebration of the couple's commitment or
union" (Shaneman, 2008). Thus troubled Buddhist couples might reflect
upon the meaning of their commitment and the prayers made as a part of
the celebration in order to enhance or maintain intimacy within their relationship. In summary, the type of commitment needed to strengthen and
maintain marital intimacy is one directed toward the relationship, rather
than commitment based on self-interest.

So far examples have been provided as to how intimacy might be better understood or enhanced by relying on any given religious framework.
However, these are general examples, and counselors should rely heavily
upon the information couples provide about their religious beliefs. Further,
counselors can inquire and promote discussions with couples about how
marital intimacy is understood within their given religious framework.
Questions to spark such discussions might include any of the following:

1. What religious resources (i.e., scripture, rabbi) do you (couple)
   rely on to help you gain greater intimacy?
2. How do you see your religious beliefs or God (or Allah) influencing your emotional, sexual, psychological, intellectual, spiritual,
   social, and physical intimacy?
3. How does your religion instruct you to self-disclose, to share your
   innermost thoughts and feelings with your partner?
4. What are the religious or cultural expectations of your gender in
   terms of being intimate with your partner?

5. When you are not feeling especially intimate, what religious tenets help you feel better or tend to make you feel worse?

6. How do your religious beliefs get in the way of your ability to be intimate with your partner?

7. When you are not feeling especially intimate, how do you use your faith to help you regain that intimacy you need and desire?

8. Do you and your partner share the same religious beliefs? How do you find the similarity or dissimilarity of those beliefs affecting the degree of intimacy you both share?

9. On a scale of 1 to 10, how committed to your partner does your religion suggest you should be, with 10 being highly committed and 1 being not committed? Where would you rate your own commitment to your partner?

10. How do you use your religious beliefs to strengthen your marriage? How do you use your beliefs to remain distant from your partner?

11. Describe the spiritual intimacy that you both share.

12. When and what have you relied on besides your religious beliefs to help you regain intimacy in your relationship? How has it worked?

13. Describe how your religious beliefs inform you about forgiving your partner when you are angry or facing conflict.

14. Would God (or Allah) be happy about the degree of intimacy you share? (examining "shoulds")

How Intimacy Is "Lost" or "Cools" Within a Religious Framework

There are various reasons why intimacy cools or is lost within a marriage. In this section I will briefly address some religious-based factors that influence marital intimacy specifically in terms of it plummeting or decreasing in intensity. The factors that will be addressed include what I refer to as the (a) faith-based differentiation of self, (b) shared religiosity, and (c) faith-based differences.

Differentiation of self has been linked to the degree of intimacy likely to be experienced in the relationship. The higher one's differentiation of self, the higher one is able to experience intimacy in any relationship. From a religious perspective, namely a Christian one, individuals have varying levels of differentiation of self in relation to God. In other words, we may understand the differences between differentiation and undifferentiation as two selves existing in each individual, namely the solid self and the pseudo-self (Gilbert, 2006). The solid self does not participate in fusing or losing self in relationships. The solid self also is quite confident in what he or she believes and does not lose these morals and values when shaken by stressors. Instead, in all circumstances this self says, "I believe that God exists, and because of my faith, I will behavior in this way when I am alone and when I am interacting with others." One's behavior and attitudes will likely be consistent in terms of "living out" one's faith. On the other hand, the pseudo-self is "negotiable" and may be influenced and altered by emotional pressures and from the environment. So, for example, in relationship conflict one partner acting from the pseudo-self may say, "I don't care what God says I should do. I'm sick and tired of forgiving other people. Besides, my partner is the one who is wrong! I am not bending on this one. Next time maybe, but today I am too stressed to forgive." So at higher levels on the faith-based scale of differentiation, the solid self will likely present itself more often than the pseudo-self, with more faith-based behaviors and thoughts consistently surfacing (i.e., forgiveness, introspection, humility, acceptance). If both partners are working from a lower level of differentiation, we can guess that the marriage will likely suffer with experiences of intimacy being lost amid strongholds detained by the pseudo-self.

One might presume that if partners share the same religious beliefs, they will have the resources to face conflict and marital challenges. However, spouses may not be at the same stage of spiritual development. That is, the Church or Spirit may have a dissimilar impact on each spouse's life (Belcher & Benda, 2003). I have witnessed Christian couples who immediately after attending a church service, supposedly feeling full of God's grace, raise their voices at each other. Although they had experienced God's power and grace during the service, they were not willing to use it to contribute to the relationship in a meaningful way. Perhaps one partner goes to church out of obligation and does not perceive the channeling of God's grace during the service to be a better spouse upon exiting the church. This would be an example of partners who may be at different ends of the spiritual development spectrum or continuum.

Interfaith couples experience their own set of challenges. Remember the particular factors mentioned at the beginning of this chapter that affect intimacy; namely, compatibility, collaboration and meaning making, and sharing of values and ideas. Each religion will provide a foundation from which followers make sense of the world, of relationships, and of themselves. Although certain values and ideas traverse religious boundaries, some differ greatly. Take for example the Catholic view of marriage, that being a sacrament in which two become one irrevocably. Values extending from this view of marriage consist of the covenant of conjugal love, exclusivity, indissolubility, or a "sanction between God and man" (May, 1995). Compare that to a humanistic view of marriage in which individuals are permitted to enter into personal relationships without the demands of culture or religious ideologies. Couples can "define them [their relationship] as they please" (Koepsell & Mercurio-Riley, 2008, p. 168). Values illustrated here are freedom, autonomy, tolerance, dignity, and free inquiry.

Other values within varying religious contexts will shape the views of gender-role expectations, family matters, death and dying, and homosexuality, to name a few. The question is whether such values and beliefs will prevent partners from collaborating or from being able to make and share mutual meaning within their coupleship. As previously mentioned, collaboration and mutual meaning making are keys in contributing to relationship intimacy.

Religious Couples Recovering From Lost or Cooled Intimacy

Counselors are encouraged to use the above-mentioned questions as a basis from which to engage couples in discussions about how to incorporate God or other religious tenets in recovering intimacy in their relationship. In this section I will address ways in which religious couples might engage in specific kinds of cognitions and behaviors that encourage intimacy.

Readjusting One's Attitudes and Perceptions

I think most of us would agree that when infidelity or some other sort of serious betrayal has surfaced within the marriage, feelings of trust and commitment will be seriously jeopardized, especially on the part of the person who was betrayed. Even years after the commitment had been breached, the betrayed partner may still struggle with believing, trusting, and feeling safe. However, regardless of where such untrusting feelings and thoughts originate, how can counselors help partners cognitively reframe their thoughts and change their behavior in order to begin moving toward a place of trust and safety, or a place where intimacy can be experienced?

Dreikurs (1974) said that one's "attitude determines the meaning of facts ... our 'biased apperception' turns reality into fiction" (p. 152). Years later, Gottman (1999) suggested something similar, which he termed as "positive sentiment override." That is, the way in which a spouse perceives the other partner's behaviors in neutral settings, as well as in conflictual ones, will determine how well the couple can repair difficult and challenging situations together, as well as how they will maintain "positive affect" during such situations.

How do we help partners reevaluate their perceptions and attitudes in ways that might help them feel closer to their spouses? How do we help partners maintain hopeful and trusting attitudes or "positive sentiments" toward their partners in both neutral and in challenging situations? More specifically and in line with the mission of this chapter, how might the religious tenets of our couples be incorporated so as to help them manifest such attitudes and perceptions?

First, counselors are encouraged to ask *the couple* the above-mentioned questions. Couples coming to counseling should be viewed as the experts of their lives. For example, they might have scriptures or resources that they rely on for help in shaping positive attitudes. Take for example Ephesians 5:1–2: "Be imitators of God ... live a life of love." Other scriptures related to one's attitudes toward others may include: 1 Samuel 1:17–27; 1 Corinthians 10:33. Partners also might consider how Muhammad or Bodhisattva Siddhartha viewed human nature. How did their attitudes contribute to building intimate relationships with those they loved? How might the virtues of Jesus or Muhammad, such as unconditional love, humility, forgiveness, and unselfishness, be more consciously emulated? Although feeling safe and feeling trustful of one's partner may take time, engaging in such discussions provides partners with a new way of thinking and feeling based on their faith-perspectives, which may essentially become the incentive for change.

Building Spiritual Intimacy: Becoming a Religiously Involved Couple

When one or both partners are struggling over the loss of intimacy in the relationship, the experience could be quite daunting. Partners might ask themselves, "Where on earth should we start?" For religious couples an excellent starting point is to focus on building their spiritual and social intimacy. Although spiritual intimacy is a rather complex construct, for the sake of brevity I will focus on the "doing" part of this dimension (which will contribute to the social intimacy dimension). For example, how can we encourage partners to come together in meaningful spiritual or religious-based activities such as becoming actively involved in the church, religious organizations, or religious-based advocacy groups? Sharing in such activities has been strongly supported in the literature as a factor in marital satisfaction, marital fidelity, conflict management, and increasing interpersonal intimacy (Dollahite & Lambert, 2007).

Couples might be encouraged to generate ideas about activities that would stimulate mutual interest. Activities such as the following cover a wide range of religious involvement. Counselors are encouraged to further exhaust the possibilities with the couples they are seeing.

1. Sharing sacred time together
   a. Praying or meditating together
   b. Studying scripture together
   c. Taking part in Islamic pilgrimage together
   d. Participating in religious ceremonies (i.e., elaborative Native American dances, or sweat lodges)
2. Attending religious services or meetings together, becoming involved in religious-based committees or organizations
   a. Volunteers for church-related organizations (e.g., St. Vincent de Paul; church council)

    b. Joining and working for religious-based advocacy groups (i.e., Free Muslims Coalition, anti-abortion groups)

    c. Attending a couples retreat or informational weekend (e.g., Retrouvaille Program, Marriage Encounter, relationship enhancement programs)

    d. Joining a Bible study group

Clinical Guidelines and Approaches

Informed Consent, Ethical Codes, and Standards of Practice

Research suggests that many religious clients might be reticent to seek secular counseling because of concerns that their religious beliefs will be ignored, discounted, or seen as pathological (Duba & Watts, 2009). Although clinicians do not have to share the beliefs of these clients to provide effective counseling, it is all the same still important to construct a climate of safety, trust, and respect for successful treatment outcomes. Demonstrating sensitivity to and respect for the couple's religious values is important from the outset of the relationship. Therefore, as counselors address the introductory issues of establishing a therapeutic relationship (e.g., providing informed consent), they can ask couples, either verbally or as an item on an intake form, if their faith is something they would like included in the therapy process. In doing so, the couple understands from the outset that these issues are welcome in the counseling process (Watts, 2008).

The foundation of all good counseling and psychotherapy is based on ethical codes and standards of practice. Consequently, a brief review of various professional codes and standards for addressing religious issues in counseling warrants attention. The 2005 American Counseling Association (ACA) Code of Ethics requires counselors to "recognize the effects of age, color, culture ... religion, spirituality" (Section E.8., Multicultural Issues/Diversity in Assessment). In 1996, the Association for Spiritual, Ethical, and Religious Values in Counseling (ASERVIC) division of the ACA developed a list of nine competencies associated with the ethical integration of religion and spirituality into counseling (Miller, 1999). The first five (as listed) pay specific attention to religious themes, suggesting that in order for counselors to be competent in helping clients address the spiritual dimensions of their lives, they should be able to:

1. explain the relationship between religion and spirituality
2. describe religious and spiritual beliefs and practices in a cultural context
3. engage in self-exploration of his/her religious and spiritual beliefs in order to increase sensitivity, understanding, and acceptance of his/her belief system

4. describe one's religious and/or spiritual belief system and explain various models of religious/spiritual development across the lifespan

5. demonstrate sensitivity to and acceptance of a variety of religious and/or spiritual expressions in the client's communication

Even Christian counselors are obliged to "work to understand the client's belief system and always maintain respect for the client ... [and to] ... strive to understand when faith and values issues are important to the client and foster values-informed client decision-making in counseling" (American Association of Christian Counselors [AACC], 2004, Section ES1-550). In summary, counselors are behooved and obligated to work toward a deeper understanding and appreciation of how the role of religion affects the couples they are seeing.

Treatment Interventions

Ribner (2003) suggested that working with a client's belief system "may necessitate creative modifications of treatment protocols in order to maximize potential for change while minimizing immutable sources of resistance" (p. 165). Such creative modifications might include adapting one's theoretical orientation, constructing genograms for the visual learner to make better sense of the situation, and using religious leaders as multicultural consultants. I will briefly address these concepts; however, counselors are encouraged to consider other adaptations that best fit for any given couple.

Theoretical Orientation   In helping religious couples, therapy techniques should be consistent with the couple's belief systems as well as their personal and mental health needs. Interestingly enough, research has indicated particular theoretical orientations that seemingly work best for religious couples. For example, the following correlations have been found: (a) orthodox Christian beliefs with cognitive behavioral and behavioral perspectives and (b) Eastern beliefs with humanistic, existential orientations (Bilgrave & Deluty, 1998). Duba and Watts (unpublished manuscript) also suggested how Christian counselors can use an Adlerian approach in counseling Christian couples.

In terms of aiding couples in recovering intimacy, I will refer to the correlation between Adlerian psychology and the Bible. Both attend to the importance of understanding one's style of life convictions and how such schemas (thoughts, beliefs, assumptions) affect one's relationships, one's sense of belonging or attachment, and one's ability to contribute to the well-being of others (the Adlerian understanding of social interest) (Watts, 2000). As previously mentioned, perceptions about one's partner and about one's sense of belonging and attachment (differentiation of self) are factors that affect intimacy. This is just one example of how a particular theory can fit into a religious context, while at the same time aiding couples in bringing intimacy back into their relationships.

Consultation With Religious Leaders Various religious doctrines will inform couples differently about interpersonal responsibility and intimate relations. Gaining an appropriate amount of knowledge and understanding how each religious couple is informed by their faith can be a very daunting task for counselors. Seeking relationships with, as well as information from, religious leaders can provide clinicians with an excellent way of gaining knowledge about the role that the faith perspective can play in a couple's experience of intimacy (Duba Onedera, Minatrea, & Kindsvatter, 2008). In addition, religious leaders might be asked to serve as multicultural consultants within the counseling session (pending the approval and comfort level of the couple). Consultants also may have suggestions about self-help books that are particularly relevant to marital intimacy within their given religious context.

Religious Lifemaps and Genograms Hodge (2005) suggested that spiritual lifemaps can illustrate a client's "relationship with God (or transcendence) over time" (p. 5). Lifemaps typically depict spiritually significant events from birth to the present. Clients are encouraged to use cutout or hand-drawn pictures, symbols, or other material to best represent such events. Lifemaps might serve as a useful technique to help religious couples who are struggling with loss of intimacy. Each partner might be encouraged to construct a lifemap that illustrates (a) times when he or she felt especially close to God or particularly distant from God and (b) times when he or she experienced a great degree of intimacy in any relationship. Not only does such an activity provide the counselor with additional information about each partner's close relationships (and struggles within those relationships) with others and with God, the activity also provides a working narrative related to each spouse's experiences, perceptions, and expectations about relational intimacy. In addition, the "working" nature of this narrative allows partners to manipulate, change, and alter it for the benefit of the relationship.

Constructing a religious or spiritual genogram with each partner can provide similar information related to relationship patterns, sources of attitudes, gender roles, morals and values, expressions of emotion, conflict management, and lines of power (Magnuson & Shaw, 2003; Wiggins Frame, 2003). Once a standard genogram has been constructed, discussions may be related to what partners have learned about intimate relationships within their families, as well as what their own emotional, physical, and intellectual experiences related to intimacy have been. Questions promoting such insight (whether it is religiously focused or not) might include:

1. What did your parents' relationship teach you about intimacy? What did other couples in your family teach you?
2. What do you admire about their relationships? What do you wish to do differently in terms of being able to intimately relate to your partner?
3. How did religion inform those couples about how to remain close to each other (i.e., how to take part in activities together, how to resolve conflict, how to display physical affection, how to forgive)?
4. What patterns of behaviors and relationships emerge as you study your genogram?
5. What are typical reactions from the family when other couples are struggling?
6. How does your relationship history connect with the present conflict between you and your spouse?
7. What new insights have you gained in regard to solving this problem? What new insights have occurred about how your faith can help you solve this problem with your spouse?

Case Example

Anne and Gary (names are pseudonyms) are practicing Presbyterians in their early 40s. They have been married for 12 years and have two children, Joanie, 11, and Tanner, 9. The couple reported feeling disengaged from each other, physically and emotionally. Although they both agreed that their sexual relationship was good, Anne stated that the more emotionally distant from Gary she feels the harder it becomes to enjoy sex as she once did.

Anne and Gary came to the first session and explained how they viewed the presenting problem. They agreed on most of the reasons why their intimacy was becoming strained. Both of them worked full time and were exhausted by the end of the work week. Anne worked as a senior loan officer at a nearby bank, and Gary was a truck driver working third shift. There could be up to 3 days during the week when the couple did not see each other. When the weekends came the couple was usually involved in either Tanner's or Joanie's athletics. Tanner was on a soccer team that traveled on weekends. Last summer and the summer previously, the entire family would make a family trip out of it. After the games they went back to a nearby campground. They had since sold the camper and would rarely attend this year's games together as a family. Either Gary or Anne would accompany him. In addition, Anne mentioned that she was very upset that they were not attending church together as a family. Gary appeared surprised. He "figured their Wednesday night Bible study was enough."

Anne also reported that since Gary's dad's death a year ago, Gary "has just not been the same. It's like he retreated into this ball. When we are having sex, everything is fine, but try to snuggle with him or have a glass of wine together after the kids go to bed. It just won't happen. Sometimes I wonder if he loves me the same way he used to." When Anne voiced this in the counseling session, Gary was quick to reply that he did indeed love Anne the same. Anne replied by rolling her eyes and saying, "Then do something about making me feel that way."

Integrating the couple's faith into the counseling process occurred in several ways. One way was by assigning subsets of the 14 questions mentioned above for homework. Due to time constraints the couple agreed to answer three of the questions separately and then briefly discuss their answers with each other before returning to the following counseling session. During the counseling sessions the couple was asked to talk about the insight they gained. Each partner was also asked to mention what he or she learned about how the other spouse viewed and experienced their intimacy.

In order to bring greater insight about each other's expectations and experiences of intimacy, each partner constructed a lifemap for homework and brought it with them to the following counseling session. Each partner was asked to illustrate the following on their lifemap: (a) times when he or she was especially close to God or particularly distant from God; (b) times when he or she experienced a great degree of intimacy in any relationship. Anne found that during the busiest times of her life (i.e., going to college, hosting family members from out of town), she did not feel especially close to God. It was easy to "forget to pray or slow down, I was on auto-pilot." Times when she felt especially close to God and to Gary included when she was in the hospital after giving birth to Tanner and Joanie, on their wedding day, and during the baptisms of her children. She recalls feeling especially close to God when Gary's father died. Anne also noted that when she was a child she felt "very close" to her parents when they would tuck her in at night or hold her. Gary, on the other hand, reported that the exercise was very difficult to do. He does not remember feeling close to any of his family members, and it was not until Anne came into his life that he felt like he could even pray. Over the next two sessions, we explored the feelings and thoughts both Anne and Gary experienced during times of intimacy and during times when were not feeling intimate with anyone or with God. Further discussion included how these experiences impacted their ability to experience intimacy with each other now, specifically in terms of the following: (a) what behaviors they learned to employ in order to move closer to another (i.e., forgiveness, giving one another a daily warm embrace, kind words); (b) what expectations they have developed of each other and how such expectations get in the way of them being able to develop and maintain intimacy; (c) what fears and apprehensions they have about behaving, thinking, or feeling in ways that beget intimacy.

Finally, the couple was asked to take a serious look at how their busy lives pose a challenge to their overall goal, namely, to "get close again." Although neither one could change their work schedule, they realized that they were going to their children's sporting and academic events more because they felt "guilty" than because they wanted to. The couple worked at exploring how it might be possible to make a "date" out of attending the events, or make conscious choices to give time to their relationship, rather than to silence their guilt. They also agreed that they needed to find a way to attend Sunday church services together.

Concluding Note

This chapter can in no way address all of the many complexities of working with religious couples who have been challenged by a loss or cooling in intimacy. For example, the term "religious couples" encompasses many persons with varying experiences, perceptions, and expectations about intimacy (sometimes even regardless of the religious affiliation). In addition, couples within one religious faith perspective (e.g., Christian) will have different ideas about how God or scripture can be incorporated into building intimacy. Gaining a knowledge base of how each individual couple defines "religion" in their lives and in their relationship is imperative at the beginning of counseling.

It also is important to remember that each partner contributes to the degree of intimacy that the couple will be able to share. Counselors are behooved to use the questions mentioned in the chapter to help individual partners understand their own experiences and expectations regarding intimacy. During these individual intrapersonal explorations, the witnessing spouse may be more inclined to have a deeper appreciation for his or her partner. Second, the experience, if conducted carefully on the part of the counselor, can become a stage for a very intimate sharing of inner personal feelings and thoughts in which the other partner serves as an empathetic and active listener. When these personal narratives about intimacy are better understood, the counselor can help the couple bridge their individual stories so as to help them construct a shared meaning around intimacy.

References

American Association of Christian Counselors. (2004). *AACC code of ethics*. Forest, VA: Author, Biblical-Ethical Foundations of the AACC Ethics Code.

American Counseling Association. (2005). *Code of ethics and standards of practice*. Alexandria, VA: Author.

Bagarozzi, D. A. (1997). Marital intimacy needs questionnaire: Preliminary report. *American Journal of Family Therapy, 25*(3), 285–290.

Balswick, J. O., & Balswick, J. K. (2006). *A model for marriage*. Downers Grove, IL: InterVarsity Press.

Belcher, J. R., & Benda, B. B. (2003). Counseling charismatic couples: Working through the charismata. *Marriage and Family: A Christian Journal, 6*(4), 497–503.

Bilgrave, D. P., & Deluty, R. H. (1998). Religious beliefs and therapeutic orientations of clinical and counseling psychologists. *Journal for the Scientific Study of Religion, 37*, 329–349.

Catholic Church. (2003). *Catechism of the Catholic Church* (2nd Ed.). New York: Doubleday.

Chapman, G. (2003). *Covenant marriage*. Nashville: B and H Publishing Group.

Chapman, G. (2007). *Now you're speaking my language*. Nashville: B and H Publishing Group.

Dollahite, D. C., & Lambert, N. M. (2007). Forsaking all others: How religious involvement promotes marital fidelity in Christian, Jewish, and Muslim couples. *Review of Religious Research, 48*(3), 290–307.

Dreikurs, R. (1974). *The challenge of marriage*. New York: Dutton.

Duba, J.D., & Watts, R.E. (2009, Spring). Therapy with religious couples. *Journal of Clinical Psychology, 65*(2), 210–223.

Duba Onedera, J. D. (2008). The practice of marriage and family counseling and Catholicism. In J. Duba Onedera (Ed.), *The role of religion and marriage and family counseling* (pp. 37–54). New York: Taylor and Francis.

Duba Onedera, J. D., Minatrea, N., & Kindsvatter, A. (2008). Collaboration between licensed mental health professionals and religious leaders. In J. D. Onedera (Ed.), *The role of religion and marriage and family counseling* (pp. 245–260). New York: Taylor and Francis.

Giblin, P. (2004). Marital health and spirituality. *Journal of Pastoral Counseling, 39*, 43–67.

Gilbert, R. M. (2006). *The eight concepts of Bowen theory*. Falls Church, VA: Leading Systems Press.

Gottman, J. (1999). *The marriage clinic: A scientifically based marital therapy*. New York: Norton.

Heller, P. E., & Wood, B. (1998). The process of intimacy: Similarity, understanding and gender. *Journal of Marital and Family Therapy, 24*(3), 273–288.

Hodge, D. R. (2005). Developing a spiritual assessment toolbox. A discussion of the strengths and limitations of five different assessment methods. *Health and Social Work, 30*(4), 314–323.

Holeman, V. T. (2008). The role of forgiveness in religious life and within marriage and family relationships. In J. Duba Onedera (Ed.), *The role of religion and marriage and family counseling* (pp. 197–211). New York: Taylor and Francis.

Kenny, D. A., & Acitelli, L. K. (1987). Measuring similarity in couples. *Journal of Family Psychology, 8*(4), 417–431.

Koepsell, D. R., & Mercurio-Riley, D. (2008). The practice of marriage and family counseling and Humanism. In J. Duba Onedera (Ed.), *The role of religion and marriage and family counseling* (pp. 165–177). New York: Taylor and Francis.

Madathil, J., & Sandhu, D. (2008). The practice of marriage and family counseling and Islam. In J. Duba Onedera (Ed.), *The role of religion and marriage and family counseling* (pp. 119–133). New York: Taylor and Francis.

Magnuson, S., & Shaw, H. E. (2003). Adaptations of the multifaceted genogram in counseling, training, and supervision. *Family Journal, 11*(1), 45–54.

May, W. E. (1995). *Marriage: The rock on which the family is built.* San Francisco: Ignatius Press.

Miller, G. (1999). The development of the spiritual focus in counseling and counselor education. *Journal of Counseling and Development, 77*(4), 498–501.

Patrick, S., Sells, J. N., Giordano, F. G., & Tollerud, R. T. (2007). Intimacy, differentiation, and personality variables as predictors of marital satisfaction. *Family Journal, 15*(4), 359–367.

Rampage, C. (1994). Power, gender, and marital intimacy. *Journal of Family Therapy, 16*, 125–137.

Ribner, D. S. (2003). Modifying sensate focus for use with Haredi Jewish couples. *Journal of Sex and Marital Therapy, 29*(2), 165–171.

Schnarch, D. (1997). *Passionate marriage.* New York: Holt.

Shaneman, J. (2008). The practice of marriage and family counseling and Buddhism. In J. Duba Onedera (Ed.), *The role of religion and marriage and family counseling* (pp. 105–117). New York: Taylor and Francis.

Waring, E. M., & Chelune, G. J. (1983). Marital intimacy and self-disclosure. *Journal of Clinical Psychology, 39*(2), 183–190.

Watts, R. E. (2000). Biblically-based Christian spirituality and Adlerian therapy. *Journal of Individual Psychology, 56*, 316–328.

Watts, R. E. (2008, June). Counseling conservative Christian clients: A spiritually sensitive perspective. *Counseling Today, 50*(12), 10–11, 13.

Wheat, E., & Wheat, G. (1997). *Intended for pleasure* (3rd ed.). Grand Rapids, MI: Baker Book House Company.

Wiggins Frame, M. (2003). *Integrating religion and spirituality in counseling.* Pacific Grove, CA: Brooks/Cole.

Appendix
Clinician's Resource Guide: Popular Self-Help Books on Intimacy

JONATHAN SPERRY and LEN SPERRY

Over the years, bibliotherapy (i.e., the adjunctive use of books, usually popular self-help books) has increasingly become part of the therapeutic process in couples therapy. It is not uncommon for clients to ask therapists to recommend books that might be of particular help to one or both partners. Similarly, therapists will occasionally, or even regularly, recommend a particular book to a couple. For example, therapists who practice imago therapy typically recommend Hendrix's book *Getting the Love You Want: A Guide for Couples* as an adjunctive to the therapeutic process. Other times, couples will asks their therapists whether they agree with the advice of a particular book. The presumption is that therapists are familiar with all the popular books on intimacy, infidelity, and the like.

Several years ago, most therapists doing couples therapy would have had little problem recommending a book or giving an opinion on the advice of a particular book, since there were only a few such books available. That has all changed in the past decade or so, and now there are dozens of such books in print. This appendix describes a dozen of the popular self-help books on the loss and recovery of intimacy, whether originating from infidelity or other factors. Each book is described in terms of these topics:

- Definition of intimacy,
- View of infidelity or loss of intimacy,
- Strategies for recovery of intimacy,
- Other significant topics covered.

All such books are in paperback and the cover price is indicated in parentheses in the full reference at the end of each review. Our hope is that couples therapists who utilize bibliotherapy as an adjunctive therapy will find our "bird's eye view" of these popular books helpful in working with couples with intimacy issues.

10 Lessons to Transform Your Marriage

John M. Gottman, Ph.D., Julie Schwartz Gottman,
Ph.D., and Joan DeClaire, Ph.D.

Definition of intimacy: Intimacy is the ability for partners to experience positive and negative emotions in daily interactions and ultimately growing as a couple after conflict. Intimacy is viewed as an emotional closeness in which passion and communication are significant features. The authors identified two simple truths about marriages: happily married couples behave like good friends and happily married couples handle their conflicts in gentle positive ways. Relationships are characterized by respect, affection, and empathy, while conflict is inevitable in any marriage.

View of infidelity or loss of intimacy: Infidelity is a significant relational stressor that is suggestive of other relational problems, such as unmet needs, conflict avoidance, and lack of communication, all of which contribute to lower levels of intimacy. Responsibility is assigned to one or both partners who contributed to a lack of communication and intimacy.

Strategies for recovery of intimacy: A couple who is attempting to improve their relationship after infidelity, loss of a job, exhaustion from working too hard, struggles with depression, and so forth can utilize the 10 lessons discussed. The methods to improve a relationship and possibly recover intimacy are: (1) Practicing healthy complaining without criticizing and being able to express and accept appreciation. (2) Communicating your needs and feelings to your partner and problem solving when appropriate. (3) Adjusting your lifestyle (exercise, healthy dieting, dating, set boundaries on work hours, etc.) to lower stress, which can ultimately promote intimacy enhancement. (4) Communicating what you want rather than what you do not want, responding to your partners statements of need with open-ended questions, and expressing appreciation to the partner who was listening. (5) Recognizing dreams and feelings within a conflict with your partner to possibly uncover hidden dreams. (6) Rather than avoiding emotional intensity, practicing expression of negative feelings and discussing conflict while still attending to both partners' needs. (7) During conflict, practicing a "softened start-up," which is a neutral type of confrontation that has a less accusatory undertone. (8) Expressing anger in productive ways. (9) Practicing identification and expression of needs to each other. (10) Establishing a dialogue about the conflict by being able to talk about disagreements on an ongoing basis.

Other significant topics covered: The dialogue in the case vignettes contains a column that provides clinical insight and knowledge on each interaction. The book offers many practical exercises, statistics, and quizzes toward improving a marriage.

Gottman, J. M., Gottman, J. S., & DeClaire, J. (2006). *10 Lessons to Transform Your Marriage.* New York: Three Rivers Press. ($13.95).

After the Affair: Healing the Pain and Rebuilding Trust When a Partner Has Been Unfaithful

Janis Abrahms Spring, Ph.D.

Definition of intimacy: Intimacy is identified as primarily sexual and emotional and is the opening of one's self to love, commitment, honesty, physical touch, fulfillment, realistic expectations, and a spiritual attachment. Intimacy is carried out through kindness and availability to one's significant other. Because the book focuses on recovering from infidelity, Spring emphasizes the impact infidelity has on the individuals, particularly the sense of betrayal. A three-stage model of healing and growth is offered: reacting to the affair, reviewing your options, and recovering from the affair. This last stage directly addresses the recovery of intimacy.

View of infidelity or loss of intimacy: Individuals should cease from "pointing the finger at each other" and stop calculating the percentage of fault in regards to the infidelity; rather, they should evaluate their individual past experiences and start searching for solutions. The author suggested that no one can make another person breach intimacy, which suggests that personal ownership of attitudes and actions should be taken. Ultimately, responsibility should be taken by both individuals through a process of evaluating their own dynamic history and behaviors that were active in their relationship.

Strategies for recovering intimacy: If a couple chooses to remain together after an infidelity, specific exercises can help rebuild that relationship. Several chapters address various aspects of recovering intimacy: restoring trust, how to talk about what happened, learning to forgive, and sex after infidelity. The directives and exercises presented offer potential relief and growth for couples who are struggling to mend a compromised relationship. Central to healing, the directives can address and validate the pain that results from the unfaithfulness. Suggestions for improving the relationship or ending it are sensitively discussed.

Other significant topics covered: The book provides a wealth of exercises that can be practiced to improve a relationship or elevate one's level of self-awareness. Other areas covered in this book are ideas about love, confronting fears and doubts, and the hurt and unfaithful partner's response to the infidelity.

Spring, J. A., & Spring, M. (1996). *After the Affair: Healing the Pain and Rebuilding Trust When a Partner Has Been Unfaithful.* New York: Harper. ($14.00).

Emotional Infidelity

M. Gary Neuman, LMHC

Definition of intimacy: Intimacy is an expression of love by two persons in a marriage when they ultimately place each other first. Intimacy is genuine love, which is a feeling of completeness by being with a person and having a sense that you have known them forever. The focus on intimacy is presumably a relational improvement or "affair-proofing method" that could be achieved by following the suggestions in this book.

View of infidelity or loss of intimacy: Infidelity is discussed in the context of reservations individuals may have in their relationship because they have made some unconscious or conscious decision to place their relationship second. Responsibility is assigned to individuals who "hold back" their true thoughts and feelings. Communication barriers, lack of trust, lack of boundaries, lack of intimacy, and extramarital relationships are a few of the many elements that can adversely impact relationships.

Strategies for recovery of intimacy: Putting the relationship before children, work, and friends is a suggested technique that promotes recovery of intimacy after an infidelity. The 10 secrets listed can serve as a proactive approach toward a successful marriage or relationship; similarly, these concepts can be applied to a struggling relationship to promote growth and relationship effectiveness. Intimacy can be recovered through the assistance of counseling and the application of the 10 secrets and different activities discussed.

Other significant topics covered: Other significant topics covered in this book are organized in the format of 10 secrets designed to foster an effective relationship. The secrets discussed are: commitment, healthy codependence, relational goals, defined roles, putting the marriage first, childhood influence, sexual intimacy in regard to trust, children and their role in a great marriage, and stages of marriage.

Neuman, M. G. (2001). *Emotional Infidelity: How to Affair-Proof Your Marriage and 10 Other Secrets to a Great Relationship.* New York: Three Rivers Press. ($14.00).

The Fight From Intimacy

Janae B. Weinhold, Ph.D., and Barry K. Weinhold, Ph.D.

Definition of intimacy: Intimacy encompasses all relational experiences whether they are positive or negative. Intimacy is meaningful emotional contact with another person. Couples who work together to heal their developmental wounds from childhood can experience intimacy.

View of infidelity or loss of intimacy: Counter-dependency suggests that an individual with counter-dependent and co-dependent features may promote infidelity due to enmeshment or the lack of emotional closeness. Responsibility can come from the individual with unmet needs from childhood, which potentially can develop into co-dependent or counter-dependent features. These behavioral patterns often lead to relationship failures.

Strategies for recovery of intimacy: Conflict resolution and communication are foundational strategies toward intimacy. Recovery of intimacy can be promoted through both partners committing to the relationship and learning and implementing skills to resolve conflict.

Other significant topics covered: Counter-dependent stages of development, the disease model of relationships, the counter-dependent culture, empathy, setting boundaries, reclaiming projections, self parenting, and sexual communication.

Weinhold, J. B., & Weinhold, B. K. (2008). *The Flight From Intimacy: Healing Your Relationship of Counter-Dependency—The Other Side of Co-Dependency.* Novato, CA: New World Library. ($14.95).

Getting Past the Affair

Douglas K. Snyder, Ph.D., Donald H. Baucom, Ph.D., & Kristina Coop Gordon, Ph.D.

Definition of intimacy: Defined as an emotional and physical closeness. Physical touching and sexual connection are part of physical intimacy. Emotional intimacy is sharing thoughts and feelings as a couple, working and playing together.

View of infidelity or loss of intimacy: Infidelity is a violation of the expectations or standards of a relationship by being involved with someone else on an emotional or physical level. Responsibility is assigned to the partner who chose to have the affair. Couples can examine their relationship to identify how it became vulnerable to an affair (e.g., examining negative influences, stressors, and the absence of adequate protective factors) to heal pain and promote future intimacy.

Strategies for recovery of intimacy: One method suggests that both partners list major ways in which they have acted in the past that influenced feeling emotionally close. A strengths building exercise suggests that both partners make a list of any tasks or behaviors they have strength in. Another tool toward recovering intimacy is the steps toward moving on past hurt and anger: recognition, responsibility, remorse, restitution, reform, release, and reconciliation. When an individual or couple is deciding whether to continue or end a relationship after infidelity, they should make a list of the reasons to move on together and a list of reasons to move on separately.

Other significant topics covered: Communication, conflict resolution, self-care, exploring why affairs happen, external stressors on relationships, relational roles, and making sense of the affair.

Snyder, D. K., Baucom, D. H., & Gordon, K. C. (2007). *Getting Past the Affair: A Program to Help You Cope, Heal, and Move On Together or Apart.* New York: Guilford. ($14.95).

Getting the Love You Want: A Guide for Couples

Harville Hendrix, Ph.D.

Definition of intimacy: Intimacy is found within the context of pleasure and safety. It is displayed through sexual experiences, sharing pains and sorrows of childhood, experiencing trust, communicating with empathy, and listening without judgment.

View of infidelity or loss of intimacy: Although the book does not discuss infidelity, it has a minor focus on avoiding intimacy. Hiding one's vulnerabilities is an attempt to avoid intimacy. Intimacy is commonly avoided by fear and anger. Fear can stem from the emotional pain one experienced in childhood. The anger is potentially from not having one's needs met and retaliating with an emotional barricade.

Strategies for recovery of intimacy: After an infidelity the couple must learn to create pleasure and safety (intimacy) within the culture of the relationship. Essentially intimacy can be recovered through imago therapy and the 18 exercises toward a conscious partnership listed in this text: Your Relationship Vision, Childhood Wounds, Imago Workup, Childhood Frustrations, Parent-Child Dialogue, Partner Profile, Unfinished Business, The Imago Dialogue, The Commitment Decision, Reromanticizing, The Surprise List, The Fun List, Positive Flooding, The Behavior Change Request Dialogue, The Holding Exercise, Owning and Eliminating Your Negativity, Self-Integration, and Visualization of Love.

Other significant topics covered: The Mystery of Attraction, Childhood Wounds, Romantic Love, The Power Struggle, Becoming Conscious, Commitment, Creating a Safety Zone, Increasing Your Knowledge of Yourself and Your Partner, Defining Your Curriculum, Creating a Sacred Space, and a Portrait of Two Relationships.

Hendrix, H. (2008). *Getting the Love You Want: A Guide for Couples.* 25th Anniversary Ed. New York: Holt Paperbacks. ($15.00).

How Can I Forgive You?

Janis Abrahms Spring, Ph.D. (with Michael Spring)

Definition of intimacy: In the context of forgiveness, intimacy can be achieved after genuine forgiveness occurs within a couple followed by interpersonal growth after conflict or adversity. Individuals' ability to speak up about who they are, how they are hurting, and what they need is an essential part of what intimacy means.

View of infidelity or loss of intimacy: Includes the scope of any "violations of human connection." Infidelity can occur in any significant relationship in which at least one individual's rights are violated. "Cheap forgiveness" can only exacerbate relationship problems after infidelity. Responsibility is primarily assigned to the unfaithful partner, but this book provides multiple case scenarios and exercises toward forgiveness and ultimately a recovery of intimacy.

Strategies for recovery of intimacy: If a couple has decided to mend a relationship after an infidelity, the offending partner should practice genuine forgiveness with his or her partner. Genuine forgiveness involves both partners' heartfelt participation after a violation. The book described the Six Critical Tasks for Earning Forgiveness: Looking at your mistaken assumptions about forgiveness and see how they block your efforts to earn it, bear witness to the pain you caused, apologize genuinely, seek to understand your behavior and reveal the inglorious truth about yourself to the person you harmed, work to earn back trust, forgive yourself for injuring another person. The healing process toward recovering intimacy will take patience, dedication, work, and sacrifice.

Other significant topics covered: Cheap forgiveness, refusing to forgive, acceptance, and how the offender's childhood wounds shape the way he or she treated the other.

Spring, J. A., & Spring, M. (2004). *How Can I Forgive You?: The Courage to Forgive, the Freedom Not to.* New York: Perennial Currents. ($13.95).

Infidelity: A Survival Guide

Don-David Lusterman, Ph.D.

Definition of intimacy: Intimacy is a commitment that promotes sexual, emotional, and physical exclusiveness that is reserved for a couple that cannot be shared with others.

View of infidelity or loss of intimacy: Infidelity is a violation of a relational agreement and ultimately a breaking of trust. Responsibility of infidelity is primarily assigned to the partner who participated in the affair. Since fault is not assigned to the unfaithful mate, the other partner should evaluate his or her own actions to observe how they may have contributed to a readiness of an affair.

Strategies for recovery of intimacy: Three phases in the recovery model after an infidelity has occurred are: Restoring trust through honesty, reviewing the marriage (communication, conflict resolution, and journaling), and a final decision about a better marriage or a divorce. Social support and therapy are two significant methods of recovery of intimacy after infidelity.

Other significant topics covered: Impact of infidelity on children, the shock of discovery, family and friends, disclosure of infidelity, divorce, feelings, and choosing a competent therapist.

Lusterman, D. (1998). *Infidelity: A Survival Guide.* Oakland, CA: New Harbinger Publications. ($14.95).

Intimacy After Infidelity

Steven D. Solomon, Ph.D., & Lorie J. Teagno, Ph.D.

Definition of intimacy: Intimacy is having trust in emotional, sexual, and behavioral areas in a committed relationship.

View of infidelity or loss of intimacy: Infidelity ranges from a one-night stand to a continuing affair. Any action taken by a partner in a committed relationship that violates the agreement of sexual or emotional exclusivity constitutes an infidelity. Responsibility is discussed in the context of the couple as an active system; both partners should investigate how their behavior or lack of behaviors may have contributed to the infidelity. Personal ownership of individual actions and improved self-awareness should be promoted to assist in healing a relationship.

Strategies for recovery of intimacy: Recovering intimacy is fostered by individual improvements, which are complemented by both partners restoring relational balance, opening communication, and growing in awareness. Strategies for recovering intimacy are: emotional identification, the Emotional Self-Awareness (ESA) tool, identifying whether the individuals love style is need love or being love, developing self-intimacy, developing healthy conflict intimacy, and establishing the relationships stage of relational progress.

Other significant topics covered: Conflict intimacy, affection intimacy, conflict intimacy, the three infidelities, infidelities of fear, infidelity of loneliness, infidelity of anger, the stages of love, and loving with security.

Solomon, S. D., & Teagno, L. J. (2006). *Intimacy After Infidelity: How to Rebuild and Affair-Proof Your Marriage.* Oakland, CA: New Harbinger Publications. ($14.95).

The Five Love Languages

Gary Chapman, Ph.D.

Definition of intimacy: Intimacy is what makes you feel most loved by your significant other. The five love languages all communicate different forms of intimacy in the context of this book. Intimacy is the satisfaction of having a mutual understanding and the display of different love languages in a relationship.

View of infidelity or loss of intimacy: If infidelity occurs and intimacy declines, the love language of the unfaithful partner should be observed. If the unfaithful partner's love style is expressed by physical touch and he or she is unable to fulfill or communicate that with his or her current partner, he or she is responsible for the infidelity. The inability to express one's needs in regard to the way a person wants to be loved is a significant factor that can influence infidelity.

Strategies for recovery of intimacy: The method of recovering intimacy can be accomplished by learning your partner's love language and his or her specific dialect of it. Once partners realizes that their love language is inconsistent with what the other actually wants, they can adjust their love language to meet their partner's needs. Forgiveness is a primary factor in recovering intimacy. Journaling and communication exercises to help identify each partner's love language can potentially optimize the expression of intimacy in the relationship.

Other significant topics covered: The five love languages are words of affirmation, quality time, receiving gifts, acts of services, and physical touch.

Chapman, G. (2004). *The Five Love Languages: How to Express Heartfelt Commitment to Your Mate.* Chicago: Northfield Publishing. ($14.99).

Not "Just Friends": Rebuilding Trust and Recovering Your Sanity After Infidelity

Shirley P. Glass, Ph.D. (with Jean Coppock Staeheli)

Definition of intimacy: Intimacy is present through emotional intimacy, secret sharing, and sexual chemistry. Intimacy also is present in a relationship when a couple is open and honest about significant areas in their individual lives. Intimacy is influenced by trust in which a partner maintains faith that he or she can believe what he or she is being told from the significant other. Intimacy is maintained by adhering to appropriate boundaries with other relationships outside of the relationship. When a couple shares intimacy they are more likely to share their deepest thoughts and feelings with each other more readily than they would turn to anyone else.

View of infidelity or loss of intimacy: Infidelity is any emotional or sexual intimacy that violates trust. Three types of vulnerabilities for infidelity are: relationship issues, individual factors, and social-cultural influences. Responsibility is primarily assigned to the unfaithful partner, yet this book suggests that both partners are responsible for healing the relationship if they choose to repair it after an infidelity.

Strategies for recovery of intimacy: The recovery process requires equal participation from both partners in order to achieve true intimacy again. The gradual process of forgiving, increasing compassion, recommitment, and reducing resentment are some of the primary ingredients in the recovery of intimacy. Abstaining from any contact with the affair partner and communicating about any unavoidable encounters are essential in reestablishing safety. Discussing the story of the affair to enable understanding of the meaning of the infidelity is a significant strategy for recovery of intimacy.

Other significant topics covered: Platonic and intimate relationships, crossing into a double life, the trauma of infidelity, staying or leaving the relationship, coping with the trauma of infidelity, importance of talking about the affair, marriage, individual stories, and healing alone.

Glass, S. P., & Staeheli, J. C. (2003). *Not "Just friends": Rebuilding Trust and Recovering Your Sanity After Infidelity.* New York: Free Press. (15.95).

Private Lies: Infidelity and the Betrayal of Intimacy

Frank Pittman, M.D.

Definition of intimacy: Intimacy can grow through confessions, explanations, and soul searching. Intimacy is supported by equality and trust. Intimacy can be displayed through sexual behaviors, emotional closeness, and emotional sharing with honesty of one's innermost secrets. Society's conditioning of male expression of intimacy rivals their ability to achieve intimacy.

View of infidelity or loss of intimacy: Infidelity is a breach of trust, a betrayal of a relationship, a breaking of an agreement. Intimacy is an agreement a couple accepts as an ideal for their relationship. Infidelity is the breaking of the agreement. If an act is lied about, done in secrecy, or done over the partner's objection, then it is viewed as an infidelity. The individual being betrayed cannot make an affair happen, cannot make the betrayer stop, and can only make him- or herself available for solving problems remedially.

Strategies for recovery of intimacy: Marriage can survive if affairs are exposed. Honesty promotion is a central factor toward reestablishing intimacy. Clarifying the agreement between spouses about what is and what is not infidelity can organize expectations if a couple chooses to repair their relationship. After an infidelity the couple should dispute personally held assumptions about their partner and actually communicate them. A primary basis for a good relationship is having a positive friendship.

Other significant topics covered: Myths about infidelity, jealousy and infidelity, monogamy, the turning point in marriage, infidelity around the world, accidental infidelity, philandering, romantic affairs, divorce, romance to remarriage, and what will the children think?

Pittman, F. (1990). *Private Lies: Infidelity and the Betrayal of Intimacy.* New York: Norton. ($15.95).

Index